THE CAVENDISH Q & A SERIES

'A' LEVEL LAW

Cavendish
Publishing
Limited

TITLES IN THE Q&A SERIES

BUSINESS LAW
CIVIL LIBERTIES
COMMERCIAL LAW
COMPANY LAW
CONSTITUTIONAL & ADMINISTRATIVE LAW
CONTRACT LAW
CRIMINAL LAW
EMPLOYMENT LAW
ENGLISH LEGAL SYSTEM
EQUITY & TRUSTS
EUROPEAN COMMUNITY LAW
EVIDENCE
FAMILY LAW
INTERNATIONAL TRADE LAW
JURISPRUDENCE
LAND LAW
PUBLIC INTERNATIONAL LAW
REVENUE LAW
SUCCESSION, WILLS & PROBATE
TORTS LAW
'A' LEVEL LAW

THE CAVENDISH Q & A SERIES

'A' LEVEL LAW

Penny Booth, Paul Cappi,
Mary Collins, Gordon McLeish,
Simon Payne, Jill Spencer

Edited by
Peter Shears, BA, LLB, LLM
Director of Legal Studies
University of Plymouth

Cavendish
Publishing
Limited

First published in Great Britain 1995 by Cavendish Publishing Limited,
The Glass House, Wharton Street, London, WC1X 9PX
Telephone: 0171-278 8000 Facsimile: 0171-278 8080

© Booth P, Cappi P, Collins M,
McLeish G, Payne S, Spencer J 1995

All rights reserved. No part of this publication may be reproduced, stored in a retrieval system, or transmitted in any form or by any means, electronic, mechanical, photocopying, recording or otherwise, without the prior permission of the publisher and copyright owner.

The right of the authors of this work has been asserted in accordance with the Copyright, Designs and Patents Act 1988.

Any person who infringes the above in relation to this publication may be liable to criminal prosecution and civil claims for damages.

British Library Cataloguing in Publication Data

'A' Level Law - (Q & A Series)
I Shears, Peter II Series
344.2

ISBN 1-874241-32-5

Printed and bound in Great Britain

Preface

This is an unusual 'Questions and Answers' book – it has been written by six authors.

The questions answered for you here are not particular past questions from particular examinations. They are examples of the kind of questions that often appear on 'A' Level papers as set by all the examination boards. They have been devised and answered by authors who are subject area specialists.

If you follow the general guidelines in the introduction to each of the areas covered in this book and set the material against the particular requirements and past papers of the examination board whose examinations you are preparing to sit, then you should be able to enter the examination room with confidence!

Good luck!

Peter Shears
April 1995

Contents

Preface — v
Table of Cases — ix
Table of Legislation — xix

1	The English Legal System	1
2	English Legal System: Sentencing	67
3	General Principles of English Law	79
4	European Law	113
5	Constitutional Law	145
6	The Law of Contract	165
7	The Law of Tort	197
8	The Criminal Law	247
9	The Law of Civil Liberties	297
10	Family and Welfare Law	315
11	Labour Law and the Workplace	339

Index — 347

Table of Cases

Adams v Lindsell (1818) 174
Adomako (1994) 255, 260, 292
Aero Zipp Fasteners v YKK Fasteners (1973) 121
Airedale NHS Trust v Bland (1993) 57, 99, 111
Alcock & Others v Chief Constable of South
   Yorkshire Police (1992) 61, 101, 107, 108,
                                                                  198, 236, 242
Alexander v NE Rly 232
Alhaji Mohammed v Knott (1968) 328
Alphacell Ltd v Woodward (1972) 294
American Cyanamid v Ethicon (1975) 208, 217, 224
Andrews v DPP (1937) 255, 260
Anglo-Continental Holidays v Typaldos (London) Ltd (1967) 194
Argyll v Beuselinck 242
Arrowsmith v Jenkins (1963) 289
Ashington Piggeries Ltd v Christopher Hill Ltd (1972) 178
Attorney General for Hong Kong v Ng Yuen Shiu (1983) 161
Attorney General for Northern Ireland v Gallagher (1961) 268
Attorney General v Guardian Newspapers (1988) 301, 309
Attorney General v News Group Newspapers Ltd (1988) 59
Attorney General v PYA Quarries (1957) 206, 215, 222
Attorney General's Reference (No 1 of 1988) 18
Ayredale NHS Trust v Bland (1993) 263

Bamford v Turnley (1860) 207, 212, 215, 223
Barclays Bank v Taylor (1989) 307
Barnett v Chelsea Hospital (1968) 237
Benjamin v Storr 206, 222
Bestobell Paints v Bigg 234
Birmingham Six case 82, 83, 85
Bisset v Wilkinson (1927) 182
Bolam v Friern Hospital Management Committee (1957) 201, 219, 236
Bolton v Stone (1951) 201, 225, 227, 237, 242
Bourhill v Young (1948) 236, 242
Boyle v Kodak 202
BRB v Pickin (1974) 149
British Westinghouse Electric Co v Underground Electric
   Railway Co of London (1912) 171
Bromley LBC v GLC (1983) 149
Bulmer v Bollinger (1974) 14
Burton v Winters 217

Cambridge Water Co v Eastern Counties Leather (1993) 60, 109, 219, 244
Caparo v Dickman (1990) 201, 205, 209, 225, 236
Carlill v Carbolic Smoke Ball Co (1893) 173
Cassidy v Daily Mirror (1929) 230, 232, 244
Castle v St Augustine's Links (1922) 219
Caswell v Powell Duffryn (1940) 203

Century Insurance Co v Northern Ireland
  Road Transport Board (1942) 211, 245
Chandler v Webster (1904) 169
Chief Constable of Avon & Somerset v Shimmen (1986) 291, 292
Chilton v Chilton (1990) 322
Christie v Leachinsky (1974) 313
Cilfit case (1983) 118
Cole v Turner (1704) 225, 241
Cole v Turner (1969) 249
Collins v Godefroy (1831) 175
Collins v Wilcock (1984) 313
Coltman & Another v Bibby Tankers Ltd (1987) 18
Corbett v Corbett (1970) 328
Corcoran v Anderton (1988) 275
Council of Civil Service Unions v Minister for the Civil Service (1984) 161
Cresswell v BOC (1980)...16
Cummings v Granger (1977) 226
Cundy v Le Coq (1884) 293
Cundy v Lindsay (1878) 188

D v D (1979) 329
Daborn v Bath Tramways 243
Dann v Hamilton (1939) 210, 227
Davis Contractors Ltd v Fareham UDC (1956) 168
Davis v Johnson (1978) 15
Delany v Delaney (1990)..324
Derbyshire County Council v Times Newspapers Ltd (1993) 61
Donnelly v Jackman (1970) 249, 313
Donoghue v Stephenson (1932) 61, 177, 179, 200,
                                              219, 225, 236, 241
Doughty v Rolls-Royce Plc (1992) 128
DPP v Beard 267
DPP v Camplin (1978) 256, 262, 267
DPP v K (a minor) (1990) 290
DPP v Little (1991) 250
DPP v Majewski (1977) 250, 252, 267
DPP v Maxwell (1979)...276, 277
DPP v Morgan (1975) 251, 293
DPP v Taylor & Little 250, 259, 276
Draper v Hodder (1972) 225
Dunlop Pneumatic Tyre Co Ltd v New
  Garage & Motor Co Ltd (1915) 185
Dunlop v Selfridge Ltd (1915) 174
Duxbury v Duxbury (1990)...325

Edgington v Fitzmaurice (1885)...183
Elliott v C (1983) 291
Emmett v Hollywood Silver Fox Farm (1936) 216

Table of Cases

England v Davidson (1840) 175
Entick v Carrington (1765) 307
Esso Petroleum v Kingswood Motors Ltd (1974) 120
Eves v Eves (1975) 319
Ex parte Equal Opportunities Commission (1994) 14
Ex parte Smith (1990)..58, 105, 111

F v West Berks Health Authority (1989) 249
Fardon v Harcourt-Rivington 225
Felthouse v Bindley (1863) 173
Fibrosa case (1943) 170
Flaminio Costa v Enel (1964) 122
Ford Motor Co Ltd v Armstrong (1915) 185
Foster and others v British Gas (1991) 128, 129
Fothergill v Monarch Airlines Ltd (1990) 15
Fowler v Lanning (1959) 240
Francovich v Italian Republic (1992)..129
Fuller v Fuller (1973) 323

Gammon (UK) Ltd v AG of Hong Kong (1984) 294
Gardiner v Sevenoaks RDC (1950) 17
GCHQ Civil Service Unions case (1984) 301, 309
Gibbons v Proctor (1891)..174
Gissing v Gissing (1970) 319
Glasbrook Bros v Glamorgan County Council (1925) 175
Goodman v Gallant (1986) 319
Gorris v Scott (1874) 17, 202
Grant v Australian Knitting Mills (1936) 179
Grant v Edwards (1986) 319
Grappelli v Derek Block Holdings (1981)...230
Groves v Lord Wimborne (1898) 202
Guildford Four case...82, 82

H, Re (A minor) (Parental Responsibility) (1993) 320
HK, Re (an infant) (1967)..162
Hale v Jennings (1938)...219
Halford v Brookes 241
Halsey v Esso (1961) 206, 207, 215,
                                                                            219, 220, 222, 223
Harlingdon & Leincester Enterprises Ltd v Christopher
  Hull Fine Art Ltd (1990) 178
Harris v Sheffield United Football Club (1988) 175
Haseldine v Daw & Sons (1941)...210
Herne Bay Steamboat Co v Hutton (1903) 168, 169
Heydon's Case (1584) 16
Hills v Ellis (1983) 288

Case	Pages
Hobbs v Winchester Corporation	293, 294
Hollins v Fowler	244
Holloway (1849)	255, 260, 292
Horton v Horton (1947)	329
Hughes v Lord Advocate (1963)	202, 209
Hui Chi-ming v R (1992)	277
Hulton v Jones (1910)	244
Hyde v Hyde (1866)	328
Ingram v Little (1961)	189, 190
James & Son Ltd v Smee	294
JCC (a minor) v Eisenhower (1983)	251
Joel v Morrison	211
John Lewis v Tims (1952)	313
John Summers v Frost (1955)	202
Julie Ward case	82
Kaur v Singh (1972)	329
Kennaway v Thompson (1981)	208, 212, 217, 224
Kings Norton Metal Co Ltd v Edridge Merrett Co Ltd (1897)	188
Knowles v Liverpool City Council (1993)	18
Knuller v DPP (1973)	96, 98
Knupffer v London Express (1944)	231
Krell v Henry (1903)	168
Kyte v Kyte (1987)	325
Latimer v AEC Ltd (1953)	201, 243
Lawrence v MPC (1971)	274
Laws v Florinplace Ltd	208, 217, 224
LBC v Thomas (1992)	18
Leadbeater v Leadbeater (1985)	324
League against Cruel Sports v Scott (1985)	225
Leakey v National Trust (1980)	220, 244
Letang v Cooper (1965)	241
Lever Finance Ltd v Westminster City Council (1971)	162
Lewis v Avery (1972)	189, 290
Lewis v Daily Telegraph (1964)	231
Liversedge v Anderson (1941)	301, 309
Livingstone-Stallard case (1974)	323
Lloyds Bank v Rossett (1990)	319
Lord Aldington v Tolstoy (1989)	234
Lynch v DPP	276
M v M (1994)	332
Maguire Seven case	82, 83
Malone v MPC (No 2) (1985)	303
Marr & Another, Re (bankrupts) (1990)	19

Table of Cases

Massmould v Payne (1993) 19
McArdle, Re (1951) 175
McKinnon v Walker Industries (1951) 216
McLoughlin v O'Brian (1983) 61, 101, 107, 109
Merivale v Carson (1887) 233
Mesher v Mesher (1980) 324
MH Marshall v Southampton and South West Hampshire
   Area Health Authority (Teaching) (1984) 128
Monie v Coral Racing Ltd and Saunders v Scottish
   National Camps (1980)..345
Morton v Wheeler 207, 216, 223
Mouncer v Mouncer (1972)..323
Murphy v Brentwood (1990) 209

Nance v British Columbia Electric Rly 203
Nettleship v Weston (1971)..242
Newstead v London Express (1940) 234, 244

Oscar Chess Ltd v Williams (1957) 178

Page Motors v Epsom & Ewell 207
Paradine v Jane (1647)...167
Paris v Stepney Borough Council (1951) 201, 225, 243
Parker v British Airways Board (1982) 59
Parmiter v Coupland (1840) 229
Patel v WH Smith (Eziot) Ltd...217
Pepper v Hart (1993) 15, 19, 20, 112, 149
Pettitt v Pettitt (1970) 319
Phillips v Brooks Ltd (1919) 188, 189
Phillips v William Whiteley (1938) 209, 219
Polkey v AE Dayton Services Ltd (1987) 344
Powell v Kempton Park Racecourse Co (1899) 17
Prentice (1994) 255, 260, 292

R v Ahluwalia (1993) 262, 267
R v Bailey (1983) 250, 252, 255
R v Bainbridge (1960) 276
R v Becerra (1976)..276
R v Benge (1865) 253, 254, 265
R v Bingham (1991) 279, 281
R v Blaue (1975) 253
R v Bourne (1952)...276
R v Brown (1993) 110, 249, 263
R v Burgess (1991) 261, 279, 280
R v Byrne (1960) 262
R v Caldwell (1981) 255, 260, 290, 291, 292
R v Carr Briant (1943) 64
R v Charlson (1955) 279

R v Cheshire (1991) 254, 266
R v Chief Constable of South Wales ex parte Merrick (1994) 270
R v Clarke (1927) 174, 261, 279, 280
R v Cogan & Leak (1975)...276
R v Coney (1882) 276
R v Cunningham (1957) 252, 276, 290
R v Curr (1967) 258, 273
R v Deller (1952) 256, 258, 265, 274
R v Duffy (1949) 266
R v Edwards (1975) 63
R v Gaming Board for GB ex parte Benaim & Khaida (1970) 162
R v Ghosh (1982) 274, 275, 292
R v Gibbins & Proctor (1918) 259, 260
R v Gibson (1990) 98, 299
R v Gomez (1993)...274
R v Governors of the Bishop Challoner Roman Catholic Girls'
  Comprehensive School & Another ex parte Choudhury (1992) 106
R v Gross 270
R v Hancock & Shankland (1986) 254, 259, 269, 289
R v Hardie (1984) 250, 252, 255
R v Hayward (1908) 265
R v Her Majesty's Treasury ex parte Smedley (1984)..............................10, 13
R v Holland (1841) 266
R v Hollinshead (1985) 273
R v Home Secretary ex parte Bentley (1993) 108
R v Home Secretary ex parte Brind (1991) 161
R v Home Secretary ex parte Cheblak (1991) 301, 309
R v Hyde (1991) 277
R v Ibrams (1981) 266
R v Independent Television Commission ex TSW case (1992) 161, 162
R v Inhabitants of Sedgley (1831) 17
R v Johnson (1989) 262, 267
R v Kemp (1956) 279
R v Latimer (1886) 255, 269
R v Lawrence (1981)...291
R v Legal Aid Board ex parte Bruce (1992) 44
R v Leicester City Justices ex parte Barrow & Another (1991) 50
R v Leicester Crown Court ex parte DPP (1987) 307
R v Lipman (1969) 250, 252
R v Liverpool Corp ex p Liverpool Taxi Fleet
  Operators' Association (1972) 162
R v McNaghten (1843) 63, 261, 277, 278, 278
R v Miller 259
R v Mitchell (1983) 255, 256, 265, 269
R v Moloney (1985) 250, 251, 252, 259, 275, 254, 289
R v Morris (1983) 274
R v Mowatt (1967) 252
R v Nedrick (1986) 250, 251, 252, 260, 269, 275, 289

| Table of Cases | xv |

R v Newell (1980) 267
R v O'Grady (1987) 268
R v Pagett 266
R v Parmenter (1991) 250, 251, 252, 314
R v Ponting (1985) 300
R v Quick (1973) 261, 279, 281
R v Registrar General ex parte Smith (1990) 16
R v Reid (1992) 290, 291
R v S of S for the Home Department ex p Khan (1985) 160, 162
R v Samuel (1988)..270
R v Sargeant (1974) 271, 282
R v Savage (1991) 250, 251, 252, 276, 314
R v Secretary of State for Transport ex parte
  Factortame Ltd (1991) 124, 125, 128
R v Self (1992) 311, 314
R v Seymour (1983) 260
R v Shivpuri (1986) 275
R v Siracusa (1989) 273
R v Smith 253, 266
R v Stone & Dobinson (1977) 259, 261
R v Sullivan (1983) 279, 281
R v Sulman 255, 260, 292
R v Summers (1952) 64
R v Thornton (1992) 262, 267
R v Towers (1874)...265
R v Tyrell (1894) 258
R v Venna (1975) 249, 250, 251
R v Wardrope 268
R v White (1910) 253, 259, 265
R&B Customs Brokers Co Ltd v United Dominions
  Trust Ltd (1988) 195
Re Sigsworth 58, 105
Read v Lyons (1947)...219, 245
Ready Mixed Concrete v Ministry of Pensions (1968) 210
Registrar General ex parte Smith (1990) 18
Rice v Connolly (1966)..304, 305
Ricketts v Cox (1982) 305, 312
Riggs v Palmer (1889) 58, 105
Rivers v Cutting 218
Robertson v Minister of Pensions (1949) 162
Robinson v Kilvert (1884) 216
Roe v Minister of Health (1954) 236
Rose v Plenty (1978)..211, 245
Rossminster Ltd v IRC 307
Rylands v Fletcher (1868) 60, 109, 198, 218, 219, 220, 244, 245

Santos v Santos (1972) 323
Sayers v Harlow UDC (1958) 227

Sedleigh-Denfield v O'Callaghan (1940) 207, 208, 216, 223, 224
Sekhon v Alissa (1989)..319
Shah v Barnet LBC (1983) 17
Shaw v DPP (1962) 96, 98, 299
Sherras v De Rutzen (1895)..294
Sidaway v Bethlem Royal Hospital (1985) 237
Sim v Stretch (1936) 229
Simmenthal case (1979) 123, 124, 128
Slipper v BBC (1990) 231
Smith v Baker (1891) 202
Smith v Eric Bush (1989) 193, 194
Smith v Land & House Property Corp (1884) 183
Solle v Butcher (1950) 182
Southport Corp v Esso (1956)..206, 222
Stefan Kiszko 82
Stevenson Jordan & Harrison v MacDonald Evans (1952) 210
Stewart Gill Ltd v Horatio Myer & Co Ltd (1992) 195
Sturges v Bridgman (1879) 207, 212, 216, 223
Suter v Suter and Jones (1986) 324
Sweet v Parsley (1969) 15, 293, 294

Tanner v Tanner (1975) 320
Taylor v Caldwell (1863)..167, 168
Tesco v Nattrass (1972) 200
The Carlgarth (1927) 227
The Wagon Mound (No 1) (1961) 202, 209, 225
The Wagon Mound (No 2) (1961) 207, 208, 216, 223, 224, 243
Tinsley v Milligan (1993) 61, 111
Tolley v Fry (1931) 230
Tottenham Three 82, 83

Vacwell Engineering Ltd v BDH Chemicals Ltd (1966)..............................180
Van Gend en Loos case (1963) 122, 127

W (a minor) v Dolbey (1983) 291
W v W (1967)..339
Walters v WH Smith (1914) 311, 314
Ward v Tesco (1976) 64, 210
Waterman v Waterman (1989) 325
Watt v Hertfordshire County Council (1954) 201, 243
Watt v Longsdon (1930) 234
Wednesbury case 162, 163
Western Fish Products v Penwith DC (1981) 162
Wheat v Lacon (1966) 209, 226
Whitbread and Company v Thomas (1988) 345
Whitehouse v Jordan (1981) 237, 238
Whitehouse v Lemon 293
Whittington v Seale-Hayne (1900)..183

Table of Cases

Wieland v Cyril Lord Carpets (1969) 227
Williams v Carwardine (1833) 174
Williams v Compair Maxim (1982) 344
Wilsher v Essex Area Health Authority (1988) 237, 238, 242
Wilson and Clyde Coal v English (1938) 201
With v O'Flanagan (1936) 183
Woodman v Photo Trade Processing Ltd (1981)....................................194
Woolmington v DPP (1935) 63, 64, 268, 273, 295
Woolwich Building Society v Inland Revenue
  Commissioners (No 2) (1992) 60, 110, 155

Yip Chiu-Cheung v R (1994) 273
Young v Bristol Aeroplane Co Ltd (1944) 56
Youssoupoff v MGM (1934) 229

Table of Legislation

Accessories and Abettors Act 1861
  s 8 ....276, 277

Administration of Estates Act 1925 16

Administration of Justice Act 1970
  s 4 7

Administration of Justice Act 1985 32

Adoption Act 1976
  s 51 111

Animals Act 1971..226, 245
  s 4 243

Appellate Jurisdiction Act 1876..154

Bill of Rights 1688..110
  Article 9 ....19, 112

Child Support Act 1991 ....323, 325

Children Act 1989
  s 1 326
  s 2 ....320, 325
  s 4 320
  s 8 325
  s 17 331
  s 20 332
  s 22 332
  s 31(2) 332, 333
  s 34 332
  s 43 332
  s 44 333
  s 47 331

Children and Young Person Act 1969 ....70, 72

Civil Liability (Contribution) Act 1978................................211, 227

Company Securities (Insider Dealing) Act 1985
  s 1(3) 18

Legislation	Pages
Consumer Protection Act 1987	219, 220, 237, 240, 243, 245
s 1	180
s 2	180
s 3	180
s 5	180
s 4	180, 181
Contempt of Court Act 1981	
s 8	24, 26
Courts Act 1971	155
Courts and Legal Services Act 1990	36, 154
s 8	234
s 17	38, 39
ss 21-26	32
ss 27-33	27, 35
s 27	35
s 28	33
ss 34-53	33
s 54	33
s 55	33
s 61	28, 31
s 62	31
s 66	34
Criminal Attempts Act 1981	275
s 1	275
s 15	68
Criminal Damage Act 1971	289
Criminal Justice Act 1967	
s 8	252, 254, 259, 269, 288, 293
Criminal Justice Act 1988	
s 39	249, 275

Table of Legislation

Criminal Justice Act 1991 ....73, 286, 287
   s 1 ....69, 75, 76
   s 2 ....70, 76
   s 5 ....70, 75
   s 18 ....71, 76
   s 29 72

Criminal Justice Act 1993 ....71, 72, 74

Criminal Justice and Public Order Act 1994 308
   s 1 ....72, 305
   s 34-39 ....84, 86, 312
   s 48 ....71, 77, 87
   s 54-60 88
   s 145 98
   s 156 98

Criminal Law Act 1977 273
   s 1 258
   s 3 312

Criminal Procedure (Insanity and Unfitness to Plead) Act 1991 278

Criminal Procedure (Insanity) Act 1964 278

Criminal Sentencing Act 1991 ....282, 284, 285

Defamation Act 1952
   s 4 ....212, 232, 233
   s 5 232

EC Directive on Unfair Terms in
Consumer Contracts 1993/13 191

Employer's Liability (Defective Equipment) Act 1969 201
   s 1 18

Employment Protection (Consolidation) Act 1978
   s 57 ....343, 344
   s 58 344

Employment Protection Act 1975 6

European Communities Act 1972 ....13, 121
    s 2(1) 121
    s 2(2) 127
    s 2(4) 121
    s 3(1) 121

European Community Treaty
    Article 3(a) 139
    Article 6(1) 115, 121
    Article 8 303
    Article 8(a) 117
    Article 12 ....122, 128
    Article 30 ....123, 128
    Article 37 122
    Article 52 ....124, 128
    Article 53 122
    Article 93 122
    Article 100 ....115, 126
    Article 102 122
    Article 103 140
    Article 104(c) 140
    Article 105 140
    Article 108(a) 140
    Article 109 ....140, 141
    Article 115 5
    Article 121 5
    Article 127 5
    Article 128 5
    Article 130 136
    Article 137 ....133, 136
    Article 138 136
    Article 144 133
    Article 145 131
    Article 148 131
    Article 155 132
    Article 158 136
    Article 169 128
    Article 173 ....138, 139, 142
    Article 174 139
    Article 175 142

Table of Legislation xxiii

Article 177 117
Article 177 118
Article 177 122
Article 177 123
Article 177 124
Article 177 139
Article 177 143
Article 189 ....115, 116, 117, 123, 127, 131, 132, 135, 136

European Convention on Human Rights
   Article 8 303
   Article 10 ....299, 300, 308
   Article 11 303

Finance Act 1976
   s 63 19

Homicide Act 1957
   s 2 ....262, 271, 277, 280, 281
   s 3 ....262, 266, 267, 269, 281

Housing Act 1985
   s 87 18

Inheritance (Provision for Family and Dependants) Act 1975 321

Interception of Communications Act 1985 ....300, 301, 308

Interpretation Act 1985 ....11, 14

Judicature Act 1873-75 30

Judicial Pensions and Retirement Act 1993 154

Juries Act 1974..24

Law of Property Act 1930..320

Law Reform (Contributory Negligence) Act 1945......................................203

Law Reform (Frustrated Contracts) Act 1943...170
   s 1(2) 170

Legal Aid Acts 1949, 1979 and 1982 43

Legal Aid Act 1988 .... 41, 43, 146
    s 1 43
    s 3 43
    s 11 45
    s 16 45
    s 22 47
    s 27(2) 50
    s 34 44
    s 58 49

Libel Act 1843 232

Limitation Act 1980 238

Magistrates' Courts Act 1980
    s 38 69
    s 101 63
    s 133 69

Matrimonial Causes Act 1973 .... 318, 322
    s 1(2) 323
    s 3 323
    s 11 .... 327, 328
    s 12 328
    s 13 328
    s 17 .... 327, 330
    s 18 330
    s 23 .... 323, 328
    s 24 .... 323, 324, 328, 330

Merchant Shipping Act 1988 124

Misrepresentation Act 1967
    s 2(2) 184
    s 3 194

Obscene Publications Act 1959 299

Occupier's Liability Act 1957 .... 218, 219, 220
    s 2 .... 209, 210, 226

Occupier's Liability Act 1984 .... 218, 219, 220

Offences Against the Person Act 1861
    s 18 .... 249, 251, 252, 290
    s 20 .... 98, 110, 249, 251, 252, 290, 292
    s 47 .... 98, 110, 249, 250, 251, 275, 276, 277, 290, 314
Official Secrets Act 1989 300

Police Act 1964
    s 51 .... 305, 311, 313

Police and Criminal Evidence Act 1984 .... 48, 307
    s 1 312
    s 24 .... 304, 311
    s 25 .... 305, 312
    s 28 .... 312, 313
    s 56 270
    s 58 270
    s 76 .... 89, 306
    s 78 89
    s 116 270

Powers of Criminal Courts Act 1973 76
    s 35 70

Prosecution of Offence Act 1985 84

Rehabilitation of Offenders Act 1974 286

Rules of the Supreme Court
    Order 53 .... 157, 159

Sale and Supply of Goods Act 1994 .... 178, 179

Sale of Goods Act 1979
    s 35 179
    s 35A 179

Single European Act 1986 .... 13, 115, 117, 131, 133

Social Security Administration Act 1992 334

Social Security Contributors and Benefits Act 1992 334

Supply of Goods and Services Act 1982
    s 13 .... 178, 179
    s 3 178
    s 5A 179

Supreme Court Act 1981 154
    s 31 159
    s 50 .... 217, 224
    s 69(1) 25
    s 69(3) 25

Theft Act 1968
    s 1 .... 69, 273, 285, 292
    s 2 274
    s 3 274
    s 8 .... 275, 285
    s 9 .... 285, 311
    s 10 285
    s 22 285

Treaty of European Union 1993 13

Unfair Contract Terms Act 1977 192
    s 1(3) 193
    s 2 193
    s 3 .... 194, 195
    s 4 .... 194, 195
    s 5 193
    s 6 .... 193, 194
    s 7 .... 193, 194
    s 8 194
    s 12 195
    s 13 195
    s 10 195

Chapter 1

The English Legal System

Introduction

For those taking the AEB examination, English legal system questions may be asked as part of a problem question in Paper II and for others also it is advisable to take a flexible approach and not conclude that when Paper I has been attempted you will not be called on to demonstrate any further knowledge of the legal system. Thus in a problem question on contract you may be asked to advise the plaintiff of the appropriate court in which he would start his action and whether he/she would be eligible for legal aid.

Given that the subject English legal system is vast and complex you will need to ensure you have a thorough knowledge and understanding of several areas. Those include: the role of the law makers, the courts and Parliament; the provision of legal services; state assistance and the unmet need for legal services; the alternatives to court action and the involvement of the layperson in the administration of justice.

Within these themes a variety of questions may be asked. For example taking laypeople and the law, you may be asked a general question on their role or a more specific one about particular laypeople or you may be asked about reform of whole or part of layperson involvement. You will not only need an overview of the legal system but a thorough knowledge and understanding of its parts together with the ability to offer critical assessment of its merits and defects. It is not sufficient merely to explain and describe the system we have but necessary to appreciate how it has developed and how it should change.

You can bring your studies alive by observing changes or proposals for change as they happen. Law should not be a dry arid subject to study but rather a critical study of how the system works and with what effects. Law is said to be 'a means to an end'; this applies just as much to the legal system.

The 1980s and 1990s have already seen much change notably with statutes such as the Courts and Legal Services Act 1990 and the Legal Aid Act 1988 and with the publication of the Runciman Report on Criminal Justice more changes will follow. We live in an age where people are more aware of their legal rights, and defects in the legal system are being subjected to scrutiny. Awareness of 'law in action' will make your studies more interesting albeit that you are not required by the examination boards to know the most recent changes.

Knowledge of the legal system, particularly of precedent and statute, can be cross-referenced and used in the study of substantive areas such as contract, tort and criminal law.

Question 1

Critically assess the effectiveness of alternatives to litigation in the resolution of disputes.

General approach

This question involves a very topical issue namely the alternative means available for the resolution of disputes. You will need to consider briefly the traditional methods of resolution, ie the courts and tribunals whereby parties in dispute will have their problem adjudicated and a decision in favour of one will be reached.

It would be useful to note that the question concerns civil law as opposed to the criminal law in that reference to disputes assumes a civil action in tort or contract for example. However, increasingly, the traditional purpose of the criminal law to punish offenders for offences against society is being questioned and, in its place, the notion of rehabilitation has at different times found favour. Also the plight of the victim of crime is receiving attention and victim support groups, community service and meetings between offender and victim are initiatives that are being taken in attempts to reduce offending.

Some of the alternatives in the civil law area include mediation, conciliation, arbitration and mini-trials. Mention should be made of ACAS (the Advisory, Conciliation and Arbitration Service) which is available for employers and employees in dispute. The Citizens' Advice Bureaux, Consumer and Housing Advice Centres may also be mentioned together with administrative and commercial agencies who offer advice and counselling services.

An important point to note is that the alternatives available in the United Kingdom are as yet in their infancy and may not have general application in all types of dispute. However the concept of alternative dispute resolution (ADR) has received official recognition by the Lord Chancellor, for example in the recent Green Paper recommending changes in the divorce laws and for the use of mediation in the settlement of marital disputes. In discussing ADR, it will be essential to show awareness of the weaknesses in the present system, not only cost, delay and the inability of the majority of the population to qualify for legal aid but also any disadvantages arising from undertaking litigation such as the souring of future relationships. It does not follow that ADR in its various forms will be the ideal cure for such weaknesses or disadvantages and it may be that it would be better to improve on the present system. It also does not follow that ADR is appropriate in all types of dispute, in which case, after attempts are made to negotiate a settlement, litigation will be the only option.

Answer plan

- the question refers to the alternatives to litigation in the resolution of disputes - this suggests that the emphasis is on civil law such as contract, tort, family disputes, property matters for example; brief mention should be made of criminal law and its purposes and initiatives such as victim support groups
- outline of the traditional court and tribunal system - the courts and tribunals, appeals, adversarial (as opposed to inquisitorial) system; the role of the advocate; proof of facts relied on; the outcome of a civil trial (winner and loser); burden and standard of proof; the role of the judge; defects of the system - cost, delay, availability of legal aid and advice, complexity of the law, the costs rule (the loser pays the winner's costs); the perception of the process by the parties and what they want from the system - are their purposes best served?

- ADR-definition and examples including arbitration, mediation, conciliation and mini-trials; the uses of each, their advantages and disadvantages, their origins and development; proposals for extension in use; comparison between negotiation and settlement on the one hand and adjudication on the other
- role of ACAS and other agencies able to advise or act as go-betweens in the settlement of disputes; disadvantages of the present system which make the prospect of alternatives appear attractive - the need to improve on present system or develop alternatives?
- advantages and disadvantages of the alternatives to litigation presently available or which are proposed drawing on the experience of other legal systems and the types of cases where alternatives are appropriate; recent proposals for reform
- conclusions

Answer

As this question refers to the alternatives to litigation in the resolution of disputes it will be assumed that it is civil law disputes which are in point and not criminal law offences where the main purpose of the law is to impose a penalty on an offender found guilty of a criminal offence.

In passing it is to be noted however that where rehabilitation of the offender takes precedence over punishment and where the concerns of the victim receive attention even in the criminal justice system there may be room for alternative courses of action such as victim support groups, arrangements for victim and offender to meet at supervised sessions and for community service in place of sentences of imprisonment.

It is in the area of civil law that the use of alternatives to litigation have become prominent in recent years. The traditional means of settling disputes whether concerning breach of contract, tort, family matters or disputes over property has been by way of court action. Ours is an adversarial system whereby the parties to a dispute present evidence to the court, both orally and by means of documentary or other evidence, and on which the judge then arbitrates so as to declare a winner. The judge's role is that of an umpire who listens to the evidence provided by the parties or their representatives and who then weighs up that evidence and applies the law to the facts as proved so as to reach a reasoned solution. The judge does not conduct his/her own investigations into the matters in dispute as in inquisitorial systems.

In recent years one of the defects of our system has been said to be the very limited role of the judge but an advantage of this has been that the judge is seen to be impartial and aloof from the parties and can make a decision in favour of one of the parties solely on the quality of the evidence presented to the court. One problem with this is that the court is not primarily concerned with establishing the truth but rather deciding the legal rights and duties of the parties on the basis of the facts and law presented. How good such presentation is of course depends on the knowledge, skill and experience of the advocates presenting the case.

The nature of litigation, whether in adversarial or inquisitorial systems, is that one party wins and the other loses. Legal action under the former is likened to a battle or gladiatorial fight and in one sense this ensures that justice is done in that both parties will have had 'their day in court' and the issues in dispute will have been fully aired. It is an adjudicatory process where the court imposes on the parties a decision. This in itself ensures certainty, subject in appropriate cases to the right of the losing party to lodge an appeal to a higher court on questions of fact, law or a mixture of both.

However there are crucial defects with the present civil justice system and this has been the subject of close scrutiny in the Civil Justice Review established in 1985 and which culminated in the Courts and Legal Services Act 1990. The high costs and delay have been well documented as has the ever increasing unmet need for legal services.

State provision of legal aid and advice schemes are currently costing some £1.1 billion per annum and this has resulted in the Lord Chancellor in 1992 and 1993 taking stringent action to cut provision on legal aid and advice schemes. Rules of court ensure that the loser pays the costs of the winner ('costs follow the event') as well as his/her own and this in itself may well be off-putting for any intending litigant.

Given the difficulties with litigation, recent years have seen moves to provide alternatives to court action as a means of resolving disputes. In a strict sense the usual alternatives to litigation coming within the term 'alternative dispute resolution' include mediation, conciliation and mini-trials.

Before considering each of these it is useful to note that alternative dispute resolution is not a term of art and in many ways is only in a developmental stage in Britain. Thus it is worthwhile noting the role played by tribunals (administrative and domestic) and arbitration.

The former offer methods of adjudication of disputes similar to the courts and were established after the second world war to relieve the courts of disputes in the main relating to social welfare legislation and which involve the application of technical provisions. The courts exercise a supervisory jurisdiction over tribunals so as to ensure consistency and compliance with the law and in some cases a right of appeal may exist to the High Court or Court of Appeal from a tribunal decision. Most tribunals reach decisions by way of a panel of three (the chairperson is usually legally qualified) but the rules of evidence are less strict than in a court. Tribunals are not strictly alternatives to litigation in that statute invariably provides for their use and in many ways their procedures are akin to that of a court of law.

It is worth mentioning here the Advisory, Conciliation and Arbitration Service (ACAS) set up under the Employment Protection Act 1975. The main functions of ACAS are conciliation, arbitration, the offering of advice, powers of inquiry and the issuing of codes of practice.

In respect of the first, ACAS may offer to assist the parties to a trade dispute in bringing about a settlement. Where a complaint is brought before an industrial tribunal concerning unfair dismissal, trade union membership, racial or sexual discrimination, maternity or redundancy rights for example a conciliation officer appointed by ACAS is under a duty to attempt to promote a settlement. Any agreement formally entered into and signed by the parties will then preclude proceedings before the tribunal. So far as arbitration is concerned, a party to a dispute may request settlement by arbitration and, provided all parties consent, either an independent arbitrator not connected with

ACAS will be appointed or the Central Arbitration Committee. Conciliation procedures must have been exhausted unless special circumstances apply.

ACAS is also an advisory body for both employers and employees on all employment matters and has the power to inquire into industrial relations both generally and in particular industries and undertakings. ACAS also has power to issue codes of practice laying down guidelines as to good practice. As with all such codes they are not legally binding but failure to comply with the provisions of a code can be used in evidence.

Arbitration is an alternative to court proceedings most often used to settle commercial disputes; landlord and tenant matters; insurance and supply of goods and services. It may be quicker and cheaper than resort to court action and under the Arbitration Acts 1950-1979 the decision of an arbitrator can be enforced by the court. Two types are of particular interest: the arbitration procedure of the small claims court involving claims of no more than £1,000 (or larger sums where both parties agree and the matter is not a complex one); and s 4 of the Administration of Justice Act 1970 which provides for the appointment of judges of the Commercial Court as arbitrators in commercial matters subject to release from court duties. Most arbitrations result from the prior written agreement of the parties. A provision in a contract stipulating that reference to arbitration is a condition precedent to court action is enforceable. This is the so called *Scott v Avery* clause from the case in 1856 which established its validity. Any attempt to oust the court's jurisdiction by preventing a party to a dispute from referring matters of law to a court is however void as it is contrary to public policy. Arbitration is long established and may well provide an alternative to litigation and one which is conducted in private and where the decision reached is not subject to publicity.

A further advantage is that no precedent will be created as the decision is reached on the facts of each dispute. However the costs of the arbitration have to be met by the parties and, as with the majority of tribunals, no public assistance with costs is available. In the small claims procedure in the county court, the parties are encouraged not to employ solicitors but to act for themselves in the preparation and presentation of the case.

This brings us to what can strictly be described as 'alternative dispute resolution'. By a Practice Statement of the Commercial Court of 17 December 1993, it is provided that parties to commercial proceedings should in appropriate cases be encouraged to consider using alternative dispute resolution as an additional means of resolving disputes. It was noted that the Commercial Court was the primary forum for resolving commercial disputes but that mediation, conciliation and other ADR services ought to be considered. It was further noted that the judges would not be involved in any of the ADR procedures but would in appropriate cases invite parties to consider their use and that the court would maintain lists of suitable providers for this purpose.

This suggests that parties to a dispute may have ultimately to resort to litigation but that there may well be disputes where it is appropriate for other avenues to be exhausted first. Most parties to a dispute will enter into negotiations, either before or after seeking legal advice, and it may be possible to agree a settlement 'at the door of the court' but the 'threat' remains that if all else fails litigation will result and this will produce an answer. The emphasis is altogether different with alternative dispute resolution where, instead of a decision being imposed on the parties, they effect (usually assisted by trained professionals, but not necessarily lawyers) a settlement of the points in issue.

Mediation is at present most used in family disputes where it is recognised that a confrontational stance may not be the most effective way of handling such matters. The National Association of Family Mediation and Conciliation Services with some 57 local agencies offer support to parties who wish to retain control of a dispute rather than relying on lawyers whose initial role is only an advisory one.

The Centre for Dispute Resolution founded in 1990 by the Confederation of British Industry and several commercial law firms offers mediation services in commercial disputes. Mediation UK is a registered charity which provides an information and referral service for individuals or groups interested in mediation and other conflict resolution methods. Mediation is primarily concerned with communication and the facilitation of common ground between the parties. This process may take a more active form and this may be described as 'conciliation' where it is not only the parties but the 'adviser' who makes suggestions as to compromise or agreement. The greater the input of the adviser the more control he/she may be able to exert over the final outcome with the result that the process closely resembles more formal dispute resolution techniques. Not only lawyers are interested in offering mediation and conciliation services but also accountants, valuers, social workers and therapists.

Two other initiatives are worthy of note. Firstly the use in commercial disputes of the 'mini-trial' and secondly the use of ADR as a prerequisite to litigation. The mini-trial was described in a report prepared by Henry Brown for the Courts and Legal Services Committee of the Law Society in 1991 and this involves the legal teams of each party presenting their cases to the parties in the presence of a 'neutral adviser' (a retired judge or a neutral lawyer) with the aim of assessing the strengths and weaknesses and entering into discussions with a view to settling the matter. This can be undertaken at any stage of the formal litigation process and may well suggest that it would not be wise to continue on the litigation path. An example of the second is the Practice Statement already referred to but other initiatives can be found in the divorce county courts where district judges go beyond the 'pre-trial review' procedure and attempt to effect early settlement of property matters and those relating to the children. There is however no consistent practice although the benefits of such procedures are well recognised and the Report of the Committee on Alternative Dispute Resolution chaired by Sir Roy Beldam in 1991 recommended the use of 'facilitatory mediation' early on in the court process whereby the mediator would help the parties reach a solution rather than suggesting solutions to them.

The recently published Green Paper on Divorce reform emphasises the use of mediation services and stipulates a compulsory hour-long interview for those wishing to divorce. Refusal could result in refusal of legal aid. Present spending on legal aid in divorce amounts to £180 million and the policy behind the Green Paper is a drastic reduction in spending.

Having described in some detail the types of alternative dispute resolution available or proposed it is necessary to assess their effectiveness. A traditional view of litigation is that it ensures justice as between the parties in dispute and that the party with the stronger case will have judgment made in his or her favour. However, given the defects in the formal system, it might be argued that, in disputes involving relatively small amounts of money, family disputes where acrimony should be avoided, particularly where children are involved, neighbourhood disputes and consumer complaints, alternatives should be promoted either by private individuals or groups or in conjunction with the court process. Much the same arguments as those raised in favour of tribunals and arbitration, namely speed, cost and informality can be called in aid here to suggest that alternative dispute resolution may be appropriate in some disputes and its use will enable the courts to concentrate on those disputes where litigation is necessary.

Two points against its use should be noted. Firstly the parties may not be well equipped to effect a settlement and one party may well have greater bargaining power than the other. This necessitates careful use of the process and the involvement of the mediator or conciliator. Secondly court-inspired mediation may well cloud the role of the court and the judge in the eyes of the parties. The judge may no longer be seen as impartial and aloof but rather involved in the negotiation process and this may result in parties feeling they have been deprived of the best solution arrived at by dispassionate argument and having settled for a compromise solution.

Question 2

'It was the function of Parliament to legislate and legislation was necessarily in written form. It was the function of the courts to construe and interpret that legislation. In popular language, it was for Parliament to make the laws and for the courts to tell the nation including members of both Houses of Parliament, what those laws meant' *per* Sir John Donaldson, Master of the Rolls, in *R v Her Majesty's Treasury Ex parte Smedley* (1984).

Critically assess the approach of the courts to their role in interpreting statutes.

General approach

This question necessitates a full discussion of the rules applied by the courts in interpreting legislation, the reasons for their development and consequences of their use. The rules of statutory interpretation are to be found in judicial decisions and in that sense are part of the common law. The constitutional position is governed by the doctrine of sovereignty of Parliament which limits the role of the courts to interpreting statutes, there being no power to declare them unlawful. This doctrine however is now of limited effect where a statute conflicts with European Community law and, as established in the *Factortame* case (1991), the English courts will be obliged to apply European Community law. The courts have developed canons of construction to assist them in putting meaning to words, phrases or sentences used in statutes.

The traditional rules are the literal rule, golden rule, mischief rule, the *ejusdem generis* rule, the *noscitur a sociis* rule, the *expressio unius est exclusio alterius* rule and various presumptions together with the limited effect of the Interpretation Act 1978. Each of these deserve some explanation and illustration of their use. In recent years, largely as a result of membership of the European Community, the courts have on occasion adopted a more liberal approach to statutory interpretation known as the purposive approach. This reflects the different traditions of the Continental systems of law whereby legislation is drafted with less concentration on detail than in English law. The judge is concerned with general principles and in addition is not subject to the rules of binding precedent. The main concern of the judge is to look to the purpose of the legislation and this may not simply be gauged from the words used but by reference to extrinsic information leading up to the enactment.

English judges have traditionally taken a much more cautious view of their role particularly in the use of extrinsic aids to construction. They have primarily been bound by the words used in the statute and, until the House of Lords case of *Pepper v Hart* (1993), felt bound not to consult *Hansard*, the official journal of proceedings in Parliament.

Similar rules apply to the interpretation of delegated legislation but here the courts are not bound by the doctrine of parliamentary sovereignty and can- declare delegated legislation *ultra vires* and void. Dicta in *R v Her Majesty's Treasury ex p Smedley* (1984) is authority for the proposition that an aggrieved citizen adversely affected by delegated legislation may challenge its validity by way of judicial review. Alternatively an aggrieved party may defend an action brought under the provision on the ground that it is ultra vires and has no effect.

The interpretation of statutory provisions nevertheless vest considerable power in the courts who may be able to extend or narrow the scope of a provision. An illustration is the case of *R v Registrar General ex p Smith* (1990).

Answer plan

- explanation of the statement and outline of the constitutional role of Parliament and the courts; doctrine of parliamentary sovereignty in relation to statutes; compare delegated legislation and the doctrine of *ultra vires*
- the traditional approach to statutory interpretation - extrinsic and intrinsic aids to construction; the rules and presumptions; case-law illustrations
- the purposive approach derived from European jurisdictions; comments by Lord Denning in *Bulmer v Bollinger* (1974); case-law illustrations of its use and advantages and disadvantages; recent developments as a result of *Pepper v Hart* (1993)
- conclusions

Answer

The traditional theory of the constitution of the United Kingdom has been that Parliament is the supreme law-maker. This ensures that the courts have no power to question the validity of legislation and only have the role of interpreting statutory provisions which are called into question in disputes as and when they come before the courts for decision. As there is no written constitution, the courts are not able to strike down legislation as unconstitutional and thereby void. However in interpreting the meaning of statutory provisions, and similar rules apply to legislation and delegated legislation, the courts have potentially considerable power to widen or narrow the meaning to be attached to the words used by Parliament.

Traditionally the attitude of the judges has been cautious, confining themselves to the words used and not generally attempting to find the meaning from other sources. It is worth mentioning two points at this stage. Firstly that, in respect of delegated legislation, the court can question its validity on the premise that Parliament is the supreme law-maker and may grant power to make law to others for example government ministers. It does not follow that the delegate has unbridled power, rather the delegate's power is limited by the statute authorising the delegate to make law. Thus the court is concerned to see that the delegate has not exceeded or abused its power. If a comparison of the words of the enabling Act and the purported exercise of the power granted do not match the court may hold the delegated legislation to be *ultra vires* and void. This may be either as the result of an application for judicial review under Ord 53 of the Rules of the Supreme Court by an aggrieved citizen or where the citizen defends an action brought against him or her in reliance of the delegated legislation.

An illustration of the former is R v *HM Treasury ex parte Smedley* (1984) in which the applicant for judicial review questioned a draft Order in Council purported to be made under the European Communities Act 1972. The court held that although the applicant had *locus standi* to bring the claim, according to its terms it would, when made, be *intra vires*. Sir John Donaldson, Master of the Rolls, after discussing the respective roles of Parliament and the courts, went on to note that delegated legislation which was not authorised by statute or the common law would not have legal effect.

Secondly the traditional doctrine of supremacy of Parliament has been eroded, if not removed altogether, following membership of the European Community and subsequent developments culminating in the Single European Act 1986 and the Treaty of European Union 1993. In so far as European Union matters are concerned the courts of the United Kingdom will be obliged to recognise the supremacy of European legislation even where it conflicts with domestic legislation.

This was established in the *Factortame* case (1991) and more recently in *R v Secretary of State for Employment ex parte Equal Opportunities Commission* (1994).

In so far as domestic legislation does not involve a European element, then the traditional doctrine continues to apply and the court will be limited to interpreting the meaning of the words used in accordance with the rules developed by the courts. However since membership of the European Community in 1972, the English courts have become increasingly aware of the differences in drafting style of European legislation and that of the United Kingdom. The former tends to be much more widely drawn based on general principle whereas the latter is more specific and detailed. The approach to interpretation has therefore been quite different.

This difference in approach was commented on by Lord Denning in the case of *Bulmer v Bollinger* (1974) where he stated that 'meticulous detail' and 'precise grammatical sense' were to be ignored. The court should look to the 'purpose or intent'. He continued by saying that it was the spirit rather than the letter of the provision which was in question. The judge should put himself in the position of the legislator so as to fill a gap and arrive at a decision which the legislator would have done if they had thought about it. This has become known as the purposive approach but, in so far as domestic legislation with no European element is concerned, it is only at a developmental stage. The English approach is to apply the various rules of interpretation developed by the courts and which appear in the case-law so as to arrive at the meaning of a statutory provision which is the subject of a dispute.

We will now consider the main rules of statutory interpretation. The starting point for the judge in interpreting the words of a statutory provision (used in a wide sense to include delegated legislation) is the statute itself.

Generally extrinsic sources are not consulted to assist the judge in deciding the meaning of the words used. A judge may be assisted by so-called statutory aids to construction such as an interpretation section contained in the Act. The Interpretation Act 1978 itself may be of limited assistance and the long title of the Act which sets out its objectives may be useful. Limitations have traditionally been placed on judges consulting extrinsic aids to construction although in the case of *Davis v Johnson* (1978) it was recognised that a judge could properly consult Law Commission reports and the reports of committees and commissions appointed by Parliament or the government with a view to reform of the law. At that time it was recognised that judges would not consult *Hansard*, the official journal of proceedings in Parliament, but following the House of Lords case of *Pepper v Hart* (1993), in limited circumstances, this is now acceptable.

The case of *Fothergill v Monarch Airlines Ltd* (1990) illustrates the reluctance of the English courts to make use of extrinsic materials. Dicta stating that *Hansard* should not be consulted must now be read subject to *Pepper v Hart* (1993). It was noted by Lord Diplock that where an Act had been preceded by an official committee or commission report to Parliament which resulted in legislation the court could consult such a report so as to identify the 'mischief' which the Act was intended to remedy. These were the only acceptable *travaeux preparatoires* which could be consulted. However where legislation gave effect to an international treaty, the court should have access to the 'legislative history' (as it is called in the United States) to resolve ambiguity or obscurity. The court will not be free to consult extrinsic materials in any case where the meaning of the provision is clear. Only where there is some ambiguity or obscurity will the court be able to resort to extrinsic materials.

Another means of assistance is for the court to call on various presumptions which have become recognised, for example, that an Act will have prospective effect unless it expressly provides to the contrary. Another example is that an Act will not bind the Crown unless it expressly so provides. Another oft quoted presumption is illustrated in the case of *Sweet v Parsley* (1969) against the imposition of criminal liability in the absence of *mens rea*.

More usually assistance will be had from the rules of statutory interpretation including the literal, golden and mischief rules, the *ejusdem generis* rule, the *noscitur a sociis* rule and the *expressio unius est exclusio alterius* rule.

The literal rule is the logical starting point in interpreting the words of a statutory provision. The judge attempts to place on the words their literal or grammatical meaning and if this produces a desirable result the judge will look no further. In *Cresswell v BOC* (1980) a rating exemption on livestock was held not to apply to fish farms. A later provision expressly included fish farms.

However in the time-honoured phrase, if this results in absurdity, repugnancy or inconsistency, then the golden rule is applied. This is an exception to the literal rule and an example of its use is *Re Sigsworth* (1935) where a son murdered his mother and claimed as her next-of-kin to be entitled to her estate under the Administration of Estates Act 1925. On the literal meaning of the words used in the Act the son was entitled to inherit but the court decided that this would be repugnant and that the principle that a person should not profit from his own wrongdoing should take precedence.

It should be noted that in the case of *R v Registrar General ex parte Smith* (1990) the court held that an applicant who sought information in connection with his birth certificate was not entitled to such information despite a clear statutory duty on the registrar to supply such information because Parliament could not have intended such a duty to be absolute. Public policy demanded a limitation to be placed on this duty where compliance would give rise to a real risk of the commission of a serious crime or danger to a member of the public in the future.

This case was decided not by reference to the golden rule but rather by way of public policy whereby the court looked to the purpose of the provision and concluded that the duty was to be limited not only where past criminality had been proved but where there was a real likelihood of future criminality. This can be likened to the purposive approach. More will be said about this later. If neither the literal or golden rules provide a solution to a question of interpretation the judge must resort to one of the other rules. The mischief rule derives from *Heydon's Case* (1584) and involves the judge asking four questions: what was the law before the Act was passed?; what was the defect not remedied by the common law?; what remedy does the Act attempt to provide? and what is the reason for the remedy? In using this rule the judge is confined to the statutory provision itself together with accepted extrinsic aids such as Law Commission reports. It does not allow the judge a free hand to attach a meaning he or she thinks desirable. This rule has a narrow scope as is illustrated in the case of *Gorris v Scott* (1874) where sheep were washed overboard as a result of the ship owner not providing pens. The owner of the sheep claimed for his loss but it was held that the Act aimed at preventing the spread of disease not preventing sheep being washed overboard. In the case of *Gardiner v Sevenoaks RDC* (1950) an occupier of a cave used it to store films and disputed the local authority's claim that, as the cave was a premises, it was subject to safety legislation. The court held that a cave came within the meaning of the word 'premises'.

Three other rules deserve brief mention. The *ejusdem generis* rule provides that general words in a statute when preceded by particular words which form a class or genus are interpreted in accordance with the class words as, for example, in *Powell v Kempton Park Racecourse Co* (1899) where Tattersalls open-air racecourse was held to be outside a provision which prohibited the keeping of 'a house, office or other place for betting purposes'. Only covered accommodation was included.

The *noscitur a sociis* rule simply provides that the meaning of a word should be gathered from its context as in *Muir v Keay* (1815) where premises providing public entertainment were to be licensed and it was held that a cafe which at night supplied cigars, coffee and minerals needed a licence.

The *expressio unius* rule provides that where a provision lists specific matters this list will be exhaustive as in *R v Inhabitants of Sedgley* (1831) where rates were imposed on 'lands, tithes and coal mines' and the House of Lords held that no other type of mine was covered.

Having looked at the main rules of statutory interpretation it is time to consider the use by the English courts of the purposive approach and the extent to which the court has a creative role to play in the interpretation of statutes and development of the law. Lord Scarman in *Shah v Barnet LBC* (1983) said that this approach involved the court in looking at the general purpose of an Act so as to guage the intention of Parliament. The Act should be read as a whole in the light of permitted extrinsic aids to construction, if appropriate, so as to discover the intention or policy of Parliament. The court was not however permitted to interpret provisions so as to give effect to the judge's view of policy.

Although no reference to the purposive approach was made in the case of *Registrar General ex parte Smith* (1990), the court clearly applied itself to the question of what public policy demanded, that is what Parliament would have enacted if it had addressed itself to the problem before the court. The conclusion was that although the words on their face were clear the court was able to look to the general purpose of the statute and give effect to the principle that 'a man should not profit from his own wrong'.

Other cases illustrate that the courts are adopting a more liberal approach to statutory interpretation. In *Knowles v Liverpool City Council* (1993), the Court of Appeal in deciding a claim in damages for injuries which resulted from a faulty flagstone brought by an employee against his employer was asked to hold that 'equipment' included a flagstone. The court said that the term equipment should be interpreted broadly so as to give effect to the general purpose of the legislation. This case has subsequently been affirmed by the House of Lords.

The earlier case of *Coltman & Another v Bibby Tankers Ltd* (1987) also involved the interpretation of the word 'equipment' in s 1 of the Employer's Liability (Defective Equipment) Act 1969 and the House of Lords held that a ship in which the plaintiff's husband was lost at sea was included within this term.

In considering statutory provisions it is useful to note that the courts are often called on to interpret no more than one word as seen above. On other occasions a phrase, sentence or paragraph may be the subject of interpretation. The interpretation of one word is also illustrated in *Attorney General's Reference (No 1 of 1988)* which concerned the word 'obtained' in s 1(3) of the Company Securities (Insider Dealing) Act 1985. The court held that the recipient of inside information who dealt in the relevant securities committed an offence regardless of how he had come by the information. The word 'obtained' was to be given a broad meaning so as to give effect to the intention of Parliament.

Another recent illustration of the willingness of the House of Lords to adopt a purposive approach is *Waltham Forest LBC v Thomas* (1992) which concerned the interpretation of s 87 of the Housing Act 1985. Lord Templeman, giving the leading judgment, held that the defendant was entitled to a right of succession having resided with the deceased tenant for 12 months prior to the death although part of this time had not been at the house for which succession was claimed.

The Court of Appeal in *Re Marr & Another (bankrupts)* (1990) stated *per curiam* that 'the rule of last resort', that is where two sections of an Act are repugnant the last prevails, no longer applies. Nicholls LJ stated that 'such a mechanical approach to the construction of statutes is altogether out of step with the modern, purposive approach to the interpretation of statutes and documents'. The court should attempt to find which is the leading and which is the subordinate provision so as to give effect to the purpose of the statutory provisions.

Perhaps the most important development that has taken place in respect of judicial attitudes to statutory interpretation is the House of Lords judgment in *Pepper v Hart* (1993) where it was held that reference may be made to *Hansard* in construing a statute if the Act is ambiguous or obscure or the literal meaning leads to an absurdity and the materials relied on contain clear statements by a minister or other promoter of the Bill. Use of Parliamentary materials was held not to be an infringement of Art 9 of the Bill of Rights 1688 as the courts were not attempting to 'question' Parliamentary proceedings. The aim of the courts was to give effect to the true intention of Parliament and there was no good reason to prevent resort to Parliamentary materials where the words used were capable of bearing more than one meaning.

The case involved school teachers at Malvern College who were taxed on the value of a concessionary scheme under which their children were educated at the school. The teachers claimed that the value of the benefit they received was nominal whereas the Inland Revenue claimed that it was the average cost to the school. It is interesting to note that the statutory provision in question, s 63 of the Finance Act 1976, appeared on its face to be clear and that this was in favour of the Inland Revenue. However on consulting *Hansard* ministerial statements clearly showed that the intention was that such benefits would be taxed on their nominal value. The House of Lords held that the preferred interpretation was in favour of the taxpayers in the light of Parliamentary debates.

In the case of *Massmould v Payne* (1993) which was decided some days later the High Court held that the *ratio decidendi* in

Pepper v Hart required that there be ambiguity on the face of the legislative provision if reference was to be made to *Hansard*. This was again confirmed in *Sheppard v IRC* (1993). Thus the courts at the moment have restricted the use to which *Hansard* may be put and, as the Lord Chancellor pointed out in *Pepper v Hart*, as a matter of policy use of *Hansard* was not desirable as it would inevitably increase cost and delay in litigation. *Pepper v Hart* is to be seen only as a limited exception to the general rule.

It will be for the House of Lords in future to decide whether or not to restrict the use of *Hansard* to cases where ambiguity or obscurity appears on the face of legislative provisions or whether, as a matter of course, to compare legislative provisions with relevant Parliamentary materials as a means of assisting the court in reaching a decision. Greater development of the use of *Hansard* will involve the courts in policy issues and ensure a creative role in law-making.

In conclusion we have seen that the narrow literal approach to statutory interpretation has given way to a broader approach where courts are willing to give effect to legislative intention not simply by construing the words used but by looking outside the statutory provision. Such developments are at an early stage and there may well be good reason, particularly questions of cost and delay, for confining the role of the courts. Ultimately it is for Parliament to change the law to give effect to its policy decisions not for the courts to second-guess what Parliament might have intended.

Question 3

'The layperson plays a fundamental role in the administration of justice.'

Discuss.

General approach

This is a general essay, inviting you to discuss the role of the layperson in the administration of justice. You need to consider juries in both civil and criminal trials; the role of the lay magistrate as compared with stipendiaries and other judges and you might also include mention of lay members of tribunals, coroners and lay assessors. Your answer should not simply be descriptive of the roles of each and their contributions to the administration of justice but should also critically assess the role of each.

You should attempt to weigh up their relative worth, calling in aid any studies or other information you are aware of. You may decide to concentrate on one or more laymen to the exclusion of the other(s) but you should make this clear at the outset with your reason(s). For example you may know more about the workings of the jury in the Crown Court and decide to concentrate on the jury (comparing civil and criminal trials) and at the start of your answer informing your reader that 'for the purposes of this question' you will devote most attention to the jury mentioning the role of other laypeople in passing.

This is a fairly typical type of question but one which allows for plenty of variations; thus a question on laypeople may be restricted to any one group, or you may be asked about the role of the jury (generally, or in civil or criminal trials) or you could be asked about some reform proposal involving laypeople and their role.

Answer plan

- laypeople; lay magistrates; juries; lay members of tribunals; lay assessors; coroners
- for the purposes of the question concentration on lay magistrates and juries in Crown Court trials; civil juries, lay members of tribunals, coroners and lay assessors to be noted
- lay magistrates; number, appointment, qualifications and training, functions, role of court clerk; cost; effectiveness; criticisms; reform proposals; alternatives
- Crown Court trials; selection, jury in waiting, challenge, swearing in, vetting, 'nobbling', number, deliberation and role, foreman, relationship with judge, facilities, reform proposals particularly Runciman Royal Commission
- civil court trials; use of juries, criticisms and reform

- brief mention of lay members of tribunals, coroners and lay assessors
- conclusions; your own supported by research/findings of others or simply an assessment of the findings of others where you do not wish to disclose your own (your own views alone, most inadvisable!)

Answer

The involvement of the layperson in the administration of justice can refer to lay magistrates, juries, lay members of tribunals, lay assessors and coroners. It would be difficult in the time and space to cover each fully so for the purposes of this question we will concentrate on examining the role of lay magistrates and juries in Crown Court trials. Brief mention will be made of the role of each of the others later and it is not intended to suggest that they have an insignificant role in the administration of justice. Apart from anything else laypeople bring a non-legalistic approach to the resolution of disputes and free-up the time of the professionals so that they are able to make better use of their time.

There are some 566 magistrates' courts in England and Wales, staffed by some 29,441 lay magistrates and 76 stipendiary magistrates with jurisdiction to try all summary criminal cases; hold committal proceedings for all indictable offences and triable either way offences where the defendant elects for jury trial at the Crown Court. Magistrates' courts also have a limited civil jurisdiction in matrimonial matters and administrative functions including the granting of licences for gambling and sale of alcohol. Magistrates also sit in what is now called the 'Youth Court', formerly the Juvenile Court.

The stipendiary magistrate sits alone in the courts in larger towns and cities. They are full-time paid members of the judiciary appointed by the Lord Chancellor from barristers or solicitors of at least seven years' standing. They have all the powers of two or more lay magistrates.

The alternative title for a lay magistrate is 'Justice of the Peace' (abbreviated to JP). This signifies the ancient origins of the office and their original role in maintaining good order. Lay justices are not lawyers but, on appointment by the Lord Chancellor, undergo training to enable them to act 'judicially'. A major criticism in the past has been the system of appointment of lay magistrates and that only those well established in the community would be able to put themselves forward for appointment by the Lord Chancellor's Commission.

In recent years, however, there has been a publicity drive on the qualifications and attributes needed with the intention of opening up the ranks to people from all walks of life. It remains a salient question as to the extent that this has been, or could be, successful. Lay magistrates in particular have the reputation of being 'case hardened' and all too easily swayed by police evidence; this may well be an idea propagated by legal advisers suggesting to some defendants that they would receive a fairer trial in the Crown Court.

Three lay magistrates usually sit one of whom will be experienced and act as chairperson. They are assisted by a Clerk to the Justices who must be a barrister or solicitor of at least 5 years' standing. His or her role is to advise on points of law and procedure but should not attempt to make a decision for the justices or retire with them during their deliberations (other than to offer advice). He/she also administers the work of the court and keeps records of evidence and prepares depositions.

It can be seen, therefore, that magistrates perform a vast array of functions and have both civil and criminal jurisdiction. Their powers of sentencing in criminal matters is limited to a fine of £5,000 and/or six months imprisonment on summary conviction and the question must be asked, albeit that there are defects, what would be the alternative if lay justices were to be abolished?

Certainly the criminal justice system is already hard pressed to meet the demands on it and this would be more true if the 98% of all criminal trials dealt with were to be handled by legally trained personnel. It is interesting to note the implications of the proposals by Lord Runciman, should they become law, for abolition of the right of defendants in 'triable either way' offences to elect trial by jury. This may well increase the number of summary trials and, where the prosecution and defence do not agree on mode of trial, the matter will be referred to the magistrates.

At present it is alleged that many defendants faced with a 'triable either way' offence (the most important one is theft) will elect for trial by jury in the Crown Court. Ours is an adversarial system and it has been shown in the many examples of miscarriages of justice that the trial court is only as good as the evidence presented to it. The role of the jury of 12 laypeople, selected at random from the electoral register, is to listen and weigh up the evidence presented to them. They are described as arbiters of fact, whereas the judge is the arbiter of the law and who passes sentence where a defendant is found guilty. The jury should be guided in the law by the judge but should then be free to make up their minds as to the verdict. As was shown in the *Clive Ponting* trial in 1985 a jury can bring in a verdict in direct conflict with the judge. As Lord Chief Justice, Lord Taylor, has spoken, in support of retaining the right of a defendant to elect jury trial, and Lord Devlin once said of the jury, it is 'the lamp that shows that freedom lives'.

Such glowing statements are not always easily justified, and there is a serious limitation to research into the workings of the jury by s 8 of the Contempt of Court Act 1981. Despite such limitations, the studies that have been conducted tend to show that juries often reach the right decision but possibly for the wrong reasons. This is not a good reason for its retention but might suggest that the system could be improved and, again, the Runciman Commission suggested that better facilities be provided to ensure that evidence is ably presented and the provision of writing materials should be standard. Selection of at least three jurors from ethnic minorities in exceptional cases where there are compelling reasons should be allowed.

The Roskill Committee on Fraud Trials 1986 recommended the use of assessors in complex criminal fraud trials to replace the use of juries and recent trials such as the *Guinness* and *Blue Arrow* trials demonstrate the complexities that might better be dealt with by a tribunal headed by a judge assisted by two lay members.

Other points worthy of mention are majority verdicts (10 to 2 after a minimum of 2 hours and 10 minutes deliberation); the qualifications for sitting on a jury and the right to be excused under the Juries Act 1974 as amended; the ability of the prosecution to challenge without showing cause ('to stand by for the Crown'), whereas since the Criminal Justice Act 1988 the defence can only challenge for cause; the Attorney General's guidelines of 1980 (as amended in 1988) on jury vetting by the prosecution in terrorist trials and those involving national security so as to guard against bias and the proper administration of justice. The question of bias and personal prejudices is a crucial one and no doubt some members of some juries do not act from the best of motives all of the time. Another factor is the pressure that may be put on jury members to reach a particular decision, so-called nobbling by defence witnesses or supporters.

All in all, lay involvement in criminal trials in the form of a jury is a laudable one but which is in need of support and improvement to ensure that its members can act as impartial and informed arbiters of the facts and evidence presented to them. Along with the presumption of innocence, the right to jury trial is a fundamental part of English criminal justice.

It now remains briefly to consider the role of the jury in civil trials and the role of laypeople in tribunals, the use of coroners and lay assessors.

The right to a jury trial in a civil case is limited to cases of libel, slander, false imprisonment, fraud and malicious prosecution and, even here, there is an overriding proviso contained in s 69(1) of the Supreme Court Act 1981 that, at the discretion of the judge, jury trial can be denied in complex cases. By s 69(3), all other cases are to be tried without a jury unless the judge exercises his discretion. It has been accepted that jury trial is appropriate in defamation trials but in recent years the huge damages awarded to plaintiffs such as Sonia Sutcliffe and Jeffrey Archer has had the effect of weakening the assumptions on which this view is based. Such awards have resulted in a change in the rules whereby the Court of Appeal can substitute its own award for that of the jury.

Discussion of the role of laypeople in the law cannot be concluded without some mention of their part in tribunals where two laypeople experienced in the area in question are assisted in reaching decisions by a legally qualified chairperson. The main advantage of the layperson is his/her knowledge or experience in the areas dealt with including social welfare, employment and pensions, state benefits, the national health service, transport and rents.

Coroners must be barristers, solicitors or doctors of at least five years' standing and are appointed by a local authority to inquire into, by way of inquest, suspicious deaths occurring in their area. Where it is suspected that death was caused as a result of murder, manslaughter, poisoning or a road accident for example, a jury must be summoned. Coroners can also inquire into the ownership of property discovered in their area which has no apparent owner and may make a finding that certain classes of property are 'treasure trove', which reverts to the Crown.

Finally lay assessors may sit in the Admiralty Court of the Queen's Bench Division of the High Court to advise on technical shipping matters and also in the Restrictive Practices Court two laypeople experienced in business matters may assist the High Court judge. As was noted earlier, the Roskill Committee recommended the use of lay assessors in complex fraud trials.

In conclusion the involvement of the layperson in the administration of justice is long established and seen to be beneficial in itself. So far as criminal trials are concerned, although there are defects, some of which have been addressed by the Runciman Report, the use of juries ensures a sense of balance and may well give the benefit of the doubt to a defendant. This is important given the presumption of innocence and the requirement that the prosecution prove guilt beyond all reasonable doubt. The proposal to remove jury trial for 'triable either way' offences can be said to detract from this, but lends support to the value of lay magistrates in serving the interests of justice.

The involvement of lay magistrates is also long established and provide, if nothing else, quick and cheap justice. This should not however be an argument for extending their jurisdiction but rather ensuring that the system accords with and promotes the underlying principles of fairness and presumed innocence. Recent cases indicate the weaknesses of jury trial in the Crown Court but this should not necessarily be an argument for their abolition but rather their improvement. Not such a strong case exists for retention of the jury in civil cases, and the amount of damages recently awarded in defamation cases has seriously brought their effectiveness into question. Section 8 of the Contempt of Court Act 1981 has seriously hampered research into the effectiveness of jury trial and commentators have called for its abolition. Lord Runciman recommended amendment of this provision.

Question 4

The Bar has promoted the idea of retaining the independent barristers' and solicitors' professions so as to ensure that the needs of the public are best met.

(a) Consider the functions of each of the professions and the recent changes that have been made in their roles. (16 marks)

and

(b) Critically assess the advantages and disadvantages of fusion and whether this would best provide for the needs of the public. (9 marks)

General approach

This question invites a discussion of the traditional functions of barristers and solicitors together with the changes proposed and given effect to by the Courts and Legal Services Act 1990. Some knowledge of the proposals which preceded the Act should be mentioned including the Benson and Marre Reports, Green and White Papers and the main provisions of the Act itself which affect the legal profession. The question of fusion should be considered and the main arguments put forward by both sides of the profession for change or retention of the present system.

Implementation of the 1990 Act by way of delegated legislation should be considered and in particular the decision in December 1993 of the Lord Chancellor's Department under ss 27-33 to end the barristers' monopoly of rights of audience in the higher courts.

You are asked to critically assess the advantages and disadvantages of fusion. Assuming that this is in prospect in the near future, some reference should be made to other jurisdictions where a fused profession operates. The second part of the question refers to the needs of the public and you will need to consider whether the public's needs will be best met by a fused profession. In the past the barristers' side of the profession has resisted change on the basis that the needs of the public have been best met by a divided profession. Given the present defects of the legal system, in particular high costs, reductions in legal aid provision and delay in cases coming to court, a fused profession may appear attractive at first sight in that lower costs and greater efficiency might be achieved.

Answer plan

- tackling part (a) first, and taking into account that it is worth seven marks more than part (b), consider the traditional roles of solicitor and barrister; brief mention to be made of the historical development of the divided profession; the solicitor operates alone or in partnership in the high street, the barrister in sets of chambers as sole practitioners; solicitors approached directly by the lay client for advice, preparation of documents and in difficult cases referral to a barrister; contract entered into between solicitor and lay client; limited rights of audience in the lower courts; immunity from suit when acting as an advocate; liability in the tort of negligence for faulty service other than litigation or matters leading to litigation; the Law Society, the governing body; barristers offer specialist advice following instructions from a solicitor; exclusive rights of audience in all courts; traditionally no contract entered into with solicitor for payment of fees (an honorarium) but s 61 of the 1990 Act now applies; role of the barristers' clerk; governing body, the General Council of the Bar; education and training of both sides of the profession; relationship between both sides

- proposals for reform of the divided profession; the Benson Report 1979, the Marre Report 1988, the Lord Chancellor's Green Papers of 1989, the White Paper, a framework for the Future 1989, the Courts and Legal Services Bill and the Act 1990; the main provisions of the Act and their coming into effect, in particular ss 27-33 of the 1990 Act

- taking part (b) consider the advantages and disadvantages of fusion; how is the public interest best served - by reforming the present system or by fusion?

  Advantages: the lay client retains one professional rather than two; reduction in delay and cost; less room for error or misunderstandings; specialisation according to area(s) of law rather than function; continuity and increase in trust between professional and lay client; market forces and the ending of monopolies and restrictive practices; removal of out-dated traditions; impact on judicial appointments

Disadvantages: confusion between old and new system; need for transitional provisions; the divided profession has stood the test of time and it is steeped in history and tradition which enhances its authority; disappearance of the 'cab rank' rule; loss of objectivity and independence of the Bar; loss of expertise built up over time; lowering of standards; the traditional links between Bar and judiciary will be lost; reduction in availability of specialist advice and advocacy skills

- conclusions; the present system and the state of reform; fusion in all but name?; future developments

Answer

(a) The traditional division of the legal profession is between barristers and solicitors. The barrister has, until recent times, been seen as the senior member of the profession acting as the specialist or consultant to whom the solicitor refers legal questions for opinion. The solicitor operates in partnership or alone usually from a high street office directly with the lay client seeking advice or the preparation of documents such as a will or a contract. The solicitor has been likened to a general practitioner with only limited rights of audience that is a right to represent clients in court. These have been limited to magistrates' courts and the county court and, in very limited circumstances, the High Court. At the present time there are some 7,000 practising barristers, some 55,000 solicitors holding practising certificates from the Law Society and some 10,000 solicitors' firms in England and Wales. Not all barristers and solicitors practise their profession and, of those who do, not all are in private practice. Some are to be found in industry, local and central government, Law Centres, the Crown Prosecution Service and education.

The division between solicitors and barristers may be said to have stood the test of time, at least for over 100 years in its present form, but it has evolved and so there appears to be no reason for it not continuing to change in the future. The extent and pace of change may well be in question and it might be argued that radical changes should be brought about gradually after due consideration of the issues.

Before the Judicature Acts 1873-75 barristers with rights of audience in the superior courts were known as 'Serjeants-at-Law' and others were 'Apprentices-at-Law'. After the 1873-75 Acts the term 'barrister' was used to refer to those with rights of audience in all courts and with the monopoly in the higher courts.

The term 'solicitor' referred to those who solicited clients and who conducted business in the Chancery courts. 'Proctors' performed similar functions in the Ecclesiastical and Admiralty courts and attorneys worked in the common law courts. All three were primarily concerned with the preparation of cases for trial and were non-advocates. The Law Society was incorporated in 1831 and was granted a Royal Charter in 1845. Following the Judicature Acts, solicitors, proctors and attorneys merged and adopted the title 'solicitor'.

An appreciation of the historical development of the divided profession shows that it has not been static and that future changes may well be warranted to meet changing needs in the provision of legal services. Whether such change should take the form of fusion of both sides of the profession will be considered more fully in the second part of the question.

What then does it mean to say that the legal profession is a divided one? We need to consider briefly some of the differences between the two sides of the profession before moving onto their functions. The intending barrister after he or she completes the academic stage (obtaining a qualifying law degree or a degree in a non-law subject and completion of the Common Professional Examination) seeks admission to an Inn of Court (Gray's Inn, Lincoln's Inn, Inner Temple and Middle Temple) where 12 terms are kept and by dining in hall on at least 18 occasions. In addition, a full-time one year course organised by the Council of Legal Education is undertaken and on completion of this and dining the student is 'called to the Bar'. One year is then spent in pupillage. This is a period of 'apprenticeship' with a senior barrister, the first six months of which is usually spent drafting documents under the pupil master's supervision and accompanying him or her to court. In the latter six months the pupil may be able to conduct his or her own cases.

The intending solicitor having completed the academic stage (qualifying law degree, non-law degree and Common Professional Examination or Legal Executive route) undertakes the vocational stage of training, the Legal Practice Course, which is a full-time one year course (or a part-time two year course) run by some universities and the College of Law. There normally follows two years of practical training, now described as 'Articles of Training', but formerly called 'Articles of Clerkship', in which the trainee enters paid employment under the supervision of a solicitor. During this time a Professional Skills Course is completed and on completion of the two year training the trainee is admitted to the Solicitors' Roll. Following admission the solicitor may take up a position in private practice or an appointment in local or central government, industry or the court service. The barrister similarly may take up such appointments.

Barristers in private practice operate from sets of chambers which traditionally were located in London close to the Inns of Court. Sets of chambers are now located in all large cities and towns and work comes to the barrister via the Clerk to Chambers from an instructing solicitor. Instructions are in the form of a written document called a 'brief' on which will be marked the fee. The so-called 'cab-rank' rule applies with the effect that a brief should not be refused if the fee is a proper one, the case is of a type normally handled and the barrister is not otherwise engaged.

Traditionally the fee was a honorarium that is binding on the solicitor in honour only. By s 61 of the Courts and Legal Services Act 1990 barristers may now enter into contracts for the provision of services. Advocates (whether a barrister or a solicitor) have in the past been immune from claims for damages in the tort of negligence in respect of work conducted in court or which is preparatory. The cases of *Rondel v Worsley* (1969) and *Saif Ali v Mitchell* (1978) are authority for this proposition which has now been given statutory effect by s 62 of the Courts and Legal Services Act 1990 which applies to all those who in future may obtain advocacy rights under this Act.

This is not to say that members of either side of the profession will escape claims that they have not provided a service of a high standard. Solicitors are governed by the Law Society and barristers by the General Council of the Bar and the Inns of Court. In addition the Solicitors Complaints Bureau and the Solicitors' Disciplinary Tribunal oversee complaints of shoddy work by solicitors. By ss 21-26 of the 1990 Act a Legal Services Ombudsman has been established to oversee the way in which both sides of the profession handles complaints. The Ombudsman does not deal with complaints direct but can recommend compensation to be paid where it is shown that the complaints procedure is itself defective. It was announced in January 1994 that the Bar intended to offer clients a complaints procedure and a report of the committee chaired by Lord Alexander QC which considered this and conducted a review of professional standards was issued in mid-1994.

After 10 years practice, a barrister may apply to the Lord Chancellor to 'take silk' (ie become Queen's Counsel). This entitles the barrister to be more selective in the cases he or she takes, to be accompanied in court by a junior barrister, to wear a gown adorned with a strip of silk and to be addressed as 'QC'.

Having discussed some of the distinguishing features of barristers and solicitors, it is now necessary to explain more fully their functions. The solicitor in private practice would be expected to offer advice to a lay client on a wide variety of matters including wills and probate, conveyancing and property matters, personal injury claims and other tortious claims, company and commercial matters, employment matters and seeking counsel's opinion in complex matters or where litigation in the higher courts was a possibility.

Before the Administration of Justice Act 1985 the 'bread-and-butter' work of solicitors in private practice was said to be in carrying out land transactions (conveyancing). The Royal Commission on Legal Services, the Benson Report of 1979, had recommended not only retention of the monopoly but its extension to preparation of contracts for sale of land in addition to transfers of ownership. This Commission also recommended retention of the divided profession ensuring continuance of the traditional barristers' monopoly of rights of audience in all courts. However, the Farrand Committee in 1984 recommended the establishment of a professional body of licensed conveyancers and this was set up under the 1985 Act. Solicitors considered that this would make serious inroads into their conveyancing monopoly but a greater threat was yet to come. This took the form of a proposal to permit banks and building societies to conduct conveyancing transactions having solicitors as members of their staff. In 1989, the Lord Chancellor published three Green Papers one of which was entitled 'Conveyancing by Authorised Practitioners'. This proposed a simplified authorisation procedure regulated by the Lord Chancellor in accordance with a code of conduct. This was welcomed by those who wished to see 'one-stop shops' in which a house purchaser could obtain the services of an estate agent, solicitor and lender under one roof. It received a less than enthusiastic response from the Law Society whose main criticisms were the likelihood of a conflict of interest and decimation of the high street solicitors' firm.

The White Paper of 1989 entitled 'Legal Services: A Framework for the Future' attempted to address both issues and offered greater protection to solicitors and safeguards to the public against conflicts of interest. The Courts and Legal Services Act 1990 ss 34-53 set up complex machinery for the provision of conveyancing services. The Authorised Conveyancing Practitioners Board, responsible to the Lord Chancellor, supervises the workings of the system and there is provision for Conveyancing Appeals Tribunals and a Conveyancing Ombudsman.

Other provisions which change the traditional role of the solicitor are contained in the Courts and Legal Services Act 1990. By ss 54 and 55 the solicitors' monopoly in probate work has been removed. Banks, building societies and insurance companies are now permitted to offer such services as are legal executives.

Section 28 of the Act removes another monopoly of the solicitor that is in the conduct of litigation. This is not to be confused with rights of audience. Conduct of litigation involves preparations for trial such as the issue of a writ and the performance of ancillary functions during the course of proceedings whereas rights of audience involve the right to appear before a court to represent a litigant. 'Authorised bodies' have the right to authorise others to conduct litigation and, at the moment, this means the Law Society which is able to grant rights to those who comply with stated criteria.

Section 66 of the Act established multi-disciplinary partnerships (solicitors will be able to enter into partnership with other professionals such as surveyors or accountants) and multinational partnerships which will allow solicitors to enter into partnerships with foreign lawyers (in particular with those in the European Union).

Having noted the traditional functions of solicitors and how these have been affected by the Courts and Legal Services Act 1990 it is time to look at the functions of barristers and how their traditional role has been affected. Barristers, or counsel as they are often referred to, act as advocates and they have had a right to appear in all courts and a monopoly on rights of audience in the High Court, Court of Appeal and in most areas of work in the Crown Court. It follows that the rights of audience of solicitors have been limited. They have been able to appear in the magistrates' courts and county courts and, in limited circumstances, in the Crown Court. In 1984, in the light of the proposed reforms, the Law Society decided to fight for rights of audience in all courts for solicitors. The Law Society published 'Lawyers and the Courts: Time for Some Changes' in which it was suggested that the intending lawyer should receive a common education and training. The Bar would be reserved for specialists following further examinations. The Bar rejected out of hand any suggestion that it should lose its monopoly over rights of audience. The Marre Committee Report was published in 1988 and recommended rights of audience in the Crown Court for solicitors and that they should be eligible for appointment as High Court judges. This was a committee established by both sides of the profession to report on the state of legal education, the profession and provision of legal services. The Lord Chancellor's Green Papers and White Paper followed which put forward the proposition that rights of audience should be granted to those properly trained and who demonstrated competency, not according to a division between barrister and solicitor.

Generally the proposals did not find favour although the Law Society continued to press for the extension in the rights of audience. The Bar considered that such reform would threaten the continuance of the junior bar and would not be in the public interest.

The Courts and Legal Services Act 1990 ss 27-33 provide for a statutory framework for granting rights of audience by the 'appropriate authorised body' and permitting the Lord Chancellor to designate 'authorised bodies' as provided for under Sched 4 of the Act. Existing rights of audience are preserved so that the Law Society and the General Council of the Bar are deemed to be 'authorised bodies'. As already mentioned s 28 relates to the right to conduct litigation.

The provisions of the 1990 Act have been or are being brought into effect by Regulations put before Parliament by the Lord Chancellor. Given the far-reaching nature of the changes in respect of rights of audience, both sides of the profession have had to review the likely effects of the changes. The Bar has responded by relaxing many of its practice rules in respect of advertising, the establishment of chambers and training of pupils.

In early December 1993, it was announced that the Lord Chancellor and four senior judges had approved the Law Society's application for solicitors in private practice to be given rights of audience in civil and criminal proceedings in the House of Lords, Court of Appeal, the High Court and Crown Court under s 27 of the Act. Solicitors employed by the Crown Prosecution Service or elsewhere have not been granted rights of audience and the decision on this has been deferred. The Law Society has not been able to estimate how many solicitors in private practice might wish to take up such rights but certainly those who regularly appear in the magistrates' courts and those engaged in commercial work may do so. A register has been set up to gauge likely demand. The Bar says that it is ready to face competition noting that barristers are the pre-eminent advocates and that solicitors will be expected to point out to clients that they can choose to be represented by a barrister.

The Regulations provide for the grant of higher courts' qualifications in civil proceedings, in criminal proceedings or in both. It is intended that only existing solicitor advocates will apply for the grant of such rights and they will have to demonstrate experience, knowledge of evidence and procedure and complete an advocacy training course.

In conclusion, therefore, the traditional roles of solicitor and barrister are changing and we are about to enter an era when solicitors may well be competing with barristers as advocates in the higher courts. In the long term this will no doubt not only have implications for the legal profession but also the composition of the judiciary which traditionally in the main has been drawn from the ranks of barristers.

(b) In any discussion of the effectiveness of the legal profession the question of fusion always seems to arise. At the root of the discussion is the need to provide legal services which the public can afford and trust. Much criticism has been levelled not only at the legal profession but the legal system generally and inevitably the attainment of justice has to be weighed against cost. The present system has undergone major reforms as a result of the Courts and Legal Services Act 1990 and many would argue that we have gone far enough along the path of reform and that fusion is undesirable.

Fusion would entail drastic changes at all stages of training and practice so as to arrive at one body of legal professionals. The traditional titles might or might not be retained, but the essential change would be in the recognition that there would no longer be a division based on function. Essentially, at present, the distinction is between on the one hand the advocate and on the other the desk-lawyer offering advice, preparing documents and conducting business matters. Instead, the lawyer would be able to take a case on and deal with it from start to finish whether or not that entailed resort to the higher courts. The client would then only need to have one lawyer to handle the case and, on first impression, this may offer the advantages of simplicity, speed and lower costs. The likelihood of error or misunderstandings would be reduced as would delay whereas the lay client would develop trust with one professional rather than, at a crucial stage, being handed over to another who might appear distant and disinterested in the client's problem.

However, the reality may be quite different in that specialisation is likely to result, not only as to legal knowledge but also as to function. Thus some lawyers will specialise in advocacy and others in desk-work. Firms will need the expertise of both so that the client's needs can be met from within the firm rather than passing the client to an expert outside the firm. It may be that only the large firms will be able to command the services of specialists with the likely result that small firms will cease and it is possible that costs will increase.

Certainly if the titles of barrister and solicitor are no longer used the system could be seen to be much more straightforward but such change would need to be made very gradually so as to avoid confusion between the old and the new and for it to become accepted given the mystique and history attached, not only to the titles, but the roles of each. It might be argued that fusion has been achieved in all but name following the announcement that solicitors will now be able to have advocacy rights in the higher courts. The last bastion of monopoly has been broken and free market forces will be able to operate so that rights of audience will in future be granted to those who demonstrate proper training, experience and who comply with codes of conduct. The test will be one of merit and not an archaic distinction between barrister and solicitor. However time will tell as to how many solicitors choose to seek advocacy rights and in any event they are to be limited to those with at least three years post-qualification experience.

The Benson Report in 1979 recommended that the two branches of the profession should remain distinct and that the needs of the public would be best met by a divided profession. It is important to note however that Benson also recommended a huge increase in the number of Law Centres and extension in the legal aid and advice provision. In rejecting calls from the Law Society to extend the rights of audience of solicitors the Benson Report concluded that such extension would not be in the public interest because advocacy involved specialist skills which could not be acquired or retained by solicitors. Furthermore the livelihood of junior barristers would be put at risk if solicitors were granted rights of audience in the Crown Court and lastly the client was better served by a solicitor who sought counsel's opinion on the client's behalf than in a system where the client was able to choose an advocate from amongst those offering advocacy services. Again on first impression the notion of a free market is attractive in that demand will govern supply but the harsh reality often is that there will be losers and this may not only be legal practitioners but also the lay client unable to find or pay for the best advice.

The object behind proposals for the reform of the legal profession must be the quality and availability of legal services to the public. Both sides of the profession have put forward their respective cases on the basis that they represent the public interest. The solicitors' side of the profession, having lost its traditional conveyancing, probate and conduct of litigation monopolies, sought extension in the rights of audience. The Bar attempted to prevent such extension on the ground that the independence and objectivity of the Bar would be lost and this would be detrimental to the public interest. Critics have concluded that each side of the profession has promoted its own interests in an attempt to ensure its own survival.

In response to the Green Papers, the Bar published 'Quality of Justice' in which it was said that the public interest would be best served by an independent Bar. The Law Society published 'Striking the Balance' in which it was suggested that the proposals put too much power into the hands of the government although it was in favour of extending the rights of audience.

What then are the aims of the Courts and Legal Services Act 1990? In s 17 of the Act, the general objective of Part II is the development of legal services 'by making provision for new and better ways of providing such services and a wider choice of persons providing them, while maintaining the proper and efficient administration of justice'. In s 17(3)(c), those with rights of audience or rights to conduct litigation are required not to withhold those services on any of three grounds, namely, that the case is objectionable to him or her or to any section of the public, or that the conduct, opinions or beliefs of the prospective client are objectionable, or on any ground relating to the source of funding for the prospective client, such as legal aid.

This is a statutory form of the present 'cab-rank' rule which is to apply to all advocates. At the time when the Bill was before Parliament the Bar attempted to have a similar provision apply to all legal services but a compromise was agreed so that in the conduct of matters, other than advocacy and the conduct of litigation, no such rule is to apply.

One of the main disadvantages of fusion is said be the loss of the 'cab-rank' rule. However other commentators point out that it has not always been strictly applied and in any event has always had very limited effect on those appointed Queen's Counsel. Section 17 of the 1990 Act ensures that in respect of advocacy and the conduct of litigation those providing those services will be subject to this rule so as to retain their objectivity and independence.

In respect of other legal services, even under a fused system, these would be provided in much the same way as under the present divided system and the quality of service would depend, as it does now, on funding.

Other disadvantages of fusion put forward include the charge that it will result in a lowering of standards, not only because those with little advocacy or litigation expertise will come into the marketplace but also because members of the junior Bar will have to compete with greater numbers of advocates and will not be able to acquire experience as easily as in the past.

Another is that as the present system, albeit with defects, has stood the test of time there is no purpose served in such a radical change. That would necessitate transitional provisions and would increase the likelihood of confusion between the old and new systems. In any event such a change would discard centuries of tradition and custom and this would do untold damage to the authority and respect for the profession and legal system. Such tradition has moulded a special trust between the Bar and the judiciary and members of the judiciary have been almost exclusively drawn from the ranks of barristers. On fusion this would be lost but already, with the extension in advocacy rights recently announced, judicial appointments will in the future no doubt be made from the ranks of advocates generally.

One argument in favour of fusion might be the experience of other countries. Almost universally other countries, including Commonwealth countries based as they are on the common law, have fused professions. However this may not provide a suitable model given the different origins and traditions, legal system and judicial structure of some of systems with fused professions.

Ultimately the question has to be resolved by reference to public interest and here there may be no one interest at stake. For instance the interests of a commercial client may be quite different from those of a private individual. This must not be confused either with the interests of barristers and solicitors wishing to perpetuate their side of the profession. In addition complete fusion will necessitate a major overhaul of the provision for education and training of lawyers and the codes of conduct governing the provision of legal services. Given the financial strictures on state assistance by way of legal aid and advice schemes it might be argued that rather than debating the issue of fusion it would be more profitable to improve further on the system as it has now developed as a result of the Courts and Legal Services Act 1990.

Recent initiatives in the use of alternative dispute resolution and the drastic cuts in funding of legal aid and advice schemes suggest that those providing legal services will have to diversify so as to compete in a marketplace free of many of the traditional monopolies and restrictive practices which had perpetuated the divided profession.

Question 5

In the light of recent developments, critically examine the statutory schemes for legal aid, advice and assistance in criminal and civil matters.

General approach

The main issue concerning state assistance for those unable to afford legal services is that of the cost to the taxpayer of providing state assistance and the changes made in funding which has resulted in the numbers of people who are eligible for assistance being reduced.

In 1992/93 the total budget for the Legal Aid Board was reported to be more than £1 billion. The legal profession received £1.1 billion, the taxpayer meeting £900 million of this bill and £200 million having been raised from contributions, the statutory charge and costs.

This would suggest that the legal system is being used to capacity but it is probable that there remains considerable unmet need for legal services. Discussion of legal aid and advice provision must now take account of the statutory instruments which took effect at Easter 1993 aimed at drastically cutting the legal aid bill. The Law Society subsequently challenged these measures by way of an application for judicial review. The court held that the Society had *locus standi* to bring the application but no relief was granted as the Lord Chancellor had acted within his statutory powers.

The Legal Aid Act 1988 governs provision of the state schemes and this is updated annually by way of statutory instrument presented to Parliament by the Lord Chancellor.

State schemes include legal aid in civil matters; legal aid in criminal matters; the legal advice (Green Form) scheme and Advice By Way of Representation (ABWOR) scheme and the Duty Solicitor scheme to be considered and the rules for assessment. Disposable income and capital limits and 'merits' tests apply for civil and criminal legal aid schemes.

Administration is by the Legal Aid Board of civil legal aid and by the magistrates' court of criminal legal aid. The proposal is to transfer responsibility for criminal legal aid from the magistrates' courts to the Legal Aid Board.

There is a reduction in the availability of assistance: some 27,7000 people were no longer eligible under the Green Form scheme with effect from 12 April 1993. No one with more than £61 a week (income support level) will qualify. The Green Form scheme covers preliminary advice, letter writing and applying for legal aid up to a maximum of two hours (three in matrimonial disputes). Those with complex cases will in future have to fund the preliminary work themselves.

Brief mention should be made of voluntary schemes, for example the £5 fixed fee interview and also the alternatives to conventional dispute resolution such as use of the citizens advice bureaux; Law Centres; administrative agencies and alternative dispute resolution. The use of a 'McKenzie Friend' may also provide an alternative for some litigants as illustrated in the *Peggy Wood* case brought against the Law Society.

The question of costs for those eligible for legal aid should be considered and also for those not eligible who will be subject to the normal rule that 'costs follow the event'. Taxation of costs should also to be noted.

Providers of legal aid and advice services, the system of franchising and fixed fees and the effect of changes in the system should be considered.

Answer plan

- outline of the state schemes for civil and criminal legal aid and legal advice schemes including duty solicitor scheme and ABWOR; assessment of entitlement, recent changes in entitlement and other changes including franchising and fixed fees
- major criticisms of the schemes with effect from April 1993; challenges mounted by the Law Society by way of judicial review
- alternatives to the state schemes and alternatives to traditional forms of dispute resolution including the increasing resort to 'McKenzie Friends' from the case of *McKenzie v McKenzie* (1971) and commented upon in the case of *R v Leicester City Justices ex p Barrow & Another* (1991)
- conclusions

Answer

It is a fundamental principle of a legal system that those who need to resort to law for the resolution of disputes should have access to the legal system and those who provide legal services. Given the ever-increasing complexity of society generally and the means by which it is regulated by law in particular, it is imperative that efficient legal services be available. It follows that those who are unable to fund themselves in obtaining legal services must look either to alternative sources of funding or alternative methods of resolving their problems.

Taking the alternative means of funding first, we will note later that, given the pressures on state assistance and the need to cut costs, alternative means of resolving disputes are receiving attention and these may well avoid resort to litigation but at the same time ensure an acceptable result.

The Legal Aid Act 1949 replaced previous provisions for those unable to afford the cost of legal services by providing a state scheme to assist those who satisfied a means test taking account of income and capital. Many of the earlier provisions had been voluntary and varied widely throughout the country. This was subsequently amended by Acts in 1974, 1979 and 1982 which extended the scope of assistance to legal advice as well as litigation in civil and criminal matters. In 1988 a new Legal Aid Act was passed and its provisions came into effect on 1 April 1989.

The aim of this legislation was to replace all previous legislation, establish the Legal Aid Board with responsibility for the administration of civil legal aid and assistance and to provide a framework within which later amendments to the system could be made by way of regulations put before Parliament by the Lord Chancellor.

Section 1 of the 1988 Act states that its purpose is to establish a framework for state funded advice and assistance so as to help those who are otherwise unable to obtain such help on account of their means. Section 3 provides for the establishment of the Legal Aid Board to oversee the administration of civil legal aid, the legal advice scheme and the Advice By Way of Representation (ABWOR) scheme. This has a membership of between 11 and 17 members drawn from lawyers and non-lawyers but with at least two solicitors and two barristers. England and Wales is divided into areas each with a Legal Aid Office and an Area Committee made up of practising solicitors and barristers. The Legal Aid Office decides whether or not an applicant is eligible for assistance and administers the Green Form scheme. The Area Committee deals with appeals against refusal of legal aid and supervises the remuneration of solicitors. It is in the administration of the schemes where drastic cuts in staffing has been seen in recent years.

As we have seen, state assistance takes various forms, the central distinction being between those schemes administered by the Legal Aid Board and criminal legal aid administered by the courts under the supervision of the Lord Chancellor.

Taking each scheme in turn we will examine the main provisions. It is important to draw a distinction between legal aid and advice schemes. The former provide assistance to those wishing to bring or defend a claim or, in the case of criminal law, to defend a prosecution. The latter, which is known as the 'Green Form' scheme (from the colour of the form filled in by the solicitor on behalf of an applicant as to his or financial means), covers preliminary advice, letter-writing and making application for legal aid.

Under this scheme, two hours worth of work (or three in undefended divorce proceedings) can be provided where the applicant satisfies a means test taking into account his or her disposable capital and weekly disposable income. The case of *R v Legal Aid Board ex parte Bruce* (1992) established that legal advice would only be paid for out of public funds if provided by a professionally qualified person. It follows that advice offered by non-qualified personnel would not be paid for out of the state scheme. Thus, on the facts, a person who provided advice on welfare benefits to solicitors was not entitled to be paid out of the scheme.

With effect from 12 April 1993 contributions by those over the 'free' limit were abolished with the effect that an applicant who is over the disposable income or capital limits is ineligible for any assistance. Also, with effect from that date, new income and capital limits were imposed which drastically reduced the numbers of those entitled to assistance. Those on income support, family credit or disability working allowance automatically qualified providing disposable capital did not exceed £1,000. Those not on benefits would be eligible if their disposable weekly income was no more than £61 and disposable capital no more than £1,000 (with no dependants). Disposable income and capital refers to earnings and savings respectively left after deducting appropriate allowances for a partner or dependants.

The changes were brought about by the Legal Advice and Assistance (Amendment) Regulations 1993 made under s 34 of the Legal Aid Act 1988 by the Lord Chancellor and was one of a package of measures designed to drastically reduce eligibility not only under the Green Form scheme but also the other schemes. The Regulations were challenged in the High Court by the Law

Society which alleged that the Lord Chancellor had acted *ultra vires* in making regulations which frustrated, rather than promoted, the purposes of the 1988 Act. It was held in *R v The Lord Chancellor ex parte The Law Society* (1993) that the Law Society had *locus standi* to bring a claim for judicial review and that it had a legitimate expectation to be consulted before the regulations were introduced by the Lord Chancellor, but in the particular circumstances, judicial review should not be granted. For 1994 new regulations came into effect on 11 April 1994 which increased the weekly income limit from £61 to £70. Weekly dependants' allowances were also increased but capital limits remained unchanged. For 1995, the weekly income limit is increased to £72.

The ABWOR scheme provides assistance for preparation and representation of the client in most non-criminal matters in the magistrates' courts (now called Family Proceedings courts) such as for maintenance and for some cases in the county court, the Mental Health Tribunal and disciplinary charges against prisoners. To be eligible, a person with no dependants should have savings of no more than £3,000 and a weekly disposable income of no more than £147 (£153 for 1994). Dependants' allowances are the same as for the Green Form scheme but a contribution towards the cost of assistance of one-third of the amount by which weekly income exceeds £61 will be payable where weekly disposable income is between £61 and £147 (£63 and £153 for 1994). For 1995, the lower income limit is £64 and the upper weekly limit is £156. In addition, a statutory charge may be imposed on the value of property recovered or preserved. This is provided for in ss 11 and 16 of the 1988 Act and applies to each scheme and ensures that, except for certain exempt property such as furniture, the family home, tools of trade or maintenance payments, property which is the subject of a claim and which has been recovered can be used to meet any shortfall between a contribution paid by the assisted person and the actual cost of the service. In addition to financial eligibility, an applicant will have to satisfy a merits test that reasonable grounds exist for bringing, defending or being a party to proceedings.

Civil legal aid covers claims in the High Court and county court, the Lands Tribunal, Commons Commissioners and the Employment Appeal Tribunal but not claims in defamation, inquests, arbitration or tribunals. As provided for under Part IV of the Act, an applicant will have to satisfy both a means and a merits test. The former is assessed by the Department of Social Security and the latter by the Legal Aid Board. The applicant's solicitor will estimate the likelihood of eligibility and will submit the appropriate forms to the area office of the Legal Aid Board.

There are two parts to the merits test: the client has to show reasonable grounds for bringing or defending the action; and that it is reasonable in the circumstances for legal aid to be granted. If the merits are in doubt, a limited legal aid certificate may be granted requiring authorisation for any further work. The criteria for deciding merits include a proper motive, the cost effectiveness of proceedings and that no alternative help is available. Financial eligibility again depends on disposable income and capital. After deducting allowances for dependants, if disposable income is £6,800 or less (£7,500 in personal injury claims) the applicant will qualify on income.

No contributions are payable where disposable income is £2,294 or less. If between £2,294 and £6,800 (or £7,500 in personal injury claims) contributions are due monthly. The lower income limit was increased to £2,382 for 1994 and £2,425 for 1995 and the higher income limit to £7,060 (£7,780 for personal injury) in 1994 and to £7,187 (£7,920 for personal injury) in 1995. To qualify on capital this should not exceed £6,750 (£8,560 personal injury) although, in cases which are likely to be expensive, legal aid may nevertheless be granted. The capital limits remain unchanged for 1994 and 1995. Those on income support automatically qualify and no contributions are payable as is the case where disposable capital is £3,000 or less. When a contribution is due it is a one-off payment of all disposable capital in excess of £3,000.

Special rules apply to pensioners which allows net income earned from capital to be disregarded in computing annual disposable income. When an applicant satisfies both merits and financial tests, the legal aid office issues a legal aid certificate or makes an offer if contributions are due. If this accepted contributions from capital are due immediately and from income by monthly instalments.

Two issues are of particular importance: the application of the rule that 'costs follow the event' and the imposition of a statutory charge. The general rule in litigation is that the loser pays not only his own costs but those of the winner. Where the winner is legally aided the loser will probably be ordered to pay the winner's legal costs but it does not follow that the loser will in fact pay such costs. If he/she does so, invariably, the costs as taxed by the court and will produce a shortfall which the winner will have to meet either from contributions or from damages or property recovered which will be made subject to the statutory charge. If the loser does not pay, for example the loser has been made bankrupt or has disappeared, the winner will have to pay his/her own costs from contributions or by way of the statutory charge and the effect may be that all damages or property recovered are used to pay legal costs.

Much criticism has been made of the statutory charge which cannot be waived, particularly as it applies in matrimonial disputes and regardless of the fact that some property is exempt.

Where the loser is legally aided he may be ordered at the judge's discretion to pay 'a reasonable amount' towards the winner's costs. His own costs will be paid by the Legal Aid Board.

Part V of the 1988 Act provides for criminal legal aid for defendants. Private prosecutions are not covered. Again a merits test and a financial test determine eligibility. The former is contained in s 22 of the Legal Aid Act 1988 which provides that assistance must be 'desirable in the interests of justice'. Several criteria are mentioned including that the case involves complex legal issues, that on conviction, the defendant is likely to go to prison or lose his livelihood, or where the defendant is vulnerable or under a disability. Application is made to the magistrates' court or Crown Court and an appeal against refusal lies to the Area Committee. Some time ago, the Lord Chancellor had proposed to transfer responsibility for criminal legal aid to the Legal Aid Board but, in December 1993, it was announced that responsibility would remain with the courts.

The financial test is that, after dependants' allowances (as for the Green Form scheme) have been deducted, the disposable capital limit is £3,000 and the weekly income limit is £45 (£47 for 1994). Contributions from capital and income start when these sums are exceeded. Those on income support, family credit or disability working allowance are exempt from contributions.

Having looked at the main provisions of the state assistance schemes brief mention needs to be made of the '24 hour duty solicitor' scheme which offers free legal advice to those being questioned by the police at a police station or elsewhere and whether or not arrested. This is provided for under the Police and Criminal Evidence Act 1984 and the Codes of Practice require suspects to be informed of their right to advice. No contributions or means test applies and a suspect may choose to be advised by his or her own solicitor or the duty solicitor or one whose name is on a list supplied by the police. Attendance at the magistrates' court is also covered although, more usually, this will be covered by the criminal legal aid scheme.

Other schemes operate on a voluntary basis. The most well known was the £5 fixed-fee interview whereby some solicitors charged £5 for 30 minutes of advice, but this was withdrawn by the Law Society in November 1993. Others operate a free or low-cost initial interview, for example the ALAS scheme (Accident Legal Advice Scheme) or Union-Law. Such schemes highlight the stark fact that, for the vast majority of people, only the initial interview may be free or charged at a nominal rate.

Thereafter advice, preparation of documents (such as a will or a conveyance) and litigation will be charged at the full rate. Even if a person qualifies for legal aid or advice under the statutory schemes there may well be contributions to be made following a means test and should a shortfall result between the costs incurred and sums paid by the loser the legally aided client may well have to meet this by way of statutory charge. It is rarely appreciated that a loser who is ordered to pay the winner's costs will not in practice pay the full costs as these will be assessed by the court (this is called 'taxing' the costs) not on an indemnity but a standard basis. The result can be unfair and it is the winner who may be out of pocket as a result.

These are not the only criticisms that have been made of a system which has been described as being 'in crisis'. Legal aid practitioners point to under-funding and low levels of remuneration; the client finds the system too restrictive (many tribunals are not covered). The Lord Chancellor has said that the system is far too costly and the regulations brought into effect in 1993 were aimed at cutting costs. Generally the charge is made that the system denies access to those most in need and is far too complex. As a result of the latest changes, some 27,7000 people are no longer eligible for assistance under the Green Form scheme.

Such criticisms raise the question as to how the system should be reformed. The Lord Chancellor's Review of 1991 in a consultation paper suggested five major alternatives to the present system. These were: reliance on litigants' own resources; bank loans; a contingency fee system; compulsory legal expenses insurance and the 'safety net' in which a litigant who is above the legal aid limit is required to pay an agreed sum towards the cost of legal services and then apply for legal aid. This left unanswered what would happen if legal aid was refused or a client gave up before the safety net was reached.

Contingency fees provide for payment of fees only if the claim is successful. In American jurisdictions the fee charged is a percentage of the value of the claim. Draft regulations made under s 58 of the Courts and Legal Services Act 1990 provide for conditional fees which in effect are on a 'no win, no fee' basis (the contingency) but payment will be in accordance with the normal hourly rate or fixed sum fee uprated by a proposed maximum of 100% to compensate the practitioner for the risk of getting no fee if the claim is not successful. At one time it was proposed to uprate by no more than 20%, but the draft regulations allow a maximum uprate of 100%. Where a conditional fee agreement has been made and then legal aid is granted the former will cease to have effect. This may have two benefits in that the solicitor will be able to conduct work without waiting for legal aid to be granted and if on a change in the client's circumstances he or she qualifies for legal aid this can take over from a conditional fee agreement.

Other alternatives which have been put forward include contingency legal aid where winners subsidise the funding of the system and a sliding scale of eligibility depending on the type of case involved. Where costs are likely to be high, eligibility levels would increase, for example in personal injury cases.

Given the many criticisms of the legal aid system, in particular the cutbacks in provision, and the ever-increasing costs of litigation, other alternatives not only to legal aid but to resort to the courts should be considered. The Lord Chancellor has set up a working party to review alternative dispute resolution (ADR) and he has recently published a Green Paper on mediation and divorce. In addition to ADR, which attempts to deal with disputes by way of mediation or conciliation, either in conjunction with, or separate from, the court, other alternatives may be available to a person seeking legal advice. Some examples are Legal Advice Centres, the Citizens' Advice Bureaux, Law Centres and Housing Advice Centres.

A more recent initiative was reported in the *Solicitors' Gazette* of 7 July 1993 known as the Legal Advice Service (LAS) and based in the East End of London. It is staffed by volunteers and offers a free legal advice service to members of the public. Those who qualify for legal aid are referred to local law firms and others are offered advice by the volunteers, who at the discretion of the court, may be able to appear on their behalf.

One other alternative must be mentioned and that is the so-called 'McKenzie Friend' which received much publicity at the time in connection with the claim in negligence brought by an elderly widow, by the name of Peggy Wood, against the Law Society. Miss Wood was represented in the High Court by Ole Hansen, former director of the Legal Action Group, under s 27(2)(c) of the Courts and Legal Services Act 1990 which permits a court to grant rights of audience to those who do not generally have such rights. An appeal was later made to the Court of Appeal in 1994.

The title 'McKenzie Friend' derives from the case of that name in 1971. The court in *R v Leicester City Justices ex parte Barrow & Another* (1991) disapproved of this title stating that it 'suggested an unjustified status and mystique'. However such a person should be referred to as an assistant or friend to denote that he or she could act as the adviser to a party appearing in court in person. The administration of justice required that a party in person be given reasonable assistance in the conduct of his or her case and this included the help of an adviser unless there was good reason for the court to order otherwise.

At the start of this question we noted that the person unable to pay their own legal costs would either need to qualify under one of the legal aid or advice schemes or seek a remedy by using alternative means to litigation. Having looked at the main provisions and the criticisms that have been made of them, one other area remains to be discussed. In respect of statutory schemes for legal aid and advice it is not only the client who may feel aggrieved but also the providers of the services. We have already mentioned the claim brought by the Law Society in June 1993 challenging the validity of four sets of regulations introduced by the Lord Chancellor under the Legal Aid Act 1988 with the aim of cutting the legal aid bill. The Law Society alleged that the package of measures, which changed eligibility limits, would deny millions access to justice but its claim for judicial review was rejected.

In another action, the Law Society attempted to challenge regulations made by the Lord Chancellor which would change the way in which solicitors were paid for legal aid work in magistrates' courts. Previously, solicitors were paid hourly rates but this was to be replaced with standard fees. It was held that the Lord Chancellor had 'a broad discretion' and that in making the regulations he had acted lawfully. It was not denied that the Law Society which represents some 59,000 solicitors had a sufficient interest in bringing the claim and that it had a right to be consulted.

Another major area of concern for practitioners has been the decision to franchise legal aid provision. In October 1993, the Legal Aid Board had circulated its franchise contract and anticipated that some 2,500 to 3,000 franchise applications to operate publicly funded legal services would be made. The first franchises were granted in June 1994. Towards the end of 1993, it was still not clear whether the Lord Chancellor's proposals for competitive tendering by franchisees for legal services were to be adopted. The Legal Aid Board was not supportive of this proposal and the Legal Action Group called for a clear statement of policy to be agreed by the Lord Chancellor and the Legal Aid Board as to future plans. Franchising will have implications not only for practitioners who will have to satisfy the criteria on quality of service, costs and standard of management within the firm, but also for other advice providers such as citizens advice bureaux who will have to decide whether or not to seek franchises.

In July 1994 the Social Market Foundation published a report entitled 'Organising Cost-Effectiveness-Access to Justice' which stated that 'the root cause of the poor state of legal aid is the high and increasing cost of legal services'. In late 1994, the Lord Chancellor proposed to set up a regional network of 'fundholders' under the auspices of the Legal Aid Board. Their function will be to process all applications for legal aid in an attempt to cut costs and waste.

A Green Paper is planned; this will address the need for greater use of alternative dispute resolution (in the form of mediation, the ombudsman, arbitrators and advice workers such as Law Centres and the Citizens' Advice Bureaux) and the closing of loopholes in legal aid provision. The most notable is in respect of the 'apparently wealthy' who, as a result of technically owning little or no property, qualify for state assistance. Other alternatives are also to be investigated such as legal expenses insurance, conditional fees and the use of tribunals. Emphasis is to be placed on the needs of the consumer, and control over the system exerted by solicitors is to be removed.

In conclusion, we have seen that publicly funded legal services are in a state of great change and (many would say) crisis. The major problem is the increasing cost of legal services coupled with financial stringency and the need to reduce public spending. In a society highly regulated by law where, over many years, people have been encouraged to know and enforce their rights, the legal system is under pressure.

Thus new ways of funding legal services will have to be found and alternatives to litigation investigated. Such alternatives however will not necessarily mean that lawyers' services will not be called on (or those of other professionals) in which case there will remain a need for public funding to assist those unable to afford mediation or conciliation services.

Question 6

Consider the extent to which the common law is capable of adapting and expanding to meet the changing needs of society. Illustrate your answer with suitable examples.

The English Legal System

General approach

This question invites a discussion of the role of the judge in making law. The common law refers to judge-made or case-law and not the common law in a narrow sense as excluding equitable rules and principles. The implication behind this question is that it is a desirable end for case-law to be adaptable and to expand to meet changing needs. Adaptability is less controversial than expansion. The latter taken to extremes may be considered a usurpation of the role of Parliament.

There must be a balance between the common law and role of the judge and that of Parliament in passing legislation. The judges should not attempt to act as legislators. In addition, there is a need for the law to achieve a degree of certainty so that those who are subject to it and wish to plan their activities in accordance with it can do so with a degree of certainty as to the outcome.

Case law develops not only by reference to common law principles and rules but also as a result of statutory interpretation. This highlights again the relationship between the judge and the legislator. Parliamentary sovereignty ensures that the court's role is to interpret statutory provisions and not strike them down as illegal. However this vests considerable power in the judges to attach meaning to statutory provisions. Delegated legislation on the other hand may be declared *ultra vires* and void.

The hierarchy of the courts and the role of law reporting should be considered so as to explain how the common law is developed. Binding and persuasive precedent also needs explanation together with the means by which an otherwise binding precedent can be avoided. The position of the House of Lords as the highest appeal court and the use of the 1966 Practice Statement allows for expansion and adaptation in the law.

Some useful judicial statements are to be found in *Attorney General v News Group Newspapers* (1988) Watkins LJ; *Parker v British Airways Board* (1982); *Woolwich Building Society v Inland Revenue (No 2)* (1992); *Cambridge Water Company v Eastern Counties Leather plc* (1993); *Derbyshire County Council v Times Newspapers Ltd & Others* (1993); *McLoughlin v O'Brian* (1982); *Alcock & Others v Chief Constable of South Yorkshire Police* (1992); *Tinsley v Milligan* (1993).

Answer plan

- define common law noting equity and legislation; role of the judge in making law; hierarchy of the courts; law reporting; the development of precedent
- binding and persuasive precedent; ways in which an otherwise binding precedent may be avoided; adaptation and expansion distinguished; consequences of each and their advantages and disadvantages
- the extent to which the judge should attempt to develop the common law; the boundary between judge-made law and legislation; the place of policy and how well equipped the judge is to decide on policy
- judicial statements suggesting that in appropriate cases the judges have a contribution to make to the development of the law; reference to the cases mentioned above which concerned the following areas of law: common law criminal contempt; the rights of the finder of property; the right of a taxpayer to a refund of unlawfully demanded tax; strict liability under the rule in *Rylands v Fletcher*; a local authority claim in defamation; claims in damages for nervous shock; application of the equitable maxim 'he who comes to equity must come with clean hands'

Answer

The reference here to the common law indicates that a broad definition of the term is needed so as to include not only the rules and principles developed by the common law courts but also those developed as part of equity. Thus it is case-law or judge-made law that is in question. This has to be further distinguished from law made by Parliament in the form of an Act or statute and rules which take the form of delegated legislation made by those to whom Parliament delegates law-making power such as government ministers. However the judge has an important role to play in relation to both legislation and delegated legislation.

So far as the former is concerned, the traditional doctrine of the sovereignty of Parliament prevents the courts from questioning the validity of Acts of Parliament but this does not prevent the court from interpreting statutory provisions should a dispute involve the application of such provisions. This power may, at different times or by different judges, be used narrowly or widely. If widely, the judge may see his or her role as one of developing the law according to the spirit rather than the letter of law as laid down by Parliament.

So far as delegated legislation is concerned, the Queen's Bench Division Divisional court of the High Court, has the power to strike this down as invalid if it purports to vest powers in the delegatee which have not been granted by Parliament. The doctrine of *ultra vires* allows the court to check administrative abuse or excess of power on the principle that a delegate must act in accordance with the power granted by Parliament and that it is for the court to interpret the meaning and extent of the words used to convey such power.

Having noted that the role of the judge in interpreting statutory provisions may permit development of the law, this is also true in respect of case-law although a distinction should be drawn between adaptation and extension. It is generally assumed that the law will need to change to meet the changing needs of society. Law is, after all, a social phenomena and is a means to an end rather than an end in itself. However adaptation suggests gradual change whereas extension suggests more radical change. Changes in the law will have to be balanced by the need for certainty. Those in need of legal advice will look to their legal advisers for solutions to a legal problem and the legal adviser will offer advice on the basis of what he or she is able to predict as the likely outcome. This will depend on the state of the case-law and the likely interpretation of statutory provisions.

The common law as defined is based on precedent so that like cases are decided alike. This has the advantage of consistency and continuity and allows development of the law over time. The disadvantage is that the law may become too rigid.

Two factors play an important part in the workings of precedent namely an accurate and comprehensive system of law reporting and the hierarchy of the courts and the appeal structure.

The decisions of a higher court will be binding on a lower court asked to decide a case concerning similar facts. Where a court is faced with a binding precedent which cannot be distinguished on its facts from the case to be decided this precedent will have to be followed unless it can be shown to have been decided *per incuriam* or has been superseded by Parliament. Where no binding precedent applies the court asked to make a decision will have to reach a decision either on the basis of logical consistency or by taking into account policy considerations.

In reality, a court will have to weigh up all the arguments which no doubt will have been argued persuasively by the advocates for each side. Discretion will also arise where the judge has to decide whether or not he is bound by the *ratio decidendi* of an earlier case of a higher court. He will have to weigh the degree of similarity and dissimilarity between the two cases. If he concludes that there is a sufficient degree of dissimilarity then he may choose not to follow the earlier precedent. The complexity is compounded in that in decisions of the higher courts, particularly the House of Lords, although all the judges may agree on a decision they may give different reasons. The *ratio decidendi* may not be at all clear to a later court which will have to decide how the law is to develop.

The appeals structure also plays its part in allowing the law to develop. On appeal, it may not only be the decision which affects the parties to the dispute which is in question. Their position may depend on an interpretation of the law binding on all lower courts. The appeal court may then overrule this precedent and in so doing create new law. An important means of avoiding an otherwise binding precedent is found in the House of Lords where there is a limited power not to follow its previous decisions 'when it appears right to do so', as provided for in the Practice Statement of 1966.

At one time, it was suggested that the Court of Appeal should have a similar power but the only exceptions now recognised are those mentioned in the case of *Young v Bristol Aeroplane Co Ltd* (1944). Although certainty in the law is certainly an advantage, flexibility also is desirable particularly where Parliament is slow to initiate reform. Another tool at the disposal of the judge is that of persuasive precedent, for example decisions of lower courts, decisions of courts in other jurisdictions and *obiter dicta* in cases decided by English courts. There is a growing willingness on the part of the judiciary to call in aid persuasive authorities, particularly the decisions of Commonwealth courts as is illustrated in *Airedale NHS Trust v Bland* (1993). This not only assists the judge in reaching a decision but ensures a full examination of the issues raised and the possible solutions.

The role of the judge in law-making and his or her relationship with Parliament as the supreme law-maker has in the past been put in the form of a question. Generations of jurists would pose the question 'do judges make law?'. The so-called declaratory theory (of the common law in the narrow sense) stated that judges merely declared what the law was and this has for some considerable time been rejected. Both Jeremy Bentham and John Austin rejected this theory. Bentham described the common law as 'the product of Judge & Co' and was not impressed with it, likening it to 'dog's law'. It was only when something was found to be wrong that the law imposed a sanction or an adverse result followed. Austin concluded that judges made law as a result of the implicit command of the sovereign.

Even though it has long been accepted that judges do make law, the debate has ensued as to the extent to which the judge may properly make law. Should the judge have a free hand in shaping future developments so as not only to be able to adapt the law but to extend the scope of existing rules to new situations as they arise? Or should the role of the judge be a limited one so that in a novel situation where the existing rules offer no solution the judge would proceed on the basis of logical consistency and not by reference to extra legal values such as morality, justice, public policy or expediency?

The positivist school suggested a limited role for the judge in that his or her main concern is to decide cases on the basis of what the law is, not what it ought to be. This assumes that there is a clear rule governing a case, but, where there is none, the judge will have to use his or her discretion in arriving at a decision. The positivist insists that the judge excludes from his or her reasoning non-legal issues such as morality. However, it might be argued that a judge is a product of the society of which he or she is a part and, although judges should be independent and impartial in their decision-making and should use an objective approach, values nevertheless must play some part in the decision-making process.

Professor Dworkin analysed amongst other things the nature of the judicial function and concluded that law consists not merely of rules (as explained by Professor Hart) but also non-rule standards. In deciding a hard case the judge draws on moral and political standards (principles and policies) to reach a decision but his or her role is to discover the one right answer to the legal problem.

Professor Dworkin considered that the role of the judge is an interpretative one and rejects the notion that judges do or should make law. The law is seen as a rich fabric of standards some of which are rules but others are open-ended principles which may lead to the development of rules. Principles are concerned with rights and establish standards based on morality, justice or fairness. It might be said that Dworkin, in stating that judges do not make law, rejected the notion that the judge is concerned with policy issues. These he defined as standards which set out a goal to be achieved in an economic, political or social context or an area which is deemed to be desirable on the grounds of expediency or efficiency. Policy is the province of Parliament. It is for Parliament to decide how the law should develop as this involves drawing a line or mapping out a new path. Such questions are not justiciable.

Professor Dworkin refers to the American case of *Riggs v Palmer* (1889) where the court held that although the legal rule permitted a murderer to benefit under the will of his victim the overriding principle that a man should not profit from his own wrong applied. This was said to be a hard case where the court was faced with a dilemma. Such a dilemma was answered in a similar way in the English cases of *Re Sigsworth* and *Ex parte Smith*. It might be argued that, in such cases as these, the court was faced with a clear rule but one which it considered unable to apply given a more fundamental and far-reaching principle. Failure to give effect to the principle would result in injustice in that particular case and future injustice if Parliament failed to legislate quickly. In giving effect to the principle it could be said that the court was acting in place of the legislature and as a matter of policy had decided to act rather than give way to injustice. This is certainly true in *Ex parte Smith* where the court recognised that it could prevent the disclosure of information where a crime had been committed in the past but it decided that it was also right to do so where there was every likelihood of the commission of an offence in the future.

Going back to the distinction between adaptation and extension of the law, it may well be a matter of degree. Far-reaching social change should be made by Parliament but judges may have to make choices and in so doing shape future developments. The courts decide cases on an *ad hoc* basis and therefore reform and development may be gradual and piecemeal.

This has an inherent danger in that a judge may rely too heavily on his or her view of his or her role and how the law should develop. Restraint on the part of the judge ensures judicial independence, with the advantage that the law is seen to be certain and based on continuity. Decisions are arrived at as a result of logical deduction from well established rules. Only in extreme cases should the judge attempt to act in the name of public policy.

Having discussed the nature of the judicial role, it is essential to turn to the case-law for further elaboration for it is through the cases that the law is seen to develop and the limits within which the judges perform their task.

In *Attorney General v News Group Newspapers Ltd* (1988) Watkins LJ described the common law as 'a lively body of law capable of adaptation and expansion to meet fresh needs'. He considered that Parliament and its ever increasing role in legislating did not prevent developments in the common law. The case concerned a criminal contempt of court at common law and it was not necessary for the prosecution to prove that proceedings were either pending or imminent to found liability.

Another clear statement of principle is to be found in *Parker v British Airways Board* (1982) which involved a claim in conversion by the finder of lost property at an airport which he had handed into an official of the airline. It was held that the plaintiff was entitled to the sale proceeds of the item on the basis that he had found it and the airport authority had not at any time attempted to claim rights over property lost on its premises. Donaldson LJ, having stated that the rights of the parties depended on the common law, went on to say that in theory the judge is 'a legal technician' and only has to find 'the ready made solution for every problem' but that 'the reality is somewhat different'. He continued by referring to the fact that the court was not bound by any previous decisions and so was free 'to extend and adapt the common law in the light of established principles and the current needs of the community'. He noted how the court had been assisted by persuasive precedent and the arguments put forth by counsel.

The more recent case of *Woolwich Building Society v Inland Revenue Commissioners (No 2)* (1992) illustrates the use made by the courts of decisions of foreign jurisdictions and a consultation paper of the Law Commission entitled 'Restitution of Payments made under a Mistake of Law' in deciding whether a taxpayer who had paid tax in response to an unlawful demand should have at common law a right to its return with interest. It was held by a majority of three to two that such right existed on the grounds that common justice required repayment unless special circumstances or some principle of policy required otherwise. Given the Law Commission paper the House of Lords said that should the legislature require limits to be placed on the right of recovery it was for Parliament to set such limits as a matter of policy.

Again the roles of legislature and the courts was discussed in the case of *Cambridge Water Company v Eastern Counties Leather plc* (1993) which involved a claim under *Rylands v Fletcher* (1868). Lord Goff with whom the other Law Lords agreed held that as Parliament had undertaken legislation to promote protection of the environment on the basis of the 'polluter pays' principle it did not follow that the courts were free to develop the rule in *Rylands v Fletcher* so as to impose liability for pollution. Policy demanded restriction of the rule only imposing liability on proof of foreseeability of damage. Again reference was made to a Law Commission paper and Lord Goff felt constrained by its recommendations as to how the law should develop.

Another House of Lords case of 1993, namely *Derbyshire County Council v Times Newspapers Ltd*, which concerned a claim by a local authority in defamation, illustrates that, in the absence of legislative action, the courts may be willing to extend the common law. It was held that a local authority should not have a right to sue in defamation as this would be contrary to the public interest in ensuring uninhibited public criticism of a public authority and would be an undesirable fetter on freedom of speech.

The tort of negligence which developed from the case of *Donoghue v Stephenson* (1932) continues to develop but future radical changes would be seen as matters of policy demanding legislative change. One such area is that of nervous shock. The case of *Alcock v Chief Constable of South Yorkshire Police* (1992) involving claims arising out of the Hillsborough disaster applied dicta of Lord Wilberforce in *McLoughlin v O'Brian* (1983) to the effect that limits should be placed on the reasonable foreseeability test for liability in claims for nervous shock. Lord Wilberforce had accepted four policy arguments against further extension of liability namely the floodgates argument, that Parliament should set the limits of liability, extension would be unfair to defendants and litigation would be lengthened.

One last case of interest to illustrate the role of the court in developing the law is that of *Tinsley v Milligan* (1993) in which the House of Lords by a majority of three to two held that property was to be held in trust for the parties as M did not need to rely on her own illegality in bringing her claim and had raised the presumption of a resulting trust. Lord Goff dissented stating that the equitable principle of 'he who comes to equity shall come with clean hands' applied in this case and that any change could only be effected by Parliament following a full review by the Law Commission. Lord Browne-Wilkinson giving the leading judgment of the court said 'as the law had developed the equitable principle had become elided into the common law rule'. It followed that whether a plaintiff relied on an equitable or a legal interest the rule was the same so that provided he did not need to rely on his own illegality he was entitled to relief.

Question 7

Explain and distinguish between the terms 'burden of proof' and 'standard of proof'. Your answer should make reference to these terms in relation to both civil and criminal proceedings.

Answer plan

- define the context in which the terms are used ie in relation to evidence in court proceedings; outline the meaning of burden and standard of proof
- explain the meanings of burden of proof; legal and evidential burden
- burden of proof in criminal cases; general rule and exceptions
- burden of proof in civil cases; *res ipsa loquitur*
- standard of proof in criminal cases; standard when burden cast upon defence
- standard of proof in civil cases

Answer

This question concerns the issues of evidence in court proceedings. Evidence is the means by which facts in issue in the proceedings are to be proved. Proof may arise from a range of evidential sources, for example, documents or the testimony of witnesses.

The facts in issue in any proceedings are the facts on which the court has to adjudicate to decide the case. In making its decision on the facts in issue the court will take into account the evidence and the burden and standard of proof applicable in the proceedings. The burden and standard of proof vary according to whether the court is dealing with civil or criminal proceedings and also according to the nature of the facts in issue and who is adducing the evidence. These matters are explored in this essay.

The burden of proof or onus of proof defines the party to the proceedings (plaintiff or defendant in civil proceedings - prosecution or defence in criminal proceedings) who has to adduce evidence to prove a fact in issue. Unfortunately 'burden of proof' has two distinct meanings. First, it is most commonly used to describe the party to the proceedings having the burden of establishing their case. For example, generally the prosecution have the burden of proving the guilt of a person charged with a criminal offence (reflecting the presumption of innocence). Secondly, there is the burden of proof in the sense of a party having to adduce enough evidence so that the matter about which they adduce evidence becomes a fact in issue. The first type of burden is typically called the 'legal' burden. The second is normally called the 'evidential' burden.

In relation to criminal proceedings it is an established principle that the legal burden is generally (see below for the exceptions) on the prosecution. The evidential burden of drawing certain facts into issue may shift. In the first instance this will reflect the legal burden. The prosecution must adduce sufficient evidence so that a *prima facie* case of guilt is established. If this is not done then the case may be dismissed by the judge (in the case of a Crown Court trial) on the basis that there is no case to answer. The evidential burden may then pass to the defence if they choose to call evidence about some matter which would constitute a defence. Alternatively the defence may call no evidence and simply argue that the prosecution bearing the legal burden have failed to discharge that burden to a sufficient degree of certainty or standard (see below). If the defence do call evidence and raise a *prima facie* case concerning that matter (thus discharging the evidential burden) the prosecution then have a legal burden to disprove the defence.

There are three exceptional cases in which the legal burden is cast upon the defence in criminal cases. First, where a defendant seeks to argue that they are insane (*R v McNaughton* (1843) and *Woolmington v DPP* (1935)). Secondly, where the crime in question creates a prohibition subject to exceptions, for example, certain persons may lawfully do this thing or may do so if holding a licence or having consent. In such cases the burden of showing that the defendant fell within the exceptional category falls on the defendant (*R v Edwards* (1975) and s 101 Magistrates Courts Act 1980). Finally particular offences created by statute may have specific provisions casting the burden of proving certain matters on the defence.

In civil cases the legal burden generally lies with the plaintiff to establish the basis of the claim. However, the position may be more complex. For example, in relation to a claim in contract the legal burden would lie with the plaintiff to make out the claim. This would involve proving the existence of the contract, breach of its terms and possibly damages. However, if the defendant's response was to argue that the contract was void because of fraud or mistake the legal burden of proving those issues would lie with the defendant.

In civil cases the legal burden may shift as result of the maxim *res ipsa loquitur*. This maxim applies in cases based on the tort of negligence where normally the plaintiff must prove the existence of a duty of care owed to the plaintiff, breach of the duty and consequent foreseeable damage. If the circumstances which gave rise to the injury or harm are under the control of the defendant or its servants and the cause of the harm or injury (usually an accident of some sort) is such that in the ordinary course of events it would not happen if proper care was taken then the burden shifts to the defendant to show how the accident occurred without negligence. This maxim was applied for example where someone slipped on yoghurt spilt on the floor of a supermarket (*Ward v Tesco* (1976)).

As to standard of proof, this simply is the degree of certainty to which the party bearing the legal burden must prove their case. The court has to apply that degree of certainty in deciding whether the party bearing the burden of proof has made out their case or not.

In criminal cases the classic formulation of the standard of proof applicable where the prosecution bear the burden of proof is that the case must be proved 'beyond reasonable doubt' (*Woolmington v DPP* (1935)). Sometimes though this has been criticised. In some cases it is acceptable to say that the standard of proof is such that the jury or magistrates are 'sure' (*R v Summers* (1952)).

In the exceptional cases mentioned above where the burden rests with the defence in a criminal case then the standard of proof is less than that of the prosecution. It is in fact the same standard as for civil cases (*R v Carr Briant* (1943)).

In civil cases (and the exceptional criminal cases) the appropriate standard is the on the 'balance of probabilities' or 'preponderance of probability'. Thus, if the court can conclude that it is more probable than not that the burden has been discharged then the party bearing the burden will succeed in that issue. If the probabilities are only equal the same party will not succeed. The seriousness of the allegations affects the degree of probability but not the appropriate standard.

Thus, if it is alleged that the defendant was in a conspiracy with high ranking government officials, this may seem improbable and thus more evidence may be needed before, on balance, the court would be satisfied that it was true.

Chapter 2

English Legal System: Sentencing

Introduction

Questions on sentencing and criminal justice are not uncommon. In general terms they may cover either the aims and principles of sentencing or the appropriate penalties applicable given a set of circumstances. In either case they may form a part or the whole of a question. The questions which require a candidate to describe the aims of sentencing or the principles on which sentence should be determined have to date always taken the form of an essay rather than problem or case study style question. They almost always require some critical appraisal of the system; this may involve making your own views known to the examiner (provided they are supported by reasoned criticism).

The other type of question which deals with the way in which a particular offender might be sentenced has always been linked to questions on criminal liability. Having discussed criminal liability the examiner then asks 'How might this offender be dealt with if found guilty?'. Normally, although you have some details of the nature and severity of the offence, there are few if any details of the offender. This does make predicting the sentence with accuracy very difficult and probably unnecessary. Instead what is required is some broad indication of the available range of sentences and the factors which the court should take into account in choosing the appropriate sentence.

The final matter which is not infrequently dealt with in either type of question outlined above is the difficult issue of juveniles. There are specific limitations on the way in which youngsters (and indeed their parents or guardians) may be sentenced. These need to be understood in order to be able to attempt the full range of questions set on sentencing.

Question 8

M who is 18 years old and O who is 15 years old decide to trick an old lady out of some money. They go around to her house and say they are collecting for a local hospital. She is so impressed that she not only gives them £10 for the hospital but also invites them in for a cup of tea. M cannot resist the opportunity to take a silver ornament from her house while she entertains them.

How might the courts deal with them on them being found guilty of any offences they may have committed.

Answer plan

This question is based on a simple set of facts concerning the offence to provide a straightforward illustration. It is likely that this type of question would form part of a question which also included a less clear set of facts relating to the offence and parts of the question addressing criminal law rather than sentencing matters.

- identify relevant offences; identify maximum penalties applicable
- identify range of applicable sentences for each defendant; both under 21; discharges (conditional and absolute); community sentences (note limited applicability because of age); custody (note age effects on 16 year old and fact that will be at young offender institution for both); secure training order; compensation order; fine (determination of amount and payment); role of parents and guardians
- factors applying to choice between sentences; custody and community sentence (role of pre-sentence report); availability based on seriousness of offence; aggravating and mitigating factors; fine and compensation order

Answer

In obtaining money from the old lady for a local hospital when in fact it was for their own purposes, both M and O have committed the offence of obtaining property by deception contrary to s 15

Theft Act 1968. In addition, M has committed theft contrary to s 1 Theft Act 1968 in taking the ornament. The maximum penalty for both offences is 10 years imprisonment. There is no maximum fine. In the magistrates' court the maximum custodial term is six months for an individual offence or 12 months for two or more offences (s 133 Magistrates Courts Act 1980). The maximum fine the magistrates court may impose is £5,000 or level 5 on the magistrates' court scales.

If the magistrates consider that they have insufficient power to sentence M or O then they can commit either or both of them to the Crown Court for sentence (s 38 Magistrates Courts Act 1980). M is a young offender being under the age of 21. O is a juvenile being under 18.

The range of possible sentences available for both M who is a young offender and O who is a juvenile include fines and custodial sentences. Custodial sentences in respect of both M and O would not be in prison but detention at a young offenders institution. In the case of the juvenile offender, the maximum period of detention (unless it is an exceptional case) is not less than two months nor more than 12 months. In making a decision on custody, the court must take into account a pre-sentence report (which will be required if custody or a community penalty is being considered) prepared by a probation officer which will provide details of the offence, offender and his background and recommendations as to an appropriate penalty taking into account any previous convictions (exceptionally a court may not proceed to obtain a pre-sentence report before sentencing of such a report is unnecessary).

In addition, the courts are restricted in their approach to custody by the Criminal Justice Act 1991. Custody may only be imposed if the offence or combination of offences (in the case of M) is so serious that only imprisonment can be justified. There is a further but irrelevant ground relating to protection of the public from violent or sex offenders. Finally custody may be imposed if the offender refuses to consent to a community sentence (see below). This is set out in s 1 of the 1991 Act. Since the 1991 Act the key sentencing principle has therefore become 'desert' (ie what the offender deserved for the offence). Thus, it would no longer be appropriate for the court to impose a custodial term simply to deter others (although public concern about a particular class of offences by the public can make an offence more serious (*R v Cox* (1992)). If the court decides in the light of any mitigating and aggravating factors (see below) that custody is appropriate for either M or O then s 2 of the 1991 Act requires the term not to be greater than that which is commensurate with the seriousness of the offence or combination of offences (in the case of M).

Thus, under the 1991 Act, the imposition of an exemplary sentence is not allowed (*R v Cunningham* (1992)). The courts will also apply the principles that the sentence length should be proportionate to the culpability of the offender and the harm caused by the offence and should be as short as is necessary to achieve the purpose for which it was imposed.

It is not possible for a suspended sentence of custody to be imposed on either a young offender or juvenile (1).

A compensation order may be made under s 35 Powers of Criminal Courts Act 1973. The Act requires the court to consider making an order. The Children and Young Persons Act 1969 provides for a court to order payment of compensation by a parent or guardian of a juvenile offender.

A community sentence might be imposed if the court considers the offence to be so serious as to warrant such a sentence (s 5 CJA 1991); the degree of restriction the sentence imposes should be commensurate with the seriousness of the offence. M might be placed on probation which would require his consent. This would require attendance for meetings with a probation officer and possibly the addition of other requirements (such as attendance for drug rehabilitation).

Another community sentence available for M is a community service order in which he might be ordered to do anything between 40 and 240 hours of unpaid work. If the court considers that the offence is too serious for a fine, a community service order working, for example, with the elderly might be a suitable sentence. In addition, there are the more unusual community sentences of a combination order (a mixture of probation and up to 100 hours community service) or curfew orders (placing a restriction on when or where the offender may go).

English Legal System: Sentencing

O is too young to be placed on probation, subject to a community service order, a combination order or a curfew order (minimum age 16). However, he might be placed on either of two remaining community sentences-attendance centre orders or supervision orders. These are available to any young offender as well as a juvenile and might therefore be used for M as well. A supervision order will place the offender under the supervision of a social worker or probation officer. Attendance centre orders can require up to 36 hours of demanding activities to be undertaken by the offender at an attendance centre on Saturday afternoons.

Finally, a fine might be imposed. The fine must take into account the means of the offender (or in the case of a juvenile the parents or guardian) and reflect the seriousness of the offence (s 18 CJA 1991 as substituted by CJA 1993 replacing the unit fines system). In the case of a juvenile, the parents are bound to pay the fine and the court is under a duty to bind over the parents to exercise proper parental control over the juvenile.

It is clear from the above that a wide range of possible sentences could be imposed. How will the court decide what is the appropriate sentence? First, it will do this under the 1991 Act on the basis of the seriousness of the offence. In determining the seriousness of the offence the court will take into account any aggravating or mitigating features of the case. For example the fact that the crime was committed against a vulnerable member of the community is an aggravating feature. So is the possibility that the elderly person has been upset by the theft and deception. Mitigating features might include reparation (the return of the ornament or repayment of the money) or a guilty plea. Section 48 of the Criminal Justice and Public Order Act 1994 requires a court when passing sentence to take into account in the case of a person who pleads guilty the stage at which the intention to plead guilty was indicated and the circumstances in which this indication was given.

This provision is intended to give effect to the Royal Commission on Criminal Justice (1993) proposal that credit for a guilty plea should be clearly indicated by the courts. It reflects the current sentencing practice of many courts. It indicates that, for example, in many cases a greater degree of credit will be given to an offender who indicates an acceptance of guilt at an early stage (perhaps on arrest) than someone who pleads guilty at court. A key aggravating feature since the amendment of the 1991 CJA by the CJA 1993 is the existence of relevant previous convictions (s 29 CJA 1991).

For O the court will be reluctant to impose custody because of his age and perhaps because of evidence that the older boy led him astray. When the court weighs all of these factors it will come to its sentencing decision.

Notes

1 Secure training orders have been introduced by the Criminal Justice and Public Order Act 1994 and might apply to O if he were under 15. These are referred to in this answer merely to draw the student's attention to these new Orders. They would not be directly relevant to this answer. They may be imposed on 12-14 year olds who are persistent offenders (s 1 1994 Act: convicted of three or more imprisonable offences) who have failed to respond to an earlier sentence (s 1 1994 Act by breaching a supervision order under the Children and Young Persons Act 1969 or by being convicted of an imprisonable offence during the currency of a supervision order).

Question 9

Critically examine the principles on which adult and juvenile offenders are sentenced by the criminal courts.

Answer plan

- introduction to the range of available sentences and restrictions on their use; introduction to CJA 1991 and White Paper 'Crime, Justice and Protection of the Public'; introduction to current trends in policy
- principles of sentencing (examined critically against background of relative importance in 1991 Act)
- deterrence, rehabilitation, desert, incapacitation, restoration, restraint in use of custody, 'equal impact', proportionality
- some conclusions

Answer

Principles on which sentencing decisions are based have to be considered in the light of the available penalties which a criminal court may impose on a defendant. Whatever principles there are will be reflected in the types of sentence available and the way in which the courts choose between alternative penalties.

The valuable penalties are first of all determined by the offence for which the defendant has been convicted: many minor offences for example will be punishable only by way of fine. In addition, if the matter is disposed of in the magistrates' court or Youth Court (for juveniles) there are additional restrictions on the powers to sentence. Generally no custodial term may exceed six months (12 months exceptionally where more than one offence is involved) nor may any fine exceed £5,000.

However in these cases if the offence is 'triable either way' the magistrates may commit the offender to the Crown Court for sentence only where the Crown Court has powers to impose any sentence permitted by the offence (although in the case of juveniles, except in very restricted cases, any custodial term must not exceed one year).

The courts broadly have a choice between a discharge (conditional or absolute), fine, community sentence (there are six types of community sentence: probation order, community service order, combination order, curfew order, attendance centre order and supervision order), imprisonment, suspended imprisonment and in the case of juveniles (up to and including 17 year olds) and young offenders (up to and including 20 year olds) detention at a youth offender institution.

The separation of young offenders from adult offenders in custody reflects a general underlying theme of treating juveniles in a different way from adult offenders (see below).

Both the courts and policy makers have recognised the existence of a range of principles on which sentencing decisions may be made. The policy underlying sentencing was subject to a major review in the late 1980s culminating in the government White Paper 'Crime, Justice and Protecting the Public'. The proposals in the White Paper were then turned into law by the Criminal Justice Act 1991 which has, as a result of wide criticism, been recently amended by the Criminal Justice Act 1993. The key effect of the 1991 Act was to make sentencing of the basis of 'desert' or what the offender deserved for the offence the basis of all sentencing decisions.

Recent government policy statements indicate that there may be further changes to the 1991 Act to reflect a tougher approach to sentencing which may permit greater reliance on the principles on deterrence and incapacitation.

Deterrence is an obvious aim of sentencing. The idea is simply that if a penalty is imposed for committing a crime this should deter both the particular offender and others from committing that type of offence. This may involve the imposition of exemplary sentences: a sentence to make an example of a particular offender as occurred in *Freeman* (1989), where a persistent pick pocket was sentenced to five years imprisonment for a theft on the London Underground.

It seems unlikely that such an approach would be permissible under the 1991 Act because of the desert-based approach. It is also the case that exemplary sentencing with a view to punishing one offender particularly harshly to deter others is undesirable as it is unjust to the person who is being made an example. In addition deterrence as a basis for sentencing is not well-founded empirically. Although it is difficult to show the effect of sentences on individuals or society generally (as if there is a deterrent effect the person deterred commits no offence and is therefore untraceable) it seems that offenders are more motivated by the risk of being caught rather than the fear of punishment. In answer recently the Home Secretary has made it clear that he believes on a common sense basis that harsh sentences do deter.

Another established aim and principle of sentencing is rehabilitation. This is applicable to all offenders but is of particular relevance to juvenile offenders. The courts may be anxious to attempt to quickly rehabilitate juveniles before they become hardened criminals. Rehabilitation may involve counselling typically by probation officers via probation orders (for those over 16) or by social workers (via supervision orders for those up to 21 but particularly those under 16) on the offenders' attitudes, behavioural problems (for example drug abuse) or help with education or training. For those over 16 rehabilitation might also be combined with more rigorous restrictions on liberty via community service order (between 40 and 240 hours of voluntary work) or a combination of community service and probation.

For those under 16 (or indeed up to 21) an attendance centre order can require attendance at a centre for up to 36 hours of demanding activities. All of these community sentences are based on rehabilitation and are only likely to be ordered by the court where the probation service's pre-sentence report favours a rehabilitative approach. Rehabilitation is based on the needs of the offender rather than the seriousness of the offence although the 1991 Act makes it clear (s 5) that community sentences should only be imposed where the offence is so serious as to justify such an approach and the restrictions placed on the offender in the order should reflect the seriousness of the offence. These principles reflect the underlying importance of the desert approach even in rehabilitation sentencing.

'Desert' as a principle underlying sentencing has always been very important. Now it has become, under the 1991 Act, the central pillar of sentencing policy which can be disapplied in only a few cases. The idea of desert-based sentencing is that the penalty should reflect the seriousness of the offence and should represent a punishment for breaking the rules.

It is criticised by some theorists as being unfair as it will often assume individual culpability for an offence when in fact the offence may be due other causes such as poverty or unemployment. Desert-based sentencing will involve an element of general deterrent as the more serious offences will be punished more severely. Indeed in *Cox* (1992), even under the restrictions of the 1991 Act (see below), it was held that the prevalence of a particular class of offence and public concern about them could be regarded as an aggravating feature of an offence which made it more serious, thus justifying a higher sentence on a desert-based approach.

The 1991 Act restricts the use of custody (both for juveniles and adults) to three circumstances (s 1 of the 1991 Act): first, where the offence is so serious that only imprisonment can be justified; secondly, where the offence is a violent or sex offence and imprisonment is necessary to protect the public from serious harm; and, finally, where an offender has refused to consent to a community sentence.

Thus, imprisonment in the case of a non violent or sex offence cannot be justified on the basis of public protection or exemplary deterrent, only on the basis of giving the offender what he deserves for that offence. This new approach was aggravated by provisions since repealed by the 1993 Criminal Justice Act which restricted the courts' ability to take into account previous convictions in considering the seriousness of the offence. Previous convictions may now be regarded as features which make the offence more serious. The length of imprisonment should reflect the seriousness of the offence(s 2 of the 1991 Act) and in the case of violent or sex offences such longer period as is necessary to protect the public.

Similarly both community sentences and fines (s 18 of the 1991 Act as amended) are based on a desert basis in setting the terms of the community sentence or the amount of fine.

Incapacitation is a further principle of sentencing. The idea is simply that, whilst an offender is in custody, they cannot commit further offences. This principle seems to have recently found favour with the government although, given the cost of keeping persons in prison, it may be regarded as an expensive way of keeping crime figures down.

This approach has always been hampered by gross overcrowding in many prisons. The curfew orders community sentence introduced by the 1991 Act (but not yet in force) may be another way of achieving the same end. Section 1 of the 1991 Act permits the use of incapacitation as a reason for sentencing to custody in cases of sex or violent offences. It seems from the empirical studies that prediction of those likely to re-offend is 'hit and miss' (for example Floud and Young) which does make the use of incapacitation both expensive, as several offenders may have be placed in custody to ensure that the one likely to re-offend is imprisoned, unreliable and unfair to those imprisoned when they were not likely to re-offend in any event.

Restoration or reparation is a further principle on which sentencing may be based. The ideas is that victims should receive justice. The Powers of Criminal Courts Act 1973 allows courts to make compensation orders in favour of victims of crime, and requires the court to give reasons when it fails to do so and a person has suffered loss, injury or death, and to give priority to the compensation order when considering the amount of a fine. The principle does face difficulties in application to crimes when the state or community rather than an individual is a victim. In those cases compensation may not be required.

A further principle relating to custodial sentencing is that there should be restraint in the use of custody. This is sometimes expressed more broadly as the principle of minimum intervention. In *Bibi* (1980) the court said that the sentence should be the minimum to be consistent with its purpose of protecting the public and punishing and deterring the criminal.

The principle of equal impact is based on the idea that the effect of the sentence on an offender should be the same regardless of the particular circumstances of the offender. This became a key principle in relation to fines (where it is of most relevance) under the 1991 Act through the infamous 'unit fines' system. This has now been abolished. The idea was that magistrates decided how serious the offence was by assigning to it a number of units. The offenders income was then multiplied against the number of units to produce the fine. Thus, a rich defendant would pay a much larger fine than a poor offender, reflecting the idea that the proportionate impact on each should be the same. The means of any defendant remain relevant to the setting of a fine under the new system but this principle has lost some credibility.

Proportionality is a principle which is closely linked to desert. Proportionality simply requires that, in deciding on the severity of the offence and therefore penalty, all aggravating and mitigating factors should be taken into account. These might include co-operation with the police or guilty plea on the one hand or pre-meditation or the use of violence or a weapon on the other. Guilty plea has taken on a new significance since the introduction of s 48 Criminal Justice and Public Order Act 1994. This requires a sentencing court to take into account, when a guilty plea is entered, the stage and circumstances in which the guilty plea was indicated by the accused.

This reflects the policy of rewarding offenders who save court time and spare the worry of the victim. The earlier guilt is indicated, the greater may be the sentence reduction. A guilty plea but without acceptance of the prosecution's version of facts might lose some, or all, credit if a 'Newton hearing' is forced (1).

The principles used in setting appropriate sentences for individuals are wide ranging. Whilst desert appears to have been crucial under the 1991 Act, along with a greater range of more flexible rehabilitative sentences particularly for juveniles, it seems likely that incapacitation and deterrence are likely to be given greater prominence in the government's forthcoming legislation on criminal justice.

Notes

1 A 'Newton hearing' is held when the facts on which a guilty plea were based are in dispute; for example, the extent of damage or injury might be disputed.

Chapter 3

General Principles of English Law

Introduction

In this section you are most likely to meet with essay style questions which will require both breadth and depth of knowledge and understanding on your part. An appreciation of recent developments is very useful and you should attempt to keep abreast of not only changes in the law but the legal system itself and its role in society. You will need to be able to analyse the concept of law, its role and functions, the need for law and its relationship with other social phenomena such as justice and morality.

The questions selected attempt to be representative of those you will be asked but there may well be variations on the themes running through them. Thus when asked to discuss law and morality we may argue that there must be a close relationship between law and morality so as to achieve justice. We have not been asked directly to discuss justice but it would be appropriate to include it. Similarly when asked about miscarriages of justice we may need to tackle the moral dilemma this creates. The question of reform and the need for law to change runs through this area and requires an understanding of the mechanisms for law reform.

You will need to be certain of the level of your knowledge and understanding of what often are elusive concepts. In addition to the well known theories of jurists and others you will need to have worked out your views well in advance and have ready data in support. Well thought out and supported arguments will earn high marks. A well structured plan at the outset could ensure you keep to the point.

Miscarriage of justice is currently a live issue but one that is not new and no doubt one that will engage lawyers, jurists and others for a long time to come. Following the report of the Runciman Royal Commission we should be better able to address the issues and critically assess the reforms proposed.

This brings us to the underlying principles of the criminal justice system and the policy to be brought into legal effect. At its heart is a moral issue namely that the innocent should not be wrongly convicted and that justice should be done. Questions on miscarriages of justice may in their terms be specific to particular incidents but you should not conclude that the wider issues are of no importance. Those issues include the role of law in society; relationship of law and morality; law and justice; change and law reform and the principles underlying the law and the effect it gives to policy.

Question 10

The criminal justice system is clearly in crisis. In the light of recent serious miscarriages of justice consider the major defects and proposals for the reform of the system.

General approach

This question highlights the serious criticisms that have been made of the criminal justice system in recent years. The Royal Commission on Criminal Justice (the Runciman Commission) reported on 6 July 1993 making some 352 recommendations for reform of the system. The Runciman Commission was set up in 1991 amid much disquiet about the state of the system following appeals in cases such as the *Guildford Four*, the *Birmingham Six*, the *Maguire Seven*, the *Tottenham Three*; the *Judith Ward* case; the *Cardiff Three* and the case of *Stefan Kiszko*. It was anticipated that the Report would be followed by a government White Paper setting out proposals for reform but, instead, the Criminal Justice and Public Order Bill was presented to Parliament containing *inter alia* provisions to remove the right of silence of suspects when in police custody and at trial, abolition of the rules of corroboration, abolition of committal proceedings and their replacement with a transfer for trial procedure and the creation of a new offence of juror and witness intimidation.

The statement refers to serious miscarriages of justice but any failure in the criminal justice system may have dire effects on a suspect or person wrongly convicted of an offence. No doubt miscarriages have occurred at all times and in all systems, due to human fallibility, and will occur in the future. This is not an argument for not attempting to reduce as far as possible such failures whether at the investigative or trial stage.

Consideration should be made as to the nature of the criminal justice system: the accusatorial system as opposed to an inquisitorial system as in Continental jurisdictions; the role of judge and jury; the presumption of innocence, the right to silence during interrogation and at trial; the right to jury trial; the disclosure of information as between prosecution and defence; the role of the police and the Crown Prosecution Service; the use of forensic evidence; the trial and the role of the Court of Appeal; the safeguards and shortcomings of the Police and Criminal Evidence Act 1984; the admissibility of evidence.

The main recommendations of the Royal Commission should be considered including limitations on the right to jury trial; sentence discounts for guilty pleas; the retention of the right to silence; the composition of juries; the judges' warning concerning uncorroborated confessions. Also the provisions of the Criminal Justice and Public Order Act 1994 with particular reference to the right of silence.

The emphasis in any criminal justice system should be to ensure that the scales of justice, if not tipped in favour of a defendant, are at least evenly balanced and the presumption of innocence is surely the most fundamental of all principles. Thus criticisms of the proposals for reform of the system should be considered and whether or not they will be effective in minimising future miscarriages.

Answer plan

- Examples of serious miscarriages of justice - what went wrong?; proposals for reform contained in the Runciman Commission Report of 1993; provisions of the Criminal Justice and Public Order Bill and its, often stormy, passage through Parliament; subsequent developments in the Criminal Justice and Public Order Act 1994
- The nature of the criminal justice system and where defects exist both at the investigative and trial stages; consideration also of the appeals structure and its shortcomings; procedure for rectification of mistakes

- The effectiveness of the proposals for reform and the provisions of the Criminal Justice and Public Order Act 1994; what other reforms could be justified?; has there been a fundamental re-think or merely a tinkering with the system?; if the latter, what are the reasons for short-term measures?

Answer

Following some very notable miscarriages of justice including the *Guildford Four*, the *Maguire Seven*, the *Birmingham Six*, the *Tottenham Three*, the *Julie Ward* case and the case of *Stefan Kiszko*, the Commission on Criminal Justice, which was set up in 1991 (the Runciman Commission), reported in 1993 with some 352 recommendations for reform of the criminal justice system.

The Royal Commission was set up to examine the effectiveness of the criminal justice system in England and Wales and in particular to consider conviction of the guilty, acquittal of the innocent, efficient use of resources and whether or not changes were needed in the following matters: the conduct and supervision of police investigations; the role of the prosecution in supervising the gathering of evidence and the decision whether to proceed and the arrangements for disclosure of evidence; the role of experts and the forensic science service; the arrangements for the defence and access of defendants to legal aid; the opportunities for the defendant to state his position and the inferences to be drawn by the court on failure by a defendant to speak; the powers and role of the court and the possibility of the court having an investigative role before and during the trial; the role of the Court of Appeal and the arrangements which should be made for considering and investigating allegations of miscarriages of justice following the exhaustion of rights of appeal.

On publication of the Runciman Report the chairman, Lord Runciman, stated that, if implemented, it would significantly reduce the risk of the innocent being convicted and the guilty from going free. Most observers are agreed that the underlying principle of the criminal justice system must be the attainment of justice and this is reinforced by the principles that all are presumed innocent until proved guilty and that it is for the prosecution to prove guilt beyond all reasonable doubt. Where opinions diverge however is in relation to the means of attaining these goals and, given human fallibility, no system would ensure absolutely against the occurance of some form of injustice or miscarriage of justice. Again general agreement exists that such injustices should be kept to a minimum and that mechanisms should exist to rectify those that do occur speedily and adequately.

Before going on to consider the main recommendations and subsequent proposals for reform, some consideration must be made of how miscarriages of justice arise and how they are dealt with.

It is not only cases such as the *Guildford Four*, the *Birmingham Six*, the *Maguire Seven* and the *Tottenham Three*, for example, which have received much press coverage where miscarriages of justice have occurred. Many other cases highlight defects in the system from the investigative stage through to trial and appeal which result in innocent persons being accused of crimes they did not commit. The main purpose of the system must be to secure justice and not merely to ensure convictions. Given the fallibility of any system, this will result in some who have committed crimes going undetected or, if accused of an offence, being acquitted. This may be said to be the price that has to be paid to ensure that the innocent are not wrongly convicted or that, if a miscarriage results, it is rectified quickly and effectively. At the present time the criminal justice system is under pressure - both financial and in respect of detection and sentencing - and it might be argued that miscarriages arise as a result of an ineffective system allowing those who have committed crimes to go free or with very little in the way of punishment for those convicted. This can certainly be a criticism of the effectiveness of the system and one where victims rightly feel aggrieved that their interests carry very little weight. However for the purposes of this question we will confine ourselves to the issues concerning failures in the system whereby the innocent are wrongly convicted of criminal offences. It is to be noted that any system cannot afford conviction of the innocent not only as far as the innocent are concerned but also because it follows that the perpetrator of the crime remains undetected and free to continue committing offences and this will result in the system coming into disrepute.

Miscarriages of justice may arise at any stage of the criminal process, from the start with the police investigation, the interrogation at the police station of suspects, the gathering of evidence, charge, preparation for and the trial itself and at the appeal stage. Many commentators suggest that it is time for a major overhaul of the system with a re-examination of first principles. The presumption of innocence lies at the root of our system and this must be protected together with the right to jury trial. Before the enactment of the Criminal Justice and Public Order Act 1994, the right to remain silent, both at the interrogation stage and during trial, was considered by many to be fundamental but the government took the view that it assisted the hardened criminal and was removed by ss 34-39.

It was thought that the reforms made by the Police and Criminal Evidence Act 1984 and the Prosecution of Offences Act 1985 would cure the defects which had previously existed but this has proved unfounded. It is a feature of the accusatorial system that the court (judge and jury) is only as good as the evidence presented to it. If the investigative process and the evidence presented to the court is flawed the court will be unable to prevent miscarriages arising. If, then, the appeal process is limited, and no independent body exists to review alleged miscarriages, those wrongly convicted may only be able to rely on the support of the press, members of parliament or pressure groups to bring the case to public view.

Despite the protections afforded to the suspect under the Police and Criminal Evidence Act 1984 and the Codes of Practice it is argued, for example by Michael Mansfield QC in his book *Presumed Guilty*, that the police make serious errors - they target suspects and their perception is clouded and they intimidate often the most vulnerable members of society. This can be compounded by members of the judiciary having a tendency to believe the police in the face of conflicting evidence. Given such a blinkered view based on prejudice and bias, the presumption of innocence becomes one of guilt and the primary purpose becomes the achievement of a conviction. The Prosecution of Offences Act 1985, which set up the Crown Prosecution Service, was passed so as to ensure an independent review of the evidence and of the decision whether or not to prosecute. In the result much criticism has been levelled at this body which is seen to be costly and ineffective. Calls have been made for the creation of an inquisitorial system whereby the investigation of crime is conducted by an independent person, as in France, where the juges d'instruction attempts to find the truth, and not construct a theory of who committed the crime and then attempt to find evidence in support. On the face of it, this is an attractive idea but would need a major overhaul in the system, notably reforms in the appointment and functions of the judiciary. Investigation could remain with the police but would be under the supervision of the independent body appointed by a Ministry of Justice. Whether or not an inquisitorial system of trial should be established has been much debated and there is certainly an argument, given the inadequacies of evidence gathering, that the judge should take a more active role in the trial process.

Other criticisms of the present system concern the inadequacies of the jury system; the restrictions on the granting of bail; the overuse of remand; the need for reform of both the legal profession and the judiciary; the monopoly of the prosecution of the forensic science service; the non-disclosure of evidence by the prosecution; reform of the appeals structure and an independent mechanism for correcting mistakes.

Some suggest that flaws in the system can be rectified via the appeals structure. An appeal can be lodged within 28 days on a point of law or on the basis that fresh evidence has been discovered. The Court of Appeal when considering the issue of fresh evidence puts itself into the position of a jury considering the new evidence and decides whether the original verdict was safe and satisfactory. Once 28 days has elapsed or an appeal is refused application can only be made to the Home Secretary who has power to refer the case to the Court of Appeal for consideration. As was shown in the *Birmingham Six* case the questioning of the integrity of the criminal justice system is not a pleasant one and one which many judges of the highest rank have difficulty contemplating. Having said that, to do nothing in the face of the most strenuous allegations of miscarriage of justice, can only in the long-term do irreparable damage to the legal system and the judiciary. Calls for reform may come from interested parties but, if the worth of the system is to be retained, the system itself must ensure that the likelihood of miscarriages is minimised and, if mistakes arise, they are dealt with promptly and satisfactorily.

Having considered some of the defects of the system it is now time to consider the main recommendations of the Runciman Royal Commission Report 1993. Following its publication, it seemed that the recommendations pleased few and some commentators have gone so far as to suggest that some of the recommendations may cause or contribute to injustice. One of the most controversial proposals was to abolish the defendant's right to elect for trial by jury and some have suggested that the only reason for this was to cut costs. Defendants would not have been able to opt for jury trial in triable either way offences and it would have been for the magistrates to decide 'in accordance with statutory criteria'. Both the Law Society and the Bar Council denounced this recommendation, the former suggesting that this was not the way to solve the problem of defendants entering last minute guilty pleas, and the latter describing the jury as 'an essential constitutional safeguard against miscarriages of justice'. It was with some relief that the Commission recommended retention of the right to silence in police stations and that neither judge nor prosecution would be allowed to comment adversely at the trial on the defendant's silence whilst in custody. As already noted, this proposal was not accepted and ss 34-39 of the Criminal Justice and Public Order Act 1994 allows adverse comment to be made by the judge. The Report also contained a recommendation for the establishment of an independent review body to investigate alleged miscarriages of justice and for them to be referred to the Court of Appeal. The Court of Appeal itself was to be more prepared to overturn unsound verdicts and to order retrials. The review body was to be staffed by lay people and lawyers and have the assistance of specialist advisers. Appointments would be made by the Home Secretary. In the result no provision implementing this proposal is contained in the 1994 Act but the Home Secretary has promised that it will be brought into effect by legislation at a later date.

Another controversial proposal was for a more open system of sentence discounts ensuring that earlier guilty pleas attract higher discounts. The Law Society expressed concern that this could have the effect of putting pressure on defendants to plead guilty. 'Justice' said that it 'subtly undermines the presumption of innocence ... and the requirement that the prosecution proves its case'. In the result s 48 of the 1994 Act provides for this.

Criticism was also made of the recommendation for disclosure of prosecution evidence 'on the basis of the relevance to the line of defence disclosed' and which permits the prosecution to ask not to disclose 'sensitive material'. This would narrow the guidelines for prosecution disclosure laid down in the *Judith Ward* trial and leave it to the prosecution to decide whether evidence was likely to be relevant to the defence. The defence would be required to make pre-trial disclosure or risk adverse inferences being drawn by the jury.

Other proposals included: the abolition of committal proceedings; video surveillance of police station custody suites and video recording of police station interviews; judges' warning of the dangers of relying on uncorroborated confession evidence and the need for independent evidence where possible; a right of access by the defence to forensic material held by the prosecution; a Forensic Science Advisory Council should oversee forensic science standards; police powers to take saliva for DNA profiles; the setting up of a national DNA databank of samples from serious offenders; police power to remove suspicious substances from suspects' mouths.

It was thought that, after such an investment in time and money and the exhaustive research projects undertaken, the proposals for reform of the system would be brought into effect. The usual process would have involved consideration of the recommendations by the Home Secretary followed by a White Paper for legislative reform. This was not to be the case but rather an announcement by Michael Howard, Home Secretary, at the Conservative party conference in October 1993 which set out the measures to be included in a Criminal Justice and Public Order Bill. This received a stormy passage through parliament and included the very controversial proposal to end the suspect's right to silence. During the debates on this proposal in the House of Lords, the Lord Chief Justice, Lord Taylor, spoke in favour of the ending of the right to silence and that judicial comment should be allowed as to a suspect's silence and failure to disclose evidence later put forward as part of the defence. He was not, however, in favour of extending such comment to a power in the judge to question a defendant as to his or her silence.

Other proposals contained in the Bill included a new power for the police to take non-intimate DNA samples, including saliva, without consent in all recordable offences with the object of the police having a database on convicted criminals and this and other powers are contained in Part IV, ss 54-60, of the 1994 Act.

A new offence of witness intimidation is provided for in s 51 with the onus of proof on the defendant. Extensions in the powers of the police to stop and search and the creation of new terrorist offences, including an offence of possessing 'anything which gives rise to a reasonable suspicion that it is to be used for the purposes of terrorism'. Curbs are to be placed on the granting of bail to those convicted of rape, murder or manslaughter who commit the same offence. The police will have power to grant bail subject to conditions and to arrest bail fugitives.

In conclusion, it may be said that not only was the outcome of the Royal Commission Report disappointing in respect of ensuring that miscarriages of justice do not arise but also the response to the Report by the government. Although the right to jury trial is not under threat, its effectiveness is not to be improved and the fundamental right to silence has been removed.

The role of the judge in commenting on a defendant's silence also poses a threat to the fundamental presumption of innocence but at least the provision in the Bill, permitting the judge to be able to call on a defendant in court to justify his silence during interrogation, was withdrawn following the disapproval of the proposal by the Lord Chief Justice. The final version of the new, longer, caution for suspects has yet to be agreed and this will no doubt be a controversial issue for some time.

Another major drawback was that no provision was made for an independent review body and legislation is still awaited. 'Justice' promoted amendments to the Bill to ensure that such a body would be set up so as to ensure a mechanism for the release of those wrongly convicted. Greater safeguards to prevent wrongful convictions were also sought as it was recognised that these arise mainly as a result of concocted evidence and that the

General Principles of English Law

provisions in ss 76-78 of the Police and Criminal Evidence Act 1984 are not strong enough. Under the present rules, the judge has a discretion to exclude illegally obtained evidence (and has a duty only to do so in respect of confessions obtained unlawfully). New rules are needed to ensure that all evidence obtained unlawfully should be excluded, as is the position, for example, in America where this is guaranteed by the constitution. It should be noted that, although s 78 of the Police and Criminal Evidence Act 1984 providing for judicial discretion in the exclusion of unfair evidence may be considered too weak, in time, it may nevertheless provide a useful safeguard to a defendant who chooses to remain silent at the interrogation stage and who may be able to challenge the validity of evidence relating to his silence.

Question 11

Critically assess the extent to which law and morality should overlap. Illustrate your answer with examples.

General approach

This question raises an issue that goes to the root of the definition and application of law. A useful starting point is to offer definitions of law and morality and then go on to examine any overlaps that exist. The question of whether law and morality should overlap is a separate question and depends on one's view of law, the purposes of law and the legal system it serves.

For the purposes of this question, law can be defined as a system of rules deriving from an authority recognised as having the power to legislate or otherwise make rules which are binding on those subject to them. Obedience will be demanded and sanctions provided so as to ensure respect for and compliance with the rules. Law principally derives in our system from legislation and case-law and it is to be noted that law does not always simply sanction behaviour but may facilitate types of behaviour, for example with the law of contract which provides a set of rules for determining when an agreement is legally enforceable.

Morality may also take the form of rules, that is standards or boundaries, providing for proper or acceptable conduct which, if flouted, will give rise to consequences such as social censure or banishment from a group. Attempting to define morality in terms of rules, however, leads to difficulties in that there may be no general agreement as to their scope or effect. It may be better to talk about moral values, precepts, tenets or principles. This reflects the idea that morality is often a matter of personal conviction as to what is right or wrong rather than ideas that can be reduced to a code or a set of rules. Furthermore, in any particular situation, moral principles may conflict, for example to tell a lie may be considered wrong but telling the truth may hurt the feelings of another. Some examples of moral principles may be offered such as an obligation to tell the truth or to act honestly, to honour promises, not to injure or kill others, to conduct ones business affairs fairly and so on. Most usually, any mention of morality conjures up sexual behaviour and the limits of what is acceptable in relation to marriage, children and personal conduct.

Having attempted to offer some definitions, it will be possible to identify areas where law and morality overlap. The clearest example is that of the criminal law, particularly offences relating to the protection of person and property. We might ask 'which comes first, law or morality'? Moral principles evolve and the result often is that law reflects such principles. However there may be no general moral consensus on an issue and the law may then reflect the morality of those dominant in society. It does not follow that the law can never lead; it may have the effect of altering ideas generally current in society where those with reforming zeal are willing to use the force of law for the greater good.

That brings us to a consideration of the extent to which law and morality should overlap. Are there areas of conduct regulated by law which have no bearing on morality? Clearly minor motoring offences is an area of the law where it is hard to attach moral significance other than in relation to the imperative that law should be obeyed and that there is a social utility in having such laws.

Another question relates to the validity of law and whether only laws which accord with moral principles can be said to be law. An analysis of the Positivist and Natural Law schools of thought will provide different answers to this question.

Areas worthy of consideration include the relationship of law and euthanasia; abortion; the transplantation of organs; the control of pornography; the punishment of offenders; capital punishment; the use of foetal tissue in infertility treatment; sexual relationships outside of marriage; homosexuality; and the age of consent. Consideration of such issues may lead to a moral and legal dilemma and, assuming that the law should provide answers, it will be necessary to decide whether it is for parliament or the courts to draw the line between the acceptable and the unacceptable.

Answer plan

- Definitions of law and morality; overlaps and examples of legal rules and principles of morality
- Should law and morality overlap?; areas regulated by law which are morally neutral, for example motoring offences; consideration of the positivist and natural law schools' views of law and its validity
- Consideration of areas involving moral questions regulated by law or where it is argued that the law should regulate such areas as noted above; the current debate over the government's policy of 'back to basics' and the place of morality in public affairs
- Initiatives to regulate moral issues by law - the Wolfenden Committee Report 1957; the proposal to reduce the age of consent for homosexuals; the regulation of the use of foetal tissue in the treatment of disease and infertility for example; the effectiveness of law in regulating such areas
- The role of parliament and the courts; consideration of recent case-law, for example *R v Brown* (1993) and *Airedale NHS Trust v Bland* (1993)

Answer

Before attempting to assess the extent to which law and morality should overlap, it is useful to examine what we mean by the terms law and morality. Definitions of law and morality have engaged the minds of great thinkers from the dawn of time and there is no one definition suitable for all contexts but it is nevertheless useful to have a working definition of both terms so as to ensure we do not deviate from the question. We can define law as a system of rules governing people's behaviour and which is imposed by those with generally recognised authority, the breach of which gives rise to a penalty or other consequence. In defining law narrowly we may include criminal law (the imposition of a sanction by the state for breach of rules made and enforced by a sovereign body) but omit civil law which often facilitates a course of action by individuals in ordering their affairs. Examples readily come to mind including the making of contracts and wills. The rules regulating the making of a contract may be endorsed by the state but individuals will usually be free to decide whether or not to enter into a contract. If a person decides to do so the rules facilitate the transaction and can ensure that a contract is valid and enforceable. It is far fetched to conclude that where the rules are not complied with, the penalty is a void contract.

Thus a wider definition of law is useful so as to include rules which facilitate action such as the making of wills and contracts.

The positivist jurist John Austin in propounding his theory of law defined law narrowly to cover the commands of a sovereign power, breach of which gave rise to the imposition of a sanction. In addition, Austin was concerned with the idea that the study of law was itself concerned with the question of what the law is and not what it ought to be. This is the main point of this question and so we will leave this to later but suffice it to say here that, having set up a model demonstrating how law is made and enforced, Austin was then able to concentrate on analysing law and the legal system and why people obey law rather than questioning the status of a law which for one reason or another was considered 'bad'.

The writings of Professor Hart illustrate that his concern was also with what law is and he defined law as a system of rules. He drew a distinction between primary and secondary rules. The former as their name suggests regulate basic needs, for example violence, theft and deception. The latter take three forms namely rules of change which confer powers on the law-maker to effect change; rules of adjudication which regulate breaches of primary rules such as the criminal law; and rules of recognition which form the basis of the legal system and which determine its validity. In the United Kingdom, the rule of recognition refers to the Queen in Parliament and this has traditionally been accepted as the definitive standard by which law is made. This has, since membership of the European Union, had to give way to the notion of the supremacy of European law where that applies. Professor Hart was concerned with how law was perceived and drew a distinction between a person having an obligation, for example to pay a debt, and being obliged, for example to pay over a sum of money demanded by a bank robber. In the former the debtor has (or should have) a sense of obligation to his creditor whereas in the latter instance the payer does so as a result of compulsion or fear. This is not to say that compulsion or fear does not apply to law but that there is an acceptance of the rule and this is what also distinguishes law from mere habit.

Another member of the positivist school was Hans Kelsen who defined law as a system of 'oughts' or 'norms' which describe actions and decisions making up human conduct. Kelsen talked of the 'grundnorm' or basic norm whose validity was presupposed but not according to social, political or moral factors but on grounds of efficacy. Law was founded on coercion and breach of a law would result in the imposition of a sanction. Law was to be explained in terms of its form - 'if X, then Y' - rather than in terms of its meaning. This took no account of laws permitting actions or of those where no sanction is imposed.

Leaving the definition of law, we can move on to consider the definition of morality. As we have seen, law can be defined in terms of rules which guide or regulate behaviour. Reference to moral rules may be misleading in that the word rule suggests a degree of certainty and clarity in its scope and effect that may not be possible in reality. It may be better to talk of moral values or principles in recognition that there may be little consensus in a particular time or place as to the contents of a moral code of behaviour. This may be even more true when comparing different societies.

At its most general, ideas of morality concern the regulation of conduct within society and distinguishes between that which is considered good or right and that which is bad or wrong.

Several questions spring to mind about this definition. Firstly from where are such moral values derived and who or what enforces them? Secondly what is the relationship between such values and law? Is law influenced by morality or is morality influenced by law? If so, to what extent? Thirdly what are the moral values with which we are concerned? Are they relative to time and place or are some at least immutable and applicable in all places and at all times?

One view suggests that morality is personal to the individual and is acquired from an early age from parents, school and religion. Morality regulates the personal conduct of the individual and this invariably refers to sexual conduct, although some would argue that it covers such things as honesty and truth, honour and integrity and caring for others. Another view suggests that morality has a much wider remit and applies to all aspects of a person's life in both personal and public matters. At present, the debate over the government's 'back to basics' policy involves this very question. Some say that sexual morality is not purely a private matter for those in public life whereas others are of the view that what a person does in private should be of no concern to members of the public unless such conduct has a direct bearing on the performance of public duties. On this view a clear line can be drawn between public and private conduct and one should have no effect on the other.

This brings us to the main point of this question, namely the extent to which law and morality ought to overlap. We have already considered some of the ideas of the positivist school of thought which was a reaction to the natural law school. The latter, although it declined in popularity in the 19th Century in the face of positivist thought, saw a revival in its fortunes in the 20th Century.

The natural law school is concerned with the point at which law and morality overlaps and attempts to show that what is natural, according to some higher law or authority, ought to be. It follows from this that a law which fails to accord with such a higher standard either is not considered to be law at all or, if it is in form law, it need not be obeyed. The proponent of natural law measures human law according to a higher more authoritative standard and is willing to attach to it a value judgment. The positivist on the other hand is only concerned with the validity of law according to a human standard (for Austin this was the concept of sovereignty; for Hart, the acceptance of an internal view of law by officials; and for Kelsen, efficacy) for, objectively, it is impossible to know right from wrong.

If one were to trace the history of natural law this would range from Plato and Aristotle to St Thomas Aquinas to Hobbes, Locke and Rousseau to Sir William Blackstone to 19th Century decline and a revival in the 20th Century. St Thomas Aquinas suggested that human law which conflicted with natural law (God's plan for mankind) or with divine law (God's law for mankind) lost its moral binding power and the individual might be justified in not obeying it. The Greek philosophers took the view that such law need not be obeyed as it was not law. Sir William Blackstone in 'Commentaries on the Laws of England' was prepared to measure human law against God-given principles so that where the former conflicted with the latter the former had no effect.

The 20th Century saw a revival in the natural law approach given the establishment of the United Nations Charter on Human Rights and the European Convention on Human Rights and the Nuremburg War Trials where crimes against humanity were prosecuted. At one extreme therefore we have the idea that 'bad' law is not law at all and for that reason need not be obeyed and at the other that 'bad' law is nevertheless law which must be obeyed. Whether or not the citizen is morally justified in not obeying 'bad' law may be of concern to the positivist as a separate question but not one which involves the definition of law.

Professor Hart in *The Concept of Law* concluded that law and morality are different but related social phenomena. Although taking a positivist approach Hart recognised a minimum content of natural law, at the same time he rejected the idea that law derives from morality or that there is any necessary relationship between the two or that a fair or just society results from the minimum content. Professor Hart rejected the views of both Professor Fuller and Lord Devlin as to the relationship of law and morality. Professor Fuller in the *Morality of Law* talked of law's internal morality including such ideas as law's generality, clarity, non-retroactivity and the possibility of compliance. He concluded that the laws passed by the Nazi regime could not by any standard be considered to be law. Professor Hart concluded however that such law was so evil that it did not warrant obedience. Lord Devlin stated that the law, and in particular the criminal law, is connected with, and based on, moral and religious principles. Ultimate standards of right and wrong exist and the law should give effect to this binding moral code which ensures the continuance of society. Law was concerned with the suppression of vice and it was not a question of consent by the individual. Public policy demanded that law regulates undesirable behaviour and, in the absence of Parliament, it was for the courts to impose the required standards of conduct. The judge is the arbiter of public morality particularly in criminal law.

This view is seen in *Shaw v DPP* (1962) - the 'ladies directory case' - where the offence of conspiring to corrupt public morals was proved. Also, in *Knuller v DPP* (1973), where a magazine published advertisements placed by readers inviting homosexual contacts, it was held that public policy required that such publications be prohibited.

In recent times, the view that in our society one moral code binding on all exists has not found favour and it has been suggested that no one code exists but rather a diversity of moral attitudes on personal and social issues. We are left with several questions including what are the moral values applying to our society?; how is their existence determined?; and what is their relationship with law?. Certainly questions relating to sexual matters and violence involve moral issues but it can be argued that questions concerning politics, social and business relationships and the ownership and use of property do also. Law and morality may overlap but may also diverge. Immoral behaviour may be lawful; for example, traditionally, adultery has been considered to be immoral but it is not unlawful although it may result in divorce. Telling lies may be considered to be immoral but only in clearly defined circumstances will it be unlawful. In such cases, the comment 'that there ought to be a law against that' is often heard to justify the need for regulation by the law.

On the other hand the law may prohibit actions which some consider to be morally neutral and others consider to be morally acceptable, for example exceeding the speed limit or parking on double yellow lines. It might be argued that when such areas are regulated by law the moral obligation to obey the law applies regardless of the individual's view of the conduct in question. But if behaviour is considered acceptable by an individual (and more importantly, by a group) obedience may be lacking and this, together with lax enforcement will bring the law into disrepute.

How far then should the law attempt to regulate social activity? It is recognised that a line must be drawn between those who want complete freedom to do as they choose and those who want restriction so as to protect those who are seen as vulnerable members of society. At the same time, the law must attempt to keep pace with scientific and technological changes.

The Wolfenden Committee on Homosexual Offences and Prostitution reporting in 1957 stated that the function of the criminal law was 'to preserve public order and decency, to protect the citizen from what is offensive and injurious and to provide sufficient safeguards against exploitation and corruption of others especially the vulnerable ie the young, weak in body or mind, inexperienced or those in a state of physical, official or economic dependence'. It was not the function of the law to intervene in citizens' private lives or to enforce any particular pattern of behaviour other than was necessary to achieve the stated purposes.

The 1960s saw what can be described as a social revolution and some of the issues with which the law has had to grapple include abortion, surrogate motherhood and embryo experimentation, sterilisation of the mentally handicapped, homosexuality and the age of consent, 'test-tube' babies, blood transfusions, the issue of contraceptives to girls under 16 without parental knowledge or consent, euthanasia and the treatment of the terminally ill.

Three issues are of importance at the present time. The first concerns the advances in medical science so as to allow the collection of foetal tissue and that this will enable women who would otherwise not have children to do so. The Criminal Justice and Public Order Act 1994 s 156 prohibits the use of cells from such tissue. Regulation will be by the Human Fertilisation and Embryology Authority. The second concerns the reduction in the age of consent for homosexuals from 21 to 18 enacted by s 145 of the 1994 Act. When the Bill was before Parliament an amendment was promoted by Edwina Currie and on which members had a free vote permitting reduction in the age from 21 to 18 and possibly to 16. In the result the age was reduced only to 18.

The third issue presently causing concern is the availability of 'test-tube baby' treatment for women who have passed the natural child bearing age. An Italian women in her 60s has given birth as a result of such treatment and it is predicted that it will not be long before the treatment will be possible in England.

In considering the extent to which law should regulate such areas, it is important to differentiate between the roles of Parliament and the courts. It may be argued that it is the proper function of Parliament to draw the line in accordance with the generally held views in society or, if there is no one view, to give effect to that which is considered to be the most desirable. This is a matter of public interest or public policy which is outside the province of the courts. However, as was seen in *Knuller* and *Shaw*, the courts have on occasion taken on the role of legislator where Parliament has not prohibited actions which are considered to be wrong. Another example is to be found in *R v Gibson* (1990) where it was held that a strict liability offence existed at common law of outraging public decency. The case involved the display in a gallery of a model's head attached to which were two earrings made from freeze-dried human foetuses of three or four months gestation.

In the case of *R v Brown & Others* (1992) the House of Lords held that offences under ss 20 and 47 of the Offences Against the Person Act 1861 had been committed notwithstanding that the victim had consented to the sado-masochistic homosexual acts because public policy required that society be protected by the criminal law from such practices and their attendant dangers. The majority of the Law Lords took the view that such acts were unlawful and that consent was no defence. Only Parliament could make such acts lawful if that was considered desirable. The minority considered that although such acts were morally wrong they were not caught by the provisions of the 1861 Act and so were lawful. If it was considered necessary or desirable to prohibit such acts it was for Parliament and not the courts.

The most comprehensive discussion of the relationship between law and morality took place in *Airedale NHS Trust v Bland* (1993) where the court was asked to grant a declaration permitting the discontinuance of treatment keeping Tony Bland, a persistent vegetative state patient, alive. The declaration was granted but the House of Lords made clear that the taking of positive steps to end life was unlawful as was shown in the prosecution of Dr Cox and that court guidance should be sought by doctors faced with similar cases in future. In any event the moral, social and legal issues should be considered by Parliament. In the case of Dr Cox, who was found guilty of the attempted murder of a patient and sentenced to 12 months imprisonment (suspended), what he had done was clearly unlawful and ethically wrong, but in his defence it was said that he had acted from the highest of motives and in the best interests of his patient. Morally he considered that he had not done wrong. If the law were to reflect such motives it would become selective and partial and fail to take account of the opposing moral view that it is wrong to kill others for whatever reason. The law has drawn the line between administering drugs to relieve pain, or, as in the *Tony Bland* case, ceasing life sustaining treatments, and administering drugs to end life. However, future cases may determine the strength of this line and, in the absence of legislation, it will be for the courts to decide each case as it arises on its merits.

In conclusion, it is clear that law and morality may overlap and it is for the law and in particular for Parliament to shape the law so as to reflect moral values. In some cases it may be the role of the law to initiate social change in advance of moral values as in the case of discrimination for example. Hoffman LJ in the Court of Appeal in *Airedale NHS Trust v Bland* (1993) stated that, on this issue, law and morality must be the same and that the law had to reflect moral values. He made reference to Professor Dworkin's writings in which the view was put forward that law and morality is inextricably mixed. In deciding hard cases the judge draws on moral and political standards (principles and policies) -

law is not only made up of rules but also of non-rule standards. The judge does not make law but has to find the one right answer. Where the judicial decision leads to socially unacceptable results it is for Parliament to draw the line or map out a new path. Given that there may not be one moral answer to a particular question the law cannot always attempt to reflect moral values. A compromise may have to be made between competing values or the view which is considered most desirable adopted. Such decisions are properly the role of Parliament rather than the courts who can only make decisions in cases coming to them. The role of the legislator is a prospective one and one in which competing interests can be weighed and evaluated.

Question 12

(a) Professor Ronald Dworkin in *Law's Empire* distinguished rules, principles and policies. How useful is this distinction in analysing the definition of law? (10 marks)

(b) Consider the extent to which each has contributed to the development of an area or areas of law with which you are familiar. (15 marks)

General approach

(a) This part of the question calls for an analysis of the definition of law with particular reference to Professor Dworkin's distinction between rules, principles and policies.

The definition of law has engaged jurists and philosophers for centuries and the theories of the two main schools of thought - positivist and natural law - should be discussed. The positivist school exponents in the 19th Century were Jeremy Bentham and John Austin and in the 20th Century Hans Kelsen and Professor HLA Hart. The natural law school developed from the times of the Greeks and Romans to St Thomas Aquinas to Hobbes to John Locke to Rousseau and the 20th Century saw a revival in the setting up of the United Nations Charter on Human Rights and the European Convention on Human Rights and following the Nuremburg War Trials. Professor Dworkin in *Law's Empire* and his other writings takes issue with the positivist school and concludes that the definition of law as a system of rules is too narrow and that account should be taken of the part played by principles and policy in law making.

The main ideas of the positivist school should be discussed: laws are the commands of an individual or body vested with authority; no necessary connection exists between law and morality (law does not depend for its validity on moral principles); a legal system is a closed logical order where decisions are deduced from legal rules by logical means; moral judgments, unlike statements of fact, cannot be determined by rational argument. It must be noted that although there may be wide divergence on some matters, the common thread running through the writings of the positivist school is that there is no necessary connection between law and morality. The positivist is concerned with analysing the law as it is and not with what it ought to be. The positivist is not concerned with what is morally desirable and is not willing to conclude that a rule which purports to be law is invalid because it is morally indefensible. Whether or not such a 'bad' law ought to be obeyed is another, and separate, question which the individual will have to decide but one which the positivist does not attempt to answer as part of the theory.

The natural law school on the other hand considers that law and morals overlap and that man-made law can be judged by a higher natural law whether God-given or derived from an innate sense of right and wrong. Whether or not a 'bad' law should be obeyed is again a separate question. Sir William Blackstone appealed to God-given principles to gauge the legitimacy of law concluding that a conflict would nullify the law and that this need not then be obeyed.

(b) Professor Dworkin refers to the case of *McLoughlin v O'Brian* (1983) and so this would be a good starting point for an analysis of rules, principles and policy leading into the second part of the question. This case concerned a claim in the tort of negligence on the ground of nervous shock and illustrates the issues facing the court and the development of the law. Further developments are shown in the case of *Alcock & Others v Chief Constable of South Yorkshire Police* (1992).

Other cases illustrating the operation of rules, principles and policy in the development of law include: *Burton v Islington Health Authority* and *de Martell v Merton & Sutton Health Authority* (1992); *R v Home Secretary ex parte Bentley* (1993); *R v Governors of the Bishop Challoner RC Comprehensive Girls' School & Another ex parte Choudhury* (1992); *R v Brown* (1993); *Airedale NHS Trust v Bland* (1993); *Woolwich Building Society v Inland Revenue Commissioners (No 2)* (1992); *Tinsley v Milligan* (1993); *Cambridge Water Company v Eastern Counties Leather plc* (1993); *R v Registrar General ex parte Smith* (1990); *Pepper v Hart* (1993).

Answer plan

- definitions and theories of law
- outline of the positivist and natural law schools of thought
- Professor Dworkin's theory of law distinguishing between rules, principles and policy; the usefulness of this distinction in analysing law
- analysis of *McLoughlin v O'Brian* (1983) and other case-law in various areas as noted above to illustrate the development of law taking into account the role of the judge in deciding cases and in interpreting statutes and the role of Parliament as the supreme law-maker
- conclusion

Answer

(a) The definition of law and its effect has engaged jurists and philosophers from the time of the Greeks and Romans to the present day. Some of the reasons for doing so include the need to differentiate law from other social phenomena such as morality, justice and religious rules; to attempt to answer the question as to why law is or should be obeyed and to analyse the role of law in society.

It might be argued that law in one form or another has been known in all societies. Law may be seen as a civilising force or institution ensuring continuance of society and the values which underpin it. In non-complex societies, law would be unwritten and closely allied with religious or moral codes of behaviour. In complex societies, law would have to be written and cover many more aspects of life than those concerning religion and morals.

Various definitions of law may be offered but the most common suggests that law is a system of rules deriving from a generally recognised or accepted source with power to enforce the rules by the imposition of sanctions or penalties. The emphasis in such a definition is on the concept of a rule the breach of which gives rise to a right in another or in the state itself to enforce the rule and exact either compensation or a penalty. For the purposes of this question we will define a rule as a standard or measure regulating conduct the breach of which gives rise to some consequence. Breach of a rule of morality might result in social censure or the 'offender' being 'sent to Coventry' whilst breach of an ethical rule, for example where a doctor breaks the confidence of his/her patient without good reason, might result in the doctor being reprimanded by his/her professional body.

The same act or omission may result in breach of not only the law but also a moral code, religious rules, ethical rules and this is often most apparent in the area of criminal law. Thus to take the life of another human being will usually offend against the law (as defined in the offences of murder and manslaughter); but also religious rules, for example in the Ten Commandments 'thou shalt not kill'; ethical rules regulating the conduct of a doctor and the need to preserve life and a moral rule stipulating that it is socially unacceptable or wrong to kill another. It is important to note however that although the act of killing is prohibited each category may define the prohibited act differently, for example the offences of murder and manslaughter. Also it does not follow that all killing is prohibited - the law may permit capital punishment or euthanasia or abortion whereas the moral rule may prohibit the taking of all life from the moment of conception until the ceasing of life without human intervention. Again, the moral or religious rule may be left to the interpretation of individuals whereas the law will need to be more precise and well defined if it is to be obeyed and respected.

The distinction between law and morals and the effect of the latter on the former brings us to a discussion of the two main schools of thought on the definition of law namely the positivist and natural law schools. The positivist defines law as the commands of a sovereign (that is the individual or group in society recognised as having power to enforce the legal rules, by coercion if necessary) breach of which results in the imposition of a sanction or penalty. In addition, no necessary connection exists between law and morality. Moral judgments, unlike fact, cannot be proved by rational argument; they concern questions as to what is considered to be right or wrong.

A legal system on the other hand is based on logic and decisions can be deduced from the application of the legal rule to the facts. Positivists are primarily concerned with analysing the nature of law and the legal system. Although law is normative in that it requires obedience the positivist is not concerned with what ought to be, only with law as it is.

In the 19th Century, Jeremy Bentham and John Austin were proponents of the positivist school. The common thread was that there was no necessary connection between law and morality and that 'bad' law was nevertheless law which had to be obeyed or at least if it was not, the penalty would have to be borne.

In the 20th Century, Professor Hart and Hans Kelsen supported the positivist approach although Hart recognised the 'core of indisputable truths in the doctrines of natural law'. Again, the emphasis was on the notion that a rule could have the status and authority of law although it did not accord with moral rules.

The natural law approach analyses the point at which law and morals converge. The theory is of ancient origin having been expounded in the writings of St Augustine, Plato, Aristotle and Cicero who concluded that man-made law which offended natural law was not law at all and need not be obeyed. St Thomas Aquinas expounded the idea that law which conflicted with natural (divine) law would lose its moral binding power justifying the citizen in some cases not obeying the law.

Sir William Blackstone in the 'Commentaries on the Laws of England' stated that man-made law derived its legitimacy from God-given principles and any conflict would nullify man-made law. Similar ideas were put forth by Hobbes, Locke and Rousseau in propounding the social contract theory. Natural law saw a decline in the 19th Century in the face of support for positivist ideas, in particular the conclusion that moral reasoning had no rational solutions.

The 20th Century saw a revival in natural law ideas in the new-found need to expound a 'higher' law in both domestic legal systems and in international law, for example the United Nations Charter on Human Rights and the European Convention.

This now brings us to a discussion of the writings of Professor Dworkin who analysed law and the legal system, the relationship of law and morals, individual rights and the nature of the judge's role. He attacked Professor Hart's model of law as a system of rules and the separation of law and morality. He considered this to be both unacceptable and impossible. Law was to be defined as not only a system of rules but also 'non-rule standards'. In deciding hard cases the court draws on moral and political standards (principles and policies) to reach a decision. The judge's role is an interpretative one in that the judge does not make law but finds the one right answer to the legal problem. Law and morality are inextricably mixed and Hart's distinction between primary and secondary rules is inaccurate in that it fails to take account of principles and policies.

In Dworkin's view rules apply in an all or nothing fashion; they dictate a result and must be applied. A principle has weight but there may be conflicting principles between which the judge will have to decide. It provides a reason for deciding a case in a particular way. It is a standard based on justice or fairness or other aspect of morality. Principles are concerned with rights and are the remit of the courts. An example given by Dworkin is the principle that 'no man should benefit from his own wrong' and this is exemplified in the American case of *Riggs v Palmer* (1889) which prevented a murderer inheriting under the will of his victim where the legal rule was silent. In English law this is shown in the cases of *Re Sigsworth* and *Ex parte Smith*. Other examples of principles come to mind, for example that a person is innocent until proven guilty; the principles of natural justice that a man should not be a judge in his own cause and that a person is entitled to put forth his case; the polluter pays principle ensuring that those who cause pollution are made responsible for the costs of cleaning up.

A principle may take the form of a maxim or wise statement without providing a result such as a penalty for breach but it may lead to the development of a rule. Conversely a rule may lead to the formulation of a principle which will have wider scope.

Policy, like a principle, is a standard which sets out a goal which aims to improve economic, political or social facets of society or which is deemed to be desirable on the grounds of expediency or efficiency. Policy is the proper concern of Parliament, not the courts. It is often a question of drawing a line or deciding on the path to be followed in the future - this is not a matter which the courts can handle given that they decide cases only as and when a dispute arises. The legislative role is a prospective one in which considerations of the public good have to be decided on. Where the decisions of a court lead to a socially unacceptable result it will be for Parliament to legislate and draw the line.

The word 'policy' is much in vogue, whether in relation to government, local authorities and other public bodies making decisions affecting the citizen, institutions such as schools and colleges, trading companies and retail outlets in their dealing with customers. In essence, a policy is a method by which decisions are reached, a set of criteria or guidelines which assist the decision-maker in his/her task. It ensures foreword planning and may set an order of priorities to be taken into account.

In the case of *R v Governors of the Bishop Challoner Roman Catholic Girls' Comprehensive School & Another ex parte Choudhury* (1992), the question arose whether the school governors were entitled to operate an admissions policy giving preference to those of the Christian faith when they found they were over-subscribed and despite a statutory rule entitling parents to choose a school. The applicants, one a Muslim and the other a Hindu, chose this school for their daughters but were refused places and a later appeal was rejected. The parents sought judicial review but the House of Lords held that there had been no error in law. The admissions policy adopted religious criteria so as to preserve the character of the school and given that it was over-subscribed such a policy was necessary and took preference over the statutory duty to give effect to parental choice. It was for the governors, acting reasonably, to decide on the criteria of the policy.

However it is by no means easy to distinguish policies and principles and even judicial statements often use the terms interchangeably. The main advantage of Dworkin's approach is the appreciation that the law comprises not only rules in the strict sense but also more fluid concepts in recognition that the law is not static but is developing and changing to meet changing needs.

(b) Professor Dworkin refers to the case of *McLoughlin v O'Brian* (1983). This involved a claim in negligence by the plaintiff who, on reaching hospital, having been informed that her husband and three children had been involved in a road accident, found her husband and two of her children severely injured and the other child dead. The accident had been caused by the negligence of the defendant. The plaintiff suffered nervous shock as a result of what she saw on reaching hospital and claimed damages against the defendant. Her claim was upheld as the nervous shock sustained was a reasonably foreseeable consequence of the defendant's negligence.

Previous cases had permitted claims where the plaintiff had been at or near the scene of the accident at the time or shortly after the accident. This case was novel in that the plaintiff had been at home at that time. Of the five Law Lords, Lords Russell, Scarman and Bridge adopted the 'reasonable foreseeability' test as determining liability. Lords Russell and Bridge stated that no sufficient policy considerations justified the limitation of this principle. Lord Scarman considered public policy considerations to be the sole province of Parliament. It was not for the courts to draw the line as this involved 'social, economic and financial policy'. Agreeing with the reasoning of Lord Bridge, he said that legislation was needed. The role of the judge was to formulate principle and weigh up policy considerations. If the development of case-law lead to socially unacceptable results it was for Parliament 'to draw the line or map out a new path'.

Lord Edmund-Davies opined that policy issues were justiciable but he gave no indication as to where the line should be drawn other than to reject the argument that foreseeability should be limited by the floodgates argument.

Lord Wilberforce, whose dicta were applied in the case of *Alcock v Chief Constable of South Yorkshire* (1992), having reviewed the principles by which claims had succeeded in the past, stated that this was a borderline case but which was sufficiently analogous as to be assimilated into the existing law. He mentioned a common principle 'at the margin, the boundaries of a man's responsibility are fixed as a matter of policy'. Foreseeability had to have limits placed on it. The general rule was that only those within sight or sound of the accident or those in close proximity could recover. He accepted that policy played a part in limiting any extension to this rule. Four policy considerations were mentioned namely proliferation of claims; unfairness to defendants; the lengthening of litigation and that Parliament should set the limits. Three elements were inherent in all such claims namely the class of persons whose claims have been recognised; the proximity of the plaintiff to the accident and the means by which the shock was caused. Only if these are met will a claim succeed. The plaintiff in the present case fell within the recognised class of claimants and so this was sufficient for her to succeed.

In *Alcock v Chief Constable of South Yorkshire* (1992), which involved claims for nervous shock arising out of the Hillsborough disaster, the plaintiffs were relatives or friends of those in the stadium. Some witnessed the events from other parts of the stadium, one was just outside and seeing the events on television attempted to find his son, and the others were at home and either watched the events on television or seen replays after having heard about the disaster from friends or via the radio. All claims failed on the basis that no duty of care was owed to those who were unable to show a sufficiently close relationship based on ties of love and affection; proximity in time and space and proximity in the means by which the shock was caused.

Other recent cases illustrate the attitude of the courts to their role and the place that rules, principles and policy play in the development of the law. In the case of *R v Home Secretary ex parte Bentley* (1993), the Home Secretary was found to have made an error of law susceptible to judicial review when he failed to consider the appropriate form of pardon. Instead of refusing to grant a free pardon he should have considered granting a posthumous conditional pardon. It was stated that it had been long established policy for a Home Secretary only to grant a free pardon where an applicant was both morally and technically innocent of any crime and it was not for the court to attempt to interfere with this. It was however proper for the court to invite the Home Secretary to reconsider the issues given the exceptional nature of the circumstances.

As Professor Dworkin stated rules apply in an all or nothing fashion and give rise to a result. Principles are open-ended and indicate a wise, just or fair course of action, for example that a person is presumed innocent until proved guilty or that 'he who comes to equity should come with clean hands' or that a person should not profit from his own wrong. Rules would state the situations where such principles would apply and the consequences for breach.

Litigants and those with a legal problem will be concerned with knowing what rules apply and the solution to be reached. They may not be so concerned with knowing what the underlying principles of the rules are and similarly may not be concerned with questions of policy. However the jurist may be so concerned in considering how the law will develop. The latter is primarily the function of Parliament as it is (in theory at least) the supreme law maker and the representative of the people and can legislate for the future on the basis that competing interests have been taken into account. The judge in making decisions will inevitably contribute to the development of the law but must do so only on a case-by-case basis working within established principles. As Lord Scarman said in *McLoughlin v O'Brian* (1983) if this leads to undesirable results it will be for Parliament to enact legislation. The law should develop consistently and be certain but a judge who attempts to develop the law to give effect to policy may create uncertainty and usurp his or her proper role.

In *Cambridge Water Co v Eastern Counties Leather plc* (1993), although the word policy was not referred to, the court considered the respective roles of the court and Parliament in law-making. The case concerned strict liability under the rule in *Rylands v Fletcher* and the question was posed whether this rule was merely an extension of the law of nuisance (a prerequisite for liability being reasonable foreseeability of harm) or part of a wider principle of strict liability for damage caused by ultra-hazardous operations. After considering the authorities the court concluded that the rule in *Rylands v Fletcher* was to be treated as part of the law of nuisance. Development of a wider principle had not taken place and had been warned against by the Law Commission in its report on Civil Liability for Dangerous Things and Activities in 1970. Any such development would have been the province of Parliament which could have laid down the appropriate criteria. In 1990 the Environmental Pollution Act had been passed enacting rules regulating environmental pollution on the basis of 'the polluter pays' principle and so it would be inappropriate for the court to extend the common law strict liability rule.

The relationship between the court and Parliament was again mentioned in *Woolwich Building Society v IRC (No 2)* (1992) where the House of Lords held that tax paid under an unlawful demand was repayable with interest. The common law recognised a general restitutionary principle so as to give effect to common justice. The Bill of Rights 1688 was also referred to and the Bill enshrined the fundamental principle that only Parliament could levy taxes. It followed that, if this was to have full effect, a citizen who had paid tax unlawfully was entitled to recover the sum paid with interest. The leading judgment was given by Lord Goff, but Lord Keith's dissenting judgment is instructive on the question of policy. He stated that on general principle recovery of such sums could only be made where duress was proved. Any extension of the law would amount to judicial legislation. This was not acceptable since policy considerations, as to how the law should develop, was the province of Parliament.

Policy questions were dealt with in *R v Brown* (1993) which concerned sado-masochistic homosexual practices and whether consent was a defence for offences under ss 20 and 47 of the Offences Against the Person Act 1861. It was held that public policy required that society be protected from such practices and that consent was no defence. Those in the majority (Lords Templeman, Jauncey and Lowry) considered that acts above a common assault were to be treated as unlawful and consent was not a defence unless Parliament permitted such actions. It was not the province of the courts to permit such actions. Those in the minority (Lords Musthill and Slynn) considered that such acts were lawful (although morally wrong) and that, if it were considered necessary to prohibit such acts, this was the province of Parliament, not the courts.

General Principles of English Law

The most significant case to arise in 1993 was *Airedale National Health Trust v Bland* (1993) where the court was asked to decide whether life-sustaining treatment and medical support should be withdrawn from Tony Bland, the persistent vegetative state patient. The declaration requested was granted but only after a full consideration of all the issues. The court stressed that euthanasia by positive steps to end life was unlawful as was made clear in the prosecution of Dr Cox who administered a drug to a terminally ill patient in dire pain. It was also stressed that court guidance was to be sought by doctors in future cases and that the moral, social and legal issues should be considered by Parliament.

Future cases may not be as clear on the facts as the present, for example as to the extent of the incapacity of the patient, and so it was vital for a full consideration of all the issues to be made by Parliament with a view to legislation.

The principle of 'he who comes to equity must come with clean hands' was dealt a blow in the House of Lords case *Tinsley v Milligan* (1993). Here T and M had jointly contributed to the purchase of a house transferred into the sole name of T. M had represented to the DSS for housing benefit purposes that she had no interest in the house. T and M fell out and T claimed sole ownership and M counterclaimed for the property to be held in trust for both T and M.

T's case was that as M had been fraudulent she could not claim any interest in the house. By a majority of three to two, the House of Lords found in M's favour holding that as she did not need to rely on her fraud in bringing her claim the principles of clean hands and *ex turpi* did not apply.

The Court of Appeal relied on a 'public conscience' test to find in favour of M but this was described in the House of Lords as an 'imponderable factor'. In the House of Lords, Lord Goff dissented, preferring the 'clean hands' principle, and stating that this should only change as a result of the passage of legislation following a full inquiry by the Law Commission.

In the case of *Ex parte Smith* (1990), s 51 of the Adoption Act 1976 concerning information to be supplied to those who had been adopted relating to the natural parents was in question.

The court held that an absolute duty to supply information was overridden by the principle of public policy that the registrar need not comply if it would give rise to a real risk of serious crime being committed or serious danger to a member of the public. These public policy considerations were to be considered paramount.

No mention of the part played by rules, principles and policy would be complete without reference to the House of Lords' case of *Pepper v Hart* (1993) where the court held that, subject to limitations, a court will in future be permitted to consult the official journal of the House of Commons to assist it in the task of interpreting statutory provisions. This case raised issues about the purposive approach to statutory interpretation, parliamentary privilege under Art 9 of the 1688 Bill of Rights and what Lord Browne-Wilkinson referred to as the principle necessitating reference to *Hansard* namely the discovery of the true intent of Parliament where the words used are ambiguous, obscure or where the literal rule leads to an absurd result.

In conclusion, a strict definition of law to include only rules can be misleading when considering how law is made. For the litigant or person with a legal problem what the rules are and how they will affect an outcome is of the prime importance but, for those attempting to analyse the process by which law is made, account must be taken of the principles on which the legal rules are founded (largely a question for the judge) and the policy issues by which law is changed and developed (largely a question for Parliament).

Chapter 4

European Law

Introduction

Most exam papers contain at least one question on European law. The dynamic nature of the subject means that this trend is likely to be enhanced. One of the difficulties confronting students is that the original EEC Treaty (now called the 'EC' Treaty) has been gradually amended by both the Single European Act and the Maastricht Treaty on European Union. It is necessary, therefore, especially when considering European institutions, to bear in mind subsequent alterations made by these instruments.

Most 'A' level questions in this field tend to be essays. Thus the standard 'rules' of answering the question apply here, ie identifying key words in the question and framing the answer around this rather than rushing in and writing everything that you know on a topic. Therefore, four of the five specimen questions and answers provided are in essay form.

Maastricht is likely to be a source of questions in the future, and the emphasis here is upon questions that relate to institutional changes as the syllabuses all specifically mention EC institutions.

It is possible, however, to frame problem questions on EC law, for example, on direct effect. Again, as with problem questions on other topics, you have to identify the subject matter for discussion, analyse those parts which are relevant to the question and then apply them to the question; very similar, really, to writing a highly selective essay.

What makes answering questions on European law different to answering questions on English legal topics relates to the sources of law. In the syllabus areas covered there are not many cases; those that are quoted are very important and must be supplied when answering a question on supremacy of Community law or direct effect. However, most of the topics require you to quote important Treaty provisions which are largely provided by the amended EC Treaty or the Maastricht Treaty. In most situations it is sufficient to provide the substance of the Treaty provision. However, two Articles require a detailed knowledge as they are the key to an understanding of the nature of EC law: Arts 177 and 189 of the EC Treaty.

Question 13

(a) Explain the difference between the various types of secondary rules as outlined in Art 189 of the European Community Treaty.

(b) Discuss the relationship between the European Court of Justice and national legal systems as provided by Art 177 of the European Community Treaty.

General approach

Questions on the sources of Community law are quite common in 'A' level papers. In particular, the relationship between the European Court of Justice and the English legal system is often touched upon. This two-part question deals with secondary sources and, indeed, reference to the court under Art 177 of the EC Treaty.

Both questions require a very factual approach. In part (a) a knowledge of the content of Art 189 is required as is the ability to explain the different legal consequences of the various forms of secondary rules and the uses to which they are put. Similarly, in part (b) a knowledge of the content of Art 177 is required as is the ability to outline the practice of the court in the way in which it deals with preliminary rulings. Whether the question refers to the English legal system or, as here, national legal systems, the approach is the same.

Answer plan

(a)
- sources of Community law; primary and secondary rules
- Art 189 of the EC Treaty; content and distinction between secondary sources
- scope of secondary rules; qualified majority voting

European Law

(b)
- Art 177 of the EC Treaty; content and nature of preliminary rulings
- discretionary and mandatory reference; distinction and limitations on reference
- precedent; practice of the European court

Answer

(a) The European Community Treaty provisions are usually referred to as the 'primary sources' of Community law. The detailed laws made by the supra-national institutions to fulfill treaty objectives are known as the 'secondary sources' of Community law. In this context, the obligations laid down on member states by the following articles of the Treaty are important. Art 5 says: 'Member states shall take all appropriate measures ... to ensure fulfilment of the obligations arising out of this Treaty or resulting from action taken by the institutions of the Community. They shall facilitate the achievement of the Community's tasks.' Similarly, Art 6(1) says: 'Member states shall, in close co-operation with the institutions of the Community, co-ordinate their respective economic policies to the extent necessary to attain the objectives of this Treaty.'

Since Community policies are enforced through the processes of law, the member states must modify their laws in order to remove the legal constraints to the effective operation of the Community.

More specifically, the harmonisation of member states' laws is dealt with by Art 100 and Art 100(a) where the Council is given the power to issue directives for the harmonisation of laws in member states which directly affect the functioning of the Common Market (Art 100) and the internal market (Art 100(a), added by the Single European Act).

Article 189 of the European Community Treaty (as amended) explains the nature of the secondary rules. It states:

> 'In order to carry out their task and in accordance with the provisions of this Treaty, the European Parliament acting jointly with the Council, the Council and the Commission

shall make regulations and issue directives, take decisions, make recommendations or deliver opinions.

A regulation shall have general application. It shall be binding in its entirety and directly applicable in all member states. A directive shall be binding, as to the result to be achieved, upon each member state to which it is addressed, but shall leave to the national authorities the choice of form and methods. A decision shall be binding in its entirety upon those to whom it is addressed. Recommendations and opinions shall have no binding force.'

Of the rules outlined in Art 189, only regulations and directives are strictly laws.

As regards regulations, they are said to have 'general application'. This means that they are issued at all members of the Community. They enforce a policy common to all states eg agriculture. Thus, a restriction on milk quotas throughout the Community would be dealt with by means of a regulation. They are also said to be 'directly applicable'. From a legal point of view this is very important. It means that regulations have legal force in all member states as soon as they are made - no enactment measures are required by the individual states.

Directives are far more numerous. They are the means by which member states' laws are harmonised for the proper functioning of the Community. A benchmark Community standard is agreed on. Directives are then issued to any number of states from one to 15 which are required to raise their legal standards to that benchmark standard. Thus on several occasions directives have been issued solely to the UK which has been out of step with its Community partners. On the other hand, directives that regulate the internal market are generally issued to all 15 member states. Also, states are allowed a certain amount of time in which to give legal force to directives. In some cases, this can be up to five years. They are not, therefore, directly applicable. Member states can also choose the method of incorporation of a directive into national law according to their constitutions.

Decisions are binding on states, companies and individuals. Arguably, they are more administrative in character but they do have legal consequences. For example, if a company asked for an

European Law

exemption from competition policy and it received an adverse decision, then acting contrary to that decision would result in legal action against the company.

Recommendations and opinions are often given and sought. Although not legally binding, they do have persuasive authority if they are relied on in a legal action.

It should be noted that Art 189 uses the phrase 'in accordance with the provisions of this Treaty'. Therefore, the secondary rules are not unlimited in their law-making scope. However, Art 8(a) (added by SEA) introduced the internal market which 'shall comprise an area without internal frontiers in which the free movement of goods, persons, services and capital is ensured in accordance with the provisions of this Treaty'. As a result of this provision and other SEA amendments, there has been a great increase in Community legislative activity in areas other than those relating purely to the original Treaty-based policies. For example, there has recently been introduced increased protection for employees under health and safety directives.

The extension of qualified majority voting by the Single European Act and the Maastricht Treaty in relation to directives has certainly enhanced the utility of this form of secondary legislation.

(b) Article 177 of the EC Treaty is an extremely important provision. Here the European Court pronounces on the conformity of national law with Community law. It is worth noting that this is the Treaty provision by which the European court has effectively developed Community law into a federal system of law for the benefit of all citizens of the Community.

Article 177 states:

'The Court of Justice shall have jurisdiction to give preliminary rulings concerning:
a) the interpretation of this Treaty;
b) the validity and interpretation of acts of the institutions of the Community and of the ECB (ie secondary rules);
c) the interpretation of the statutes of bodies established by an act of the Council, where those statutes so provide.

Where such a question is raised before any court or tribunal of a member state, that court or tribunal may, if it considers that a decision on the question is necessary to enable it to give judgment, request the Court of Justice to give a ruling thereon.

Where any such question is raised in a case pending before a court or tribunal of a member state, against whose decisions there is no judicial remedy under national law, that court or tribunal shall bring the matter before the Court of Justice.'

As regards preliminary rulings, here, the national court does not feel that it has the expertise to rule on whether its own state's laws comply with Community law. Domestic court proceedings are suspended and the case is sent to Luxembourg to be examined by the European court. The preliminary ruling of that court will then be sent back to the national court to guide it in its decision. The European court will accept requests for preliminary rulings from any courts, however lowly in a state's hierarchy of courts.

However, different member states have different policies as to which courts can submit requests. In the United Kingdom, for example, the domestic appeals procedure must normally be exhausted before a request for a preliminary ruling is sent to Luxembourg.

Paragraph 2 of Art 177 deals with the discretion of the member states' courts to request a preliminary ruling. This is indicated by the use of the word 'may' in para 2 of Art 177. Most requests for preliminary rulings arise under this part of Art 177. By contrast, para 3 of Art 177 deals with the right of a plaintiff, once the domestic appeals system has been exhausted, to have the case referred to Luxembourg, ie mandatory reference. Exhaustion of appeals is indicated by the phrase 'no judicial remedy' and the mandatory nature of the reference is indicated by the word 'shall' in para 3 of Art 177.

The extent of mandatory reference was considered by the European court in the *Cilfit* case (1983). It stated:

' ... the third paragraph of Art 177 of the EEC Treaty is to be interpreted as meaning that a court or tribunal against whose decisions there is no judicial remedy under national law is required, where a question of Community law is raised before it, to comply with its obligation to bring the matter before the Court of Justice, unless it has established that the question is irrelevant or that the Community provision in question has already been interpreted by the court or that the correct application of Community law is so obvious as to have no scope for any reasonable doubt.'

Thus, even where the appeals procedure has been exhausted, a court is entitled to refuse to refer on the ground that the answer is clear. This is an application of the continental legal doctrine of *acte clair*.

The European court answers specific questions concerning the interpretation of Community law that are referred to it by the national court. It is left to the national courts to comply with the ruling in the context of the domestic situation. Thus, although the European court is not supposed to rule on the compatibility of national law with Community law, the effect of its ruling might well be to achieve that result. The court, following Continental practice, is not bound by its previous decisions. There is no rigid system of *stare decisis*. Also, the ruling is addressed to the courts of one particular member state. However, the court, in practice, often refers to its previous decisions where a well-developed doctrine like direct effect is under consideration. In general, however, the court has great flexibility to alter and develop its policies which are then binding on the national legal system concerned.

Question 14

What is the legal status of United Kingdom legislation which conflicts with European Community law?

General approach

This is a very typical example of an 'A' level essay question. It is quite common to find a question which deals with the situation of a conflict between United Kingdom law and Community law, however the question might be worded. Sometimes, for example, the question will ask you about the effect on the doctrine of sovereignty of Parliament arising from United Kingdom membership of the European Community. In any case, however, you will be required to examine the legal status of such conflicting legislation, ie is it valid, valid until repeal, or void?

In such a question, it is a good idea to set the scene by examining the relevant sections of the European Communities Act 1972, and commentaries thereon, to see if a clue can be provided here. You will see that these provisions effectively embody prior European Court of Justice decisions. You can then move on to examine these and subsequent decisions, especially the *Factortame* case in order to arrive at a conclusion.

Answer plan

- supremacy of Community law; definition and recognition by United Kingdom politicians and judges
- the European Communities Act 1972; the incorporation into UK law of the doctrine of supremacy by ss 2(1), 2(4) and 3(1)
- implementation of treaties by statutes; modification of the normal rules in relation to Community law
- the attitude of the European Court of Justice; elaboration of the doctrine of supremacy in *Van Gend en Loos, Costa v Enel, Simmenthal* and *Factortame* cases
- conclusion; modification to the doctrine of sovereignty of Parliament

Answer

Even before the United Kingdom joined the European Community, the European Court of Justice had decided that, in any conflict between Community law and National Law, Community law was supreme. This has had enormous implications in limiting the sovereignty of Parliament. Thus, the 1967 White Paper dealing with the United Kingdom's entry into the European Community said that Parliament will have to refrain from passing legislation which is inconsistent with Community law. Also, on entry to the Community, the United Kingdom judges clearly recognised the legal implications. In *Esso Petroleum v Kingswood Motors Ltd* (1974), Bridge J observed that, where Community law is in conflict with UK domestic law, the effect of the European Communities Act 1972 is to require that Community law shall prevail. Similarly, in *Aero Zipp Fasteners v*

YKK Fasteners (1973) Graham J said that the European Communities Act 1972 enacted that relevant common market law should be applied in the UK and should, where there is a conflict, override English law.

The European Communities Act 1972 incorporated the primary and secondary rules of Community law into United Kingdom law as required by Arts 5 and 6 of the European Community Treaty. This statute avoids any outright statement of the supremacy of Community law. It was probably thought unnecessary in view of the practice of the European Court of Justice. However, the various provisions of the European Communities Act 1972 collectively guarantee the effectiveness of supremacy of Community law within the United Kingdom constitution. Section 2(1) of the Act incorporates Treaty provisions into United Kingdom law which have direct effect. In fact, s 2(1) uses the phrase 'enforceable Community right'. As the European Court of Justice has interpreted the nature of these rights, then arguably s 2(1) also impliedly incorporates the doctrine of supremacy which has arisen out of this interpretation. Section 2(4) of the Act also gets close to entrenching Community law into the United Kingdom legal system. It provides that 'any enactment passed or to be passed, shall be construed and have effect subject to the foregoing provisions of this section'. This means that Parliament should beware of passing legislation that is contrary to Community law. Also, the effect of s 3(1) of the Act is that the courts of the United Kingdom have to defer to the European Court of Justice in matters of Community law, the court which has created the doctrine of supremacy of Community law.

Thus, the orthodox doctrine that statutes designed to implement treaty provisions are not different from other statutes and may be expressly or impliedly amended or repealed by subsequent inconsistent statutes does not co-exist very happily with implementation of the Community treaties. The European Court of Justice would not look favourably on any legislation that was contrary to Community law.

As in so many other areas of its work, the Court of Justice has adopted an evolutionary approach to this topic. It has moved from saying simply that Community law shall prevail in a case of conflict with national law to a position where it regards such national legislation as being void. Thus, in the early days of the Community, national judges would have to wait for the repeal of inconsistent national legislation in order to apply Community provisions. Now, however, they have to disapply inconsistent legislation, not await its repeal, and always apply Community provisions.

The doctrine of supremacy of Community law was elaborated gradually by the European court in the course of its interpretation of the Treaties. The stage was set in the *Van Gend en Loos* (1963) case. The case arose out of the imposition by the Netherlands government of new import duties, which, it was argued, were in contravention of Art 12 of the EEC Treaty. Article 12 states:

> 'Member states shall refrain from introducing between themselves any new customs duties on imports or exports or any charges having equivalent effect, and from increasing those which they already apply in their trade with each other.'

The plaintiff was a company affected by an increase from 3% to 8% in import duties on certain plastics despite the provisions of Art 12 of the Treaty. It paid the higher import duties and then brought an action in the Dutch court for the return of the increased import duties. The Dutch court referred the case to the European court for a preliminary ruling under Art 177 of the EEC Treaty.

The European court declared that Community law was applicable not only to the member states in the form of international law but also to the citizens of the member states in the form of a federal law.

Thus, the obligation under Art 12 was owed to the Dutch people, companies and anybody else adversely affected by the breach of Art 12. The latter provision prevailed over the contrary Dutch legislation. Therefore, the Dutch government repaid the money wrongfully taken as customs duties.

The case of *Flaminio Costa v Enel* (1964) can be regarded as the cornerstone of the doctrine of supremacy. The European court went much further. An Italian small claims court asked for a ruling whether or not the Italian law, which nationalised the electricity industry after the entry into force of the EEC Treaty, was compatible with Arts 37, 53, 93 and 102 of the Treaty. The plaintiff had argued that Italian shareholders in the private electricity companies had received a lower level of compensation than applied in other EC states.

In its preliminary ruling, the European court said that, unlike ordinary treaties, the EEC Treaty has created its own legal system which, on the entry into force of the treaty, became an integral part of the legal systems of the member states and which they are bound to apply.

The precedence of Community law is confirmed by Art 189 whereby a regulation 'shall be binding' and 'directly applicable in all member states'. This provision would be quite meaningless if a state could unilaterally nullify its effects by means of a legislative measure which could prevail over Community law. The European court went on to say that the transfer by the states from their domestic legal system to the Community legal system of the rights and obligations arising under the Treaty carries with it a permanent limitation of their sovereign rights, against which a subsequent unilateral act incompatible with the concept of the Community cannot prevail.

In the *Simmenthal* case (1979), an Italian law of 1970 imposed a charge for the inspection of beef and veal imported from France into Italy. The case concerned whether the 1970 charge was in breach of Art 30 of the EEC Treaty: 'Quantitative restrictions on imports and all measures having equivalent effect shall, without prejudice to the following provisions, be prohibited between member states.'

An action in Italy against the Exchequer for repayment of veterinary charges succeeded. However, the Italian government objected and the case was brought before the European court under Art 177.

The question was, what was the scope of Art 30 - was it so wide that it prohibits veterinary charges at the frontier? In answering yes to this, the European court said: (a) the Treaty provision (Art 30), by the very fact of entry into force, not only repealed any conflicting provisions of existing domestic law, but also (b) prevents the valid enactment of any new domestic legislation to the extent to which such legislation is incompatible with community provisions.

Thus, a duty lay on the national courts to refrain from applying subsequent conflicting legislation. A national court which is called upon to apply provisions of Community law is under a duty to give full effect to those provisions.

Further, a national court should not have to await the repeat of inconsistent legislation before giving effect to Community law.

Therefore, by the time of the *Simmenthal* decision, the European Court of Justice had moved gradually from saying that Community law prevailed over conflicting national law to a position where it stated that such conflicting law was effectively void and of no legal effect. At last in *R v Secretary of State for Transport, ex parte Factortame Ltd* the opportunity came to test United Kingdom legislation against the *Simmenthal* approach. In this case, the plaintiffs were companies which owned and operated fishing vessels. Although the ships were registered as British under the Merchant Shipping Act, and the plaintiff companies were incorporated under United Kingdom law, the majority of the shareholders and directors were Spanish. It was felt by the United Kingdom government that the use of a British 'flag of convenience' by Spanish ships was a means of access to British fishing quotas. Part II of the Merchant Shipping Act 1988 sought to deal with this situation. Section 14 of the Act provided that a vessel could only be registered in the United Kingdom if its owner were a British citizen resident in the United Kingdom or a company incorporated in the United Kingdom and having its principal place of business in the United Kingdom with at least 75% of its shareholders who were British citizens resident in the United Kingdom. The plaintiffs' vessels did not qualify for registration under the 1988 Act and, therefore, were deprived of the right to fish. They challenged the 1988 Act as being contrary to Art 52 of the EEC Treaty on the grounds that the United Kingdom statute discriminated against the right of establishment, ie the freedom to set up a business.

The question was referred by the House of Lords to the European Court of Justice under Art 177. In agreeing that the 1988 Act did contravene Art 52 of the EEC Treaty, the European court said that the statute should be disapplied to the extent that it contravened Community law. The House of Lords subsequently

European Law

issued injunctions against the United Kingdom government to prevent the application of the offending provisions of the 1988 Act against the plaintiff companies.

Factortame is a landmark decision because, historically, the United Kingdom courts have not been able to challenge the validity of legislation due to the doctrine of sovereignty of Parliament. Now, when it comes to legislation which is contrary to Community law, it seems that they have little choice but to do so.

Question 15

The Council of Ministers issues a directive to the United Kingdom which limits the working week of employees to 48 hours. The United Kingdom has five years in which to implement this directive. Six years later, implementation has still not occurred. Smith, an employee, is dismissed by the privatised Alpha Water Company for refusing to work a 50 hour week. To what extent can Smith rely on the unincorporated directive in order to claim compensation?

General approach

This is a typical example of a problem question in the area of European Community law. The first task is to locate the topic for discussion. The legal nature of directives stands out as requiring general treatment. However, the key phrase in the problem is 'unincorporated directive'. This should get you thinking about the principle of direct effect which is discussed in the text in Chapter 14 of *Lecture Notes on 'A' Level Law Paper 1* (Cavendish Publishing, 1994) on 'The United Kingdom and the European Community'. Do not try and find a solution to the problem straight away. Introduce the topic by defining your terms and trace the evolution of the doctrine from *Van Gend en Loos* to *Francovich*. Once you have done this, you will be able to apply what you have written to the facts of the problem and be able to draw some conclusions.

Answer plan

- the legal character of directives; Arts 189 and 100(a) of the EC Treaty
- implementation of directives; the United Kingdom approach; s 2(2) European Communities Act 1972
- direct effect; the attitude of the European Court of Justice; the *Van Gend en Loos* case.
- unincorporated directives; the *Marshall* case and vertical direct effect
- state responsibility; the criteria laid down in *Foster* and applied to the question
- the *Francovich* case; the criteria laid down by the European Court of Justice and applied to the question

Answer

The legal character of directives is provided by Art 189 of the EC Treaty (as amended) which states:

> 'In order to carry out their task and in accordance with the provisions of this Treaty, the European Parliament acting jointly with the Council, the Council and the Commission shall make regulations and issue directives, take decisions, make recommendations or deliver opinions. A regulation shall have general application. It shall be binding in its entirety and directly applicable in all member states. A directive shall be binding, as to the result to be achieved, upon each member state to which it is addressed, but shall leave to the national authorities the choice of form and methods. A decision shall be binding in its entirety upon those to whom it is addressed. Recommendations and opinions shall have no binding force.'

Directives are extremely numerous - they are the means by which member states' laws are harmonised for the proper functioning of the Community. Article 100(a) of the EC Treaty expressly gives the Council of Ministers the power to issue directives for the harmonisation of laws in member states which directly affect the functioning of the internal market. A benchmark Community standard is agreed on. Directives are then issued to any number of states from one to 12 which are required to raise their legal standards to that benchmark standard. The growth of qualified majority voting in the Council of Ministers has resulted in directives being imposed, in some cases, on member states. Therefore, a generous time-limit for the implementation of a directive into national law is often provided.

If the directive is incorporated into national law then it can be relied on just like any other part of United Kingdom law. For example, the provisions of the Equal Treatment Directive can be found in the Sex Discrimination Acts of 1975 and 1986. Apart from Acts of Parliament, the United Kingdom more usually incorporates directives by means of delegated legislation under s 2(2) of the European Communities Act 1972. This provision confers extensive authority upon Her Majesty in Council and upon ministers and government departments to make delegated legislation in order to incorporate directives into domestic United Kingdom law.

A problem that frequently occurs, however, is a situation where a member state fails to incorporate a directive within the prescribed time-limit (as in this question). Can such an unincorporated directive produce direct effect, ie can an individual, such as Smith, rely on it in order to obtain a remedy? At first sight you would not think so, as Art 189 deals with the obligations of member states and does not mention the rights of individual or corporations.

However, the European Court of Justice has consistently broadened the concept of direct effect of Community law, justifying its actions by Art 5 of the EC Treaty which states 'member states shall take all appropriate measures ... to ensure fulfilment of the obligations arising out of this Treaty or resulting from action taken by the institutions of the Community. They shall facilitate the achievement of the Community's tasks'. Thus, member states should not be obstructive in the creation of rights for individuals and companies in Community law.

Although concerned with treaty provisions, the *Van Gend en Loos* case was a landmark judgment as regards the principle of direct effect. Here the Court of Justice made it clear that, provided a treaty provision imposed a clear, precise and unconditional obligation on the state, it could be relied on (in this case Art 12 of the EC Treaty) by individuals and corporations against the state if it violated that provision. This was despite the opposition of the Dutch government which argued that Community Treaty provisions were merely international obligations enforceable by the EC Commission under Art 169 of the EC Treaty and by member states under Art 170 of the EC Treaty. The direct effect of Treaty provisions was also relied on, eg in *Simmenthal* (Art 30) and *Factortame* (Art 52). Similarly, regulations, being directly applicable, also are directly effective if clear, precise and unconditional in nature.

The Court of Justice has extended this approach to directives. Provided the time-limit for incorporation has run out and provided that the directive is clear, precise and unconditional then it may be relied on - but only against a body for which the state is responsible. Thus, these unincorporated directives have vertical direct effect. In *MH Marshall v Southampton and South West Hampshire Area Health Authority (Teaching)* (1984), Art 5(1) of the unincorporated Equal Treatment Directive was held by the ECJ to have direct effect - it could be relied upon against the state authority acting in its capacity as an employer. In this case, however, the European court confirmed that unincorporated directives do not have horizontal direct effect, ie they cannot be utilised against individuals or bodies for which the state is not responsible.

In this question, therefore, the problem is whether or not the privatised Alpha Water Company is a body for which the state is responsible. If so, then the unincorporated directive can be used against it as it appears to be clear, precise and unconditional in nature. In *Foster and others v British Gas* (1991), Lord Templeman, in applying the European court's ruling, said that the directive in question could be relied on in a claim for damages against a body, whatever its legal form, which has been made responsible, pursuant to a measure adopted by the state, for providing a public service under the control of the state and which has for that purpose special powers beyond those which result from the normal rules applicable in relations between individuals. In this case, the directive was held to be directly effective. However, in *Doughty v Rolls-Royce Plc* (1992), the principles laid down by the European Court of Justice and as applied by the House of Lords in *Foster v British Gas* produced a different result. The directive concerned was held not to be directly effective against Rolls-Royce as this organisation was not regarded as providing a public service and did not possess any 'special powers' of the type enjoyed by the British Gas Corporation.

Does the Alpha Water Company meet the three criteria established in *Foster*? Firstly, is it 'made responsible pursuant to a measure adopted by the state for providing a public service'? Certainly, legislation privatised the water companies and they do provide a public service. On the other hand, like Rolls-Royce, they act as independent commercial undertakings to a large extent. Secondly, is this 'service under the control of the state'? This is debatable. Privatisation was the means of shedding state control of water companies. On the other hand, water companies are regulated to some extent as regards the charges that they can levy. Thirdly, does the water company enjoy 'special powers beyond those which result from the normal rules applicable in relations between individuals'? To some extent, they do, eg the power to dig up gardens in order to gain access to pipes.

It is, therefore, unclear as to whether the unincorporated directive on working hours has direct effect or not. If, as is possible, the Alpha Water Company is not regarded as being a body for which the state is responsible then a claim for compensation against it would fail as it would be horizontal in nature.

However, the decision of the European Court of Justice in *Francovich v Italian Republic* (1992) would certainly enable Smith to make a claim, not against the Alpha Water Company, but against the United Kingdom for its failure to implement the directive in time. In *Francovich* the European court held that the directive in question was not capable of producing direct effect against the Italian state. However, the court held that the plaintiffs could obtain compensation for the damages they had suffered by reason of the state's failure to implement the directive. The court held that in order to give rise to liability for damages: (a) the result required by the directive includes the conferring of rights for the benefit of individuals; (b) the content of these rights may be determined by reference to the provisions of the directive; (c) there must exist a causal link between the breach of the obligation of the state and the damage suffered by the person affected.

These three conditions would seem to be fulfilled in our question and Smith would be able to claim damages against the United Kingdom state for its failure to implement the directive within the five year period.

Question 16

To what extent does the Maastricht Treaty on European Union continue the process of extending the European Parliament's role in the Community legislative process?

General approach

The changes introduced by the Maastricht Treaty are many and varied. However, half of its text is devoted to amendments to the original EEC (now EC) Treaty. Of these amendments, quite a substantial part is devoted to institutional changes. At the centre of these is a package of measures designed to enhance the involvement of the European Parliament in the law-making process and the way in which Community law is implemented. These changes tend to be mainly at the expense of the Council of Ministers and, to a lesser extent, at the expense of the Commission.

To answer the question 'To what extent?' it is, therefore, necessary to examine the Parliament's original powers under the EEC (now EC) Treaty, the way in which these were increased under the SEA and other provisions and how Maastricht has built upon these as part of an evolutionary process of change.

The Parliament's pre-Maastricht powers can be found in *Lecture Notes on 'A' Level Law Paper 1* (Cavendish Publishing Limited, 1994) in Chapter 13 on 'The European Community'. The changes made by Maastricht can be found in the same *Lecture Notes* book in Chapter 14 on 'The United Kingdom and the European Community'.

European Law

Answer plan

- legislative powers of the Council of Ministers; Art 189 of the EC Treaty, Art 148 and qualified majority voting
- legislative power of the Commission; Arts 189 and 155 of the EC Treaty
- the European Parliament; Arts 137 and 144 of the EC Treaty and extension of status and powers
- the Single European Act; extension of Parliament's legislative powers by the co-operation procedure
- the Maastricht Treaty; amendments to Art 189 - the co-decision procedure; powers provided by Arts 138 and 158

Answer

Article 189 of the EEC Treaty stated: 'In order to carry out their task the Council and the Commission shall, in accordance with the provisions of this Treaty, make regulations, issue directives, take decisions, make recommendations or deliver opinions.'

Under the EEC Treaty it is the Council whose task it is to 'ensure that the objectives in this Treaty are attained' (Art 145); in this context, it is the major law-making institution of the Community (not the Parliament), utilising the power conferred by Art 189 of the EEC Treaty. However, this power is balanced by the fact that in most cases the Council can only act on the basis of a proposal from the Commission and under the judicial control of the Court of Justice. Council legislation is, therefore, undertaken on the basis of a draft placed before it by the Commission. If the Council wishes to amend the draft proposal it may only do so by acting unanimously.

Article 148 of the EEC Treaty says 'Save as otherwise provided in this Treaty, the Council shall act by a majority of its members'. However, since the passing of the Single European Act, there has been an extension of the system of qualified majority voting. Most of the Council's legislative powers have now to be exercised by this method, for which a weighted voting system is used. Under this system each member state is given a number of votes according to size. A total of 65 votes is required for the Council to adopt a measure. The system means that the large states cannot, between them, force through a measure - they need the co-operation of some of the smaller states. A total of 25 votes will, therefore (since the accession of the three new states), block a measure:

Member states	Votes
France	10
Germany	10
Italy	10
United Kingdom	10
Spain	8
Belgium	5
Greece	5
Netherlands	5
Portugal	5
Denmark	3
Ireland	3
Luxembourg	2
Sweden	4
Austria	4
Finland	3

Also, under Art 189 of the EEC Treaty, the Commission can make regulations, issue directives and take decisions. However, this has to be in accordance with the provisions of this Treaty. Most of the Commission's legislative activity takes place within the sphere of Community competition and anti-dumping policy.

Article 155 of the EEC Treaty also states that the Commission shall 'have its own power of decision and participate in shaping of measures taken by the Council and by the European Parliament in the manner provided for in this Treaty'. This is one of the most significant roles of the Commission because, in most instances, the Council may only pass Community legislation when it is based on a proposal from the Commission. The Commission formulates its proposals for submission to the Council only after lengthy deliberation involving consultation with interested parties and representatives from the member states.

Article 137 of the EEC Treaty states: 'The European Parliament, which shall consist of representatives of the peoples of the states brought together in the Community, shall exercise the advisory and supervisory powers which are conferred upon it by this Treaty.'

The establishment of this body, originally referred to as the Assembly, reflected the desire of many in the Community to develop towards closer political union; it was also seen as a means of exercising some degree of democratic control over the Commission and the Council. For example, Art 144 of the EEC Treaty gave the Parliament the power to force the Commission to resign by a motion of censure if earned by a two-thirds majority of the votes cast.

However, the Assembly lacked authority because it was comprised of nominees of the member states (originally 142 members, 198 following the accession of the UK, Ireland and Denmark). Also, at most, the Council of Ministers only had to consult the Assembly when making laws. Its limited role in the legislative process has always been at the heart of the debate concerning how to make the European institutions more susceptible to democratic control.

A series of steps increased the status and power of the Assembly. First of all, on 30 March 1962 the European Assembly decided to describe itself as the European Parliament. In 1975 new budgetary powers were acquired for the Parliament. In 1976 the Council approved direct elections to the Parliament which took place between 7-10 June 1979. The first meeting of this directly elected Parliament of 410 members took place on 17 July 1979. The number increased to 518 following the accession of Greece, Spain and Portugal. The second direct elections took place between 14-17 June 1984, and the third between 15-18 June 1989. The next elections took place between 9-12 June 1994. Of equal significance, the entry into force of the Single European Act in 1987 allocated increased legislative powers to the Parliament. It also gave Treaty status to the title 'European Parliament'.

There are currently 626 members of the European Parliament (MEPs) who are directly elected for a term of five years. All member states, apart from the United Kingdom, use various systems for proportional representation to elect their members. Proportional representation is also used in Northern Ireland. The remainder of the UK uses the traditional 'first past the post' system of voting. Members sit in multinational political groupings. The Parliament holds its plenary sessions in Strasbourg but has offices and staff in both Brussels and Luxembourg. From 1994 there was an increase to 567 MEPs, reflecting demographic changes within the Community, principally the re-unification of Germany. The number increased to 626 MEPs with the accession of Sweden, Finland and Austria to the Community on 1 January 1995.

The Parliament's role in the legislative process was largely consultative. Commission proposals were sent by the Council to the Parliament for its opinion. Although persuasive, the Parliament's role was very limited. The extension of the Parliament's powers in the legislative process at the expense of the Council of Ministers has been argued by those who wish to see a transfer of power from national governments to elected representatives of the peoples of Europe.

The Single European Act introduced an important extension to the Parliament's legislative powers - the co-operation procedure involving the Commission, Council and the Parliament. Whilst allowing the Parliament to exercise greater influence over the legislative process, this influence, however, was limited. The co-operation procedure only extended to Community legislation regulating the following areas:

(a) the elimination of discrimination on the grounds of nationality;
(b) the freedom of movement for workers;
(c) the right of establishment (the right to set up a business);
(d) the freedom to provide services, and
(e) harmonisation measures relating to the establishment and functioning of the internal market.

The process still depends on the Commission formulating a proposal which is submitted to the Council which in turn obtains the opinion of the Parliament. The Council of Ministers is then required to reach a 'common position', a consensus on the basic elements by qualified majority voting.

The Parliament is then informed of the 'common position' and within three months may approve the Council decision, amend it or reject it. If the Parliament has rejected the proposal, the Council has to agree unanimously on the 'common position' in order to proceed to a second reading.

The Commission, within a period of one month, re-examines the proposal in the light of amendments suggested by the Parliament and sends back the re-examined proposal to the Council.

Within three months, the Council can either adopt the re-examined Commission proposal by qualified majority or adopt Parliament's amendments not approved by the Commission by unanimous voting or otherwise amend the Commission proposal, again by unanimous voting.

The emphasis in Maastricht is to increase the powers of the European Parliament in order to increase the democratic accountability of the European Community. This is recognised in a new Art 189 of the EC Treaty where the first paragraph is altered to 'In order to carry out their task and in accordance with the provisions of the Treaty, the European Parliament acting jointly with the Council, the Council and the Commission shall make regulations and issue directives, take decisions, make recommendations or deliver opinions'.

This amendment to Art 189 is due to the Parliament's new powers of co-decision with the Council of Ministers provided by Art 189(b). This effectively allows the Parliament to reject certain proposals for legislation by an overall majority, eg in the field of single market legislation and health and safety. The procedure is similar to the existing co-operation procedure in that the Parliament may approve the common position of the Council or propose amendments. However, the new element is that the Parliament, by an absolute majority of its members, may reject the common position. In this case, or if the Council does not approve the amendments, the matter must be referred to a Conciliation Committee, composed of equal members of the Council and Parliament. The Commission is required to take part in the proceedings with a view to reconciling the positions of the Council and Parliament. If a joint text is approved then the Council and Parliament may jointly adopt it. However, if they cannot agree on a common proposal the Parliament may reject the text by an absolute majority of its members.

The co-operation procedure is now contained in Art 189(c) of the EC Treaty. Many new areas of legislation, eg environmental protection laws made under Art 130(r), are brought within the qualified majority voting/co-operation procedure for the first time.

The Parliament's increased authority is recognised by the new Art 137 of the EC Treaty where 'shall exercise the advisory and supervisory powers which are conferred upon it by this Treaty' is altered to 'shall exercise the powers conferred upon it by this Treaty'.

In legislative areas covered by the co-decision and co-operation procedures of Art 189(b) and Art 189(c), Art 138(b) of the EC Treaty provides that 'The European Parliament may, acting by a majority of its members, request the Commission to submit any appropriate proposal on matters on which it considers that a Community act is required for the purpose of implementing this Treaty'.

This is an important provision which places the Parliament close to being an initiator of policy.

Also, Art 138(c) gives the Parliament the power to investigate, by means of a Committee of Inquiry, 'alleged contraventions or maladministration in the implementation of Community law'.

Article 138(d) allows any citizen of the Union residing in a member state or company registered in a member state to petition the Parliament 'on a matter which comes within the Community's fields of activity and which affects him, her or it directly'.

Article 138(e) gives the Parliament the power to appoint an Ombudsman to receive complaints 'concerning instances of maladministration in the activities of the Community, institutions or bodies, with the exception of the Court of Justice and the Court of First Instance acting in their judicial role'.

Finally, in relation to the Commission, Art 158 says that 'The President and the other members of the Commission ... shall be subject as a body to a vote of approval by the European Parliament'. Maastricht, therefore, consolidates the Parliament's powers, building upon the twin pillars of direct elections and the co-operation procedure.

Question 17

Explain why the provisions on economic and monetary union in the Maastricht Treaty have necessitated updating the jurisdiction of the European Court of Justice.

General approach

The initial jurisdiction of the European Court of Justice can be found in the *Lecture Notes* book (see p 130). The major areas are those altered by Maastricht: Arts 173, 175 and 177. After an explanation of their uses, it is necessary to examine the Maastricht provisions on economic and monetary union. It will be seen that these provisions provide for a European system of central banks (ESCB) with a law-making European Central Bank (ECB), preceded by the European Monetary Institute (EMI) already set up (1 January 1994) in Frankfurt. The character of the ECB can only be explained in the context of the general provisions in Maastricht on economic and monetary union.

It will then be necessary to look at the amended jurisdiction of the European Court of Justice under Arts 173, 175 and 177 which takes into account the existence of the ECB and its law-making powers. (Until the ECB comes into existence, references to it in these articles will be taken to refer to the EMI.) So, the question requires a fairly straightforward before-Maastricht and after-Maastricht approach to explain the changes in the jurisdiction of the European court.

Answer plan

- initial jurisdiction of the European Court of Justice; Arts 173, 175 and 177 of the EEC Treaty
- Maastricht; provisions on a single economy
- Maastricht; provisions regarding monetary policy - the ECB and law-making under Art 108(a)
- Maastricht; transitional arrangements for economic and monetary union - the EMI

- Maastricht; the third stage of EMU - Art 109(1) and setting up of ECB
- amended jurisdiction of the European Court of Justice; new Arts 173, 175 and 177 of the EC Treaty taking into account the ECB

Answer

The EEC Treaty imposes a framework of legality around the actions of the EC Commission and Council. If these bodies exceed their powers then an action can be brought against them under Art 173. Also, if those bodies fail to act where they have a duty to act then an action can be brought against them under Art 175.

Art 173(1) states:

'The Court of Justice shall review the legality of the acts of the Council and the Commission other than recommendations or opinions. It shall for this purpose have jurisdiction in actions brought by a member state, the Council or the Commission on grounds of lack of competence, infringement of an essential procedural requirement, infringement of this Treaty or of any rule of law relating to its application, or misuse of powers.'

What are the grounds for challenge?

(a) *Lack of competence* - this means that the body does not have the legal power to make the secondary legislation. It is thus equivalent to the English doctrine of substantive *ultra vires*.

(b) *Infringement of an essential procedural requirement* - this means that a legally required procedure has not been complied with in the formulation of the secondary legislation and is equivalent to the English doctrine of procedural *ultra vires*.

(c) *Infringement of this Treaty or of any rule relating to its application* - this provides a very broad ground for challenge and encompasses a breach of general principles of law recognised by member states, eg breach of the rules of natural justice.

(d) *Misuse of powers* - there is no precise English equivalent and this ground for challenge is rarely successful. However, it embraces the concept of abuse of discretionary powers.

What is the result of a successful action?

Article 174 of the EEC Treaty states: 'If the action is well founded, the Court of Justice shall declare the act concerned to be void.'

Also, Art 175(1) states: 'Should the Council or the Commission, in infringement of this Treaty, fail to act, the member states and the other institutions of the Community may bring an action before the Court of Justice to have the infringement established.' Less widely used than Art 173, this action is broadly similar to that of *mandamus* in English law.

Article 175(2) gives the institution concerned two months to react to a call to act. The action can only take place if nothing happens during this time period.

Article 177 of the EEC Treaty is an extremely important provision. Here the European court pronounces on the conformity of national law with Community law. Article 177 states:

'The Court of Justice shall have jurisdiction to give preliminary rulings concerning:
a) the interpretation of this Treaty;
b) the validity and interpretation of acts of the institutions of the Community;
c) the interpretation of the statutes of bodies established by an act of the Council, where those statutes so provide.

Where such a question is raised before any court or tribunal of a member state, that court or tribunal may, if it considers that a decision on the question is necessary to enable it to give judgment, request the Court of Justice to give a ruling thereon.

Where any such question is raised in a case pending before a court or tribunal of a member state, against whose decisions there is no judicial remedy under national law, that court or tribunal shall bring the matter before the Court of Justice.'

Economic and monetary union is the most controversial and potentially most important aspect of Maastricht. It is mainly dealt with by Arts 102-109(m). New institutions are provided for which have an important bearing on Community law.

As regards a single economy, the scene is set by Art 3(a) which mentions the 'irrevocable fixing of exchange rates leading to the introduction of a single currency, the ECU, and the definition and conduct of a single monetary policy and exchange rate policy the primary objective of both of which shall be to maintain price stability'.

Article 103 says 'member states shall regard their economic policies as a matter of common concern and shall co-ordinate them with the Council'. This article goes on to say that the Council of Ministers, acting by a qualified majority, can adopt recommendations setting out broad guidelines for the economic policies of the member states and of the Community.

Article 104(c) provides that 'member states shall avoid excessive governmental deficits'. This provision also provides that the Council of Ministers, acting by a qualified majority on a recommendation from the Commission, has the power to decide whether an excessive deficit exists. If so, the Council can require the state concerned to make a deposit with the Community until the excessive deficit has been corrected or to fine the state.

As regards monetary policy, Art 105 deals with the tasks of the European System of Central Banks (ESCB) 'which shall be composed of the European Central Bank (ECB) and of the national central banks ... These tasks shall be to define and implement the monetary policy of the Community; to conduct foreign exchange operations; to hold and manage the official foreign reserves of the member states; to promote the smooth operation of payment systems'.

Article 105(a) says that the ECB shall have the exclusive right to authorise the issue of bank notes within the Community.

Article 108(a) has important ramifications for Community law-making. It says: 'In order to carry out the tasks entrusted to the ESCB, the ECB shall, in accordance with the provisions of this Treaty ... make regulations ... take decisions ... make recommendations and deliver opinions.'

Article 109(a) says that the Governing Council of the ECB shall consist of the members of the Executive Board of the ECB and the Governors of the national central banks. Only nationals of member states can be members of the Executive Board which will consist of a President, Vice-President and four other members appointed for a non-renewable term of eight years.

Transitional provisions provide for a gradual changeover to economic and monetary union.

Article 109(e) provides that the second stage for achieving economic and monetary union will begin on 1 January 1994. On that date a European Monetary Institute (EMI) was established (in Frankfurt) to smooth the path towards a single currency by (Art 109(f)) *inter alia*, strengthening the co-ordination of monetary policies of the member states and facilitating the use of the ECU and overseeing its development.

Article 109(j) provides that a meeting of Heads of state or government will take place no later than 31 December 1996. By a qualified majority this meeting will decide whether a majority of the member states fulfil the conditions for the adoption of a single currency and decide a date for the beginning of the third stage of economic and monetary union if appropriate. If by the end of 1997 the date for the beginning of the third stage has not been set, the third stage will start on 1 January 1999, the European Council having confirmed which states fulfil the conditions for the adoption of a single currency.

Article 109(k) provides that member states which do not fulfil the conditions for the adoption of a single currency will be called 'member states with a derogation'. Such a member state and its national central bank will be excluded from rights and obligations within the ESCB, and the state's voting rights within the Council on related matters will be suspended.

The third stage of economic and monetary union is dealt with by Art 109(1) which provides that, as soon as the date for the entry into force of the third stage of economic and monetary union has been decided upon, the governments of the member states without a derogation will appoint the Executive Board of the ECB. As soon as this happens, the ESCB and the ECB will be established and their powers exercised from the first day of the third stage. As soon as the ECB is established it shall take over the tasks of the EMI which shall go into liquidation.

Article 109(l) provides that 'at the starting date of the third stage, the Council shall ... adopt the conversion rates at which their currencies shall be irrevocably fixed and at which irrevocably fixed rate the ECU shall be substituted for these currencies, and the ECU shall become a currency in its own right'.

The third stage of economic and monetary union will limit states' sovereignty tremendously. The conduct of economic policy in many important areas will have to be carried out within a more integrated European framework. For this reason, in one of the protocols to the Maastricht Treaty, the United Kingdom is stated not to be obliged to move to the third stage of economic and monetary union without a separate decision to do so by its government and parliament.

A new Art 173 of the EC Treaty takes account of the court's case-law and also of new institutions created by the Maastricht Treaty.

Paragraph 1 now reads: 'The Court of Justice shall review the legality of acts adopted jointly by the European Parliament and the Council, of acts of the Council, of the Commission and of the ECB, other than recommendations and opinions, and of acts of the European Parliament intended to produce legal effects *vis-a-vis* third parties.'

Paragraph 2 now reads: 'It shall for this purpose have jurisdiction in actions brought by a member state, the Council or the Commission on grounds of lack of competence, infringement of an essential procedural requirement, infringement of this Treaty or of any rule of law relating to its application, or misuse of powers.'

Paragraph 3 now reads: 'The Court shall have jurisdiction under the same conditions, in actions brought by the European Parliament and by the ECB for the purpose of protecting their prerogatives.'

For the same reasons, a new Art 175 of the EC Treaty has been created whose para 1 now reads: 'Should the European Parliament, the Council or the Commission, in infringement of this Treaty, fail to act, the member states and the other institutions of the Community may bring an action before the Court of Justice to have the infringement established.'

A new para 4 reads: 'The Court of Justice shall have jurisdiction, under the same conditions, in actions or proceedings brought by the ECB in the areas falling within the latter's field of competence and in actions or proceedings brought against the latter.'

Again, a new Art 177 of the EC Treaty takes account of changes elsewhere in the Maastricht Treaty. The provision is essentially the same except that Art 177(b) now reads: 'The validity and interpretation of acts of the institutions of the Community and of the ECB.'

Thus, the jurisdiction of the European Court of Justice is updated by the Maastricht Treaty to take account of the provisions on Economic and Monetary Union, especially the existence of the ECB.

Chapter 5

Constitutional Law

Introduction

To illustrate the scope of constitutional law and the relationship with administrative law a problem and an essay question have been selected. For those wishing to demonstrate the extent of their knowledge and understanding a problem question can be ideal. It will allow you to apply the law (case-law and/or statute) to fact and reach a reasoned solution; but several dangers may exist. The problem may be long and involved and the 'facts' may be vague or conflicting. You may be asked to advise one or more parties and you may not be clear about all the parts of the problem.

Should you tackle a problem question well you will be assured of high marks but it may be safer to consider attempting an essay if the dangers outweigh the benefits.

A plan or diagram may assist and should you find yourself running short of time this can act as a handy reference for points you do not have time to cover more fully. The 'facts' in a problem question will nearly always be vague so you must be willing to argue the point both ways. Assume the role of an advocate! Put forth the strengths of your 'case' but remember that the weaknesses of your case can be the strengths of your opponent's case.

You will be asked to advise not on the basis simply of your personal opinions but on the law so you must support your 'case' where appropriate with cases and statutory references. If you are not very good at remembering case names, comfort yourself with the idea that the case name alone is perhaps the least important piece of information. What you should remember are sufficient facts, the decision and the *ratio decidendi* so as to support your line of argument. It is also helpful to remember the court that made the decision.

So far as subject matter is concerned you will need to be aware of the nature and characteristics of the UK constitution and in particular appreciate the changes brought about by membership of the European Union.

A critical awareness of the defects of the constitution is useful in particular the debate concerning the need for a Bill of Rights and/or written constitution. Appreciation of the role and relationship of the three arms of government is necessary, in particular the judges and their powers of judicial review. This has seen much of a revival in recent years and continues to be extended to novel situations where decisions of public bodies adversely affect the citizen.

A notable example in 1993 were the challenges by the Law Society of decisions made by the Lord Chancellor to amend legal aid provision under the Legal Aid Act 1988 and another the challenge of the Home Secretary's exercise of the Royal Prerogative of Mercy and the use of his sentencing powers in respect of prisoners sentenced to life imprisonment.

Question 18

Critically assess the constitutional position and the role of the judiciary in the United Kingdom taking into account the means by which the judges are selected, appointed and dismissed.

General approach

The United Kingdom is known for its unwritten constitution (New Zealand and Israel are other countries with unwritten constitutions).

This is not to say that the UK does not have a constitution but it is to be found in the ordinary law of the land, principally statute and case-law. There is no one document or series of documents which set out the respective roles of the three arms of government: the legislature, the executive and the judiciary. These roles and the relationship between them, have evolved and are evolving, and, to analyse the place of the latter, such doctrines as the rule of law, separation of powers, parliamentary sovereignty and judicial independence must be examined.

We need to ask who are the judges?; are they an homogeneous group?; how are they selected, appointed and dismissed?; by whom and with what authority?

Constitutional Law

Are the judges independent of the executive power of government? To what extent can/should the judges question government actions? What is the relationship of the judiciary with Parliament? By what means can judges make law? How effective are the judges in protecting the citizen against abuses of power?

Lord Hailsham described British government as 'an elected dictatorship' whereby parliamentary sovereignty over the Crown has given way to executive control in the form of ministerial government. The judiciary therefore must protect the citizen from abuses or excesses of power.

Lord Denning suggested that the judges should be trusted with the task of guarding our freedoms but it is noticeable that in the UK the citizen has nothing more than just 'freedoms'.

Thus, calls have been made for at least a Bill of Rights if not, in addition, a written constitution that will guarantee civil rights. One suggestion is for incorporation of the European Convention on Human Rights into UK law. The main stumbling block for any such change is the doctrine of sovereignty of Parliament which would allow its repeal (express or implied) by later conflicting legislation. Major constitutional reform is urged by others so as to ensure entrenchment of such provisions. The role of the judges would have to change and there would be need for a 'constitutional' court along the lines of the American Supreme Court.

Answer plan

- nature and characteristics of the UK constitution; unwritten; constitutional law founded in the ordinary sources of law; the absence of formal documents setting out the separation of powers; the rule of law and sovereignty of Parliament; role of the judiciary as interpreters of statutes; development of the common law; supervisory jurisdiction of the High Court - judicial review and control of delegated legislation
- the judiciary as guardians of the constitution and freedoms of the citizen?; the need for a Bill of Rights and/or within constitution?; entrenchment of such provisions; impact of the European Convention on Human Rights?; establishment of a supreme court?

- selection, appointment, dismissal of the judiciary; judicial independence and impartiality; role of the Lord Chancellor; the Queen and Prime Minister; proposals for reform of appointments system; who are the judges?; are they drawn from a narrow social group?; are/should they represent society?; independence and impartiality; the extent to which the judiciary are/should be concerned with policy and questioning government abuse or excess of power
- conclusions

Answer

Lord Denning in his Richard Dimbleby lecture of 1980 entitled 'Misuse of Power' painted a scenario of a future Prime Minister packing the bench with judges of his own extreme political colour. He asked the question whether such judges would be tools in the hand of the Prime Minister. The answer given was a resounding 'no!'. Lord Denning put his trust in the judges suggesting that in the past, as in the future, the judges would be vigilant in protecting the freedoms of the citizen.

On appointment, the judge discards 'all politics and all prejudices'. These are indeed laudable sentiments and ones which aim to inspire faith in the judiciary as upholders of the law and justice. However such sentiments are extremely hard to prove or disprove and this is in large part due to the nature of the judicial and constitutional system of the United Kingdom.

The United Kingdom has not known major political upheavals since the 17th Century, but Lord Hailsham has written of an 'elected dictatorship' whereby Ministerial government, and in recent times, the power of the Prime Minister, has usurped the doctrine of parliamentary sovereignty. The theory remains intact in that Parliament can pass any law it chooses or repeal any existing law, subject to the inroads on this doctrine resulting from membership of the European Union. The reality, however, is that when a government is in power with a strong majority it can ensure that its policies become law by relying on the support of its party members. The government controls the parliamentary timetable thereby ensuring that its Bills pass into law. Private members' Bills rarely stand any real chance of becoming law, unless the subject matter finds favour with government and time and resources are allocated for its passage through Parliament.

Parliamentary sovereignty ensures that the judges have a limited role in law-making. Statutes cannot be declared void and the role of the judge is to interpret the meaning of statutory provisions which are called in question in cases coming before the courts. The case of *BRB v Pickin* (1974) established the notion that an Act that has passed all stages in the House of Commons and the Lords and received the Royal Assent cannot be challenged in a court of law. It is to be noted however that statutory interpretation nevertheless vests in the courts considerable power to narrow or extend the scope of statutory provisions and since the House of Lords decision in *Pepper v Hart* (1993) it is permissible, in given circumstances, for the court to consult *Hansard*, the official journal of the House of Commons so as to assist it in attaching meaning to a statutory provision.

In addition to interpretation of statutes, the judges have traditionally made law by way of developing the common law or case-law. However two limitations apply here. The common law can only develop on a case-by-case basis and will in any event be subject to statute. In controversial areas, the judges may excuse themselves from developing the common law by suggesting that policy issues are at stake and that these should be settled by legislation.

One area where the common law has developed in recent years is that of judicial review whereby decisions of public bodies can be questioned by an aggrieved individual. The role of the court is to ensure that public bodies act in a fair manner and according to law. The court is not concerned with the merits of the case or with substituting its decision for that of the decision-maker unlike a case which goes to appeal. Another aspect of the High Court's ancient supervisory jurisdiction is the control it exerts over delegated legislation and its ability to find that there has been an excess or abuse of power which it declares *ultra vires*. Unlike Parliament, which is supreme, the delegate of power must act only in accordance with that power otherwise the action can be found to be *ultra vires* and void as in *Bromley LBC v GLC* (1983).

The United Kingdom constitution is an unwritten one (New Zealand and Israel also have unwritten constitutions) there being no one document or series of documents in which powers and duties of each of the arms of government are set out.

Invariably, in countries with written constitutions, the constitution is accepted as fundamental law of a higher order than law regulating citizens one with another or as between the citizen and the state. This higher law may be entrenched so that, in order for it to be changed, a special mechanism will have to be gone through, for example a 75% vote in each house of the legislature. In such systems, the judiciary not only make and apply the ordinary law but are vested with the power of acting as the guardians of the constitution. Laws which do not accord with the principles of the constitution can be declared unconstitutional and void. The notion of the rule of law takes on special significance in that government can only make law which accords with the principles of the higher law as interpreted by the judiciary. The judiciary in the UK system have no such power and are bound to apply the law as enacted by the legislature. This is not to say that the courts do not exert control over government actions.

The doctrine of sovereignty of Parliament does not apply to delegated legislation which, if found to be exercised in excess of the powers granted by the enabling legislation, can be declared *ultra vires* at the suit of an individual or group who are aggrieved. In addition, the High Court can question the actions of public bodies (or those exercising public functions) by means of judicial review where the court may order *certiorari, mandamus*, prohibition or injunction to prevent an abuse, or intended abuse, of power. It must be noted however that such challenges can only be made where a dispute arises and the courts have no general power to review or question government actions.

Recent years have seen calls for a fundamental change in the legal order which would vest the judges with power to strike down legislation where it was shown to conflict with fundamental principles. Some argue that as the United Kingdom is a signatory to the European Convention on Human Rights that this should be ratified and given effect to in domestic law by way of enabling legislation. If this were done it would obviate the need of an aggrieved citizen seeking redress by application to the Commission and European Court of Human Rights and claims could be dealt with by domestic courts. The Convention establishes general, but well recognised, rights, including, the right to freedom of expression, the right to life, the right not to be tortured or subjected to inhuman or degrading treatment, the right to marry and found a family and the right to liberty and security of person. In the present system, citizens have no rights, as such, but only freedoms.

A citizen is only permitted to do something in so far as the law does not prohibit it. Even where statute confers rights, these can be removed by new legislation. Given the doctrine of parliamentary sovereignty and the limited role of the judiciary in challenging legislation, this vests considerable power in the executive in whose control Parliament operates. This doctrine also points to a limitation of the effectiveness of passing legislation giving effect to the Convention. Unless a mechanism was provided guaranteeing its continued existence, such legislation could be repealed as it would have no higher status than ordinary legislation. One mechanism would be the creation of a written constitution entrenching such provisions or, as Professor Wade suggested, the judges should swear an oath promising to act as the guardians of fundamental rights and of the constitution. In either case, the role of the judiciary would be fundamentally different and there would be need for the establishment of a supreme or constitutional court which would have the ultimate say on the legality of legislation. The result would be a drastic shift in the balance of power between legislature, executive and judiciary. No longer would Parliament be supreme in the way in which that is presently understood although, if Parliament establishes the constitutional document as representative of society, it could be said that the courts as its guardians would simply be protecting the citizen from incursions by an over zealous executive.

Supposing such changes were brought about, the question remains as to the suitability of the judiciary to act as constitutional guardians. It might be argued that, as a body, the judiciary as presently composed is ill-suited to this task. In considering the selection, appointment and dismissal of the judges, it should be noted that so far as jurisdiction is concerned the judges do not form an homogeneous group although many commentators have over the years noted that the majority of judges are drawn from a narrow social and educational background reflecting upper-middle class values. This it is said results in the judges being out of touch with changes in society and should not have vested in them wider powers enabling them to shape future changes.

Taking appointment first, Lords Justices of Appeal, who sit in the Court of Appeal, are appointed by the Queen on the advice of the Prime Minister. There are some 27 Lord Justices drawn from the ranks of High Court judges or barristers of at least 15 years standing. The Lords of Appeal in Ordinary (of which there are 11) are also appointed by the Queen on the Prime Minister's advice. The 'Law Lords', as they are more often called, are drawn from the ranks of existing judges or barristers of at least 15 years standing. On appointment they become life peers and members of the Judicial Committee of the Privy Council. The Lord Chancellor, the Lord Chief Justice, the Master of the Rolls, the President of the Family Division and the Vice-Chancellor of the Chancery Division are also all appointed by the Queen on the advice of the Prime Minister. The origins of this system stem from all power (whether judicial, legislative or executive) being vested in the Monarch. Since the 17th Century the Monarch has exercised power through, and on the advice of, her government ministers. The monarchy is described as a 'constitutional' or 'limited' monarchy. However this raises the question as to the suitability and wisdom of having the highest judicial appointments made by the Prime Minister. It might be argued that to ensure judicial independence of the executive, not only in name but in reality, appointments should be made by the judiciary itself, for example by way of a Judicial Appointments Body which would act openly and ensure that their decisions were subject to public scrutiny.

When considering the appointment of High Court judges, the doubts raised earlier are again in question. High Court judges, of which there are some 73, are appointed by the Queen on the advice of the Lord Chancellor from barristers of at least 10 years standing. In June 1993 Sir Michael Sachs made legal history when he was appointed as a High Court judge having been a Circuit judge for 10 years and a solicitor. Circuit judges and Recorders are also appointed by the Queen on the Lord Chancellor's advice. The former are drawn from the ranks of barristers with 10 years standing or who have held the office of Recorder for 5 years. The latter are drawn from the ranks of barristers or solicitors of 10 years standing or from solicitors appointed as Recorders for 5 years. The Courts and Legal Services Act 1990 provided for advocate experience of 10 years for High Court judges and 15 years for Law Lords. This should ensure that superior court judges in the future are drawn from the ranks of solicitors. Magistrates are appointed by the Lord Chancellor.

The Law Officers of the Crown, that is the Attorney General, Solicitor General and the Director of Public Prosecutions are, together with the Lord Chancellor, political appointees. On a change of government the occupants of these offices will change so as to reflect the policies to brought into effect by the new government. The role of the Lord Chancellor which combines executive, judicial and legislative functions has been the subject of criticism in recent years. Proposals have been made for a Ministry of Justice to be set up so as to ensure more open appointment of judges and as a guarantee of judicial independence.

So far as the selection of judges is concerned, this is a more highly charged subject, given the amount of secrecy which surrounds appointments. The present Lord Chancellor has attempted major reforms of the legal system, notably the passage of the Courts and Legal Services Act 1990. His reforms of legal aid and advice have been much criticised and made the subject of an application for judicial review by the Law Society. This highlights the fact that his political, legislative and judicial roles do not sit easily together and emphasises the lack of separation of powers.

Recent months have seen greater openness in selection procedures with the announcement by the Lord Chancellor that appointments of District Judges and Circuit Judges will be filled following advertisement of posts and publication of the criteria by which appointments will be made. The convention whereby judges refrain from making public statements of criticism of the legal system and commenting on matters of public interest has been relaxed and one notable recent critic of the Lord Chancellor and government policy has been the present Lord Chief Justice, Lord Taylor.

Much has been written, for example by Professor Griffiths in *The Politics of the Judiciary* (1), about the backgrounds of the judges and that generally they are drawn only from the upper-middle class, who have been educated at public school and Oxbridge and who are predominantly middle-aged, white and male. This stereotype of the judge supports the notion that he/she is remote and has little, if any, appreciation of how the vast number of people live and conduct their affairs. This is particularly acute when considering sentencing for criminal offences. We do not have career judges, but ones drawn traditionally from the ranks of barristers, and who will have reached perhaps their earlier 50s before appointment. The charge has been made that more women judges should be appointed and that those from the racial minorities should be better represented. There is a strong argument in favour of more openness in the appointments system and for it to accommodate a wider range of candidates so as to ensure respect for the administration of justice.

It is likely that, in time, given the changes made by the Courts and Legal Services Act 1990 permitting solicitors' rights of audience, that the judiciary will become more representative of society. The judiciary is not alone in the criticism that there are too few women and members of racial minorities; the Bar also has had to review its policies in a bid to achieve greater equality of access. Helena Kennedy writing in *Eve Was Framed* (2) also comments of this stereotype of the judge and the adverse effects it can have not only in preventing access to the judiciary but on those who come to the courts for decisions, whether they be defendants or plaintiffs. The public perception of the judiciary and of the legal system is also tarnished, in particular criminal court sentencing, in that there appears to be a lack of accountability on the part of the judiciary.

Given the principle of independence, it is important that judges can make decisions without fear of recrimination or unwarranted removal by the executive. The Supreme Court Act 1981 and the Appellate Jurisdiction Act 1876 provide that the salaries of the superior court judges are fixed by statute and form a charge on the Consolidated Fund. They hold office 'during good behaviour' and may only be removed by the Crown on an address presented by both Houses of Parliament. Retirement is provided for by the Judicial Pensions and Retirement Act 1993 providing for a retirement age of 70. Circuit judges and Recorders can only be removed by the Lord Chancellor under powers in the Courts Act 1971 for incapacity or misbehaviour. Magistrates may be removed by the Lord Chancellor 'if he thinks fit' but, by convention, this only happens where there is good cause.

Questions of removal bring into question the constitutional position of the judiciary and its independence and impartiality in decision-making. It is essential that there be respect for the law and for those who administer it but, in turn, members of the judiciary must be seen to be accountable for their decisions. The case of *Woolwich Building Society v Inland Revenue (No 2)* (1992), where the House of Lords by a three to two majority held that, where tax had been paid as a result of an *ultra vires* demand, the common law recognised a right to repayment unless special circumstances or policy required otherwise, is instructive on the role of the judiciary and its relationship with the executive and Parliament.

Lord Goff referred to one of the most fundamental principles of law namely that enshrined in the Bill of Rights 1688 that taxes should only be levied with Parliament's authority. Full effect could only be given to this if payments wrongly exacted were to be repaid. He further referred to the traditional boundary between the judges and the legislature separating 'the legitimate development of the law by the judges from legislation'. He concluded, however, that in order to do justice between the parties it was acceptable for the court in this case to find in favour of the Woolwich Building Society and to establish the principle of repayment.

It will be for the executive to decide policy issues and to have legislation passed through Parliament giving effect to its decisions. The court has a limited role to play in developing the common law and in interpreting statutes, and should not overstep the boundary by attempting to make policy decisions. It is a fine line to draw and, in recent years, the courts have become far more assertive in balancing government power and the rights of the citizen. Much greater use has been made of its judicial review powers in questioning how public decisions are reached. The time may come that judicial review will be used not only to check procedures of public decision-makers but also to question the substance or policy of decisions, more along the lines of its use in constitutions which are written. This would necessitate a major shift in thinking and would bring judges into the political forum but hints of such a change can be seen with reference to the European influence and use of concepts such as 'proportionality' and 'legitimate expectation'.

Notes

1 (1991) 5th ed, Fontana Press
2 (1992) Chatto & Windus Ltd

Question 19

The Broadcasting Licensing Council is empowered by the Broadcasting Act 1972 to grant broadcasting licences in the television regions throughout England and Wales. Its members have expert knowledge of the broadcasting industry and, in granting licences, the Council is obliged to ensure that successful applicants will provide a high standard of service throughout the 10 years duration of a licence.

ABC Ltd applies for renewal of its licence for West Region which it has successfully operated in the past 10 years. Negotiations take place between ABC Ltd and the Council following the issue of a statement to all applicants by the Council setting out the criteria to be used in reaching its decisions. This states that the Council will take into account 'the financial information and forecasts supplied by applicants, the intended programme mix and the relevance of programmes for the region to be covered by the licence'. No indication is given as to the weight to be attached to these criteria and ABC Ltd does not attempt to seek clarification as part of its negotiations. It concludes that it is in a strong position having submitted the highest bid and having long experience of operating a licence in its region. In the result the licence is granted to XYZ Ltd which submitted one of the lowest bids and has no previous broadcasting experience.

ABC Ltd wishes to challenge this decision, alleging that the licence was granted to XYZ Ltd. only because the company was a newcomer to the industry. Advise ABC Ltd of its legal position.

General approach

This question concerns public decision-making and the means available to an aggrieved citizen (an individual or group) for challenging decisions of bodies performing public powers and duties. The emphasis is on the decisions made by public bodies and this is an area of administrative law. The decision-making body may, for example, be a government minister, a statutory body empowered to make decisions or a local authority. The aggrieved citizen may have a right of appeal provided by statute, otherwise he/she will have to rely on Ord 53 of the Rules of the Supreme Court. This is an application, for which the leave of the High Court is required, for judicial review. Unlike an appeal the High Court, on an application for judicial review, is not concerned with the merits of the case. It does not try the issues and substitute its decision for that of the decision-making body. Instead, the court is primarily concerned with ensuring that the law has been complied with and that the decision-making body has acted fairly.

Assuming that ABC Ltd has no right of appeal to the courts or a tribunal or other body from decisions of the Broadcasting Licensing Council, its only means of challenge will be by invoking the Ord 53 procedure. Leave of the High Court will be required and the burden of establishing a *prima facie* case sufficient for the grant of leave rests with ABC Ltd. Assuming that this is met, the High Court will then hear the allegations that the decision was reached unfairly and in breach of the rules of natural justice.

Judicial review actions may arise where it is alleged that a body making public law decisions has misdirected itself as to the facts or the law or where the decision-making process has been unfair.

We are not concerned here with mistakes of law or fact but whether the Council reached a decision by fair means. ABC Ltd alleges that the Council failed to reach its decision to grant a licence in accordance with its stated criteria, eg it took into account a criterion not mentioned in the statement issued to all applicants. The question arises whether ABC Ltd can substantiate a claim for judicial review on the ground that it had a legitimate expectation that the decision made by the Council would be made in accordance with the criteria mentioned in its statement issued to applicants. If the Council was permitted by statute to take account of other criteria it could be argued that ABC Ltd could expect to be informed of the change and, together with other applicants, be given a chance to make representations or amend its application. For the Council to publish criteria and then apply others, even where others are permitted, would not appear to be fair or reasonable.

When considering judicial review claims the question of remedies is important. Judicial review is primarily a procedural claim and the orders that the court can make are prohibition, *certiorari, mandamus* and injunction. An award of damages can only be made where a civil law right has been infringed. On the facts of this case, ABC Ltd would seek an order of *certiorari* quashing the decision of the Council. The matter would then be referred back to the Council for reconsideration.

Answer plan

- recognition of relevant facts; a public decision-making body with statutory power to grant licences; an application for the renewal of a licence; published criteria on which decision is to be based; a criterion taken into account which is not mentioned in the published list; refusal of renewal of licence; aggrieved party wishes to challenge the decision-making process

- identification of relevant areas of law; Ord 53 Rules of the Supreme Court; application for judicial review; leave to apply; judicial review and appeals distinguished; situations where the doctrine of natural justice applies and reliance on legitimate expectation; consideration also of 'Wednesbury unreasonableness' and the use of estoppel in public law

- application of law to facts of present case; ABC Ltd not a 'mere applicant' as in *Re H K (an infant)* (1967) and *R v Gaming Board for GB ex p Benaim and Khaida* (1970); question of legitimate expectation illustrated in the cases of *R v S of S for Home Department ex p Khan* (1985), *AG for Hong Kong v Ng Yuen Shiu* (1983), *R v S of S for Home Department ex p Ruddock* (1987), *R v Brent LBC ex p McDonagh* (1989), *Council of Civil Service Unions v Minister for the Civil Service* (1984), *R v Liverpool Corp ex p Liverpool Taxi Fleet Operators' Association* (1972), *R v*

Independent Television Commission ex p TSW Broadcasting Ltd (1992); consideration of the case of *Associated Provincial Picture Houses Ltd v Wednesbury Corporation* (1948) and the doctrine of estoppel
- remedies sought and likely outcome

Answer

In this question, the Broadcasting Licensing Council (BLC) is empowered to grant broadcasting licences throughout England and Wales by the Broadcasting Act 1972. The provisions of the Act ensure that licences should only be granted to applicants who are able to convince the BLC that they will provide a high standard of service throughout the duration of the licence.

ABC Ltd apply for the renewal of its licence to broadcast in the West Region and, following negotiations and the issue of a statement setting out the criteria to be used in the decision-making process, the licence is awarded to XYZ Ltd.

ABC Ltd wishes to challenge this decision alleging that the decision was not made in accordance with the stated criteria issued by the BLC to all applicants. From the available information there appears to be no mechanism for an appeal from the BLC to another body whether that be a court, tribunal or a government agency. In the absence of a right to appeal the only means of challenge open to ABC Ltd will be to seek judicial review under Ord 53 of the Rules of the Supreme Court as provided for in s 31 of the Supreme Court Act 1981.

The courts have stressed on many occasions that judicial review does not permit the court to substitute its decision for that of the decision-making body. The role of the court is simply to ensure that the licensing procedure was fairly conducted.

The first step is to seek the leave of the High Court to bring the claim and the burden of proving a *prima facie* case rests with the applicant for judicial review. In addition, ABC Ltd will have to show a sufficient interest in the subject matter of the claim if the court is to grant leave for ABC Ltd to proceed. This will not be a major obstacle as clearly ABC Ltd has held a licence in the past 10 years and has not had it renewed. The company has suffered a detriment and providing it can offer some evidence for its allegation that criteria other than those mentioned in the BLC's statement were relied on it should be able to establish a *prima facie* case.

Assuming that leave is granted to ABC Ltd to challenge the decision of BLC by way of judicial review, ABC Ltd will have to prove that BLC either misdirected itself or otherwise made a mistake as to the facts or the law or that the decision was reached by unfair means. On the facts, BLC issued a statement to all applicants of the criteria to be used in reaching a decision. This stated that three criteria would be taken into account, namely financial information and forecasts supplied by applicants, intended programme mix and the relevance of programmes for the region for which the licence was being applied. ABC Ltd allege that BLC made its decision that XYZ Ltd was a suitable applicant on the basis that it was a newcomer to the industry without previous experience. It is therefore open to ABC Ltd to claim a legitimate expectation that BLC would act in accordance with its stated criteria or, assuming that it wished to change these (and that it was empowered to do so), ABC Ltd and the other applicants for licences would have been given the opportunity to revise their applications in the light of the new criteria.

The case of *R v S of S for the Home Department ex p Khan* (1985) illustrates the concept of 'legitimate expectation'. Khan and his wife wished to adopt a Pakistani child and were referred to a Home Office standard form letter by a Citizens' Advice Bureau. The letter specified four criteria to be taken into account by the Home Secretary in deciding whether or not to allow an adoption. Khan's application was refused but he was able to prove that a criterion not mentioned in the letter was taken into account. It was held that the letter was sufficiently certain in its terms to afford a 'reasonable expectation' that on satisfaction of the four named criteria an adoption would be permitted. Watkins LJ dissented on the ground that the letter amounted to no more than helpful guidance in that it stated that the Home Secretary 'may exercise his discretion and exceptionally allow adoption'. Dicta by Dunn LJ suggests an alternative approach in that he referred to '*Wednesbury* unreasonableness', one heading of which is that the decision-maker takes into account an irrelevant consideration.

Certiorari was granted to Khan with the result that the refusal of Khan's application was quashed. The Home Secretary would then either have to reconsider the application on the basis of the four criteria published in the letter and afford Khan a hearing or allow Khan to make representations as to the decision to be reached using the new criteria.

It is important to note that the court is not concerned with the decision itself but rather with the process by which it was reached and the court does not attempt to prevent decision-makers from changing their previous conduct or statements for the future providing that those who may be adversely affected are notified and given an opportunity of making representations.

Legitimate expectation that natural justice will be complied with can arise as in *Khan* from a published statement or express assurances as in the case of *Attorney General for Hong Kong v Ng Yuen Shiu* (1983) where an illegal immigrant was assured that his case would be considered on its merits but where he was not allowed to put forward facts in his favour. Previous conduct may also give rise to a legitimate expectation that this will not change without notification and an opportunity for those affected to make representations. In *Council of Civil Service Unions v Minister for the Civil Service* (1984) an attempt to ban unions at GCHQ, although permitted on the grounds of national security, would in normal circumstances not have been allowed without the workforce having had notice of an intended change in practice. Lord Diplock in this case classified the grounds on which judicial review controls public decision-making under the heads of 'illegality, irrationality and procedural impropriety' and Lord Donaldson MR in *R v Home Secretary ex p Brind* (1991) and *R v Independent Television Commission ex p TSW* (1992) suggested that legitimate expectation is not a separate head of judicial review but 'is a particular aspect of natural justice or fairness which would probably ... be included in ... procedural impropriety'. In the *TSW* case, it was noted that 'legitimate' does not simply refer to 'reasonable'. There must be some injustice to an applicant for judicial review who has been misled as to likely results of an action.

In this case clearly, ABC Ltd is not a 'mere applicant', having operated a licence in the past and, although mere applicants may not have a right to be heard, dicta in *R v Gaming Board for GB ex p Benaim & Khaida* (1970) and *Re HK (an infant)* (1967) suggest that they should be treated fairly and be given sufficient information so as to put forward their case.

A case which concerned an applicant for the renewal of a licence but in which legitimate expectation was not referred to is *R v Liverpool Corp ex p Liverpool Taxi Fleet Operators' Association* (1972). The Corporation decided to increase the size of its fleet but undertook not to do so until a private Bill was passed. It was advised that the undertaking had no effect and so went ahead and granted new licences without first consulting the Association. It was held that the undertaking was to be honoured until the association had been given an opportunity to make representations. An order of prohibition was granted. The reason given for the decision was on the ground of estoppel whereby the Association relied on the undertaking to its detriment and the Corporation was prevented from going back on its word without first consulting those affected. Lord Denning relied on the cases of *Robertson v Minister of Pensions* (1949) and *Lever Finance Ltd v Westminster City Council* (1971) but in later cases the doctrine of estoppel with its origins in private law has not found favour: *Western Fish Products v Penwith DC* (1981).

Before considering the application of the *TSW* case to the present facts, it is worth noting the dicta of Dunn LJ in *Ex p Khan* (1985) where he considered the alternatives of estoppel and the taking into account of an irrelevant consideration. Estoppel was rejected in that Khan had not spent money on the faith of the Home Office letter but Dunn LJ considered that '*Wednesbury* unreasonableness' was applicable. This could be applied to the facts of the present case if it can be proved that the Council departed from the criteria listed in the statement issued to applicants.

The *TSW* case would appear on the face of it to have relevance here in that both concern applications for the renewal of TV licences. However, that is where the similarity ends in that the nature of the allegations diverge. Two grounds of challenge were made in the *TSW* case: the first (which was rejected) concerned an allegation that the ITC had applied more stringent criteria to the TSW bid than indicated in its 'Invitation to Apply'; that TSW had a legitimate expectation that bids would be dealt with on the basis of the Invitation. The second, which went to appeal to the House of Lords and was then rejected, concerned a staff paper taken into account by the ITC in making its decision. The House of Lords held that the procedure adopted for consideration of the applications was of a high standard and there was no evidence of *Wednesbury* unreasonableness' by the ITC.

On the facts of the present case, only if ABC Ltd can show that criteria other than those contained in the statement issued to applicants were taken into account in breach of its legitimate expectation arising out of that statement will the company have a claim for judicial review. The nature of this claim is not one as to the merits of the case and so it is not open to the court to impose its decision on the BLC. It is likely that an order for *certiorari* will be granted, quashing the decision and requiring the matter to be re-opened so as to permit ABC Ltd, and the other applicants, an opportunity of putting forward fresh applications. The BLC will also be required only to take into account the criteria in its statement or, if it intends to amend these, to give notice to all applicants.

Chapter 6

The Law of Contract

Introduction

The questions which might arise in this area require, in the first instance, an understanding of the law of contract: its concepts, their development, and how they have been applied in specific instances to provide practical outcomes in cases. A further requirement for those whose syllabus extends beyond the law of contract itself is an understanding of the principal ways in which the law controls trading activities and the extent to which it offers protection to consumers.

Most of contract is based on case-law. Where this has been altered or developed by statute, eg the Misrepresentation Act 1967, the statutory addition generally presupposes the existence of a well defined set of common law principles. You cannot hope to be able to tackle successfully questions on the operation of the statute without a sound understanding of the pre-existing case-law.

Much trading/consumer protection law on the other hand is to be found in statute. Good answers to questions based on these statutory rules will not only refer to the relevant sections but will, whenever possible, illustrate the way the section has been interpreted in actual decisions.

It is important that your answers display your knowledge of case and statute law in a manner which demonstrates an understanding of all the issues involved and an ability to use rational argument to reach a conclusion. In the heat of the moment it is difficult to remain calm when a topic you have 'spotted' in revision turns up on the paper, eg the 'postal rules' relating to acceptance of an offer. Remember that the question may well have other (more important) issues which require attention but which are not so obvious at first sight. For an example of where this might happen see Question 21 below.

When tackling a 'problem' question, work out not only what you need to include but the order in which issues must be addressed. It is not appropriate to discuss the remedies open to a purchaser of goods or services until you have first established what obligations exist on the part of the seller/supplier and whether (on the facts) these have been broken: see Question 22. When answering an 'essay' question, pay attention to the 'angle' the examiner has chosen and use your material accordingly: see Question 25.

Question 20

Alice and Betty are amateur wildlife enthusiasts. They planned to spend two weeks holiday in June in a rented cottage on the Cornish coast in order to be able to study the famous seal colony at nearby St Piran's Cove. They intended to write an article which they hoped would be published in *Wildlife* magazine.

The rent for the cottage, which was owned by Trelawney, was £200 per week. Of this, £100 was payable when the booking was made and the balance on arrival at the cottage. At the time they booked Alice and Betty told Trelawney that they intended making a study of the seals.

A few days prior to the start of their holiday Alice and Betty heard that due to an oil spill from a tanker, St Piran's Cove had been polluted. Public access to the area was forbidden while seal rescue and clean-up operations were in progress. Alice and Betty telephoned Trelawney to say they were cancelling the booking and wanted their £100 back. Trelawney refused to accept their cancellation and said he was holding them to the agreement made.

Advise Alice and Betty.

Answer plan

First note that this question is fairly typical of questions which are set on the termination of contractual liability with special reference to the doctrine of frustration. When answering the question it is important not to rush to the conclusion that it is a case of frustration of contract and merely deal with the consequences. Display your understanding of all the issues involved, as well as the rationale of the doctrine (if you have the time).

- set the context; termination of contract and discharge of liability
- explain the nature of the doctrine of frustration
- outline the kinds of situations in which it operates and its applicability to the question
- consider whether frustration has occurred here
- if it has, consider the consequences for the parties involved; in particular consider the Law Reform (Frustrated Contracts) Act 1943, and its provision for the return of money paid in advance
- if the contract is not discharged by frustration, note that Alice and Betty may be sued for damages for breach
- comment on the measure of damages necessary to compensate the plaintiff

Answer

There are a number of ways in which a contract may end and the parties be discharged from further liability under it. The most obvious is where both fully perform all their respective obligations. However, circumstances may arise where, before this can occur, an external event beyond the control of either party intervenes to thwart their common intention. This may result in preventing performance of the contract completely or in making performance radically different from that which the parties originally intended. When this happens the contract is said to be 'frustrated' and the parties are discharged from any further obligations due to be performed under it.

The primary issue in this problem is whether the contract Alice and Betty have with Trelawney is discharged by the doctrine of frustration and if so what the consequences are for the parties. A secondary issue is what the effect of Alice and Betty's cancellation is if the contract is not discharged under the doctrine.

It is perhaps important to remember that the doctrine of frustration dates only from *Taylor v Caldwell* (1863). The original rule at common law, known as the rule in *Paradine v Jane* (1647) was logical if somewhat harsh. The attitude taken by the early law was that as contractual obligations were incurred voluntarily the parties should have had the foresight to provide for situations which made those obligations more burdensome to perform or even pointless or impossible. If they did not do so the ensuing difficulties were of their own making and the law should not interfere.

From *Taylor v Caldwell* this rule was mitigated by a series of cases in which the courts did intervene. At first this was justified on the basis of an 'implied term', ie what the parties must have intended to happen but did not expressly mention in their contract. Later the test for intervention became objective, ie whether there had been a radical change in circumstances which justified discharge: *Davis Contractors Ltd v Fareham UDC* (1956).

Taylor v Caldwell itself was a case where the contract became physically impossible to perform. The plaintiff agreed to hire a concert hall from the defendant on specified dates but before the first of these arrived the concert hall was destroyed by fire, no blame attaching to either party. It was held that they were both discharged from their obligations under the contract.

In a similar way a contract may become impossible to perform lawfully. Perhaps due to an event, such as the outbreak of war, a contract perfectly lawful when made is rendered illegal because it now involves 'trading with the enemy'.

In a group of cases dating from 1903, and generally referred to as the 'coronation cases', the concept of frustration was extended to situations where, although it was still possible and lawful to perform the contract, performance had become useless and futile because the whole object or purpose, which both parties knew to be its basis, had been destroyed by the frustrating event. In these cases the frustrating event was the cancellation of the coronation of Edward VII and attendant celebrations due to the King's serious illness. The hiring of rooms for the day along the route of the coronation procession was still possible but clearly pointless. Hirers sought to cancel, thus escaping payment, or to claim the return of deposits already paid. In *Krell v Henry* (1903) the hirer was successful in using the doctrine of frustration by way of defence when sued for non-payment of the hire fee. However, in *Herne Bay Steamboat Co v Hutton* (1903) it was held that a contract to charter a steamboat to take passengers for a day's cruise around the fleet and to see the naval review by the King was not frustrated by the King's illness and consequent cancellation of the review. The fleet remained and so one of the stated purposes of the contract could still be achieved. The contract was not discharged and the charterer was still liable to pay the agreed fee.

The first issue for Alice and Betty is whether the contract with Trelawney has been discharged through frustration. The hire of the cottage remains physically possible and the contract is lawful to perform, unless the cottage is so close to the cove that it actually comes within the boundary of the prohibited area of the clean-up operation. If this is so and there is no likelihood of the ban being lifted during the time of Alice and Betty's planned holiday, then the contract is indeed frustrated and they are discharged from any further liability. They may properly treat the contract as having terminated.

If the cottage is outside the restricted are, the doctrine can apply only if both parties knew and understood that the foundation of the contract was the study of the seal colony, not merely the motive which inspired it. After all, Alice and Betty are still liable to have their summer holiday in the cottage: compare *Herne Bay Steamboat Co v Hutton* (1903) and to sample the attractions of the Cornish countryside. It is unlikely that merely telling Trelawney at the time they made the booking would be sufficient to enable Alice and Betty to substantiate a claim that their seal study was the foundation of the contract. If they cannot show this to be the case the contract will not be frustrated and they will have no right to regard it as cancelled.

If the contract is frustrated, either through supervening illegality or, because of facts not disclosed on the face of the question, Alice and Betty are able to show their seal study formed the basis of the contract, the consequences of frustration need to be considered.

Both parties are discharged from the date of the frustrating event. Alice and Betty do not have to pay the outstanding sum of £300 for the cottage. However, the contract is not void *ab initio* nor may they claim to be entitled to rescind it. Obligations which have been performed before the frustrating event are unaffected. Obligations which should have been performed and were not remain outstanding: *Chandler v Webster* (1904). At common law the loss lay where it fell. Money paid before frustration could not be recovered. Money due to be paid was still payable. The House of Lords reduced the full effect of this rule by holding in the *Fibrosa* case (1943) that it was possible in certain circumstances for the payer to recover (or cease to be liable) for payments in advance. The House held that, if the payer had received nothing at all from the other party, money could be recovered on the quasi-contractual ground of its having been paid for a consideration which had totally failed. The result, although of benefit to the payer, was not regarded as a satisfactory solution as the burden now fell solely upon the party required to return the money. He might very properly have stipulated for an advance payment to cover expenses likely to be incurred in preparing for performance of the contract. The result of the dissatisfaction was the passing of the Law Reform (Frustrated Contracts) Act 1943.

The Act applies only to cases of discharge through frustration. By s 1(2) whether there is a total or partial failure of consideration money paid in advance is recoverable. Money payable in advance ceases to be payable. However, the court may, if it thinks it just, award to the party to whom the money was paid or payable a sum to cover his expenses (if any) incurred in proceeding with performance of the contract before frustration. The amount awarded must not exceed sums paid or payable in advance. If, therefore, the contract between Alice and Betty and Trelawney is frustrated Alice and Betty are entitled to the return of the £100 they paid when booking the cottage. (If they had not paid it when frustration occurred the obligation to pay would have ceased.) However, this is subject to the right of Trelawney to claim from the £100 an amount to cover his expenses, if he actually incurred any, in performing his part of the contract prior to discharge.

Finally, what is the position where Alice and Betty cancel the booking and the contract is not discharged under the doctrine of frustration? They are repudiating liability where they have no right to do so. They are in breach and may be sued by Trelawney for damages.

The purpose of awarding damages is to put the plaintiff in the financial position he would have been in if the contract with Alice and Betty had been completely performed. However, Trelawney is expected to act as a reasonable person to mitigate the damage caused by their breach. He will not be able to recover for a loss which resulted from his failure to mitigate: *British Westinghouse Electric Co v Underground Electric Railway Co of London* (1912). If Trelawney can with reasonable ease find someone else to rent the cottage during the two weeks booked by Alice and Betty he should accept the new customers. His damages will be reduced accordingly. The amount he is entitled to by way of compensation for the breach is his net loss. If the cottage is in great demand it is possible that Trelawney's loss will be minimal and he may have to return most, if not all, of the £100 already paid.

The outcome for Alice and Betty depends on whether or not their contract with Trelawney has come to an end under the doctrine of frustration. If it can be shown that the contract has become illegal to perform, or that its foundation has been destroyed their action of cancelling it will have been justified. They will not have to pay the £300 outstanding and will probably be able to claim the whole of the £100 already paid. If, however, the contract has not been brought to an end by frustration, Alice and Betty are in a weak position. They have repudiated the contract without justification and are liable to be sued by Trelawney for damages by way of compensation.

Question 21

Barbara's horse was stolen. Barbara was very upset. She advertised in the 'lost and found' column of a local newspaper for his return, stating she would pay £100 to anyone who supplied information which assisted in the recovery of the horse. The advertisement indicated the reward would remain open until the end of June.

Detective Constable Jones, assigned to the case, traced the horse's whereabouts and reported back to police headquarters so that the horse was recovered and the thief arrested. Back at the police station someone mentioned the reward to Detective Constable Jones. He wrote to Barbara and claimed the £100, posting his letter on Friday 30 June. It arrived at Barbara's house on Monday 2 July.

Advise Detective Constable Jones whether under contract law he is entitled to the £100 reward.

Answer plan

There will be few examinations on the law of contract which do not feature questions on the formation of agreement (offer and acceptance) or the doctrine of consideration. This question covers both and raises some fundamental issues concerning the concept of contract. Do not be deceived into thinking that the problem is centred around the rules relating to acceptance through the post. This is only a minor point to be covered.

- state the fundamental assumptions that a contract is (a) founded on agreement, and (b) a bargain
- note the formula for agreement (offer and acceptance) and deal with unilateral offers contained in advertisements
- consider what constitutes acceptance here; is communication needed?
- indicate the nature and effect of acceptance sent by post
- question whether a person may accept an offer by an act done prior to becoming aware of the offer
- explain the doctrine of consideration and question whether it is possible here to link, as part of a single transaction, the act done and the promise to pay the reward
- question whether the act done by DC Jones is sufficient (real) consideration if he was merely doing his duty as a police officer

Answer

Two fundamental assumptions of contract law are (a) that a contract is founded on an agreement, and (b) that a contract is a bargain. Both are in issue in this problem and Detective Constable Jones (DC Jones) will not be entitled to the £100 reward unless he can establish that he was party to a contract to pay him this sum.

To see if an agreement has been made the facts must be examined to ascertain whether one party made a proposal, or offer, which the other accepted in the precise terms in which it was made. An offer must show a willingness on the part of its maker to be bound and be certain in the sense that its terms are clearly defined.

Statements made in advertisements frequently fail to demonstrate any such intention and may often be expressed in vague and perhaps exaggerated language. Exceptionally, though an advertisement may be framed in clear words which show a definite intention to be bound. Such was the case in *Carlill v Carbolic Smoke Ball Co* (1893). The company offered, by means of an advertisement, a reward of £100 to anyone who, having used their product correctly, contracted 'flu. Carlill adhered to the directions but caught 'flu. She claimed £100 which the company refused to pay. The Court of Appeal held that the advertisement constituted a general or 'unilateral' offer which was capable of being accepted by any member of the public who fulfilled the conditions contained in it, thus forming an agreement.

Although the exact wording of Barbara's advertisement is not given, the question seems to indicate that a definite offer of reward was made with the terms being clearly set out.

A contract formed in this manner is referred to as a 'unilateral' contract, the acceptance being signified by the performance of an act by the offeree. There needs to be some outward sign by the offeree that he has accepted. The general rule is that mere silence cannot constitute acceptance: *Felthouse v Bindley* (1863). Furthermore it is possible that the decision to accept must also be communicated to the offeror. The point was raised in *Carlill v Carbolic Smoke Ball Co* where the defence argued that Carlill had not informed the company. It was held that in the circumstances the company had, by implication, waived the need for communication of acceptance by the offeree. Fulfilling the conditions laid down in the advertisement was all that was required.

Normally this will constitute acceptance in the case of a unilateral contract but an issue now raised is whether in the question the advertisement impliedly dispensed with the need for DC Jones to communicate acceptance to Barbara. Did his act of supplying information itself fulfil the conditions laid down in the offer? Even if the exact wording of the advertisement reveals that communication to Barbara is required all is not lost.

Although the offer of reward has been expressed to last only until the end of June, and will automatically terminate then, the rules applicable to communication of acceptance by post will assist DC Jones. The decision in *Adams v Lindsell* (1818) means that his letter claiming (accepting) the reward is deemed to be communicated the moment it is posted. As this was done on 30 June when the offer was still open it is irrelevant that his letter was not delivered until 2 July.

However, a more fundamental fact affecting the validity of DC Jones' claim is that he appears not to have been aware of the existence of the offer of reward until after he had assisted in the recovery of the horse. Is it possible to 'accept' an offer while being ignorant of it? The Australian case *R v Clarke* (1927) suggests the answer is 'no'. The government of Western Australia offered a £1,000 reward for information leading to the arrest of the murderer of two police officers and a pardon should this be supplied by an accomplice. Clarke, an accomplice, who saw the offer of £1,000 but admitted having forgotten about it when he supplied the information, saying he was concerned only about saving himself, was held not entitled to the reward. 'There cannot be assent without knowledge of the offer; and ignorance of the offer is the same thing, whether it is due to never hearing of it or to forgetting it after hearing' said Higgins J.

Following this reasoning it would seem therefore, (if acceptance is taken to be the act of supplying the information required by the advertisement), that DC Jones will not be entitled to the £100 reward. He was unaware of its existence when he performed the act in question. However, might it be the case that acceptance occurred when DC Jones wrote to Barbara claiming the reward? Much depends on the wording of the advertisement and whether this was one of the conditions set out in the offer. If this is so it may be argued that the decision in *R v Clarke* should not be followed and that whenever possible the individual who fulfills the requirements of the offer should receive the reward: *Williams v Carwardine* (1833) and *Gibbons v Proctor* (1891).

Even if these arguments are successful, DC Jones faces a further obstacle. In addition to being an agreement, a contract is also a bargain. There must be a *quid pro quo*. The law will not enforce a defendant's promise unless the plaintiff has 'bought' that promise by himself supplying consideration: *Dunlop v Selfridge Ltd* (1915). Consideration is said to be 'executory' when plaintiff and defendant exchanged mutual promises, 'executed' when the plaintiff performed an act in return for the defendant's promise. Whichever formula is used it is essential that the defendant's promise and the plaintiff's counter-promise or act are related as part of a single transaction. An act and a promise which are unconnected will not be regarded as constituting a bargain: *Re McArdle* (1951).

In the question, DC Jones gives information leading to the return of the horse but it is not done in response to Barbara's promise. At this point in time he is unaware of its existence. The act done by DC Jones was not executed in reply to the promise (offer) of reward. It seems therefore that it would be extremely difficult for him to establish the act and promise formed a single transaction, a bargain.

A further and final problem posed to DC Jones' claim is whether his actions amount to consideration at all. Consideration must be sufficient or real. It must have some value. If a person promises to do or does something which he is already obliged to do he may be regarded by the law as not having provided anything of value; the 'price' for which the promise of the other is bought.

In circumstances where a person is bound by operation of law or because of his status to behave in a certain way he is supplying nothing of value by carrying out what he is, in any case, duty bound to do: *Collins v Godefroy* (1831). However, in *England v Davidson* (1840) the defendant offered a reward to anyone who gave information leading to the conviction of a criminal. The plaintiff, a police officer, supplied the information. The defendant argued that the officer was not entitled to the reward as he was merely doing his duty and that such a contract with a member of the police was contrary to public policy. It was held that there was nothing about the contract which offended public policy and that the plaintiff had rendered a service over and above that which duty demanded.

Instances of successful actions brought by the police for the recovery of payments, (although not rewards), include *Glasbrook Bros v Glamorgan County Council* (1925) and *Harris v Sheffield United Football Club* (1988). The courts seem very favourably inclined to find, if they can, for police plaintiffs who have done more than their status apparently obliged them to do.

Nevertheless, the onus is on DC Jones to convince the court that, although he was working on the case in the line of duty (the question says he was assigned to it) he did more than his status demanded of him, thus supplying valuable consideration in return for Barbara's promise.

It is possible that DC Jones may be successful in his claim to the £100 reward offered by Barbara but substantial weaknesses in his case stem primarily from the fact that he was unaware of the existence of the reward until after he had given the information it requested. It is difficult to argue that an agreement was made or a bargain struck when one party acted in ignorance of the other's intentions.

Question 22

X plc, a company which manufactures pharmaceutical products, last year put onto the market a new medicine for the relief of symptoms of the common cold. Y purchased and used the preparation on numerous occasions throughout the winter months. Unfortunately he now appears to have suffered a permanent impairment to his hearing and research conducted this year indicates it is most likely to have been caused by use of the medicine. The deterioration in Y's hearing was substantial enough to make him visit the Z Hearing Centre to be examined, advised and fitted with a hearing-aid. However, the hearing-aid was fitted badly. It made Y's ear ache for hours after use. Furthermore, the hearing-aid used up batteries at twice the rate specified by the Z Hearing Centre when they supplied it.

What are Y's rights in law in relation to the manufacturer of the drug and the Z Hearing Centre?

Answer plan

This problem demonstrates the distinction between consumer redress for the poor quality of goods and services and for unsafe goods which cause harm. The answer should show an awareness of this and deal with the contract-based and tort-based remedies which the law provides.

- identify the essence of the contract with Z; the supply of a service
- consider which provisions of the Supply of Goods and Services Act 1982 apply and whether they have been broken
- discuss the remedies available to Y as a consequence of the breach
- identify the ways in which tort, through negligence and Consumer Protection Act 1987, would assist Y in a claim against X for the injury he has sustained
- consider in more detail the important elements needed to establish liability under Consumer Protection Act 1987
- discuss the possibility of X using the 'development risks' defence available to producers

Answer

The civil law provides for consumers to seek redress from producers and suppliers of both goods and services. Consumer rights are based either on contractual or on tortious remedies.

Y has entered into a contract with Z under which they have agreed to supply him with a service (professional advice on his hearing difficulties) and with goods (the hearing-aid). Questions which need to be addressed are: what obligations does Z owe Y?; have these been broken?; if so, what remedies are available to Y?

There is no privity of contract between Y and X. Such remedies as Y may have are tort based. In *Donoghue v Stevenson* (1932) the House of Lords held that a manufacturer owes a duty of care to the ultimate consumer of his products to see that the product is safe to consume or use. If the duty is broken and the consumer suffers injury as a consequence the manufacturer is liable to compensate him. The Consumer Protection Act 1987 Part I has extended the protection available to consumers by not requiring the plaintiff to prove the defendant's negligence. Questions which will need to be addressed include: is the product defective and did it cause the injury to Y? If so, could X have discovered, in the light of scientific knowledge available at the time, that the product was defective when it was launched?

In his contract with Z, Y is looking to Z to supply a professional service, not merely sell him a hearing-aid. Contracts of this kind are governed by the Supply of Goods and Services Act 1982 as amended by the Sale and Supply of Goods Act 1994. By s 13 a term is implied that Z, who is acting in the course of a business, will provide the service with reasonable skill and care. It appears from the question that the hearing-aid itself was not of poor quality. It was lack of skill on the part of Z which resulted in the supply on an unsuitable, ill-fitting device. The obligation under s 13 requires Z to show a level of competence normally associated with the provision of such services; Z appears to be in breach of this obligation.

By s 3 there is an implied condition that goods transferred by description will correspond with the description. 'Description' covers statements made by the supplier relating to the goods and the section applies where the buyer places reliance on the description. Not all descriptive words take effect as contractual terms and some may amount to a misrepresentation only: *Oscar Chess Ltd v Williams* (1957). In order to be incorporated as a contractual term the words used have to identify the item supplied: *Ashington Piggeries Ltd v Christopher Hill Ltd* (1972). 'Reliance' by the consumer on the description is crucial: *Harlingdon & Leincester Enterprises Ltd v Christopher Hull Fine Art Ltd* (1990), where the buyer did not rely on the description, and *Beale v Taylor* (1967), where the buyer relied heavily on the information given as to its age by the seller of a car.

Assuming Y was told by Z, prior to supply, the rate at which this make of hearing-aid consumed batteries, it is reasonable to argue that the information was a factor in obtaining Y's agreement to its supply. This gave rise to an implied condition on the part of Z that the hearing-aid would fit the description under which it was supplied. As the hearing-aid does not fit this description there has been a further breach by Z.

What remedies are available to Y as a consequence of these breaches of contract by Z? The law offers two possibilities: repudiation of the contract and damages. Repudiation, which involves rejection of goods and recovery of the price paid lies only for a serious breach or breach of condition. An action for damages may be brought whether the breach is of a condition or a warranty (a less serious obligation). Section 13 contains the neutral word 'term' and the position will depend on whether Y has been substantially deprived of the benefit of the contract. The implied obligation in s 3 is a condition. Even if this breach had been slight, which it is not, Y, who deals as consumer, would retain his *prima facie* right to reject under the new s 5A enacted by the Sale and Supply of Goods Act 1994.

In contracts of sale of goods the Sale of Goods Act 1979, as amended by the 1994 Act, precludes a buyer from rejecting goods for breach of condition once he has 'accepted' them as set out in s 35 and 35A. There is no equivalent section in the Supply of Goods and Services Act 1982 with the result that the common law rules of affirmation apply. Under these an individual is not normally held to have affirmed a contract until, knowing of the breach and therefore his right to terminate, he nevertheless confirms the contract.

The question is silent on the time which has elapsed since the service was supplied and on whether Y has yet paid Z. If Y has paid, has complained and has acquiesced in Z's suggestions for remedy he will probably be too late to repudiate. However, the measure of damages applicable to the case should ensure that Y is put financially in the position he would have been if the contract had been properly performed. The device is useless to Y. He needs to start again with a competent supplier and should therefore be awarded damages to enable him to obtain this service without further expense on his part.

Y's claim against X, the manufacturer of the medicine, which apparently caused his deafness, could be pursued through the tort of negligence under the principle in *Donoghue v Stevenson* (1932). However such a claim would not be successful unless Y could show that X actually had been negligent, ie broken the duty of care owed to consumers. The question does not suggest that there was a manufacturing problem; that the wrong quantities were used or that some noxious substance entered the product. The inference is that the problem lies in the design of the product. The courts have been ready to infer negligence in the case of a manufacturing defect where there is no direct evidence as to how the defect occurred: *Grant v Australian Knitting Mills* (1936). It has been otherwise in the case of a design defect which is likely to have arisen as a consequence of inadequate research by the manufacturer: *Vacwell Engineering Ltd v BDH Chemicals Ltd* (1966). It is a heavy burden for a plaintiff to discharge.

In the circumstances Y would be better advised to bring a claim based on the Consumer Protection Act 1987. X is a 'producer' as defined in s 1 and is liable under s 2 for any damage caused by a defect in its products.

The first important hurdle for Y is to establish that the medicine was 'defective' as defined by s 3. Essentially, a product is defective if its safety 'is not such as persons generally are entitled to expect'. Factors to be taken into account include the purposes for which the product was marketed and instructions and warnings issued, or, by inference, which should have been issued, with it; also what might reasonably be expected to be done with the product. The time at which to judge whether or not a product is defective is the time when it was supplied by the producer.

The question indicates that recent research points to the product having been the cause of Y's loss of hearing. Presumably, the research was undertaken because the problem is widespread. Many users have impaired hearing. This may have similar dimensions to the Thalidomide and Opren disasters. Was it the frequency with which the medicine was used which caused the problem? Why were there no warnings, or inappropriate warnings, given on dosage? If there were warnings did Y ignore them?

Many more facts need to be established before anything approaching an answer can be given as to whether the product was defective. If it is assumed, for the sake of argument, that it is and that it was the cause of Y's injury, Y should *prima facie* be entitled to damages He has suffered personal injury, which is defined by s 5 as damage giving rise to liability.

Is there a way by which X may escape liability? By s 4(1)(e) it is a defence for the defendant to show that the state of scientific and technical knowledge at the time of supply was such that no producer of such products could reasonably have detected the defect.

The fact that the research establishing the likelihood of a causal link between product and injury was carried out after the supply and use of the product indicates that X may be able to use the defence successfully. It is, nevertheless, better for Y to base his claim on the Consumer Protection Act where the burden of proof is upon X to establish the defence than to sue using the tort of negligence where the burden of proof would be upon Y to establish X's fault (lack of appropriate care) in the first instance.

The law does provide a remedy in the form of compensation for Y in respect of the breach of contract by Z. However, in the case of the drug company the position is not nearly so clear. Although Y may be able to establish a *prima facie* claim under the Consumer Protection Act, it could be defeated if X is successful in using the 'development risks' defence available to producers under s 4.

Question 23

Advise Tom in each of the following sets of circumstances:

(a) He buys a car from his neighbour Rob who innocently misleads Tom into thinking that the car is in good condition. A week later the car breaks down and Tom is advised by a reputable garage that substantial repairs are needed.

(b) He enters into a contract to build a workshop for Sam who intends setting up a small engineering business. The date stated in the contract for completion of the work is 1 May. Tom is to pay £250 by way of agreed damages for every week's delay beyond the date agreed.

Tom has not met the deadline and Sam is seeking to enforce the contract.

Answer plan

(a) The question is concerned with the law relating to misrepresentation. The answer should demonstrate an understanding of the conditions which must be fulfilled before the law will recognise a misrepresentation and the remedy available for innocent misrepresentation. The answer needs to cover:

- misstatement of a material fact, contrasting it with a statement of law, future intention and opinion
- when silence amounts to misrepresentation; inducement
- the remedy of rescission; its essential characteristics and bars to relief, the court's discretion under s 2(2) Misrepresentation Act 1967

(b) This problem is about a very specific area of contract law: liquidated damages and penalty clauses. Do not assume that just because the words 'agreed damages' appear in the question that this automatically provides the answer.

Introduce the topic by a general comment on the function of damages: to compensate the plaintiff and why agreed damages clauses are used. Then proceed with:

- a discussion of the differences between liquidated damages and penalty clauses and the consequences for the parties
- the rules set out in the *Dunlop* case for distinguishing between the two
- an application of the rules to the contract between Tom and Sam and advise Tom accordingly

Answer

(a) Not everything said during negotiations which lead to the making of a contract became contractual terms. A statement may be made, which is relied on, but which never becomes an obligation in the contract itself. In such circumstances the party misled may be able to pursue a claim for misrepresentation.

For a misrepresentation to be operative, ie to have legal effect, it must be a misstatement of an existing fact and have induced the representee to enter into the contract. The misstatement must be of fact not law, although sometimes the distinction is difficult to see: *Solle v Butcher* (1950). A statement of opinion is not one of fact: *Bisset v Wilkinson* (1927) where the seller of a farm not previously used for sheep said he believed it capable of carrying 2,000 sheep. If, however, a person who has first hand knowledge expresses an opinion it will amount to a misrepresentation if that opinion could not honestly have been held by him: *Smith v Land & House Property Corp* (1884). A person who makes a statement of intention but, when making the statement, plans to do otherwise is guilty of a misrepresentation: *Edgington v Fitzmaurice* (1885).

Silence will not, as a general rule, amount to misrepresentation, although there are exceptional situations in which the law imposes a duty of disclosure: contracts *uberrimae fidei* and fiduciary relationships Silence will constitute misrepresentation when it results in the distortion of a positive statement. Thus a half-truth may be a misrepresentation as will a statement, true when made, which subsequently becomes false due to a change in circumstances: *With v O'Flanagan* (1936).

For a false representation of fact to constitute a misrepresentation it must have been made to the representee and acted upon his mind so as to induce him to enter into the contract. It need not have been the sole reason provided it had some effect upon him. If a representee acts upon his own judgment or relies upon advice given by a third party there will be no inducement: *Attwood v Small* (1838).

More information is required to advise Tom fully. What did Rob actually say which led Tom to believe the car was in good condition? Was Rob's statement merely an honest opinion? Or has Rob specialist knowledge? Did he state some good things about the car and omit to tell Tom others which would have altered the picture? The question indicates that Tom relied on what was said and was therefore misled and induced into making the contract. Provided it can be shown that Rob made a false statement in the sense discussed above a misrepresentation will have been established.

The question indicates that Rob acted innocently. The remedy the law provides for such circumstances is rescission. This is a cancellation of the contract; a giving back and a taking back on each side so that the parties are restored to their pre-contractual positions. In addition the plaintiff may claim an indemnity in respect of obligations created by the contract: *Whittington v Seale-Hayne* (1900). Rescission, being an equitable remedy, is granted at the discretion of the court. There are three 'bars' to rescission, ie situations in which the court in exercise of its discretion will withhold the remedy. These are (i) where the injured party has affirmed the contract, (ii) where restitution is impossible, eg because the subject matter has been consumed or substantially altered in character and (iii) where rescission would harm a third party fitting the description of a *bona fide* purchaser for value without notice of the misrepresentation.

In any proceedings where a plaintiff would be entitled to rescind the court has a discretion conferred on it by s 2(2) Misrepresentation Act 1967. The court may declare the contract still subsisting and award damages instead of rescission. Tom should be advised therefore that the remedy open to him is to seek rescission of the contract with Rob, giving the car back and reclaiming his money. It would seem that none of the bars to rescission exist. The car is substantially the same as when Tom received it. It has not been involved in an accident, for example. Its faults, which were hidden when Tom bought it, have now manifested themselves but its essential nature remains unaltered. Tom should be further advised that if the matter cannot be settled and the case comes to court the court would have a discretion under s 2(2) Misrepresentation Act to award him damages instead of the rescission he seeks.

(b) The purpose of awarding damages for breach of contract is to compensate the plaintiff, not to punish the defendant. Sometimes when breach occurs it is difficult to calculate the amount of the plaintiff's loss. In such circumstances the parties, anticipating this difficulty, may agree in the contract itself that a specified sum will be payable on breach. If the sum is a genuine attempt to estimate the amount of the plaintiff's loss it is properly referred to as a 'liquidated damages' clause. In the event of breach the plaintiff is entitled to recover this sum and this sum alone. He cannot be heard to argue that the amount should be disregarded because his actual loss turned out to be greater than was originally estimated.

If the sum stipulated is out of all proportion to the likely amount of the plaintiff's loss, the object being to punish the defendant, to use it as a threat, forcing him to complete the contract, it is called a 'penalty'. The sum is not recoverable. The plaintiff is free to sue the defendant for damages in the normal way, which means he will need to establish the value of his loss.

The Law of Contract

The question indicates that Tom and Sam have in their contract a clause that Tom is to pay '£250 by way of agreed damages' for each week the workshop remains unfinished. It does not matter what they have called the amount. The important factor is whether in substance the sum represents a genuine attempt to calculate Sam's likely loss or whether it is penal in its proportions.

The leading case which offers guidance on how to distinguish between liquidated damages and penalties is *Dunlop Pneumatic Tyre Co Ltd v New Garage & Motor Co Ltd* (1915). Here the defendants agreed, *inter alia*, not to tamper with marks on the plaintiff's products, not to supply persons on a 'suspended' list and not to sell the goods below a fixed minimum price. For contravention of any of these the defendant became liable to pay the plaintiff the sum of £5. The House of Lords held the amount of £5 was liquidated damages. Although it might appear large for a single item sold in breach of the agreement the effect on Dunlop's organisation, once the news became known among traders, was incalculable. £5 was not in the circumstances an extravagant amount.

In his judgment Lord Dunedin summarised the position and set out rules for guidance. These are:

(i) the sum is a penalty if it is unconscionable in amount and greater than the greatest lost which could result from the breach;

(ii) if on failure to pay a sum under the contract a larger sum becomes payable, the larger sum must be a penalty;

(iii) subject to rules (i) and (ii), if a single sum is payable in respect of one event only there is a presumption that it is liquidated damages. If it is payable in respect of several breaches, varying in gravity, the presumption is that the sum is a penalty;

(iv) a sum is not prevented from being liquidated damages because an accurate estimate of the plaintiff's loss is impossible; if not unreasonable in amount it is likely to be acceptable.

An interesting comparison can be made between the *Dunlop* case and *Ford Motor Co Ltd v Armstrong* (1915). Under an agreement similar to that in *Dunlop*, the Ford Motor Co sued the defendant retailer for breach where the agreed sum for every contravention of the restrictions was £250. The Court of Appeal held this sum to be a penalty.

In the question Tom has broken his contract with Sam. The workshop has not been completed by the stipulated date. The issue now is whether Sam is entitled to damages at the rate of £250 per week until the building is finished. The sum is payable in respect of a single breach. It is by no means out of proportion to the loss which might be suffered by Sam as a result of not being able to start his business venture. On the other hand it would be impossible to calculate in advance with any degree of precision what Sam's actual loss might be. As the sum appears not unreasonably large it is likely in any proceedings that a court would judge it to be liquidated damages.

Tom should be advised accordingly of his liability to pay the amount for each week that he remains in breach.

Question 24

Explain the circumstances in which a contract may be declared void on the ground of mistaken identity and comment on whether the law provides a satisfactory solution to the issues raised by such cases.

Answer plan

This question provides an excellent opportunity to display your understanding of a relatively self-contained area of law. It has developed from a series of cases involving swindlers at work on innocent victims. Diverse 'tricks' have been used but the legal structure of the cases and the central issues remain the same. At common law there is no satisfactory solution - one of two innocent parties must lose. Perhaps the best solution would be to grant by statute a wide discretion to the court to apportion the loss between the parties as it saw fit.

If you are familiar with the cases the temptation is to write down the facts and the result in each so that your answer becomes a series of brief case reports. This shows the examiner you can remember the facts. It is important that you also show your understanding of the issues involved and the difficulties the courts face in coming to a judgment. Discuss these and centre your answer around the factors the courts will use in arriving at a conclusion - did the party mistaken:

- intend to contract with someone other than the rogue?
- regard the identity of the other party as crucial?
- take reasonable steps to confirm the identity of the other party?

Answer

Virtually all cases of mistaken identity in contract law are instances of unilateral mistake in which one party fraudulently represents himself to be another person and tricks an innocent victim into contracting with him. The mistake thus engendered is unilateral because the rogue is aware of the effect his misrepresentation has. Where, to external appearances, a contract has been made the courts have been reluctant to declare it void. Drastic consequences result for third parties who rely on its validity.

In most instances the rogue obtains goods on credit or in return for a worthless cheque from his victim. He sells the goods on to a third party, who is unaware of this deceit, and absconds with the proceeds. A legal contest then ensues between the first and second victims of the fraud. If the contract is declared void the second victim will be the loser and will have to return the goods or pay their value to the first victim. If the contract is not void for mistake the first victim will have lost his title to the goods and will be left to pursue (technically) an action for the price of the goods against the rogue.

The factors upon which the court will base its decision are: whether the party mistaken intended to contract with some person other than the rogue; whether the identity of that other was crucial; whether he took reasonable steps to confirm the identity of the other contracting party. The burden of proof is upon the party who alleges the contract is void.

The first requirement is for the party pleading mistake (the plaintiff in the illustration above) to show that the person he really intended to contract with actually exists and that he has confused the two entities. In *Kings Norton Metal Co Ltd v Edridge Merrett Co Ltd* (1897) a rogue by the name of Wallis set up business under the name Hallam & Co. On company notepaper, which suggested a business of international proportions, he ordered goods from the plaintiff for which he never paid. He then sold them to the defendant. The Court of Appeal held that the contract must stand. The plaintiff must have intended to contract with the writer of the letter whether that was an entity by the name of Hallam or of Wallis.

The second requirement is that the plaintiff should be able to show the identity of the other contracting party to have been of crucial significance to him. In *Cundy v Lindsay* (1878) the plaintiffs received an order for goods sent by Blenkarn from 37 Wood Street, Cheapside, but which appeared to come from Blenkiron & Co, due to the way Blenkarn signed the letter. The plaintiffs were aware of the reputable firm, Blenkiron & Co, and knew they carried on business in Wood Street, although they were unaware of the number. The premises were in fact at 123 Wood Street. They despatched the goods to Blenkiron & Co, 37 Wood Street. Blenkarn received them and sold them to the defendants.

The case could have been decided either way. If it was inferred that the plaintiffs intended to do business with the trader at 37 Wood Street the contract was not void (even though it was voidable due to Blenkarn's fraudulent misrepresentation). On the other hand the facts could be interpreted so as to indicate that the plaintiffs had intended to contract only with the reputable firm Blenkiron & Co. The House of Lords chose the latter and held the contract to be void.

If the second requirement is difficult for a plaintiff to establish in the case of a contract made by correspondence, the task is monumental where the parties are contracting face to face. How can the plaintiff convince the court that he never intended to deal with the very person standing in front of him with whom he conversed? In *Phillips v Brooks Ltd* (1919) the rogue, North, entered the plaintiff's shop and selected jewellery to the value of £3,000. He wrote a cheque for this amount saying, 'You see who I am. I am Sir George Bullough', giving an address in St James' Square. The plaintiff who had heard of but never met Sir George found, on consulting a directory, that he was indeed listed as living at that address. The plaintiff allowed North to take with him one item, a ring priced at £450, supposedly for his wife's birthday, the next day. North pledged the ring for £350 with the defendant who was unaware of the fraud.

It was held that the plaintiff, no doubt pleased to have secured Sir George as a customer, nevertheless must have intended to sell to the man who was present in his shop. The argument that he had intended to contract with Sir George and him alone was weak especially as, beyond checking the address given, he did nothing to verify the man's identity.

Further cases which raised the same issues were *Ingram v Little* (1960) and *Lewis v Avery* (1972). In *Ingram v Little* the plaintiffs, who agreed to sell a car, refused to go through with the deal when the rogue indicated his intention to pay by cheque. They changed their decision only when he said he was PGM Hutchinson of Stansted House, Caterham, and they confirmed through the directory that someone of this name lived at the address he had given. Prior to this they had never heard of PGM Hutchinson. The cheque was dishonoured. Meanwhile the rogue sold the car to an unsuspecting third party. The Court of Appeal surprisingly held that the plaintiffs had intended to deal only with PGM Hutchinson. No contract had been made with the rogue.

In *Lewis v Avery* the Court of Appeal expressed its disapproval of *Ingram v Little* preferring to follow *Phillips v Brooks*. In *Lewis v Avery* the plaintiff sold a car to someone posing as Richard Greene, the actor and who signed a cheque for the purchase price of £450. Until the buyer produced a pass to Pinewood Studios to authenticate his identity the plaintiff was unwilling to let him take the car away. The Court of Appeal held the plaintiff had failed in his attempt to establish that no contract had been concluded with the rogue.

The third requirement-that the plaintiff took reasonable steps to check the identity of the other party-was also of direct relevance to all three cases. The court was clearly unimpressed by the efforts made in *Phillips v Brooks* and *Lewis v Avery*. It is difficult to follow the reasoning in *Ingram v Little* especially in view of the fact that prior to the issue of identity being raised the plaintiffs had no idea that a PGM Hutchinson existed. In the other cases the plaintiffs had at least heard respectively of Sir George Bullough and Richard Greene prior to the contracts being made.

These cases have been difficult to distinguish and much has been made of the difference between an individual's 'identity' and 'attributes'. To succeed in his claim that the contract is void the onus is on the plaintiff to establish that it was the identity of the other party which influenced his decision to contract. Qualities or attributes which the other may possess, such as status or creditworthiness, are insufficient. In *Ingram v Little* Pearce LJ said: 'The real problem ... is whether the plaintiffs were in fact intending to deal with the person physically present, who had fraudulently endowed himself with the attributes of some other identity, or whether they were intending only to deal with that other identity.'

The idea that a distinction can be made in these terms was vigorously rejected by Denning MR in *Lewis v Avery*: 'A man's very name is one of his attributes. It is also a key to his identity. If then he gives a false name, is it a mistake as to his attributes? These fine distinctions do no good to the law.' His preference was for all such cases to be treated as voidable, not void.

The law cannot be said to be in a satisfactory state when it is unclear how a court will choose to view the problem. There is, regrettably, no completely satisfactory solution to the problem. It is also a hard fact in all mistaken identity cases that one of two innocent victims of the swindler has to suffer. There is no halfway house. For Lord Denning in *Lewis v Avery* the second victim was more worthy of protection. The first had, to some extent, caused the problem by not being sufficiently vigilant in dealing with the rogue.

The common law is unable to offer a way out of the dilemma and must continue to make difficult choices. However, statute is not so restricted. A solution to the impasse might be through legislation to empower the court to exercise a discretion opportioning the loss between plaintiff and defendant. This would operate with greater equity than the present win/lose scenario.

Question 25

In what ways does the Unfair Contract Terms Act 1977 seek to protect consumers through the control of exclusion and limitation of liability clauses, and the content of standard form contracts?

Answer plan

The question requires a detailed look at the provisions of the Unfair Contract Terms Act from the 'angle' of consumer protection. It is therefore not just a matter of going through the Act, section by section, but of selecting the concepts and devices which apply to consumer transactions and explaining how they work. Bear in mind that the EC Directive 93/13, which will be implemented by the UK in July 1995, deals not only with exemption clauses but with 'unfair' terms in general and the use of plain, intelligible language in consumer contracts.

To demonstrate to the examiner your understanding of the context in which the Act operates explain:

- why exemption clauses and standard form contracts came about in the first place; the general policy of the Act with reference to freedom of contract
- the meaning of the terms used in the question

Next consider in detail the means of control the Act uses:

- making some exemption clauses completely ineffective
- making others subject to the reasonableness test, giving guidelines on the meaning of 'reasonableness', putting the burden of proof on the party who alleges a term is reasonable, giving a definition of 'consumer', putting the burden of proof on the party who alleges a transaction is a non-consumer transaction to show that this is the case and providing anti-evasion devices

Answer

The law of contract is based on the notion that a contract is a bargain which two parties have freely negotiated. With the rise of an industrial society engaged in the mass production and supply of goods and services for the consumer market, this notion has been somewhat strained. The result has been the 'mass production' of the terms on which such goods and services are supplied - standard form contracts which are presented to the consumer on a 'take it or leave it' basis. It is an arguable point whether this leads only to exploitation of the consumer or is a means of supplying the goods and services desired by the consumer in the most efficient way.

The policy adopted for dealing with this situation by the Unfair Contract Terms Act 1977 has been to allow suppliers freedom in the first instance to operate on terms of their choosing but to restrict considerably the ways in which they may exclude, limit or redefine obligations which otherwise would arise as a consequence of contract or negligence liability by means of exemption clauses

Exemption clauses come in many forms. They are terms which absolve a party from breach or non-performance of all or part of his obligations. Limitation clauses are those which, while not exonerating breach or non-performance, limit the extent of a party's liability to a specific sum (eg £500) or with reference to another figure (eg the price of the goods supplied).

Both these types of clause are likely to be found in standard form contracts together with terms which could operate to produce a similar effect by a different means. One such device is where the supplier, instead of using an exclusion clause, redefines his primary obligations under the contract. Another is the use of a clause under which the consumer agrees to indemnify the supplier in respect of breach of the supplier's own obligations towards a third party or towards the consumer himself.

The Unfair Contract Terms Act seeks to control the use of such terms and devices, particularly as they affect consumers, through a number of ways and by the use of various concepts such as 'reasonableness' and 'deals as consumer'. The Act covers liability arising in contract and through negligence and attempts to exclude or limit it by means of contract terms or notices. However, the scope of the Act, with some minor exceptions, is expressed to extend only to 'business liability', that is from things done or to be done in the course of a business or from the occupation of business premises: s 1(3).

The primary way in which the Act operates is to make some exemption terms completely ineffective and to make others subject to the 'reasonableness' test. The first of these is used where there is an attempt to exclude or restrict liability for death or personal injury resulting from negligence: s 2(1). It is used also in connection with attempts to exclude or limit liability for breach of statutory implied terms in contracts relating to the sale or supply of goods

Implied undertakings as to title by a seller of goods cannot be dispensed with (s 6(1)) and, where a person 'deals as consumer', in connection with the other implied obligations which cover description, satisfactory quality, fitness and sample (s 6(2) and s 7(2)).

Section 5 operates to prevent manufacturers of goods giving 'guarantees' which are worded so as actually to reduce or negative the producer's liability. For the section to apply, the goods must be of a type ordinarily supplied for private use or consumption. If they are defective due to the manufacturer's negligence and this causes loss or damage to the consumer the manufacturer cannot exclude or restrict his liability by reference to a guarantee of the goods

The 'reasonableness test' operates to protect consumers in a number of situations, most importantly in the following. First, it applies to exemption from loss or damage (other than personal injury) resulting from negligence: s 2(2). In *Smith v Eric Bush* (1989) the defendant argued that a disclaimer in his survey report on a house to a building society was not subject to s 2(2), because it did not exclude liability. Instead it defined the nature of the liability the defendant was prepared to take on. The House of Lords rejected this argument. The defendant owed a duty of care to the plaintiff (purchaser of the house) who had relied on the report, which had been negligently prepared. The section applied to attempts to prevent the duty arising as well as exempting liability when breach occurred.

Second, exemptions in contracts which fall within s 3 are subject to the requirement of reasonableness. The section applies where one of the parties 'deals as consumer' or on the other's written standard terms of business. As against that party liability for breach cannot be excluded or restricted unless the term permitting this passes the test of reasonableness. The requirement applies also to terms in the contract under which the other claims to be entitled to render (a) a performance substantially different from that which was reasonably expected, or (b) no performance at all. The type of situation which (a) was designed to cover is that found in *Anglo-Continental Holidays v Typaldos (London) Ltd* (1967) where terms allow a tour operator to change the itinerary or destination in a package holiday.

Further situations to which the concept of reasonableness applies, giving support to consumer rights, are those covered by s 4 - indemnity clauses (considered below) - and by s 8 - exclusion of liability for misrepresentation. Section 8 amends s 3 Misrepresentation Act 1967 so that a contract term which excludes or restricts any liability or any remedy arising as a consequence is subject to the reasonableness test in the Unfair Contract Terms Act.

The Act offers guidance on the reasonableness test, in general terms in s 11, more specifically in Sched 2. The time when the test is to be applied is when the contract is made: s 11(1). By s 11(4) the court should, in the case of a limitation clause, note whether the defendant has resources to meet his liability and whether he could obtain insurance cover. By far the most significant way in which the guidelines protect the consumer is contained in s 11(5). It is for the party who alleges a term is reasonable to show that it is.

Although the additional guidelines in Sched 2 are stated to apply to the reasonableness test for the purposes of s 6(3) and s 7(3) (transactions involving goods in non-consumer contracts), the tendency has been to consider them elsewhere if they appear relevant. This occurred in *Woodman v Photo Trade Processing Ltd* (1981) and *Smith v Eric Bush* (1989) where the court considered the relative strength of the parties' bargaining positions and whether it was possible for the plaintiff to have acquired the services elsewhere on different terms or at a different price.

A central feature of the Act is the way in which the person who 'deals as consumer' is singled out for special treatment. The definition of 'consumer' in s 12 is someone who: (i) neither makes a contract in the course of business or holds himself out as doing so; (ii) deals with another who does make the contract in the course of a business; and (iii) the goods supplied are of a type ordinarily supplied for private use or consumption. By s 12(3) it is for the party claiming that a person does not deals as consumer to show that he does not. The result is that the definition has been interpreted very widely. By placing the burden of proof upon the supplier (as with s 11(5)) the position of the consumer is strengthened considerably, so that even when a company purchased a car, partly for business use and partly for private use, it was held to have been dealing as consumer: *R & B Customs Brokers Co Ltd v United Dominions Trust Ltd* (1988).

Finally, in order to prevent circumvention of the provisions of the Act by clever drafting, a number of devices have been used. By s 13(1) an extended definition is given to exemption clauses. Thus in *Stewart Gill Ltd v Horatio Myer & Co Ltd* (1992) it was held that a clause which provided the defendants were not to withhold payment for incorrect or defective goods on grounds of set off or counterclaim was an exemption clause under s 13(1)(b). As a consequence, it was caught by s 3, being contained in the plaintiff's standard written terms of business, and was subject to the reasonableness test. By s 4 a clause under which a consumer is made to indemnify either the other contracting party or a third party for negligence or breach of contract is also subject to the reasonableness test. This stops the trader or supplier agreeing to take on an obligation but then, by means of the indemnity clause, throwing financial liability for its breach back on the consumer. By s 10 the consumer's rights in a main contract (eg purchase of a TV set) cannot be taken away by a secondary contract (eg associated maintenance contract). Any attempt in the secondary contract to take away the purchaser's Sale of Goods Act rights in the main contract would fail.

The Unfair Contract Terms Act is a complex statute. It requires a comprehensive understanding of the existing rules of common law to make sense of it and is not simple in its internal arrangement. Nevertheless, it has produced a major change in substantive law which has significantly improved the consumer's position through the concepts and devices outlined above.

Chapter 7

The Law of Tort

Introduction

Tort is a case-law subject concerned with compensation for wrongs. It lends itself well to problem questions, though essays can appear on general issues of fault and compensation, and of course a question can ask for a simple 'explanation' of a topic without requiring a comparison and contrast. The key words of the question must be understood and followed.

For example, Question 27, below, does not simply require an explanation; even one full of case-law and statutory evidence, it requires you to consider 'how well' the system works, an evaluation of it, is it good or bad? stating, of course, your reasons. Words like 'assess' or 'evaluate' require that treatment also, and words like 'contrast' or 'compare' mean just what they say. Also, avoid generalisations and prejudices, eg 'It is generally agreed that ... '. Examiners look for reasoned argument and evidence, especially cases and statutes.

Many marks are lost by not answering the precise requirements of the question. If a tort is mentioned in the question, stick to it. If the question says 'advise A', it does not want you to advise B.

Further marks are lost by poor order. Keep it logical. If an essay requires you to consider both sides (as they often do) then after an introduction in which you say that you are going to consider both sides, then go through the 'pros' and then the 'cons'; only then conclude at the end.

In a problem question establish the tort (the plaintiff's burden) and then go to the defences. The examiner wants to know whether you know your law but moreover whether you can apply it to the facts.

Do not underestimate the second point. Many students lurch into writing 'everything I know about the topic', ending with a brief simple paragraph of conclusion. This is bad style; the 'essay' part contains much irrelevant matter (which wastes your time and tells the examiner that you cannot apply the law to the facts of the question). Under this method your application will be scanty and general, rarely showing that a case mentioned much earlier relates to a fact in the question.

It is better to adopt 'law, cases, application' on each point as you move through the question. Adopt one of two approaches to suit the individual question; either work through each event as it comes, or deal with one plaintiff or defendant at a time.

Finally, cases and, more rarely in tort, statutes should be inserted, if relevant, to illustrate the rule under examination. The order of what to remember of a case is: (a) the point of law; (b) the brief facts; and (c) the name (but rarely the date as you would in statutes).

In the answer be brief. Practise during your course the art of combining all three parts into one sentence. Use the formula 'In (the name of the case) where (the facts) it was held that (the law)'.

For example: 'In *Alcock v Chief Constable of South Yorks*, where relatives and friends saw the Hillsborough injuries on television, or first viewed the bodies in the mortuary the next day, it was held that there was no duty of care as, although within the protected class of relatives, they were not in proximity to the defendant (there were intervals of space and time) and the means of communication were indirect.'

Hardly good 'coursework style'! But exams require leanness of style (strictly, the examiner does not need to know that this is the 'Hillsborough football case').

Favourite topics in problems are (especially) negligence, Occupiers' Liability Acts 1957 and 1984, and defences of *volenti* (consent) and contributory negligence, private nuisance and vicarious liability; but breach of statutory duty, *Rylands v Fletcher* and the Animals Act 1971 also appear in the questions chosen here.

Questions on trespass to the person appears in Chapter 9 (p 297 onwards). Aspects of compensation are useful for essays on the purpose and effectiveness of the tort system, and defamation, while only occasionally a question topic by itself, is a good topic for an essay on the balance of competing interests, being a balance of the right to reputation and the right to free expression.

Question 26

Grind Ltd operates a factory, at which Joe works. To stay competitive, Cynthia, the 'director of quality', directs that the workforce must increase its completion rate per hour for their product. Joe's machine normally needs to be stopped every fifteen minutes to take its guard off in order to brush away the iron filings. But to meet the new production levels, he keeps the machine running but with the guard off to brush the filings away. While he is doing this one time, with the guard off, someone drops a mug behind Joe. Joe jumps, and catches his thumb and a finger on his revolving machine. Several tendons are severed, after which Joe cannot hold anything firmly, so he is dismissed.

Advise Joe as to his rights in tort, and as to the basis of the compensation he will hope to recover.

General approach

This is rather a strange question. On the one hand it covers the usual duty, breach, and damage of common law negligence, although even there some knowledge of employers' liability is useful, but in a situation like this, a factory and an injured workman, there is bound to be some statutory duty or other. The question does not say that there is, but in view of this certainty, the tort of breach of statutory duty is included.

There are two possible approaches. The one adopted is preferable, clearer and less likely to get you in a muddle. This is to cover each tort at a time. If you follow the other style, combining both duties, both breaches, both 'damage', it will not be clear to which tort your rules and cases relate.

On the other hand, the defences, *volenti* and contributory negligence, are dealt with together as their application in the two torts is similar. This question would be allowed 35-45 minutes.

Answer plan

- introduction; negligence, breach of statutory duty, Employers' Liability (Defective Equipment) Act 1969; defences

- common law negligence; burden of proof, duty, *Donoghue v Stevenson*, *Caparo v Dickman* (Lord Oliver), *Wilsons Clyde v English*; safe equipment; 1969 Act
- breach; reasonable standard; skilled (*Bolam*); likelihood (*Bolton*); severity (*Paris*); social use (*Watt*); burden (*Latimer*)
- damage; causation; reasonable; foreseeability, *Wagon Mound*, *Hughes*
- breach of statutory duty; duty; class (*Groves*); sanction?; breach; standard; *John Summers*; damage: causation (*Boyle v K*); *Gorris*
- defences; no *volenti* (*Smith v Baker*); contributory negligence (*Nance, Caswell*); 1945 Act
- personal injury compensation; general damages; special damages

Answer

This question concerns the torts of negligence, in particular employers' liability and possibly breach of statutory duty, in all cases for personal injuries. (We are not told in the question of any relevant statutory duty, although one is almost certain to apply to machines in a factory.) In some respects the common law tort and the breach of statutory duty are similar as they both involve a duty, its breach and damage.

Throughout, the actions of Cynthia are considered as those of Grind Ltd, not through vicarious liability as it is doubtful whether Cynthia has committed a tort against Joe (a duty of care is unlikely), but as the acts of a director are usually construed as being those of the 'brains' of the company (as opposed to its 'hands': *Tesco v Nattrass* (1972).

The first action which Joe can take is to sue Grind Ltd in common law negligence. Joe must prove, on balance of probabilities, that Grind Ltd owed him a duty of care to avoid personal injury; secondly that Grind Ltd was in breach of that duty; and thirdly that Joe suffered reasonably foreseeable damage as a result.

Firstly, Joe must prove that a duty of care was owed him. The neighbour principle of *Donoghue v Stevenson* (1932) suggests that

Grind Ltd will owe a duty of care in effect to people it ought to have in reasonable contemplation at the time of its allegedly negligent act or omission. *Caparo v Dickman* (1990) has added to foreseeability of harm the requirements of proximity between the parties and a just and reasonable test. Lord Oliver in that case said that, in cases of direct physical harm, these are implied from the foreseeability of harm. A duty of care is therefore owed by Grind Ltd to Joe as elaborated by *Wilson and Clyde Coal v English* (1938) as a duty to provide *inter alia* safe equipment. It is worth noting that the Employer's Liability (Defective Equipment) Act 1969 imposes strict liability for defective equipment manufactured by a third party.

Secondly, Joe must now prove breach of the common law duty of care and of the duty in the Act . The standard required by Grind Ltd is that of a reasonable company in that line of work (*Bolam v Friern Hospital Management Committee* ((1957)). To establish this standard the court will consider the likelihood of injury caused by an increase in the speed at which Joe works, forcing him to leave off the safety guard (see *Bolton v Stone*: where a cricket ball being hit out of ground was held not likely), and the severity of harm even if unlikely (see *Paris v Stepney DC* (1951) where the severity of harm was held greater to a one-eyed man). Against this are weighed the social usefulness in taking the risk (see *Watt v Hertfordshire CC* (1954) where a firearm was hurt by a loose jack, but the risk was worth taking to save woman) and the burden on removing the risk on the defendant (see *Latimer v AEC* where a wet factory floor did not justify closure). It is likely here that the likelihood of Joe being injured and the severity of injury are likely to outweigh any usefulness in working without the guard on and the burden not of acquiring a guard, as one already exists, but of using it in such a way as causing a slowing down and loss of profit.

The question does not say whether the machine is defective within the Employers' Liability (Defective Equipment) Act 1969 but it might be argued that a machine so dangerous but which can be operated without its guard on is indeed defective.

Thirdly, Joe must prove damage. He must prove that the breach of duty caused the damage. The but-for test will prove this, ie but-for the pressure on Joe and but-for Joe being negligently allowed to work without a guard, he would not have been injured.

Joe must also prove in the common law action that his damage was reasonably foreseeable (*The Wagon Mound (No 1)* (1967)). While loss of fingers might not have been foreseeable, some personal injury was reasonably forseeable and this would be sufficient, as in *Hughes v Lord Advocate* (1963): where burns by an explosion were held equivalent to burns by flame. Thus the injury is reasonably foreseeable and Joe will *prima facie* succeed in the common law action. The defences available will be discussed below.

Although no statutory duty is mentioned one is bound to exist in this situation. Joe should sue in all available actions to increase his chances of success. To sue in breach of statutory duty the plaintiff must prove, again on balance of probabilities, that the statute or statutory instrument imposed a duty on Grind Ltd, not simply a prohibition or discretion. Secondly, Joe must prove that he was within the class of person which the statute was intended to protect (*Groves v Lord Wimborne* (1898) where a boy working in a factory was held to be so). A third consideration is whether the statute imposes a sanction other than the right to sue for damages.

To establish a breach of statutory duty, the standard required by the statute must be considered. This is not known here but in *John Summers v Frost* (1955) the court said that it was no defence that a machine would not work with the precaution in place. It is likely that there would be a duty and a breach here. The plaintiff Joe must also prove causation of damage on the same principles as above. In *Boyle v Kodak* it was held that where duties were imposed on both parties, who each broke them, then both parties caused the damage. If Joe was himself under a duty not to use the machine without the guard on he could be called a separate tortfeasor equally liable for causing the damage. Joe must also prove that the damage was within the kind which the statute was intended to protect him against (see, for example, *Gorris V Scott* (1874) where sheep pens were required for the prevention of disease and there was therefore no action for the loss of sheep washed overboard).

Grind Ltd might raise either or both of two defences. Firstly that of *volenti non fit injuria*, but this is unlikely to succeed in either action as it is not enough to prove that a person, especially an employee, knew of the risk; it must be proved that he voluntarily agreed to take it on (*Smith v Baker* (1891)).

More likely to succeed is contributory negligence. This is described in *Nance v British Columbia Electric Rly* as a failure to take reasonable precautions for his own safety. But in *Caswell v Powell Duffryn* (1940) the court said that where there is loss of concentration caused by the monotony, noise and distractions of a factory the court would be slow to recognise contributory negligence as a result. The decision here would be with the court in Joe's action. If the court held that Joe was guilty of contributory negligence then, after working out the total damages, it would reduce them in proportion to Joe's fault under the Law Reform (Contributory Negligence) Act 1945.

In his action, Joe would claim general damages for loss of amenity (even if he used not, say, play a musical instrument, the loss of the use of a hand is a serious disability), pain and suffering, both past and future, future loss of net earnings and future expenses; and special damages of past net earnings and past medical and other expenses including any private health care. If there is a chance of a serious disease or serious deterioration in his condition then the judge should be asked for an award of provisional and future damages. Otherwise the award will be a single lump sum, structured settlements only being obtained by private settlement and not from the judge.

Question 27

Dinetter Ltd run a transport cafe at the edge of a suburb of a big city. They convert it to a 24-hour 'drive-in' cafe with optional 'one-armed bandit' facilities. It proves very popular with lorry-drivers and locals on motorbikes alike. The cafe tends to cause noise all round the clock, but the local residents' complaints to Dinetter Ltd have so far been ignored.

Dinetter Ltd buy some coffee machines which need servicing every so often. Expresso Coffee Services obtain the contract. Expresso is a partnership between Jill and Jen. One week Jill services the valve at the outlet pipe of the coffee machine, but forgets to tighten the nut to hold it in place.

Bill, one of Dinetter Ltd's waiters, who has been told always to open the valve slowly the first time he draws coffee after a service, opens the tap quickly to draw a cup of coffee. He causes the untightened valve to come adrift, with the result that water squirts out, injuring Mary, a customer, when she slips on it.

(A) What legal action can the local residents take? (12 marks)

(B) What liability to Mary might Dinetter Ltd be under in the torts of negligence and Occupiers' Liability Act 1957 for the acts of Jill and of Bill? (20 marks)

(C) What liability to Mary is there on Jen? (5 marks)

(D) The court hearing the local residents' claim will have had to balance the competing interests of the parties. How well does the law balance these interests? (13 marks)

General approach

This is a wide question (it would be allocated 50 minutes) taking in the torts of public nuisance and private nuisance, negligence and the Occupiers' Liability Act 1957. Whenever you see smoke, noise, flooding, vibrations which interrupt people's lives or which damage land or interfere with the use of it, or even causes personal injury (public nuisance covers all types of harm), then go straight to nuisance. (If there is an accumulation and an escape, consider also *Rylands v Fletcher*; but there is none here.)

If people are hurt by the state of premises or land, or by the activities done on premises or land, this invites consideration of the Occupiers' Liability Act (of which there are two, depending on whether the plaintiff is a lawful visitor (1957 Act) or a trespasser (1984 Act)). Careless conduct in public, or where it does arise from the state or activity of premises or land, is common law negligence.

This question also covers the liability of a person for the torts of his servant or partner, or independent contractor. Contribution between defendants is another issue that springs to mind where different people's negligence cause the damage. In tackling the issues raised in the last two sentences, which all relate to parties, you must always first determine whether the person whose conduct is the cause of the damage is personally liable in tort.

Only, say, if a servant or contractor is personally liable for negligence, should you then consider whether someone else is also liable vicariously, or liable to make a contribution.

On the matter of parties where, especially in a negligence question, you find a negligent servant, look for any vicarious liability of his master. And look also for any question of liability of an independent contractor. They are favourite comparisons.

Finally, there is a lot to cover here; but you will not remember all this detail in an examination, and your language will be more concise (though still precise!).

But, as in all questions, plan well. Sort out the torts and ascribe them to each action.

Answer plan

- Local residents v Dinetter Ltd
  Public and private nuisance; noise (*Bamford v Turnley, Halsey v Esso, Page Motors v Epsom*); burden of proof (*Southport Corp v Esso*); injunction - interlocutory (*Kennaway v Thompson*)
- Mary v Bill
  Negligence; duty (*Donoghue v Stevenson*); breach, likelihood (*Bolton v Stone*), but severity (*Paris*); damage (*Wagon Mound, Hughes v Lord Advocate*)
- Mary v Dinetter (personally, and for the tort of Jill)
  Occupiers' Liability Act 1957; personal duty; reasonable to employ independent contractor?; *Woodward v Hastings*
- Mary v Dinetter Ltd (for the tort of Bill)
  Vicarious liability; master and servant relationship; in course of employment?; *Century Ins v Northern Ireland Transport*; contribution; master and contractor
- Mary v Jen (for the tort of Jill)
  If Jill is negligent, vicarious liability; Partnership Act 1890
- Contribution
- Evaluate; against defendants; reasonableness test; malice; fault; but prescription, in his favour; compromise (*Kennaway v Thompson*); defamation

Answer

(A) Local Residents v Dinetter Ltd

The local residents may be able to sue Dinetter Ltd for the noise in both public nuisance and in private nuisance. A public nuisance can be defined as an act or omission which materially affects the reasonable comfort and convenience of life of a class of Her Majesty's subjects (*AG v PYA Quarries* (1957)). It is a crime but any member of that class who can show special damage over and above that suffered by the rest of the class can sue in it as a tort. The plaintiff need not be interfered with in his use of his land. In *Halsey v Esso* (1961), the plaintiff's loss of sleep caused by the noise of tankers entering and leaving the refinery through the night in convoys of four amounted to public nuisance, even though the defendant had lawful authority to operate the refinery. We can presume that the class in *Halsey* was the residents of that road, but that the plaintiff suffered more than they did. Here, the class would be the local residents, and here lies a problem. In *Benjamin v Storr*, a case concerning horses urinating outside a cafe, it was said that the defendant must be one of that class, but one who has suffered damage over and above that suffered by the rest of the class.

If all the local residents have suffered to the same extent, the action will fail. If only some residents are affected then the burden of proof of disproving a nuisance is in Dinetter Ltd, according to Denning LJ in *Southport Corp v Esso* (1956).

The residents can also sue in private nuisance, which can be defined as indirectly and unreasonably causing either physical damage to land in the possession of the plaintiff, or substantial interference with his use and enjoyment of that land (or an interest in it); in whichever case the defendant will be the creator of the nuisance or a person responsible for it as occupier of the land where the nuisance is. The cause of the nuisance will normally be a state of affairs. The state of affairs is the nuisance, here the operation of the cafe.

The harm must be either physical injury to the plaintiff's land, or, as here, 'sensible' interference with the plaintiff's use and enjoyment of his land. We have already seen that tanker noise was held to be a public nuisance in *Halsey v Esso*, but the plaintiff's inability to sleep was also caused by the noise from the boilers and the road tankers inside the refinery, as well as the noise of the tankers while on the road. All these were held to be evidence of a private nuisance as they amounted to sensible interferences with the plaintiff's use and enjoyment of his land.

In the use and enjoyment cases only, the character of the locality is relevant in determining whether the interference is appreciable and substantial. 'What would be a nuisance in Belgrave Square would not necessarily be so in Bermondsey': *Sturges v Bridgman* (1879).

The plaintiff's user here is not a sensitive one, which would perhaps deny the existence of a nuisance. But a key factor is the unreasonableness, if any, of the defendant's use of the land. The court will here consider the ordinary and reasonable user of the land by the defendant, the duration, frequency or transience, and, as already mentioned, the locality.

In assessing the 'ordinary and reasonable user of the land' by the defendant, the court will first adopt 'a rule of give and take, and live and let live' (*Bamford v Turnley* (1860)). Under this case reasonableness of user is established if the state of affairs is 'necessary for the common and ordinary use and occupation' (operation of oil refineries in Fulham in *Halsey v Esso* (1961) or a cafe here), and the state of affairs is 'conveniently done', that is, done reasonably and not excessively

If the defendant complies with these rules, his user is reasonable, and the plaintiff must accept any harm still occurring as give and take. But the burden of proof of the reasonableness is probably on the defendant to rid himself of fault (see Denning LJ in *Morton v Wheeler*). It seems unlikely that the defendant here will be able to defend as reasonable the noise throughout the night. The fact that it arises out of a third party's conduct (the customers') is irrelevant. In *Page Motors v Epsom & Ewell* there was liability for the fact that gypsies had collected on the defendant's land.

There is no evidence of malice here to assist the plaintiffs but, as argued above and as the state of affairs is continuous, a private nuisance will be held to exist. Fault can be easily established. As required by *The Wagon Mound (No 2)* (1961) and *Sedleigh-Denfield v O'Callaghan* (1940), the fault is in failing to abate a nuisance, the existence of which the defendant is or ought to be aware as likely to cause damage to his neighbour. Dinetter Ltd know that they are open all night and have received complaints, and are therefore at fault.

The definition above indicates that the plaintiff must be in possession of the land affected; this is so here, as the plaintiffs are residents. The defendant could be either the creator of the nuisance, or the occupier of the offending land, in which last case he is liable if he knows or should have known of the nuisance arising out of his land, and fails to abate it. The customers are not trespassers or strangers. Thus, as in *Sedleigh-Denfield v O'Callaghan* (1940), where Brother Dekker saw the trespassers carrying out the work, the defendant company will be held at fault and therefore liable.

With regard to damage the plaintiff must prove both causation and reasonable foreseeability of damage (*The Wagon Mound (No 2)*).

None of the defences applies here. Nor is it a defence that the defendant's act is for the public benefit, as it was sought to justify the fried-fish shop in *Adams v Ursell*; nor that the defendant had taken reasonable care and skill.

The remedies sought by the residents would be damages and a prohibitory injunction to stop the nuisance. They may immediately seek an interlocutory injunction, which the court will grant if damages are inadequate as a remedy, as in *Laws v Florinplace Ltd* to remove the nuisance caused by the sex-shop. To apply for an interlocutory injunction the plaintiff need not make out a *prima facie* case; the rule is that the court must decide (i) whether there is a serious question to be tried, and (ii) on the balance of convenience (*American Cyanamid v Ethicon*).

In accordance with general principles, damages *in lieu* of injunction might be awarded under s 50 Supreme Court Act 1981. But any injunction will be a compromise; not closing down the day-time opening of the cafe but only restricting the night-time opening (as in *Kennaway v Thompson*, where it limited the racing to certain times of the year, to certain weekends and events) to certain times, and the noise level to certain decibels. There would be no grounds for entering the cafe to abate the nuisance, as there is no urgency.

(B) Mary v Bill

Mary must prove that Dinetter owed her a duty of care to avoid foreseeable harm, that the company broke that duty, and that the breach caused damage of a reasonably foreseeable kind. To establish a duty of care, Lord Atkin's neighbour principle would first be cited, that a duty of care is owed to persons in reasonable contemplation of suffering harm from the defendant's negligence. Thus foreseeability of harm is an essential requisite, and was said by Lord Oliver in both *Murphy v Brentwood* (1990) and *Caparo v Dickman* (1990) to be the only requisite in cases of foreseeability of direct physical harm. Bill has been warned that he must not open the tap too fast. He can foresee that if the tap is not secure, hot water will flow onto or splash bystanders. He owes a duty to anyone he knows is, or can reasonably be expected to be, close.

A breach of duty of care is a failure to take reasonable care. Bill is a waiter, and he has a duty to behave as a reasonable waiter (*Phillips v William Whiteley* (1938)). Given the likelihood of harm from his negligence, the severity of harm, and the fact that the adequate precautions are very easy to perform, ie opening the tap slowly, Bill would be held in breach.

The breach has caused damage; 'but-for' the breach there would have been no damage. The damage is of a reasonably foreseeable kind (*The Wagon Mound (No 1)* (1961), *Hughes v Lord Advocate* (1963), where actual burns by an explosion was held to be within the foreseeable burns by fire).

Mary v Dinetter (personally, and for the tort of Jill)

An occupier of land and premises may owe a duty to a person coming onto the land. His liability will depend on whether the plaintiff is a lawful visitor, in which case a duty is owed under the Occupiers' Liability Act 1957, or a trespasser. Clearly, Mary, as a customer, is a lawful visitor. She can sue under s 2(1), which imposes the 'common duty of care' on an occupier of premises, which s 2(2) defines as a duty to take such care as is reasonable to see that the visitor will be reasonably safe in using the premises for the purposes for which she is invited or permitted by the occupier to be there. The duty is on the 'occupier' of premises, whether or not also the owner. In *Wheat v Lacon* (1966), where the plaintiff, a guest, fell down an unlighted staircase, the important criteria were control and management. 'Visitor' includes all invitees and licensees, and will include Mary.

She, as plaintiff, has to prove both breach and damage on principles similar to those in common law negligence, above.

The doctrine of *res ipsa loquitur* may apply as in *Ward v Tesco* (1976), where the plaintiff slipped on yoghurt, as Mary does not know why the water she slipped on was there, but can say that it should not have been there had care been taken. Even if she cannot invoke that doctrine, she can say that the machine should not have been sited where it was, so near to customers. She can claim for injury to the person

As there is no attempt at exclusion or restriction of liability, nor warning, and her being in the cafe cannot be held to be either implied consent (*Dann v Hamilton* (1939): where it was held that there was no implied consent to getting in a drunk's car), nor contributory negligence, Dinetter Ltd will be liable to Mary under the 1957 Act for her injuries. However, the company can plead under s 2(4)(b); that it was reasonable to entrust the servicing work to an independent contractor and that it used reasonable care in choosing a competent contractor and in checking that the job had been properly done. In *Haseldine v Daw & Sons* (1941), it was held reasonable to instruct a contractor to mend a lift, thus shifting liability from the occupier.

Mary v Dinetter Ltd (for the tort of Bill)

If Bill is found to be liable to Mary in negligence, as shown above, then Mary can consider an action against his master, Dinetter Ltd. A master (or employer) is vicariously liable for the tort of his servant (or employee) acting in the course of his employment. A distinction must be drawn between servants, operating under a contract of service, for whom the master is liable and independent contractors, operating under a contract of services, for whom the 'master' is not liable (and is in truth no 'master'). There are various tests to determine which the tortfeasor is, including control, integration (*Stevenson Jordan & Harrison v MacDonald Evans* (1952)), and the economic tests of *Ready Mixed Concrete v Ministry of Pensions* (1968) such as the provision of tools etc, and payment. The question says that Bill is one of the company's waiters, so he is probably a servant.

Mary must then prove that Bill committed his tort in the course of his employment, ie if the act is authorised, expressly or impliedly. It is authorised even where the act is a wrong or prohibited mode of doing an authorised act. In *Century Insurance Co v Northern Ireland Road Transport Board* (1942), the petrol deliverer who threw the match down was doing what he was authorised to do, ie deliver petrol, and this would be so even if the master has specifically forbidden the servant to do something, as in *Rose v Plenty*, where the milkman was acting against orders in allowing the boy to ride on the float. Here, Bill is simply doing the task he was authorised to do, namely, serve hot drinks from a machine. There is no question of him being 'on a frolic of his own', as put in *Joel v Morrison*.

Dinetter Ltd will therefore be vicariously liable for Bill's negligence towards Mary.

(C) Mary v Jen (for the tort of Jill)

The Act says that partners are jointly and severally liable for the torts of any of the partners. Thus, if Jill is found to have been liable to Mary in negligence on the principles of duty of care, breach, damage mentioned above, Jen will be vicariously liable for Jill's negligence.

(D) Contribution

In circumstances such as these, whether either one or more people are held liable to the plaintiff, a sole defendant or a defendant who has had to pay what he thinks someone else should be liable for, the defendant can seek a contribution or indemnity from the other person liable under the Civil Liability (Contribution) Act 1978. The aggrieved defendant would bring in the other person as a third party in 'third-party proceedings'. This is a matter between defendants, however; it does not fetter a plaintiff in pursuing her claim where she thinks fit.

(E) Evaluate: balance of competing interests

Many torts involve the resolution of a conflict or balancing act between competing interests. In nuisance, the test of reasonable user in *Bamford v Turnley* (1860), expresses the principle of give and take, live and let live. The fact that different standards apply in different areas (Belgrave Square versus Bermondsey: *Sturges v Bridgeman* (1879)) shows that flexibility is a key factor. The harsh imposition of the burden of proof onto the defendant is mitigated and balanced by the fact that there are defences available to the defendant, for example the long-user principle of prescription. The curious fact that it is no defence that the plaintiff came to the nuisance is an aberration, but even here the courts show themselves to be in compromise mood in the form of injunctions which they are willing to impose. For example in *Kennaway v Thompson* (1981), the injunction did not rule out the water sports completely, but only put restrictions on the times and decibels of the racing.

Essentially, this is a balance between rights and duties: the rights of a plaintiff balanced against his duties towards the defendant in the interest of fairness and of respect to others' rights, especially the defendant's, but also those of society's and the public's. This balance is also found in other torts; defamation is a good example. The plaintiff's right to expect a defendant not to publish a defamatory statement about him is balanced, in the interests of freedom of speech and expression, long valued by the courts, by various defences, especially those protecting truth (justification) and fair comment (fair comment on a matter of public interest), and others which allow the important functions of state to operate (absolute privilege). An interesting balance is that between the strict liability of defamatory meaning and reference to the plaintiff, which is mitigated by the defence of unintentional defamation under s 4 Defamation Act 1952.

Question 28

Maggy and John are next door neighbours in a street of a former industrial town, where residential areas have for 100 years been interspersed with industrial development. While the heavy industry no longer exists, those plots have been taken over by light industrial and commercial concerns, thus still leaving a mixture of areas within the locality. Although the terraced houses do not have gardens, John makes a good living repairing the lawn-mowers of the inhabitants of the new houses further out of town, which all have gardens. He has done this work, in his back yard, for a few months now. The testing of the machines creates lots of noise and fumes. Maggy has complained to John that her clothes, and especially her sequinned ballroom dresses which she hangs out on the line get smutty, but John needs the money so he ignores the complaints.

Maggy has recently taken to climbing over the wall into John's yard at night to see if she can ascertain the names of John's customers so that she can ask them not to send him work. One night she treads on a roller-skate which one of John's children had left outside. The skate moves, throwing her to the ground and injuring her.

In despair, Maggy invites her brother, a chemist, to come over, bringing with him some chemicals with which he could create foul smells to waft over the wall into John's yard to annoy him. This involves heating up chemicals over bunsen burners in Maggy's yard. Unfortunately some chemicals explode, shattering one of John's windows and causing injury to his eye.

Explain the tort of private nuisance and apply them to these facts.

What liability to Maggy might John be under as occupier of his back yard?

What liability to John is there arising out of the explosion?

In the torts you have discussed explain how the nature of the damage dictates the success or otherwise of the claim.

(50 marks)

General approach

This is a wide question (it would be allocated 50 minutes) taking in the torts of private nuisance (but not public - we are not told that a class is affected), negligence and the Occupiers' Liability Act 1984, but possibly also the 1957 Act depending on whether she is a trespasser or not, and the strict liability of the *Rylands v Fletcher* and the Consumer Protection Act 1987.

Whenever you see smoke, noise, flooding, vibrations which interrupt people's lives or which damage land or interfere with the use of it, or even causes personal injury (public nuisance covers all types of harm), then go straight to nuisance.

If there is a bringing-on and an escape, consider also *Rylands v Fletcher*; and personal injury caused by a defective, ie unsafe, product invites discussion of the Consumer Protection Act 1987.

This question also expects you to be precise on the type of damage which can be the subject of the various torts. We have both personal injury, property damage and interference with use and enjoyment.

But, as in all questions, plan well. Sort out the torts and ascribe them to each action.

Answer plan

- Maggy v John
  Private nuisance, noise (*Bamford v Turnley*, *Halsey v Esso*); injunction; interlocutory (*Kennaway v Thompson*)
- John v Maggy
  Trespass to land; abatement of a nuisance
- Maggy v John
  Occupiers' Liability Acts 1957 and 1984; *volenti* and contributory negligence
- John v Maggy
  Negligence; *Rylands v Fletcher*; CPA 1987
- Effect of type of loss
  No personal injury in private nuisance; in *Rylands*? *Hale v Jennings*; *Read v Lyons*; no property damage in CPA; OLAs: 1957 plaintiff's property; 1984 no property damage

Answer

(a) Maggy v John

There can be no liability in public nuisance here as we are not told that John's activities affected a class, as required by *AG v PYA Quarries* (1957).

Maggy can possibly sue in private nuisance, which can be defined as indirectly and unreasonably causing either physical damage to land in the possession of the plaintiff, or substantial interference with his use and enjoyment of that land (or an interest in it); in whichever case the defendant will be the creator of the nuisance or a person responsible for it as occupier of the land where the nuisance is. The cause of the nuisance will normally be a state of affairs. The state of affairs is the nuisance, here the use of John's premises for the repair of lawnmowers.

The harm must be either physical injury to the plaintiff's land or, as here, 'sensible' interference with the plaintiff's use and enjoyment of his land (the noise and clothes damage). In *Halsey v Esso* (1961) tanker and boiler noise was held to be a private nuisance, which caused his inability to sleep. Both of these were held to be evidence of a private nuisance as they amounted to sensible interferences with the plaintiff's use and enjoyment of his land.

But a key factor is the unreasonableness, if any, of the defendant's use of the land. The court will here consider the ordinary and reasonable user of the land by the defendant, the duration, frequency or transience, and the locality. In assessing the ordinary and reasonable user of the land by the defendant, the court will first adopt 'a rule of give and take, and live and let live' (*Bamford v Turnley*). Under this case reasonableness of user is established if the state of affairs is 'necessary for the common and ordinary use and occupation' (operation of oil refineries in Fulham (*Halsey v Esso*) or a repair base as here), and the state of affairs is 'conveniently done', ie done reasonably and not excessively. If the defendant complies with these rules, his user is reasonable, and the plaintiff must accept any harm still occurring as give and take.

In the use and enjoyment cases only, the character of the locality is relevant in determining whether the interference is appreciable and substantial. 'What would be a nuisance in Belgrave Square would not necessarily be so in Bermondsey': *Sturges v Bridgman* (1879) Maggy and John live in an area of mixed residential and light commercial type, but the activities of John are not confined to a factory, but to a back-yard of a house. Nor is the plaintiff's user here a sensitive one, which would perhaps deny the existence of a nuisance (as did the sensitive brown paper-making in *Robinson v Kilvert* (1884)).

If the activity is a nuisance by normal standards, then sensitive damage will not be too remote; the orchid damage in *McKinnon v Walker Industries* (1951) was actionable on this basis. Further, the fact that John ignores Maggy's complaint may show malice, and thereby tend towards the state of affairs being unreasonable, as the shooting causing the vixens to abort in *Emmett v Hollywood Silver Fox Farm* (1936).

Once the nuisance is established, the burden of proof of the reasonableness is probably on the defendant to rid himself of fault (Denning LJ, in *Morton v Wheeler*). It seems unlikely that the defendant here will be able to argue successfully that noise and smut damage is reasonable. Fault can be easily established here. As required by *The Wagon Mound (No 2)* and *Sedleigh-Denfield v O'Callaghan* (1940) the fault is in failing to abate a nuisance of the existence of which the defender is or ought to be aware as likely to cause damage to his neighbour. John knows that he is causing a nuisance as Maggy has informed him of it, and he is therefore at fault.

The definition above indicates that the plaintiff must be in possession of the land affected; this is so here, as Maggy lives next door. The defendant could be the creator of the nuisance, or the occupier of the offending land, in which last case he is liable if he knows or should know of the nuisance arising out of his land, and fails to abate it. Thus as in *Sedleigh-Denfield v O'Callaghan*, where Brother Dekker saw the trespassers carrying out the work, the defendant company will be held at fault and therefore liable.

With regard to damage the plaintiff must prove both causation and reasonably foreseeability of damage (*The Wagon Mound (No 2)*).

None of the defences applies here.

The remedies sought by Maggy would be damages and a prohibitory injunction to stop the nuisance. She may immediately seek an interlocutory injunction, which the court will grant if damages are inadequate as a remedy, as in *Laws v Florinplace Ltd* to remove the nuisance caused by the sex-shop.

To apply for an interlocutory injunction the plaintiff need not make out a *prima facie* case; the rule is that the court must decide (i) whether there is a serious question to be tried, and (ii) on the balance of convenience (*American Cyanamid v Ethicon*). In accordance with general principles, damages in lieu of injunction might be awarded under s 50 Supreme Court Act 1981. But any injunction will be a compromise, prohibiting the smuts but not closing down the lawn-mower repairing during day-time hours during weekdays (as in *Kennaway v Thompson* (1981) where it limited the racing to certain times of the year, to certain weekends and events), to certain times, and the noise level to certain decibels. There would be no grounds for entering John's yard to abate the nuisance, as there is no urgency.

(b) John v Maggy

Maggy must prove that Maggy has intentionally and directly entered property of which he is in possession, without John's consent or other excuse. Trespass is actionable *per se*, so despite the fact that she causes no damage she will be held to have trespassed on John's property. Maggy's only possible defence, amounting to her right to enter, is that she was entitled to abate the nuisance. This is a self-help remedy which the courts are wary of, as it easily leads to a breach of the peace. In *Burton v Winters* it was held that it should be kept to cases of simplicity such as cutting overhanging branches, or cases of urgency. Neither situation applies here, and in any case she does not use the entry to abate the nuisance, merely to find out names and addresses, so Maggy will be liable in damages for her trespasses and can be enjoined not to trespass on his property even if she does not actually damage it, as was held possible in the unlawful car-parking case of *Patel v WH Smith (Eziot) Ltd*.

An occupier of land and premises may owe a duty to a person coming onto the land. His liability will depend on whether the plaintiff is a lawful visitor, in which case a duty is owed under the Occupiers' Liability Act 1957, or a trespasser, where the 1984 Act applies. Maggy will be held to be a trespasser unless either she has a right to abate the nuisance, and does so, or she has John's consent to enter his land. Even though she has entered his yard on previous occasions, and might claim to have implied licence to do so on account of his passive attitude; this claim would fail as she has only entered at night, in circumstances unknown to John. She will be classed as a trespasser.

An occupier of land, which John is, owes a duty to reasonably protect a trespasser, under the 1984 Act, when he knows, or should know, of the presence of a person, and of the existence of a danger, and where it is reasonable to act to protect that person. If John does not know of Maggy's nocturnal visits, nor has reason to suspect them, then he will be under no duty to ensure that any toys are left in the yard at night. Thus there is no duty under the Act, and no liability, and the questions of *volenti* and contributory negligence are irrelevant.

(c) **John v the brother and Maggy**

John will first sue for his eye injury. A claim in negligence against Maggy will fail unless he can prove that she was negligent in her choice of expert chemist. In *Rivers v Cutting*, the police were held free of liability in this tort after instructing a breakdown firm to remove a car from the motorway. The firm then damaged the plaintiff's broken-down car. Her brother is a chemist and Maggy will probably be held to have made the choice with reasonable care. But a claim under the Consumer Protection Act 1987 against the brother may well succeed for his personal injury. This Act imposes strict liability where a defective (defined as 'unsafe') product causes personal injury to a person. No issues of foreseeability or breach are relevant. This claim will succeed, but not for the broken window, unless the cost of repair is at least £275.

John could sue more sensibly for his window in *Rylands v Fletcher* (1865), where a land-owner is strictly liable for damage caused by his bringing onto his land 'things likely to do harm if they escape'. In *Read v Lyons* (1947), an explosion in a munitions factory which injured an inspector failed only because of the lack of the escape from the factory. Here there is an escape, and the chemicals brought onto Maggy's land, being a required 'non-natural' use in the back yard of a terraced house, will be held to fit the definition, as was the case in *Read v Lyons*.

The damage in this tort must have been foreseeable by Maggy, as required by *Cambridge Water Co v Eastern Counties Leather* (1991); and the damage is here is forseeable. Alternatively, a claim for the window could be brought under the tort of negligence, but would have to surmount the problem of breach of the duty of care. Given that the brother is a professional chemist, the standard required of him would be that of the reasonable chemist (*Bolam v Friern HMC* (1957)), and not merely the reasonably competent amateur (as the jeweller who did ear-piercing in *Phillips v William Whiteley* (1938)). It might be held that someone of his expected skill should have foreseen the likelihood or severity of the damage.

(d) Discussion on the influence of the type of damage in tort

We have seen above that the type of damage is influential. Personal injuries are recoverable in negligence (we need search no further than *Donoghue v Stevenson* (1932)), under the Occupiers' Liability Acts 1957 and 1984, public nuisance (by a golf-ball in *Castle v St Augustine's Links* (1922)) and under the Consumer Protection Act 1987, but not in private nuisance. In private nuisance, personal injury is evidence of unreasonable interference with use and enjoyment of the plaintiff's property, but will not lead to separate damages and will not support a claim standing alone. For instance, the refinery smell would be evidence of such interference in *Halsey v Esso* (1961) but a claim, say, of difficulty of breathing could not be brought in its own right. In *Rylands v Fletcher* the position is confused. An action succeeded in *Hale v Jennings* (1938) where a chair-o-plane escaped and flew off, causing personal injury to the plaintiff, but dicta in *Read v Lyons* (1947) disagree.

Property is also subject to similar rules. A claim will succeed in negligence (all car-damage is proof of this), public nuisance (the car in the street damaged by acid smuts as in *Halsey v Esso*), *Rylands v Fletcher* (the leading case itself), and private nuisance (*Leakey v National Trust* (1980)). But the Consumer Protection Act 1987 will only cover property damage above £275, and not the defective product itself, and while the Occupiers' Liability Act 1957 covers the plaintiff's goods which he has brought onto the defendant's land, for example the plaintiff's car, the 1984 Act is limited to claims of personal injury.

Critics of the present system and array of torts will say that these differences only place additional burdens on injured plaintiffs; an action in the wrong tort will fail and possibly when the limitation period is expired. The only precaution is to sue in each tort every time, thus causing increased costs and use of court time. But it is not simply the common law torts which show ambivalent attitudes; the statutory torts shown above are just as discriminatory.

Question 29

Ann is a tenant in Rachman's run-down tenement building. In the flat below lives Mrs Smith, an infirm widow who keeps an alsatian dog, Sheba, for protection. Because she cannot take the dog out for exercise, the dog whines continually, day and night. Ann cannot sleep on many an occasion because of the whining dog and, one night, having lain awake for three hours she gets up and goes down to Mrs Smith's flat. Mrs Smith answers the door, but only to let Sheba out in order to chase Ann away. Sheba bites Ann's heel, and as Ann runs upstairs to her own flat; the bannister on which she is leaning gives way under her weight, and she falls back down to Mrs Smith's floor, suffering further injuries.

What legal action can Ann take (a) in respect of her injuries, and (b) to stop the dog's whining?

General approach

This is a narrower question than Questions 27 or 28 (it would be allocated 35 or 45 minutes). It takes in the torts of public nuisance and private nuisance, the Animals Act 1971, battery and negligence, and the Occupiers' Liability Act 1957.

Whenever you see noise, which interrupt people's lives by interfering with the use of it, or even causes personal injury (public nuisance covers all types of harm), then go straight to nuisance.

People being hurt by the state of premises (or the activities on them, such as allowing football or cricket in a classroom or hospital ward) invites consideration of the Occupiers' Liability Act (of which there are two, depending on whether the plaintiff is a lawful visitor (1957 Act), as here, or a trespasser (1984 Act)).

But as for the bite, you must consider not only battery and negligence, but also the Animals Act 1971, which some 'A' Level syllabuses cover. But, as in all questions, plan well. Sort out the torts and ascribe them to each action.

Answer plan

- Ann v Mrs Smith and Rachman for the dog whining
  Public and private nuisance; noise (*Halsey v Esso, Bamford v Turnley*); injunction
- Ann v Mrs Smith for the dog biting
  Battery (*League Cruel Sports v Scott*); negligence (*Fardon v Harcourt-Rivington*); Animals Act 1971 and defence of guard dog (*Cummings v Granger*)
- Ann v Rachman for the bannister giving way
  Occupiers' Liability Act 1957; *The Carlgarth?*; two causes (bannister and fleeing from dog).

Answer

(a) Ann v Mrs Smith and Rachman for the dog whining

Ann may be able to sue Mrs Smith for the noise in both public nuisance and in private nuisance. A public nuisance can be defined as an act or omission which materially affects the reasonable comfort and convenience of life of a class of Her Majesty's subjects (*AG v PYA Quarries* (1957)). It is a crime but any member of that class who can show special damage over and above that suffered by the rest of the class can sue in it as a tort. In *Halsey v Esso* (1961) the plaintiff's loss of sleep caused by the noise of tankers entering and leaving the refinery through the night in convoys of four amounted to public nuisance, even though the defendant had lawful authority to operate the refinery. We can presume that the class in *Halsey* was the residents of that road, but that the plaintiff suffered more than they did. Here, the class would be the tenants as a body, and here lies a problem. In *Benjamin v Storr*, a case of urinating horses outside a cafe, it was said that the defendant must be one of that class, but who has suffered damage over and above that suffered by the rest of the class.

If all the tenants have suffered to the same extent, Ann's action will fail. If only some residents are affected then the burden of proof of disproving a nuisance is on Mrs Smith, according to Denning LJ in *Southport Corp v Esso* (1956).

Ann can also sue in private nuisance, which can be defined as indirectly and unreasonably causing either physical damage to land in the possession of the plaintiff, or substantial interference with his use and enjoyment of that land (or an interest in it); in whichever case the defendant will be the creator of the nuisance (Mrs Smith) or a person responsible for it as occupier or landlord (Rachman) of the land where the nuisance is. The cause of the nuisance will normally be a state of affairs. The state of affairs is the nuisance, having a dog which whines all day and night.

The harm must be either physical injury to the plaintiff's land, or, as here, 'sensible' interference with the plaintiff's use and enjoyment of his land. We have already seen that tanker noise were held to be a public nuisance in *Halsey v Esso*. But his inability to sleep was caused also by the noise from the boilers and the road tankers inside the refinery, as well as the noise of the tankers while on the road. All these were held to be evidence of a private nuisance as they amounted to sensible interferences with the plaintiff's use and enjoyment of his land.

In the use and enjoyment cases only, the character of the locality is relevant in determining whether the interference is appreciable and substantial. 'What would be a nuisance in Belgrave Square would not necessarily be so in Bermondsey': *Sturges v Bridgman* (1879). Nor here is the plaintiff's user a sensitive one, which would deny the existence of a nuisance. *Halsey v Esso* accepts that sleep at night is a reasonable requirement of the plaintiff.

But a key factor is the unreasonableness, if any, of the defendant's use of the land. The court will here consider the ordinary and reasonable user of the land by the defendant, the duration, frequency or transience, and, as already mentioned, the locality.

In assessing the ordinary and reasonable user of the land by the defendant, the court will first adopt 'a rule of give and take, and live and let live' (*Bamford v Turnley* (1860)). Under this case reasonableness of user is established if the state of affairs is 'necessary for the common and ordinary use and occupation' (eg the operation of oil refineries in Fulham (*Halsey v Esso* (1961)) or a guard dog, or even a pet, here), and the state of affairs is 'conveniently done', ie done reasonably and not excessively. If the defendant complies with these rules, his user is reasonable, and the plaintiff must accept any harm still occurring as give and take. But the burden of proof of the reasonableness is probably on the defendant to rid himself of fault (Denning LJ, in *Morton v Wheeler*). It seems unlikely that the defendant here will be able to defend herself as reasonable the noise throughout the night.

There is no evidence of malice here to assist the plaintiffs but, as argued above and as the state of affairs is continuous, a private nuisance will be held to exist.

But Mrs Smith's fault might be difficult to prove. As required by *The Wagon Mound (No 2)* and *Sedleigh-Denfield v O'Callaghan* (1940) the fault is in failing to abate a nuisance of the existence of which the defendant is or ought to be aware as likely to cause damage to his neighbour. Mrs Smith may be old, and slightly deaf, or might simply sleep soundly herself, and either way not be at fault if this is the first time that Ann or anyone else has complained.

The definition above indicates that the plaintiff must be in possession of the land affected; this is so here, as Ann is also a tenant. The defendant could be the creator (as dog owner) of the nuisance, or the occupier of the offending land, in which last case she is liable if she knows or should know of the nuisance arising out of her land, and fails to abate it. Thus if Mrs Smith is unaware of the noise, and not as in *Sedleigh-Denfield v O'Callaghan*, where Brother Dekker saw the trespassers carrying out the work, she will not be held at fault and will not therefore be liable.

With regard to damage the plaintiff must prove both causation and reasonably foreseeability of damage (*The Wagon Mound (No 2)*). We are talking still of Ann's lack of sleep here, not her injuries, so these tests are satisfied, at least.

None of the defences applies here. However, Mrs Smith's lack of fault may be a stumbling block for Ann.

The remedies sought by Ann would be damages and a prohibitory injunction to stop the nuisance of the dog whining. She may immediately seek an interlocutory injunction, which the court will grant if damages are inadequate as a remedy, as in *Laws v Florinplace Ltd* to remove the nuisance caused by the sex-shop. To apply for an interlocutory injunction the plaintiff need not make out a *prima facie* case; the rule is that the court must decide (i) whether there is a serious question to be tried, and (ii) on the balance of convenience (*American Cyanamid v Ethicon*). In accordance with general principles, damages in lieu of injunction might be awarded under s 50 Supreme Court Act 1981. But any injunction will be a compromise, not making Mrs Smith give up the dog but making her arrange for it to get outside every day. In *Kennaway v Thompson*, (1981) the court limited the racing to certain times of the year, to certain weekends and events, and limited the noise level to certain decibels. There would be no grounds for entering Mrs Smith's flat to abate the nuisance, as there is no urgency.

(b) Ann v Mrs Smith for the dog biting

Battery consists of an intentional, direct touching of the plaintiff without his or her consent and without lawful excuse. 'The least touching of another ... is battery': *Cole v Turner* (1704). Clearly it is not Mrs Smith who has bitten Ann but, in another case, *League against Cruel Sports v Scott* (1985) trespass to land was found where the master of hounds intentionally or negligently sent the hounds onto the plaintiff's land. It could be argued that if Mrs Smith intentionally or negligently sent her dog out at Ann, then she is liable in trespass to Ann.

Ann could also sue in the tort of negligence, under *Donoghue v Stevenson* (1932). Ann must prove that Mrs Smith owed her a duty of care to avoid foreseeable harm, that she broke that duty, and that the breach caused damage of a reasonably foreseeable kind.

To establish a duty of care, Lord Atkin's 'neighbour principle' would first be cited, that a duty of care is owed to persons in reasonable contemplation of suffering harm from the defendant's negligence. The requirement in *Caparo v Dickman* (1990) of foreseeability of harm is satisfied and there is a relationship of proximity and it is just and reasonable that a person who sets a dog on a known victim should be held to owe some care towards that person.

Ann must then prove breach. A breach of duty of care is a failure to take reasonable care. Rachman would no doubt plead *Fardon v Harcourt-Rivington* in which the lack of likelihood of damage from leaving a dog in a car negated breach. But given the likelihood of harm from Mrs Smith's act of releasing a dog without shouting for help or calling the police (*Bolton v Stone* (1951)), and moreover the severity of harm from a dog such as this (*Paris v Stepney* (1951)), and the fact that the adequate precautions are very easy to perform, *viz* not opening the door, Mrs Smith would be held in breach.

The breach has caused damage; 'but-for' the breach there would have been no damage. The damage is of a reasonably foreseeable kind as required by *The Wagon Mound (No 1)*; in *Draper v Hodder* (1972) being attacked by dogs in a pack was foreseeable, and the same probability would be arguably present here in the case of a single alsatian.

The Animals Act 1971 created four strict liability torts. As Sheba is not an animal of a dangerous species; nor is this damage by a dog to livestock; nor damage caused by straying livestock, the tort which is relevant here is that of liability for a known, but uncharacteristic, propensity to cause damage. In this tort the animal must be of a species not usually known for dangerous behaviour but the keeper knows his individual animal to be uncharacteristically dangerous. Mrs Smith's dog has bitten Ann, but Mrs Smith will argue that the species here is not simply 'dog' but 'alsatian', and that either alsatians as a species are well-known for their dangerous nature, or (as recognised in *Cummings v Granger* (1977) where a barmaid was lawfully bitten during her trespassing by a guard dog alsatian) they are not dangerous as a species except when used as a guard dog. In both of these situations the dog's keeper is not liable. Ann would in any case have to prove Mrs Smith's knowledge of Sheba's uncharacteristic dangerous propensity, and the question only hints that she expects that Sheba will be able to frighten off the caller.

(c) Ann v Rachman for the bannister giving way

An occupier of land and premises may owe a duty to a person coming onto the land. His liability will depend on whether the plaintiff is a lawful visitor, in which case a duty is owed under the Occupiers' Liability Act 1957, or a trespasser. Maggy, as one of the tenants, is a lawful visitor. She can sue under s 2(1), which imposes the 'common duty of care' on an occupier of premises; s 2(2) defines this as a duty to take such care as is reasonable to see that the visitor will be reasonably safe in using the premises for the purposes for which she is invited or permitted by the occupier to be there. The duty is on the 'occupier' of premises, whether he is resident or not. In *Wheat v Lacon* (1966), where the plaintiff, a guest, fell down an unlit staircase, the important criteria were control and management, and an absent landlord was held to be an occupier (in fact the landlord was a brewery company). 'Visitor' would include all persons in possession as tenants, and will include Maggy.

Ann, as plaintiff, has to prove both breach and damage, on principles similar to those in common law negligence, above.

Ann's main problem will be proof of breach; if the defect was latent, or hidden from view, then a reasonable landlord under a duty of reasonable care might be excused for a danger which is not reasonably likely (as the risk of people outside the cricket ground fence being hit in *Bolton v Stone* (1951)). However, if Rachman is found to be in breach, that breach will be held to have caused reasonable foreseeable damage to Ann. As there is no attempt at exclusion or restriction of liability, nor warning, and her being on the stairs and leaning against the bannisters (and not sliding down them, which would negate the duty: *The Carlgarth* (1927)) cannot be held to be either implied consent (*Dann v Hamilton* (1939) where there was held no implied consent to getting in a drunk's car), nor contributory negligence, Rachman will be liable to Maggy under the 1957 Act for her injuries. Ann may however also sue Mrs Smith for the bannister injuries.

Causation is the sole test of liability for damage under the Animals Act, and a fall in escaping is a foreseeable kind of damage from a breach of the common law duty of care (in negligence), so if her fleeing up the stairs is held to be reasonable it will not break the chain of causation leading from Mrs Smith's breaches under these two torts. Following *Wieland v Cyril Lord Carpets* (1969) where using stairs to get a son to take the plaintiff home who could not use her bi-focal spectacles properly, was not unreasonable conduct by the plaintiff. And her fleeing up the stairs in her escape does not amount to contributory negligence; it is quite a reasonable thing to do (such as climbing out of a toilet in which the plaintiff is locked: *Sayers v Harlow UDC* (1958); nor is leaning on the bannister unreasonable within that defence (as opposed to putting her whole weight on the toilet-roll holder in *Sayers v Harlow UDC*).

If Ann succeeds in suing for her banister injuries against both Rachman (under the 1957 Act) and Mrs Smith (in negligence and the Animals Act), either defendant can seek a contribution or indemnity from the other under the Civil Liability (Contribution) Act 1978. The aggrieved defendant would bring in the other person as a third party in 'third-party proceedings'. This is a matter between defendants, however; it does not fetter Ann as plaintiff in pursuing her claim where she thinks fit.

Question 30

Mouth is the editor of a newspaper called the *Daily Gossip*. The newspaper publishes an article headed 'Dirty Whirty'. Whirty is a City tycoon, and thought to be trying very hard for a knighthood. The article lists Whirty's past land speculation deals, some of which are stated to have involved the crime of conspiracy to defraud the Inland Revenue. In fact, Whirty once lived in Canada and was imprisoned there for six months after a conviction for evasion of car duty when he illegally exported several cars to the United States of America. But that was 20 years ago, and Whirty has not been in trouble since.

However, when Whirty sees the newspaper article he telephones Mouth shouting, 'You'll regret this. The city is not as safe as you think'. The following morning the newspaper's post contains a bomb, which is later defused and in fact from an animal rights group protesting over a previous article. Mouth thinks that Whirty has arranged for this to be sent and in the midday editions publishes an article headed, 'Whirty cannot gag my Mouth'. The article gives details about the bomb, stating that it came from Whirty.

What rights, if any, does Whirty have against Mouth in defamation?

General approach

This is a 'single tort' question which would take 35-45 minutes. Firstly, you should establish the causes of action. There are at least two here: the two publications (in this tort an express statement can imply a second statement). However many publications you find you must then apply the plaintiff's burden to each and consider relevant defences.

There is no hint of judicial proceedings or Parliamentary matters here, so the defence of absolute privilege should not be mentioned. As all statements are libel, no mention of slander should be made, other than that it exists. But do not simply write an A-Z of defamation; apply the law as you go along. An essay followed by a brief paragraph of application of law to facts will carry fewer marks.

However, follow the order of the tort and of the defences.

Answer plan

- statements; libel; 'dirty' and innuendos; 'Gag my Mouth' and innuendos
- defamatory meaning and innuendos (true, false)
- reference to plaintiff and innuendos
- publication
- defences; justification; fair comment on public interest; qualified; privilege; s 4 DA 1952
- remedies; damages; injunction?

Answer

This question concerns the tort of defamation, of which there are two forms: libel and slander. A libel is in permanent form, usually visible, actionable *per se* and also a crime, though only civil liability concerns us here.

Slander is in transient form, usually audible, requires proof of damage (save in four cases) and is not a crime. As all the statements published here are expressly stated in a newspaper, or arise by inference from a newspaper, then they are in permanent form and only libel needs be examined.

In all libel actions the plaintiff must prove, on balance of probabilities, firstly, that the statement was defamatory, and secondly, that it refers to the plaintiff, and thirdly, that there was publication by the defendant to a third party. Damage need not be proved as libel is actionable *per se*, though proof of actual damage would increase the damages if brought to the jury's attention.

On the first point, that the statement was defamatory, several tests have been stated. 'Would the words tend to lower the plaintiff in the estimation of right-thinking members of society generally?': Lord Atkin in *Sim v Stretch* (1936) or is it a statement 'which is calculated to injure the reputation of another, by exposing him to hatred, contempt, ridicule': *Parmiter v Coupland* (1840) or which makes 'the plaintiff be shunned and avoided': *Youssoupoff v MGM* (1934).

Whichever test is used, the standard is objective, ie the standard of the ordinary, reasonable man. It is not what the defendant intended but what he is reasonably understood to mean. Insults and jokes may or may not be defamatory, depending on circumstances. But it can be defamatory even though no-one believed it to be true. The judge decides whether the statement was capable of a defamatory meaning; and the jury decides whether it had that meaning on that occasion. The two statements as published are that Whirty is 'dirty' and might 'gag' or censor the editor. Both are likely to lower Whirty's reputation in the eyes of right-thinking members of society generally, whether dirty is taken as unwashed, or devious and unscrupulous, which is the other common interpretation of the word 'dirty'.

But the word 'dirty' might cause certain readers to make inferences, and to ascribe to this statement an innuendo, or second, hidden defamatory meaning. There are two types of innuendo: firstly, by there being further facts, known to a third party to whom the statement is published, which put the statement in a defamatory light (a true innuendo); and secondly, by the third party reasonably reading in some other meaning inherent or implied in the statement (a false innuendo).

On the word 'dirty', those readers who are aware of the further fact that he is a City tycoon, and probably very rich, may infer a true innuendo. In *Tolley v Fry* (1931) a chocolate advertisement depicting a golfer teeing off, innocent enough even if he were being paid for it, appeared in a different light to those who knew that he was an amateur and, as such, should not gain money from his sport. In *Cassidy v Daily Mirror* (1929), Mr Cassidy was photographed at the races with a lady-friend. Under the photograph when it appeared in the newspaper was the caption, 'Mr Cassidy and Miss X, whose engagement has been announced'. Mr Cassidy himself had supplied this information. But it was Miss X (later Mrs Cassidy) who sued, claiming that the innocent caption would take on an innuendo to those aware that she had been living with him all these years, and who had now been told that they were unmarried. So, here, some readers may infer that Whirty's wealth and position were acquired by dishonest means. However, it is clear from *Grappelli v Derek Block Holdings* (1981)(where the violinist's agent falsely told the public that he was ill and would never tour again), that the people alleged to have those further facts must have them at the time of publication. The public believed Grappelli's agent at that time; the fact that they later found it to be false, causing them to think less of Grappelli for double-booking, was too late to assist Grappelli's action.

Other readers might infer from 'dirty' a false innuendo, that he is a man of loose morals, or of sexual malpractice. The right-thinking member of society will read between the lines, even without knowing any further facts. After all he might only read the heading of the article. 'Logic is not the test', as Lord Devlin said in *Lewis v Daily Telegraph* (1964). These innuendos are in effect further defamatory statements which Mouth must in turn defend.

The second element of this action is that Whirty has the burden of proving that the statement referred to him. 'The only relevant rule is that ... the words must be understood to be published of and concerning the plaintiff': Lord Atkin in *Knupffer v London Express* (1944). Whirty is named in both statements so he can be easily identified, without recourse to the innuendo matters, which can apply here too. Nor are we aware of any other people called Whirty, which would mean a possible reference to those people also.

The third element of the plaintiff's burden of proof is that the defendant must have published the statement, ie made it known to any third party who understands it. Generally, the defendant has published it if he intended publication, or ought to have foreseen it. (Moreover, the usual rules of remoteness of damage apply, namely causation and reasonable foreseeability.) Thus, each repetition is a fresh publication, and a person who authorises, or can or should foresee a repetition is *prima facie* liable for it. In *Slipper v BBC* (1990), a review in the press of a defamatory television programme was a foreseeable publication causing further damage as a result of the programme. It is therefore likely that the statements about Whirty will be published elsewhere, in print or on the television, and those publications will amount to further causes of action which Mouth and his newspaper will have defend.

So far, then, both Mouth and his newspaper are each liable for the two express statements and also the innuendos. It is now up to Mouth (and his newspaper) to try to invoke the protection of one of the defences. Three of these do not apply, or in the last case offer a defendant poor protection; these are consent, absolute privilege; and apology under the Libel Act 1843.

The realistic defences are justification; innocent publication under s 4 Defamation Act 1952; fair comment on a matter of public interest, and qualified privilege (the last two of which the plaintiff can defeat on proof of malice).

In the defence of justification the plaintiff need not prove that the statement is false in order to succeed. The defendant must defend himself by proving it to be true, even if he was not aware it was true when he said it, or he said it maliciously. It need only be substantially true (so long as the false parts do not aggravate the defamation), and the justification need only meet the common sting of the statement (s 5 Defamation Act 1952 and *Alexander v NE Rly*, where it was immaterial that a report that a man convicted of travelling without a ticket on a train stated that he had been sentenced to three weeks imprisonment in default of payment of a fine, instead of two weeks). But where there are two meanings (as here, an innuendo also), the defendant must justify both.

It is likely that the errors in the actual details of the newspaper account as to whose tax authorities he was defrauding may be disregarded under s 5 and *Alexander v NE Rly*; the sting of the statement that he was devious, and the true innuendo of corruption are basically true. However, the meaning that he was unwashed, or attempting to censor the press, or of moral or sexual shortcomings, cannot be protected in this way. These last meanings amount to different stings which are not justified by his previous land deals mentioned in the question. Finally, a rumour must be proved to be true, not just that it existed; Mouth has no defence of 'existing rumour'.

A second defence is provided by s 4 Defamation Act 1952. This is called, variously, 'unintentional defamation' or 'innocent publication'. At common law, liability is strict as regards defamatory meaning (the defendant in *Cassidy v Daily Mirror* (1929) was not at fault; they had got their information from Mr Cassidy). Section 4 provides, in these circumstances, that if the 'publisher exercised all reasonable care' the defendant may make the plaintiff an 'offer of amends'. The plaintiff can accept it or not, but, effectively either way, it amounts to a defence. The court will then supervise the publication of a suitable correction and apology. But this defence only protects statements which are not defamatory on their face; thus s 4 would not protect the express or innuendo statements here, as they are all defamatory. If the judge were to decide that some are not so, it is not clear whether Mouth has evidential support for his statements (including the innuendos), which would show that he has taken reasonable care to avoid the defamatory statements.

Thirdly is the defence of fair comment on a matter of public interest. The defendant must prove that the matter is of public interest, that the statement is comment on a matter of fact, and that the statement is fair. Matters of public interest include not only government, industry, unions, churches, the courts etc; the City and the acquiring of its wealth would be included. The words must be comment, based on true fact, whether stated expressly or implied. Thus in *Merivale v Carson* (1887), a defendant who called a play immoral for the amount of adultery in it failed in his defence as there was none in it at all. Lord Esher MR in *Merivale v Carson* (1887) said that the test of fairness was, 'Would any honest man, however prejudiced he may be, however exaggerated or obstinate his views, have said that?' The statements covered by this defence are the comment that Whirty's means of acquiring wealth are devious and unscrupulous. As these terms are not measurable they will be classed as comment, but, as in justification, Mouth will have to show that the implications raised by the false innuendo are based on true fact. Mouth may not be able to show that the tax fraud facts related in the newspaper were sufficiently true, or were on the lines of the adultery in *Merivale v Carson*. In any case, Whirty can defeat this defence by proving malice; that the comment was not fair, ie not honest.

Mouth's final possible defence would be qualified privilege. Whereas the last defence was protecting free speech in public matters, this defence is mainly concerned with private matters. This is only a defence in the absence of malice, for example that the defendant was not motivated by ill-will or has properly used the occasion.

There are many situations, but Mouth's claim here would be that his statements were in performance of a duty (legal, moral or social) or in protection of an interest, to someone under such a duty or with such an interest. Normally, these concern private affairs, and the defence does not cover mischievous statements, such as to a spouse relating to the plaintiff's adultery, for example, in *Watt v Longsdon* (1930). But if Mouth can argue that he was under a moral duty to expose Whirty's fraud and his debased character to the public, and in particular to the City, then the defence might hold.

Whirty may so far be able to sue in respect of some of the statements but, as some of the decisions are questions of fact for the jury, those decisions are not predictable. However, if he succeeds, he will almost certainly claim damages. Damages are awarded by the jury and are therefore at large. They can amount to very large sums, eg £1,500,000 for libel (later reduced by consent) in *Lord Aldington v Tolstoy* (1989) and *Watts*, although s 8 Courts and Legal Services Act 1990 now gives the Court of Appeal power to decrease a ridiculous jury award. In contrast to these exorbitant awards, the award in *Newstead v London Express* (1940) was one farthing as contemptuous damages, as the jury, while agreeing that the law was on the plaintiff's side, nevertheless thought that the plaintiff was in it to make some money rather than to clear his name. The outcome of a defamation award is always in doubt. It is likely, however, that if a defendant pleads the defence of justification, then a plaintiff's claim for an interlocutory injunction will not succeed, as in *Bestobell Paints v Bigg* where the plaintiff posted a notice on his house (the paint on which was peeling off) that it had been painted with the plaintiff's paints. But once a plaintiff succeeds at trial a perpetual or final injunction may be awarded to prevent the defendant from repeating his statements. Thus Whirty may well be able to 'gag' Mouth's mouth after all!

Question 31

Assess the effectiveness of the current English system of compensation for personal injuries.

General approach

Any essay on 'compensation for personal injuries' is an essay on the tort system. 'Effectiveness' requires your view on how good the system is. An explanation of the system is only half the job; to get the high marks you must assess its value, and, as ever, show evidence to support your assessment.

What evidence? Crudely, your essay will be a contrast of 'pros' and 'cons', either as all the 'pros' first, followed by all the 'cons', or by tackling aspects in series, showing both sides of each aspect as you go along. Think, therefore, of the torts which deal with this area: negligence and breach of statutory duty are the main ones. Then choose cases which indicate the effectiveness one way or another.

Think also of the trend towards strict liability, say for products, and areas of law which deal with the practicalities of suing, such as limitation, methods of assessing damages. Briefly, then, mention the other methods. This should certainly fill an essay of 35-45 minutes!

Answer plan

- present system; negligence cases which fail in duty (*Bourhill v Young, Alcock v Chief Const of South Yorks, Roe v MoH*); breach (*Bolton v Stone*); damage; causation (*Barnett v Chelsea, Wilsher v Essex AHA*); also OLA 1957; breach of statutory duty
- strict liability (*Pearson*); CPA 1987; causation (*Wilsher*); development risks
- limitation; three years; s 33; extension
- damages; lump sum or structured settlement
- cost of system; time (*Wilsher, Whitehouse v Jordan*)
- conclusion

Answer

In this essay we will analyse the tort system with a view to assessing whether it is, as is often said, a system having as its main aim the compensation of individuals. Such a system, adversarial as it is in England, must respect the rights of both sides. It is here that the burden of proof on a plaintiff in negligence will be considered, especially the burden of proving fault. Other areas of the civil litigation system will be considered, and other systems of compensation, and after considering matters of cost and delay, a conclusion will be reached.

It is public policy in a civilised state to operate a system whereby private individuals can sue other private individuals, where there is a valid reason. For one thing this will obviate the need for private revenge. The judicial system, through the law of tort, has to follow its main aim of compensation, while not totally disregarding the rights of the defendant.

Thus we find that the tort of negligence, although applying the civil standard of proof on balance of probabilities, nevertheless puts the burden of proof on the plaintiff. Thus, the plaintiff will have to prove that the defendant owed him a duty of care, and was in breach of that duty, and thereby caused reasonably foreseeable damage to the plaintiff. Under the first test, duty of care, the plaintiff will use the well-known neighbour principle of *Donoghue v Stevenson* (1932), as elaborated upon in *Caparo v Dickman*. The test now requires foreseeability of harm, which will still deny damages to plaintiffs such as those in *Bourhill v Young* (the plaintiff was out of sight of the accident which caused her to miscarry), *Alcock v Chief Constable of South Yorkshire* (1991)(relatives of Hillsborough victims were held not to fall within the foreseeable class, or proximity but who saw the accident on TV), and *Roe v Minister of Health* (1954), where it was emphasised that duty of care is related to the foreseeable type of harm. Thus, as there, if the means of harm are undiscovered by science (eg hairline cracks in 1940s), how can a defendant foresee them?

The next problem is that of breach. Granted that professional and skilled defendants owe a higher standard of care (the *Bolam* test), but many plaintiffs have failed in their claims. Miss Stone in *Bolton v Stone* failed in her claim as her harm was unlikely; and many medical actions have proved the same point, such as the plaintiffs in *Sidaway v Bethlem Royal Hospital* (1985)(paralysed), and *Whitehouse v Jordan* (1981)(brain-damaged at birth).

Further, on the third element, damage, plaintiffs have failed to prove causation (*Barnett v Chelsea Hospital* (1968)), especially if the exact cause is not discernible out of several causes (as in *Wilsher v Essex Area Health Authority* (1988), where the baby, born premature, was blinded, but could not point with certainty to the cause).

Thus the negligence system, based as it is on fault, will often deny some victims, but of course not those who can prove all these things.

Because of the burden of the fault requirement there has been much consideration of a strict liability system. Why should one baby injured at birth recover damages while in similar circumstances another is unable to, solely because the first doctor is proved to have been negligent, but the second not? Is this fair? Both have to go through life with the same handicap. And in any case both doctors are either indemnified or insured.

The principle accordingly came under review in the 1970s: in Britain by the Royal Commission on Civil Liability and Compensation for Personal Injury (1978) (producing the 'Pearson Report'); and at the Council of Europe, and in the European Economic Community. The recommendations of the Pearson Report fell on deaf ears, but the EEC did produce a directive on strict liability for a defective product, obliging the British government to enact the Consumer Protection Act 1987. This Act is based on the strict liability causation of personal injury, dispensing with the need to prove duty of care, breach and reasonable foreseeability of damage. The Act has, however, allowed the defence of 'development risks' to allow a defendant to say that the risk was not known to science at the time the product was put into circulation.

However, liability for road accidents and for the increasingly prominent area of medical negligence (ie for negligent diagnosis, advice and treatment) is still fault-based. In any case, all torts, strict or fault-based, have the element of proof of causation of damage, and will involve the problems of *Barnett v Chelsea*

Hospital (1968), and *Wilsher v Essex AHA*, above. It is now 25 years since the Pearson Report; the decision of fault or no fault is not easy; fault is at the heart of our imposition of liability, and at the moment it holds sway. Why should a defendant have to pay damages if he has acted completely innocently?

Other potential problems for a plaintiff are limitation and the structure of the damages award or settlement. The Limitation Act 1980 is kind to a plaintiff, however. Whereas the common law said that the three year limitation period commenced at the time of causation of damage, whether noticeable or not, the Act postpones its starting time until the plaintiff becomes aware of the facts which ought to put him on enquiry. And even then there is provision for a plaintiff to seek leave to issue his writ provided that the defendant is not prejudiced by the plaintiff's delay. The matter of the form of the award will soon change.

Traditionally the judges can only award a single lump sum of damages (though interim payments and provisional damages are provided for). But the problem arises as to how long the plaintiff will live, and whether the lump sum will last that long. In 1991 one case was settled on the basis of a structured settlement. This involves an annuity providing a regular income for the plaintiff's life. Clearly, if the expectation of life is short, this is a bad idea, but not so if the plaintiff will live a long time. At the moment this arrangement can only be made out of court, but it is certain that judges will soon be able to award damages on this basis.

A further consideration is the delay a plaintiff will have to endure before the hearing of the action. The plaintiffs in *Wilsher v Essex AHA* and *Whitehouse v Jordan* (the first injured in his first few months, the latter at birth), were respectively 9 and 11 years old when the House of Lords finally rejected their actions. In the latter case, the legal aid fees paid to the lawyers were £250,000. Figures have shown that the tort system as a whole is expensive. The Pearson Commission found that social security payments account for one half of total national annual injury payments, and the tort system for one quarter; but whereas the former cost 11p for every £1 of benefit, the latter cost 86p for every £1 of damages. But whereas tort gives a chance of a big sum, social security is a modest, if regular, income.

Before concluding, it must be remembered that the present tort system is not the only means of compensation for harm. In addition, there are private insurance and pensions and social security, ie public insurance and state pensions. New Zealand has had a no-fault compensation scheme since 1974. But as described above the United Kingdom has left the fault-based tort system to take the vast bulk of claims, while introducing piece-meal schemes to cope with isolated groups of victims. Notable are the scheme under the Vaccine Damage Act 1969, the scheme for payments to haemophiliac sufferers of AIDS infected through NHS transfusions, and the Motor Insurers Bureau whereby the state and insurers agree to pay compensation where a vehicle driver is uninsured or unidentified. The final decision can only be made after considering all these factors. But even then, to a large extent, it comes down to individuals' beliefs: welfare state, or private recovery of damages, with the modest payments in the former matched by the risks of failure in the latter.

Question 32

Discuss the importance of fault in tort.

General approach

You will here need to explain, firstly, the aim of the law of tort and the role of fault in that system, what fault is in its various forms (intention and negligence), why there are these distinctions, and finally why there is strict liability in some torts. The argument along these lines should flow along quite nicely, but the better marks will be won by those who not only do this, but support their argument with case-law and statute-law as appropriate.

Answer plan
- the aim of the law of tort
- the role of fault in that system
- definition of fault; intention; negligence
- why there are these distinctions
- why there is strict liability in some torts
- conclusion

Answer

The common law has its roots in the customs of the people. One of that law's aims is to keep pace with the standards, values and interests of the ordinary people. Just as in ordinary dealings where people will indignantly claim that they are 'not to blame' or that it is 'not their fault', and will refuse accordingly to accept responsibility for something, so also in English law; the lack of fault will generally absolve a defendant for responsibility.

A clear example of damage without fault (or so it was pleaded) is *Fowler v Lanning* (1959), where the plaintiff's statement of claim simply claimed that 'the defendant shot the plaintiff' and was rejected as a valid cause of action. Without an allegation of fault the claim disclosed no tort. Fault, then, is important, whether as intention or negligence. Another aim of the tort system is compensation of the victim. Indeed the modern attitude is perhaps to see this aim as the most important, at least in some areas.

The Consumer Protection Act 1987, Part I, a strict liability tort, is an admission that in some cases the victim should be compensated irrespective of whether there is fault on the defendant's part. Faced with these two extremes, the requirement of fault in *Fowler v Lanning* (1959), and the lack of that requirement in the 1987 Act, this essay will examine the role of fault, its definition, and an examination of the various degrees of fault, and finally a review and possible justification of strict liability in this area.

As we have seen, the common law is closely identified with the standards and values of society, among which is fairness. There has emerged in the law of tort a system wherein three principles are normally essential for a successful claim; an interest deemed worthy of protection by the law (for example the person, goods, land, reputation and others); an interest must be damaged by a wrongful act; and which was committed with fault. Clearly it is better that a civilised state should adjudicate claims between citizens rather than them taking it out by violence or by self-help remedies. For this system to be respected it must be fair, and one of the important of the three principles mentioned above to give it a sense of fairness is the requirement of fault.

In tort, as we have said, fault takes one of two forms. Some torts require intention. Among these are the torts of trespass, in all its forms (against the person, goods and land). In *Cole v Turner* (1704) it was said that 'the least touching' will suffice for the interference, but *Letang v Cooper* (1965) made it clear that fault of either type was required in at least trespass to the person. Clearly people who intentionally punch or otherwise directly interfere with the plaintiff should pay for their tortious acts. But the law should be sensible; an intentional move forward which touches one person when there are several in a queue, and somebody has to move forward to let someone else through, will be tortious if the 'closeness' is abused. But if this is done modestly, though intentionally, it should be treated, as Lord Goff said in *Re F; F v West Berks AHA* (1989), as one of the trivial jostles of everyday life. The jostle might well be intentional, but a claim would only reap nominal damages.

On the other hand, a claim for intentional trespass where severe harm is caused would be recompensed in real, or substantial damages. In *Halford v Brookes* a trespass action proceeded for the alleged murder of a child. Clearly here the intention in killing someone will be treated as far more serious than, say, an intentionally unwanted kiss, and the amount of damages can express the degree of fault.

The other form of fault in tort is negligence. This again reflects common sense. Most people have heard, say, a child claim that he did not 'do it deliberately'. But since 1932 this is not enough, the plaintiff can claim that he was negligent; indeed, a common response to the child's plea mentioned above is, 'well, you should have taken more care'. This is a sensible approach considering that many road traffic accidents and many factory accidents cause hundreds of plaintiffs to suffer death or personal injury every year. Very often these incidents are not true 'accidents' at all, as that word implies a lack of fault; they are usually caused by negligence.

Negligence existed before 1932, but it was in *Donoghue v Stevenson* (1932) in that year that Lord Atkin and Lord MacMillan, two of the three Lords of Appeal who found for the snail-injured plaintiff, founded a duty of care on the principle of social justice. Thus Lord Atkin set out his 'neighbour principle' that even where we do not intend to cause someone harm, we should consider those we ought to have in mind when we do the act, and take care to avoid the foreseeable harm. Clearly we cannot see through trams (*Bourhill v Young* (1948)) or over the Pennines (*Alcock v Chief Constable for South Yorkshire* (1991)(the Hillsborough disaster claims)), but where physical harm is foreseeable, we should take care to avoid it.

Lord Atkin also pointed out in his 'neighbour principle' that this duty did not impose a great burden, simply one of 'reasonable care', thus again reflecting the common sense of the community. And as society would expect a surgeon to be better at surgery than a jeweller, and as a reasonable man would not do something he was very unsure about, so the law follows suit. Thus a reasonable man is not forgetful or inexperienced. In *Nettleship v Weston* (1971), a learner driver and, in *Wilsher v Essex Area Health Authority* (1988), a junior doctor, who negligently inserted a catheter into a baby's vein, pleaded their inexperience, but both in vain. Where a higher skill is professed, for example a medical or legal skill, then the standard must meet the higher standard of someone with that skill. Thus the *Bolam* test to this effect takes account of a professed skill while refusing to accept, for example, that all jewellers who pierce ears are self-professed surgeons. And a failure to use higher-than-reasonable skill is not negligent. In *Argyll v Beuselinck* the plaintiff instructed a solicitor-cum-author with a reputation in the literary world to advise her generally in her intention to publish her memoirs. His standard was simply a reasonable solicitor-cum-author, not that of the best; for that standard the client must enter into a contract and pay for it.

But how is the 'reasonable' standard of care determined? In considering the standard of care which the defendant was expected to meet, the court will consider four matters which should run through the mind of a reasonable man: the likelihood of injury, the gravity of the injury, the social importance of the defendant's actions, and the burden of adequate precautions. Thus some risks might be far-fetched; in *Bolton v Stone* (1951) the chances of a batsman hitting Miss Stone from the crease were not likely at all. The reasonable man would foresee the risk but ignore it. But sometimes although it may not be likely that harm would be caused, the gravity or severity of the harm which would be caused if it did occur would make it reasonable for the defendant to take steps to reduce the risk. In *Paris v Stepney Borough Council* (1951) the harm to the worker may not have been likely but would have been severe; here, the loss of his one good eye. The reasonable man would increase his care. The social usefulness of the item or practice might justify the risk, especially in emergency. In *Daborn v Bath Tramways* it was said that if all the trains in this country were restricted to a speed of five miles an hour, there would be fewer accidents, but our national life would be intolerably slowed down. Many items and practices of modern life cause harm, from trains, cars and aeroplanes to the use of gas, kitchen knives or petrol. The judge will be looking for a reasonable compromise, as that in *Watt v Hertfordshire County Council* (1954) where a firearm was injured by a vehicle jack which was loose. In *Latimer v AEC Ltd* (1953), Denning LJ said that in every case of foreseeable risk, it is a matter of balancing the risk against the measures necessary to eliminate it. It is by considering these four principles and by giving each its due weight, that the standard of the reasonable man can be set, again reflecting the standard expected by a fair, civic society.

In another tort, private nuisance, fault is also required. Lord Reid in *The Wagon Mound (No 2)* (1961) said that fault of some kind is almost always necessary, and generally involves knowledge, whether actual or reasonable, of the nuisance coupled with unreasonable failure to abate it.

It is against this background of fault that we turn to the principle of strict liability, or liability without fault. The torts discussed here relieve the plaintiff of part of the burden normally placed on a plaintiff, in that here the plaintiff need not prove that the defendant acted intentionally or negligently in causing the damage. The list of strict liability torts has grown haphazardly. The predecessor to s 4 Animals Act 1971 (liability for straying livestock) was mediaeval in origin; others are very recent, for example liability for dangerous products under the Consumer Protection Act 1987. Similarly, many consumer protection and factory protection provisions are strict. Further, while these and many other examples are statutory, the common law has been active also: the original liability for cattle trespass and the rule in *Rylands v Fletcher* (1866), being examples. We shall consider whether there is in fact some common thread, and whether the pressure towards strict liability in some areas is ill-founded.

As we have seen, the rationale in English liability in tort is that a person should only be liable where he is at fault, ie where he is blameworthy. Strict liability should be understood; these torts require intention or negligence as to some act or state of affairs, but introduce elements of strict liability. For example, conversion requires an intention to interfere, but not an intention to convert (*Hollins v Fowler*), and defamation requires an intention to publish, but not an intention to defame (*Cassidy v Daily Mirror* (1929), *Hulton v Jones* (1910), *Newstead v London Express* (1940)); and the rule in *Rylands v Fletcher* whereby a person who brings on his land and collects there anything likely to do mischief if it escapes, must keep it in at his peril.

There is a tendency to look for some common thread that these are all naturally, hazardous things, but in *Read v Lyons* an action failed in *Rylands v Fletcher* because there was no escape of the explosion from the munitions factory, thus defeating that theory. Further, there is no liability for things not 'brought on', ie for things naturally on the land. No matter how hazardous the state of the land is, if this is as a result of nature there is no liability (as there might be in private nuisance, above, *Leakey v National Trust* (1980)). Indeed, the decision in *Cambridge Water Co v Eastern Counties Leather* (1991) shows that the only strictness in the tort of *Rylands v Fletcher* is as to the escape; there still has to be reasonable foreseeability of damage. Perhaps because of the uncertainty in this tort, Parliament has clarified the liability in some areas by statute.

Thus the Nuclear Installations Act 1965 replaces the common law for liability for personal injury or property damage caused by radioactive material and channels all such liability onto the person licensed to operate the nuclear plant, who is strictly liable. Further, the Animals Act 1971 replaced a mixture of common law and statutory torts with four strict liability torts, and the Consumer Protection Act 1987, complying with an EC Directive intended to provide easier actions for such as the thalidomide victims (but only, incidentally, complying with the recommendations of the Pearson Commission on Personal Injury

Liability), created a strict liability regime for personal injury caused by defective products.

In a review of strict liability in tort, the fact should be remembered that a master is vicariously, and often strictly, liable for the torts of a servant acting in the course of his employment. This is so, even where the servant is stupid in carrying out his job (eg smoking when delivering petrol, in *Century Insurance v Northern Ireland Transport* (1942)), and even when forbidden to use a particular method (eg allowing boys to ride on a milk-float, in *Rose v Plenty* (1978)).

Finally, in conclusion, we can say that fault is a fundamental element of most common law torts, especially those where the injury is personal, but which has unaccountably spread into other common law torts. The main development, however, is the creation of strict liability torts. Despite the denial that strict liability at common law is intended to cover 'hazardous activity' (Scott LJ in *Read v Lyons* (1947)), it is the only rationalisation that can be made to link such diverse torts. Certainly there is a thread in the statutes of 'protection against hazardous things', for example, nuclear material, defective products (especially drugs), and wild animals. More important than this, however, is the question of whether strict liability should be extended in tort. Firstly, if much factory protection legislation is strict, why is road traffic liability also? Strict liability does not deny the operation of the contributory negligence defence (both the Animals Act 1971 and the Consumer Protection Act 1987 allow the defence), so could not a system of strict liability with contributory negligence work? Or is this just shifting the burden of proof of fault from plaintiff to defendant, and is that fair? In the final analysis, the choice may well be simply: who should suffer? Either a person is liable without fault, or a person is injured without compensation.

Chapter 8

The Criminal Law

Introduction

Much of what has been said in the introduction to tort questions in Chapter 7 (p 197) applies here as this also is a subject that lends itself very well to problem questions.

Criminal law, however, has more 'statute-law' than has tort. The examiner will not expect you to recite statutory provisions word for word, but you should be able to give a good paraphrase containing the main requirements of the crime. Cases should, of course, be cited as advised in the tort introduction. It is always good style, and it is logical, to state the *actus reus* of the crime first, with an application of that law to the facts, followed then by a statement of law on *mens rea* and its application to the facts. Always remember then to consider any relevant defences.

Favourite topics are murder and manslaughter, (especially causation, and intention and recklessness), provocation, intoxication and sentencing, and the purpose of criminal law. Less common are Theft Act offences, inchoate offences, and assaults.

Be on your guard when two defendants appear in a question. Consider secondary parties, and incitement and conspiracy. These inchoate offences can also be suggested by words like 'he suggested', 'they agreed'. And if any defendant fails to succeed in a crime, consider attempts.

Question 33

Dave is fed up with the usual English winter weather, so he books a cottage in Angola for three months. He has a series of inoculations against malaria and so forth at his doctor's surgery. On his way home he feels rather 'queer' and, when the bus he is waiting for arrives, he pushes Kate, the person at the front of the queue, out of the way to get on first. Kate is annoyed and trips Dave up, so that she can get on in front of him. Dave bruises his arm when he falls, but gets up and punches Kate very hard in the face, ripping her left eye brow and lid. Kate falls backwards, knocking Daphne, an old lady, to the ground. An ambulance is called for Kate and Daphne but, on the way back to the hospital, the ambulance crashes into a tree due to the bad driving of the driver, and causing a delay of one hour in arrival at hospital. Daphne, who has an illness causing her to have brittle bones, is found at hospital to have fractured her skull. Two months later Daphne dies of the effect of her fracture.

What criminal liability, if any, is there on Dave?

General approach

This question, for which 45 minutes would be allowed, covers the whole range of assaults, manslaughter or even murder, issues of causation of injury, attempts, and the defences of provocation and intoxication.

In questions such as this (which can also occur in tort, covering trespass to the person), where things happen fast, it is best to take the facts slowly, in order, crime by crime, but in all crimes, establish the *actus reus* first and then the *mens rea*: virtually all crimes have both. In the case of assaults, go through the following list of five mentally each time an assault occurs: common assault, battery, s 47, s 20 and s 18 Offences against the Person Act 1861 (OAPA). If an offence crops up twice, refer the examiner back to your previous explanation of law in that essay (though you should never cross-refer between questions; different questions may be split up between different markers).

Answer plan

- Dave pushes Kate; battery only; no ABH or GBH; intoxication
- Kate trips Dave; no wound or GBH; s 47; ABH
- Dave punches Kate; wound, or GBH?; ss 20 and 18; intoxication
- Dave causing Daphne's fall and death; transferred intent; what intent?; malice aforethought?; murder or manslaughter?; causation; provocation to murder; intoxication in both crimes
- Kate falling into Daphne; voluntary *actus reus*?

Answer

This question covers the whole range of assaults, manslaughter or even murder, issues of causation of injury, attempts, and the defences of provocation and intoxication. In each offence the prosecution must prove beyond reasonable doubt that the accused, or defendant, voluntary caused the *actus reus* of the offence having at that time the required *mens rea*.

In the case of the defences the defendant has the evidential burden of showing, on balance, that he has the defence, whereon the prosecution has the probative burden of disproving that defence beyond reasonable doubt.

Dave pushes Kate

There are five general assaults. Since the Criminal Justice Act 1988 the following now exist: common assault (or assault) 'contrary to s 39 CJA 1988'; battery 'contrary to s 39 CJA 1988'; 'assault occasioning actual bodily harm' (s 47 OAPA 1861); wounding or inflicting grievous bodily harm (s 20 OAPA 1861); and wounding or causing grievous bodily harm with intent (s 18 OAPA 1861).

When Dave pushes Kate, he does not cause her harm. Notwithstanding this, he commits the offence of battery (which should be charged as 'contrary to s 39 CJA 1988', *per DPP v Taylor & Little*, as he 'intentionally or recklessly applied force to the person of another' (see *R v Venna* (1975) where a person being arrested thrashed his legs about and kicked a policeman on the hand). The *actus reus* requires that the force must be unlawful and voluntary. Lord Goff in *F v West Berks Health Authority* (1989) excluded from battery 'all physical contact which is generally acceptable in the ordinary conduct of everyday life', such as the tap on the shoulder by a policeman, in *Donnelly v Jackman* (1970). But pushing people out of the way to jump the queue does not come within Lord Goff's exclusion. If the burden of lack of consent is on the prosecution (as to which there is uncertainty; Lord Lane CJ and Lord Jauncey disagree in *R v Brown*) then this will not be difficult to prove here. In battery, no actual harm need be proved: 'the least touching of another ... is battery': *Cole v Turner* (1969).

The *mens rea* of battery was discussed in *R v Venna*, the facts of which are set out above. This shows that intention or *Cunningham* actual foresight of some harm is required. As Dave intended to jump the queue he will be held to have intended the battery, as that was his purpose (*R v Moloney* (1985), 'going to Manchester', and *R v Nedrick* (1986)).

If Kate saw the battery coming, then she was also assaulted. An assault is an intentional or (by analogy with battery in *R v Venna*) reckless act which causes a victim to apprehend immediate unlawful touching of the victim's person, however slight. In both crimes, if the burden of consent is on Dave, the defendant, he will not be able to discharge his evidential burden as there is no evidence that Kate consented.

As these are crimes of basic intent, the effect of any intoxication from his inoculations would normally be disregarded, as said in *R v Lipman* (1969) and *DPP v Majewski* (1977). Thus *mens rea* would be assessed irrespective of the intoxication. But in *R v Bailey* (1983) and *R v Hardie* (1984) a distinction was made between drink and known dangerous drugs on the one hand, and medicinal drugs on the other. In the latter case, *R v Hardie*, where the defendant took valium but innocently, the test was stated as one of *Cunningham/Caldwell* actual foresight of harm. But it seems that the foresight required need not be foresight of *actus reus*, but simply of 'aggressive, unpredictable and uncontrollable conduct'. In *R v Hardie* (1984), there was no actual foresight of such harm.

If Dave has no actual foresight of such harm, he will not have *mens rea* in either the battery or assault of Kate.

Kate trips Dave

On the reasoning shown above, Kate is also guilty of battery, and, if Dave saw the battery coming, assault. But as Dave bruises his arm while he falls, she will be guilty of s 47 OAPA 1861, 'assault occasioning actual bodily harm'. 'Assault' in s 47 includes 'battery' (*DPP v Taylor, DPP v Little*). The *actus reus* is an 'assault', which causes actual bodily harm; 'occasioning' raised solely a question of causation, so said Lord Ackner in *R v Savage, R v Parmenter* (1991).

Actual bodily harm includes any hurt or injury calculated to interfere with the health or comfort of the prosecutor. In *R v Savage* (1991), the defendant threw her beer over another woman she did not like and was convicted of s 47.

The *mens rea* of s 47 is simply the *mens rea* of assault, either intention or actual foresight recklessness, so said the House of Lords in *R v Savage, R v Parmenter* (1991), approving *R v Venna* (1975), above. Here, it might well be proved that Kate was aware of the virtual certainty of causing some harm, in which case she will be held to have intended the ABH: *R v Moloney* (1985) and *R v Nedrick* (1986).

Dave punches Kate

This punch might *prima facie* fall within either ss 20 or 18 OAPA 1861. The *actus reus* of these two offences are similar, only differing unnecessarily in one particular. Each section is divided into two types of *actus reus*: wounding, and causing (s 18) or inflicting (s 20) grievous bodily harm.

Wounding requires a break in both layers of skin. Thus a rupture of blood vessels in the eye caused by an air pistol shot was insufficient in *JCC (a minor) v Eisenhower* (1983), but Dave rips her brow and lid; such breaks in the skin would be classed as wounding. In any case the ripping of the skin around the eye might well be counted as grievous bodily harm.

Grievous means 'really serious', which such an injury is. For s 18 Dave will be held to have caused the GBH. 'Inflicting' does not necessarily need an assault, but would be held to be proved here.

As to the *mens rea* of these two crimes, s 18 is a crime of specific intent to do some grievous bodily harm to any person, or with intent to resist.

'Intent' must be proved (on the lines of *R v Moloney* and *R v Nedrick*). The facts in the question do not state what his intent was, ie whether it was to cause her GBH or wound her, or whether he saw the virtual certainty of causing those injuries by his punch.

But he honestly thought (as in *DPP v Morgan* (1975)) that she was arresting him by the trip, but wrongly arresting him; he would not have had the intention to resist the arrest.

As to the *mens rea* of s 20 he must be proved to have acted intentionally, as defined in *R v Moloney* and *R v Nedrick* or 'maliciously', meaning that he actually foresaw that he might cause some personal injury (*R v Savage, R v Parmenter* approving *R v Cunningham* that only actual foresight is relevant here, and *R v Mowatt* (1967) that the foresight need only be of 'some' harm). It is not clear whether Dave will be held to have been aware of the virtual certainty of causing wounding or GBH, or merely actually foreseeing the possibility of some harm; the decision of intention or recklessness will be left to the jury who will decide from all the evidence, including their proper inferences under s 8 CJA 1967.

As regards s 20, a crime of basic intent, the effect of any intoxication from his inoculations is normally disregarded, as said in *R v Lipman* and *DPP v Majewski*, described above. But s 18 is a crime of specific intent. The cases of *R v Bailey* (1983), where a diabetic failed to take enough food after insulin, and *R v Hardie*, where the defendant took valium (but in both cases innocently) have divided the defence of intoxication into two groups; intoxication caused by alcohol and dangerous drugs, and that caused by non-dangerous drugs. In the latter circumstances the test stated is one of *Cunningham/Caldwell* actual foresight of harm. But it seems that the foresight required need not be foresight of *actus reus*, but simply of 'aggressive, unpredictable and uncontrollable conduct'. Thus only if Dave was actually aware of this tendency would he be guilty of ss 20 or 18.

Dave causing Daphne's fall and death

Dave might be charged with murder. This is the killing of a person within the Queen's peace with malice aforethought, the death falling within a year and a day of the last act causing death.

Of the *actus reus*, the timing of the death falls within the time limit (two months after the assault), but we have no evidence, and therefore will assume, that Daphne is not an enemy alien, but rather within the Queen's peace.

The issue is whether he voluntarily caused Daphne's death. His punch at Kate was voluntary; and the use he made of Kate was the same as if he had pushed a block of stone onto Daphne. In effect, Kate was a weapon. But two problems arise in the matter of causation. First, the brittle bones, an egg-shell condition. It has always been said that the tortfeasor or criminal 'takes his victim as he finds her'. Dave has no right to unlawfully cause Daphne to fall, and, if by his bad luck she has a medical condition, the loss falls of Dave, as in *R v Blaue* (1975), where the defendant was held to have killed a Jehovah's Witness, whose religion forbade her to have a blood transfusion to save herself.

The other problem as to causation of the result of death is that of whether the fall or the crash into the tree caused the fractured skull that killed her. If the fall caused her fatal fracture, then the *actus reus* is proved as the chain of causation is intact. But for Dave punching Kate so hard she would not have fallen into Daphne who would not have fallen fracturing her skull. But the problem arises that perhaps the skull was fractured by the crash alone. If this is the case, then the death was not caused by the fall; in *R v White* (1910), there was no causation of death when a mother being poisoned by a son had a heart attack quite independent of the poisoning.

A further problem arises if both the fall and the crash are contributory causes of the death. The defendant's act need not be the sole or main cause of death. The contributory behaviour of a third party will not relieve the defendant of liability. Thus in *R v Benge* (1865), a foreman whose failure to order the carrying out of safety measures while the track was up (at Staplehurst, in Kent), thereby causing a railway crash, could not argue that other employees also failed to take care. So here, it is irrelevant that the bad driving also contributed to the death, if Dave himself did.

On the other hand, if the fracture could have been treated satisfactorily if the ambulance had not negligently crashed, the question arises whether the negligent driving is a *novus actus interveniens*, which will break the chain of causation. But it will not be a *novus actus interveniens* if the defendant's original act is still 'an operating cause and a substantial cause' (*R v Smith*). Similarly, medical mistreatment will only break the chain of causation of death if the treatment was 'palpably wrong' and the original assault was no longer a threat to the victim's life, as in *R v Jordan* where the wrong drug was given to a patient recovered from his wound. But this case was distinguished in *R v Smith* where the victim was stabbed in the lungs with a bayonet stab in a barrack-room fight. Here, the victim was dropped twice off his stretcher; oxygen was given to him even though this was bad for pierced lungs; the doctors were harassed by having other victims to attend to, but the stab was the sole cause of death: similarly, the original shot in *R v Cheshire* (1991). In this case the court took a more robust stance, refusing to allow the defendants to off load their liability onto hard-pressed doctors, who, after all, were acting to preserve their victims' lives. How far a court will refuse to allow a defendant who made the original assault to off load liability onto a negligent ambulance driver is not clear. At the end of the day, the principle of *R v Benge* (1865) is the strongest, that even if the crash is partly the cause, so is Dave's punch at Kate.

The prosecution must also prove *mens rea*. This is called malice aforethought in murder.

The *mens rea* of murder is called 'malice aforethought', though it need be neither malicious nor pre-meditated. Malice aforethought is the intention to kill or cause grievous bodily harm.

There are two forms of intention. The first form is the state of mind where it is the defendant's purpose to bring about the death or grievous bodily harm. Thus if the defendant admits, or if the jury infers from all the evidence under s 8 Criminal Justice Act 1967, that he killed or caused grievous bodily harm on purpose, or deliberately, then he can be said to have intended that result. But Lord Bridge's example of a man intentionally going to Manchester, in *R v Moloney* (1985), shows also that purpose need not always coincide with desire.

The second form of intention arises where it is not the defendant's purpose to bring about that result (or so he says), but the result is something that could have been expected in the circumstances. Similarly, in *R v Moloney*, where a soldier at a family party shot his step-father's head off, and in *R v Hancock & Shankland* (1986), where some striking miners dropped a concrete block from a bridge onto a taxi passing underneath, the defendants were held to have purposefully or deliberately caused the deaths. Both cases discussed a second form of intent which the jury can infer, based on foreseeability of natural and probable consequences. In *R v Nedrick*, Lord Lane CJ explained it as the defendant's 'appreciation' that causing the *actus reus* was a 'virtual certainty' of his act or omission. Thus only if Dave deliberately intended to at least cause GBH, or was aware of that result as a virtual certainty, will he be guilty of Daphne's murder. It must be remembered that any intent to cause Kate GBH can be transferred to Daphne under the doctrine of transferred intent: *R v Latimer* (1886) and *R v Mitchell* (1983).

But as murder is a specific intent crime, in deciding whether Dave had this intention, they must take into account all the evidence (s 8 CJA 1967), including whether he actually foresaw 'aggressive, unpredictable and uncontrollable conduct' as a result of his inoculations, in determining his *mens rea*, as stated above for s 18.

If Dave is not proved to have killed Daphne with malice aforethought, then he might be convicted on involuntary manslaughter. There are three types: constructive manslaughter, reckless manslaughter, and gross (or criminal) negligence manslaughter.

The first, constructive manslaughter is committed where the defendant kills by an unlawful and obviously dangerous act. An assault would certainly constitute an 'unlawful act', for example pushing into a post office queue, knocking an old man into the elderly victim, who fell and later died (*R v Mitchell* (1983)).

Secondly, since 1981, reckless manslaughter has been recognised on the principle of *R v Caldwell* (1981), the leading case on recklessness by reasonable foresight.

Thirdly, the form called 'gross or criminal negligence' manslaughter, defined in *Andrews v DPP* (1937), as requiring a degree of negligence of a very high degree, was held to have survived *R v Caldwell* in *R v Sulman, Prentice* (1994), *Adomako* (1994), *Holloway*. Lord Taylor CJ said that it required proof of (a) a duty, (b) breach of that duty and causation of death, and (c) gross negligence which the jury considered justified a criminal conviction. Without purporting to give an exhaustive definition, he gave examples of this type of manslaughter, the relevant one here being indifference to an obvious risk of injury to health.

In manslaughter, a crime of basic intent, the effect of intoxication depends on the decision as to whether Dave actually foresaw 'aggressive, unpredictable and uncontrollable conduct' (*R v Bailey* (1983), *R v Hardie* (1984)) as mentioned above.

To conclude on these crimes of killing, therefore, he will probably not be found to have acted with malice aforethought, but will be held to have committed constructive manslaughter. If he has no actual foresight of aggressive etc behaviour arising from his inoculations, he will be acquitted of that. As he is not convicted of murder, he cannot use the defence of provocation under s 3 Homicide Act 1957, where his behave is assessed by a standard of a reasonable man with any permanent characteristic of which he is sensitive (*DPP v Camplin* (1978), the chapati-pan killing).

Kate falling into Daphne

The prosecution must prove that Kate voluntarily committed an *actus reus* of whatever crime she is charged with. If they cannot prove this, then *actus reus* is not proved. In *R v Mitchell*, where the defendant pushed into a post office queue, knocking X into Y, X could not be said to have voluntarily knocked Y down. As Kate does not voluntarily push into Daphne, but is pushed into her, she cannot be held to have committed any *actus reus*. If there is no *actus reus*, no crime is committed: *R v Deller* (1952), where a defendant told the truth that his car was free from encumbrances, and could not therefore be held to have misrepresented the car.

Question 34

Susan and Stephen married in 1975. In 1993 Stephen was diagnosed as having cancer. It was mutually agreed that Susan would nurse him and administer his drug, but, as they both believed in voluntary euthanasia, Susan reassured Stephen that if his illness became too painful for either of them she would humanely bring a close to his life. When that moment came, in 1994, Susan found, when her agreed promise came to be fulfilled, that she could not kill Stephen, even after three attempts, or even assist in his suicide. Her anxiety rose to such a pitch that she suddenly left one Sunday after watching his troubled body for the whole weekend. Susan returned a month later to find Stephen dead as a result. It was found later by the coroner that Stephen's death was a result of not being fed and administered his drugs.

The Criminal Law

The following day, before notifying the police, she visited her own doctor, who found her to be in a state of anxiety so intense that she probably only thought of her own position when she left, and not of Stephen's plight, either his illness or the effect of her absence on it.

What criminal liability, if any, is there on Susan?

General approach

This question, for which 35 to 45 minutes would be allowed, covers two of the inchoate offences (incitement and conspiracy; murder and manslaughter), and the defences of insanity (diminished responsibility and provocation).

Where several parties are concerned, you should also discuss secondary parties, but your discussion here would be brief given that one party is in fact a victim. On a question like this, refer briefly to the English position on euthanasia.

Where events and circumstances occur in sequence, it is best to take the facts slowly and in the order given, crime by crime or defence by defence. In all crimes, establish the *actus reus* first and then the *mens rea*: virtually all crimes have both. If a defence applies particularly to one crime, say diminished responsibility to murder, deal with it straight after the crime. If an offence crops up twice, refer the examiner back to your previous explanation of law in that essay (but never cross-refer between questions; different questions may be split up between different markers).

Answer plan

- Susan's promise; suggestion and agreement; incitement, conspiracy
- *actus reus* of murder and manslaughter; causation
- *mens rea* of murder
- involuntary manslaughter
- voluntary manslaughter and the effect of anxiety; insanity; diminished responsibility; provocation?
- English attitude to euthanasia; *Ayredale v Bland*; consent, *R v Brown*

Answer

This question covers two of the inchoate offences (incitement and conspiracy; murder and manslaughter) and the defences of insanity (diminished responsibility and provocation). In each offence the prosecution must prove beyond reasonable doubt that the accused, or defendant, voluntary caused the *actus reus* of the offence having at that time the required *mens rea*.

In the case of the defences the defendant has the evidential burden of showing, on balance, that he has the defence, whereon the prosecution has the probative burden of disproving that defence beyond reasonable doubt.

Even though the two parties have been supporters of euthanasia for some time, the common law places the killing here in the crimes of murder or manslaughter. The criminal law will firstly look for the person who suggests the crime to another, that is to say incites the other to commit it, and secondly for the several parties to any agreement to follow a course of conduct which brings about the result of unlawful death, that is to say a conspiracy.

We are not told who incited the other here, but if Susan made the initial suggestion then she cannot have incited Stephen to commit any crime, as it was not envisaged that he would commit any; the killing was to be carried out by Stephen. In *R v Curr* (1967), where the person alleged to have been incited (the women with the family allowance books who thought the plan was all legal), the lack of that person's *mens rea* meant that the accused did not incite.

Conspiracy is an agreement to follow a 'course of conduct' which, along with envisaged circumstances and results, will necessarily cause a crime to be committed (s 1 Criminal Law Act 1977). But a conspiracy solely consisting of husband and wife is not a conspiracy according to the Act, nor can an intended victim be a conspirator (*R v Tyrell* (1894)).

Susan might be charged with murder. This is 'the killing of a person within the Queen's peace with malice aforethought, the death falling within a year and a day of the last act causing death'. If any part of the *actus reus* cannot be proved, then an acquittal must ensue, as in *R v Deller* for the unwittingly truthful statement about the car, or in *R v White* where the victim of poisoning in fact died from an independent heart attack.

Of the *actus reus*, the timing of Stephen's death falls within the time-limit, but we have no evidence and, therefore, will assume that Stephen is not an enemy alien, but rather within the Queen's peace. The issue is whether Susan voluntarily caused Stephen's death by omission, which is an acceptable form of *actus reus* where there is a duty or 'responsibility' to remove a danger created by the defendant, as in *R v Miller*, where a tramp who set fire to a mattress in his sleep was held guilty for his failure, when he awoke, to remove the danger he had created by extinguishing the fire.

Examples in the crimes being discussed are *R v Stone & Dobinson*, where the accused left without medical treatment a sister of one of them, who subsequently died from that lack of help, and *R v Gibbins & Proctor* (1918) where a daughter of one of the accused died of starvation through the defendants' failure to feed her. Causation of Stephen's death by Susan's failure to feed and treat Stephen is therefore proved; thus the *actus reus* of both murder and manslaughter is proved.

The prosecution must also prove Susan's *mens rea*. The *mens rea* of murder is called 'malice aforethought', though it need be neither malicious nor pre-meditated. Malice aforethought is the intention to kill or cause grievous bodily harm.

There are two forms of intention. The first form is the state of mind where it is the defendant's purpose to bring about the death or grievous bodily harm. Thus if the defendant admits, or if the jury infers from all the evidence under s 8 Criminal Justice Act 1967, that he killed or caused grievous bodily harm on purpose, or deliberately, then he can be said to have intended that result. But Lord Bridge's example of a man intentionally going to Manchester, in *R v Moloney* (1985), shows also that Susan's purpose need not always coincide with her desire.

The second form of intention arises where it is not the defendant's purpose to bring about that result (or so she says), but the result is something that could have been expected in the circumstances. Neither in *R v Moloney* where a soldier at a family party shot his step-father's head off, and in *R v Hancock & Shankland* (1986), where some striking miners dropped a concrete block from a bridge onto a taxi passing underneath, did the defendants purposefully or deliberately cause the deaths.

Both cases discussed a second form of intent which the jury can infer based on foreseeability of natural and probable consequences. In *R v Nedrick* (1986), Lord Lane CJ explained it as the defendant's 'appreciation' that causing the *actus reus* was a 'virtual certainty' of his act or omission. In *R v Gibbins & Proctor*, the jury held that malice aforethought existed. Susan had promised to kill Stephen, but leaves, causing his death. Thus it was her purpose to kill him, but not by these means, and her leaving was because she could not face killing him. As her *mens rea* must coincide with her *actus reus* it is only if she has that purpose while she is away that she will be held to have intended the death. The other form of intention requires her awareness of the virtual certainty of the grievous bodily harm or death as a result of her failures. In view of her anxiety she may not have been aware of this. However, the existence of her intention of either type is a question for the jury on all the evidence under s 8 CJA 1967.

If Susan is not proved to have killed Stephen with malice aforethought, then she might be convicted of involuntary manslaughter. There are three types: constructive manslaughter (which is not relevant here), reckless manslaughter, and gross (or criminal) negligence manslaughter.

Since 1981, reckless manslaughter has been recognised on the principle of *R v Caldwell* (1981), the leading case on recklessness by reasonable foresight. In *R v Seymour* (1983), a motor manslaughter case of intending to frighten a former girlfriend but misjudging and crushing her with a lorry, there was a conviction of this type of involuntary manslaughter. It might be decided by a jury that Lord Diplock's test in that case, based on the existence of an obvious risk, and reasonable foresight of some harm by her leaving, is enough to obtain Susan's conviction.

But the form called gross or criminal negligence manslaughter, defined in *Andrews v DPP*, as requiring a degree of negligence of a very high degree, and which was held to have survived (*R v Caldwell* in *R v Sulman, Prentice* (1994), *Adomako* (1994), *Holloway* are probably the most relevant here). Lord Taylor

CJ said that it required proof of (a) a duty, (b) breach of that duty and causation of death, and (c) gross negligence which the jury considered justified a criminal conviction. Without purporting to give an exhaustive definition, he gave examples of this type of manslaughter, the relevant one here being indifference to an obvious risk of injury to health, as had been the form applied in *R v Stone & Dobinson* (1977), above.

Susan's anxiety might be used on which to base the defence of insanity or that of diminished responsibility. Insanity is a defence still governed by common law rules, called the '*McNaghten* rules', formed in 1843. By these rules everyone is presumed sane but can be proved to be insane if there is a 'defect of reason caused' by a 'disease of the mind' which results in the defendant not knowing what she is doing or not knowing that it was legally wrong. It might well be proved here that either of the two final clauses in this test could apply to Susan. It would then have to be proved that her reason was defective and caused by a disease of the mind.

'Defect of reason' means that the powers of reasoning must be impaired, and not as in *R v Clarke* where the old woman did not pay for some items, but put them in her own bag, simply in a state of confusion or absent-mindedness. And disease of the mind, as explained in *R v Quick* (1973), means a malfunctioning of the mind caused by some internal factor. In *R v Burgess* stress caused by a woman's rejection was held to be an internal factor, and therefore insanity, though in the same case a propensity to the disease manifesting itself in violence was said to be part of the definition. Here, the anxiety caused by having to kill a loved one might be said, as in *R v Burgess* (1991), to be an internal factor as being part of Susan's internal make-up, but it is not likely to result in violence; the facts show that it manifests itself rather in a reluctance to act. Thus it may not be held to be insanity.

However, whether she does not think about the effects of what she is doing, which would fit within the *McNaghten* rules, or does but does not think that it is legally wrong, is not stated in the question, so a final decision on this defence is not possible here. If, on the other hand, she is found to be insane on account of *R v Burgess*, the verdict would be 'not guilty by reason of insanity', against which Susan would have a right of appeal.

Quite apart from this defence, and the forms of involuntary manslaughter discussed above, there is the form called 'voluntary manslaughter', consisting of the *actus reus* with malice aforethought, but with a special defence, only available to murder, and resulting in a conviction of manslaughter. One form of this is voluntary manslaughter under s 2 Homicide Act 1957, under which the defendant must be proved to be suffering from an 'abnormality of mind' which 'substantially impaired [the defendant's] mental responsibility'. In *R v Byrne* (1960) the defendant suffered from violent perverted sexual desires which 'he finds difficult or impossible to control', and who killed and mutilated a woman. It was said that difficulty in exercising will-power to control physical actions should be assessed in a 'broad common-sense way'. This would so far cover Susan's position, but s 2 states that the abnormality of mind must arise from a condition of arrested or retarded development of mind or any inherent causes or induced by disease or injury, but persons with chronic anxiety states have been allowed into the defence such as the defendant wife in *R v Ahluwalia* who had suffered her husband's violence and degradation for a long time. As with insanity, the evidential burden of proof of the defence is on the defendant on balance of probabilities. It is likely therefore that Susan will be able to rely on the defence of diminished responsibility under s 2.

One other defence that Susan might have thought to try is 'provocation', under s 3 Homicide Act 1957, where her behaviour is assessed by a standard of a reasonable man with any permanent characteristic of which he is sensitive (*DPP v Camplin*, the 'chapati-pan killing'). Like s 2 this is a defence only to murder and results in a conviction of manslaughter. Susan might argue that the situation of extreme anxiety has provoked her into leaving, and that it is no reason to refuse the defence that the defendant brought the situation onto herself. In *R v Johnson*, the defendant was the person who made the initial threat of violence which started a sequence of quick events which led to his killing a victim. However, it is unlikely that this defence will hold, as a result of recent decisions. In *R v Thornton* (1992) and *R v Ahluwalia* (1993), where in both cases a wife had endured a history of domestic violence, the defence failed as s 3 requires a sudden, spontaneous violent act by the defendant, not a slow thought-out killing. It is likely that the latter is how the jury will view Susan's thoughts and behaviour during the time she is away, rather than a sudden eruption, and, as in the two cases mentioned, the defence will fail.

Finally, it is worth noting the House of Lords' decision in *Ayredale NHS Trust v Bland* (1993), where they gave permission for Tony Bland, in a persistent vegetative state since being crushed in the Hillsborough football disaster, to be allowed to die by having his anti-biotics withdrawn, thereby allowing illness to kill him. The House however made the point that euthanasia, whether on the Dutch model (which was based on a lax attitude to the criminal law) or not, is not a part of English law; and, as the House in *R v Brown* held that consent to sado-masochistic behaviour was void as against public policy, it is likely that an allegation of a victim's consent to his murder will similarly be void, no matter how much evidence there was for it.

Question 35

In a crowded public house Henry accidentally slips on Paul's foot. Paul responds angrily and, in his rage, slips and falls, pulling a table and five full pints of beer all over himself. In a sense of humiliation, Paul leaves and continues drinking in a nearby public house, where he brings his total for the day to 11 pints of beer. He leaves at 10.40 pm and goes to Hui Chi-ming's Flower Garden Take-Away, still with his shirt soaking wet. While he is waiting for his 'sweet and sour' in walks Henry and his pal, Seamus. Henry sees Paul and points at Paul, shouting out that Paul now had more beer on his person than in his person. Henry, Seamus, the cooks and others in the queue all laugh at this. Paul then grabs a bottle half full of 5p coins for charity from the counter. He lurches towards Henry, saying, 'I'll shut your bloody laughing for you'. Henry leaves quickly and runs into the road outside to escape. Paul throws the bottle, heavy with 5p coins. It hits Linda at a bus-stop over the road, killing her. Henry is caught in the traffic and killed by a passing lorry.

(a) In a prosecution of Paul for Henry's murder:
   (i) did Paul cause Henry's death?
   (ii) would Paul have a defence of provocation?
   (iii) would Paul have a defence of intoxication?
   (iv) who has the burden of proof in (ii) and (iii)?

(b) In a prosecution of Paul for Linda's murder:
   (i) how would Paul's *mens rea* be proved?
   (ii) would Paul have a defence of provocation?

(c) If Paul is arrested could he obtain legal advice?

(d) If the prosecution can only secure a conviction of manslaughter, on what principles would his sentence be decided and with what aims in mind?

General approach

This is a 'normal' criminal law problem, but with a difference that helps the student. Here the questions are itemised; the question does not simply ask, 'What is Paul's liability?' The student is relieved of the problem of working out an order to the answer and of ensuring that he or she keeps to it.

Note, however, that an element of police procedure is included at question (c). The topic is dealt with in Part 4 on Civil Liberties in *Lecture Notes on 'A' Level Law Paper II* (Cavendish Publishing, 1995).

Answer plan

This question is planned out for you, but, as always, use cases in support of your arguments and stick to the question. If the question asks for *mens rea*, do not include *actus reus*, and *vice versa*; and if a question requires discussion of a defence, keep to that, and do not also prove the *actus reus* and *mens rea*.

Answer

(a) In a prosecution of Paul for Henry's murder:

(i) did Paul cause Henry's death?

The prosecution must always prove an *actus reus*. It normally consists of conduct, plus consequences, plus circumstances. The *actus reus* of murder, according to Coke CJ, is the killing of a person within the Queen's peace, the death falling within a year and a day of the last act causing death. A complete *actus reus* must be proved. In *R v Deller* (1952) the defendant made a true statement about a car, but unwittingly; his intention to lie did not alter the fact that there was in fact no fraud and therefore no actus *reus* of fraud.

The *actus reus* must also be voluntary, ie willed by the defendant, as in *R v Mitchell* (1983) where a person was shoved by the defendant into an old lady, who died. That person's fall into the victim was involuntary and therefore she could not have been prosecuted. Further, causation of the killing by the defendant's voluntary act must be proved. In *R v White* (1910) the old lady died as a result of an independent heart attack, not from the defendant's poison; thus no causation was proved.

The defendant must be 'of sound memory', not able to plead the defences of insanity and diminished responsibility, and 'of the age of discretion', and not able to plead the defence of infancy. These points seem to be satisfied here.

The defendant must be proved to have caused the death or, more properly, accelerated it. The problem here is that Paul does not personally kill Henry, but frightens him into the road. But the fright of the victim can form part of the chain of causation. In *R v Towers* (1874) the baby went black in the face and died because the girl holding it screamed and, in *R v Hayward* (1908), a wife who jumped out of a window to escape her husband was held to have been killed by him.

The defendant's act need not be the sole or main cause of death. There might be a contribution by someone else, as in *R v Benge* (1865), where the foreman and others were all causes of the train crash. But the question here is whether the lorry's killing of

Henry was a *novus actus interveniens*, a 'new intervening act', to break the chain of causation. It will not be a *novus actus interveniens* if the defendant's original act is still 'an operating cause and a substantial cause' (*R v Smith*, where the victim was stabbed in the lungs with a bayonet stab in a barrack-room fight; and *R v Cheshire* (1991), where the wounds were still 'an operating cause and a substantial cause' of the death despite the new acts (medical treatment) of third parties).

In discussing the effect of a *novus actus* the question also arises as to whether the victim's unreasonable behaviour breaks the chain of causation. In *R v Holland* (1841), a defendant refused treatment, namely amputation of a gangrenous finger, but this was held to be reasonable, and not *interveniens*. Further, if the defendant's original act, is not an 'operating cause', but causes a foreseeable natural consequence (running across the road in fright) which causes the death, there will be no intervention. In *R v Pagett*, a defendant who held his girlfriend in front of him and shot at police was liable for their shooting back, killing her.

Here, therefore, it is likely that causation will be proved.

(ii) would Paul have a defence of provocation?

Section 3 Homicide Act 1957 deals with what provocation is, and allots that issue to the jury; but the effect of a finding of provocation is dealt with by the common law. It is a defence only to murder, and results in a verdict of conviction of manslaughter. The provocation can be by things done or by things said or by both together.

The two main issues are: firstly, was the defendant provoked into losing his self-control? (this is a subjective question); secondly, was the provocation enough to make a reasonable man do as he did? (this is an objective question).

Both questions are decided by the jury. On the first point, the defence protects provoked, impulsive retaliation, not carefully planned revenge. Relevant therefore are the nature of the provocative act, the sensitivity or phlegmatism of the defendant, the time elapsed between the act and the killing. The time elapsed has defeated many pleas; there must be a sudden and temporary loss of self-control (*R v Duffy* (1949)). In *R v Ibrams* (1981) the defendant took several days to kill after the so-called provocation, and in the battered wives' cases of *R v Thornton* (1992) and *R v Ahluwalia* (1993) the pleas failed; they had waited too long. Paul has responded fairly quickly, but he did have time to consider as he went to another pub.

The second point involves two questions: would the reasonable man have reacted at all?; and would the reasonable man have reacted in this way? By s 3 words or laughter can amount to a provocation, and the decision as to whether the reasonable man would have reacted at all is measured by the standard set in *DPP v Camplin* (1978), where a 15 year old boy was buggered and laughed at. He killed his attacker with a chapati pan.

This was the reasonable man, a person having the power of self-control as can be expected of an ordinary person of the sex and age of the accused, but having the accused's sensitive characteristics, say the defendant's big nose, or his impotency. In *R v Newell* (1980) such a characteristic was required to be permanent.

The relationship between the provocation and the mode of retaliation, throwing a coin bottle at the provoker, is covered by s 3: the decision of whether the response is reasonable is left to the jury. It may be said that as Paul commits the first act accompanied by *mens rea*, he induced the provocation in the 'take-away', but since *R v Johnson* (1989) this would not defeat his defence.

Paul would be able to use this defence if the jury decided that he did not respond too late, and if throwing the bottle was a reasonable response.

(iii) would Paul have a defence of intoxication?

This defence mainly concerns the influence of drink; drugs are now included but that does not concern us here. There is no automatic defence of intoxication. The sole issue is whether the intoxication prevented the defendant from forming *mens rea* or not; evidence of intoxication is only relevant to prove the presence or absence of *mens rea* (according to Lord Birkenhead LC in *DPP v Beard* and confirmed *DPP v Majewski* (1976)). The burden is, as usual, on the prosecution to prove *mens rea*.

This principle only applies to crimes of specific intent, which includes murder, the charge here. If, however, Paul drinks the beer in the second pub to give himself 'Dutch courage' to kill Henry if he sees him again that night, then the defence will not be available at all (*AG for Northern Ireland v Gallagher* (1961)).

The final consideration concerns the coincidence of intoxication and provocation. Intoxication can affect the defendant's perception of being provoked, and his retaliation. On the defendant's heightened perception of being provoked, the case of *R v O'Grady* (1987) said that his drunkenness would rule out his pleaded defence of self-defence, and, in *R v Wardrope*, the judge restricted the effect of whether he was provoked to that of 'a reasonable man, not a drunken man', while assessing the retaliation as if the mistaken facts were true.

Probably, then, Paul's drunkenness would deny him the use of the defence of provocation if a sober man would not have responded as Paul did.

(iv) who has the burden of proof in (ii) and (iii)?

In defences such as provocation, the evidential burden is on the defendant to show on balance of probabilities evidence which *prima facie* establish the defence. If that succeeds, the probative burden is then on the prosecution to prove beyond reasonable doubt that the defence does not apply.

In the 'defence' of intoxication in (iii), above, the burden of proof is on the prosecution throughout to prove *mens rea* beyond reasonable doubt, in accordance with *Woolmington v DPP* (1935), where the trial judge erred in directing the jury that if the prosecution could prove causation the defendant had to prove lack of fault. This was wrong; the burden is on the prosecution both as to proof of *actus reus* and of *mens rea*.

(b) In a prosecution of Paul for Linda's murder:

i) how would Paul's mens rea be proved?

The *mens rea* of murder is called 'malice aforethought', though it need be neither malicious nor pre-meditated. Malice aforethought is the intention to kill or cause grievous bodily harm.

There are two forms of intention. The first form is the state of mind ie whether it is the defendant's purpose to bring about the death or grievous bodily harm. Thus if the defendant admits, or if the jury infers from all the evidence under s 8 Criminal Justice Act 1967, that he killed or caused grievous bodily harm on purpose, or deliberately, then he can be said to have intended that result. But Lord Bridge's example of a man intentionally going to Manchester, in *R v Moloney*, shows also that purpose need not always coincide with desire. Paul does not deliberately kill Linda, it is not his purpose to do so; his purpose, and therefore his intention, is to kill Henry. But under the doctrine of transferred intent, the intention to kill one person can be transferred to the person actually killed (*R v Latimer* (1886) and *R v Mitchell* (1983), where the battery against one person in a post office queue was transferred to his actual victim). Thus the purposive intention to kill Henry will apply to the killing of Linda.

If (which is unlikely) that form of intention is not proved, there is a second form of intention, which arises where it is not the defendant's purpose to bring about that result (or so he says), but the result is something that could have been expected in the circumstances. The cases of *R v Moloney*, where a soldier shot his step-father's head off, and *R v Hancock & Shankland* (1986), where some striking miners killed a taxi-driver with a concrete block, were re-interpreted in *R v Nedrick* (1986), where the defendant caused death by pouring petrol through the victim's letter-box. There, Lord Lane CJ refined this second definition of 'intention'. He explained it as the defendant's 'appreciation' that causing the *actus reus* was a 'virtual certainty' of his act or omission. This form would have been difficult to establish here, as his throwing the coin bottle would not have been certain to cause at least grievous bodily harm to Linda.

Thus Paul's intention to cause grievous bodily harm, if not death, can be proved, in its 'purpose' form and transferred to Linda under *R v Latimer* and *R v Mitchell*.

ii) would Paul have a defence of provocation?

The principles of this defence, available under s 3 Homicide Act 1957 are set out above at (a)(ii), and would apply here. At common law provocation was limited to that by the deceased, towards the defendant, but s 3 has removed both barriers.

Moreover, at common law, even if the defendant's retaliation was aimed at a third party (Henry here), but missed and killed another victim (Linda here), the defence was available on the defendant's charge of murdering the victim. In *R v Gross* the defendant was provoked by her husband's blows. She shot at him, missed, and killed someone else, but was able to use the defence. It is likely that the same principle would apply here, where the provocation comes from Henry, and Linda is the actual victim.

Paul would also be able to use this defence here if the jury decided that he did not respond too late, and if throwing the bottle was a reasonable response.

(c) If Paul is arrested could he obtain legal advice?

Treatment of a suspect while in police custody is dealt with by the Police and Criminal Evidence Act 1984 and various codes of practice. By s 116, murder is classed as a 'serious arrestable offence'.

An arrested person in police custody has a right to contact a solicitor 'if [the arrested person] so requests' (s 58; s 56 contains a similar right to contact a friend or relative). The solicitor contacted may well be the duty solicitor, a solicitor available for such consultation throughout the day and night. The arrested person must be informed of this right. But a police superintendent can delay it for 36 hours in the case of a 'serious arrestable offence' where he reasonably thinks that allowing it 'will' cause interference with evidence or persons, or lead to other suspects being alerted, or hinder the recovery of property. Murder is, by s 116, a serious arrestable offence. In *R v Samuel* (1988), access to a solicitor was refused on the ground that he might inform, albeit unwittingly, an accomplice. The conviction was quashed on appeal; s 58 says that the risk must be that the solicitor 'will' inform someone. The Court of Appeal thought it unlikely that an experienced solicitor would be hoodwinked by a 24 year old into passing a message on. Section 58 only refers to police custody, but in *R v Chief Constable of South Wales ex parte Merrick* (1994) a common law right to a solicitor was confirmed to exist.

(d) **If the prosecution can only secure a conviction of manslaughter, on what principles would his sentence be decided and with what aims in mind?**

On a conviction of manslaughter the court has the whole range of sentences available, from absolute discharge at the lower end to imprisonment, even for life, at the higher end. Probation is often a fair sentence where the defendant killed under diminished responsibility (under s 2 Homicide Act 1957) a relative who is in pain from a serious and terminal disease. After all, in these circumstances, the defendant is not violent or dangerous, nor will he kill again.

In *R v Sargeant* (1974), Lawton LJ in the Court of Appeal said that all sentences should follow the four classic aims of sentencing. These were: punishment (or retribution or revenge); protection, especially of the public; deterrence, both of the defendant and of others; and reform and rehabilitation of the offender.

Question 36

Alex, Bob and Clare read the *Devon Informer*, which at the moment is highlighting the fear of attack of pensioners as they leave the post office having just drawn the weekly pension. Alex, Bob and Clare all think that stealing from these pensioners would be justifiable, because, as students, their grants have been cut to pay those pensions. In any case, they all agree that this crime, if done without personal harm, would not be a real crime, just a redistribution of government wealth. They finish by agreeing to have a try at it some day. Alex goes on a field trip the next day, but Bob and Clare decide to go to a post office in another village, 15 miles away, to see how 'it could be done', and perhaps have a try.

They get there and watch for half an hour until Bob notices an old man with a stick walk away with his bank notes still in his other hand. Bob says to Clare, 'That one', and follows the old man. Bob tells Clare to move away as they might be remembered as being together just before the snatch. Clare says she will occupy the telephone box around the corner to prevent anyone from telephoning for the police. She goes out of sight of Bob. Someone gives the old man a lift in a car, but Bob pulls the handbag of the next woman who comes out of the post office. The woman is thrown off balance by Bob's violent pull, and falls, breaking a finger. Bob is now frightened and runs off without the handbag, which was in any case empty as the woman had forgotten her pension book.

What is the criminal liability, if any, of Alex, Bob and Clare respectively?

General approach

This question, for which 35-45 minutes would be allowed, covers minor assaults, theft (especially the appropriation element of the *actus reus*), and its aggravated form, robbery.

Also, because there is a discussion followed by a frustrated attempt, the three inchoate offences, incitement, conspiracy and attempts, and moreover the liability of a secondary party (Clare, to Bob's offences) need to be dealt with. As is normally the case with problem questions, the best way to tackle this question is to work through it in the order of the incidents that appear in it.

Answer plan

- introduction: to all three
- incitement
- conspiracy; Criminal Law Act 1977
- specifically Bob: theft (s 1 Theft Act 1968); especially appropriation (*R v Gomez, Corcoran v Anderton*); robbery (s 8 Theft Act 1968); attempted theft (Criminal Attempts Act 1981); empty bag; impossibility (*R v Shivpuri*); battery or s 47 OAPA 1861
- specifically Clare: parties; Clare as secondary party to Bob's crimes; s 8 Accessories and Abettors Act 1861; aiding and abetting
- specifically Alex: parties; counselling?

Answer

This question covers minor assaults, theft (especially the appropriation element of the *actus reus*), and its aggravated form, robbery, the three inchoate offences, incitement, conspiracy and attempts, and the liability of a secondary party (Clare, to Bob's offences).

In all crimes the prosecution would have the burden of proving both *actus reus* and *mens rea* of each crime, as said in *Woolmington v DPP* (1935), where the trial judge had wrongly imposed the burden as to *mens rea* onto the defendant.

The first two possible crimes occur at the time of the initial discussion. It is not clear who first suggested to the others that they all committed the crime of theft of the pension moneys, but that person would have committed the inchoate offence of incitement to commit theft. This will be so if that person is aware of the incited person's *mens rea* and capacity to commit the crime. In *R v Hollinshead* (1985) the incitee did not have the capacity to commit the incest crime she was being persuaded to commit, and in *R v Curr* (1967) the women being persuaded to take part in the family allowance fraud did not have *mens rea* as they thought it legal. Here, these problems do not arise; all three have capacity to commit theft and are aware of the others' *mens rea*.

The second inchoate offence is statutory conspiracy under the Criminal Law Act 1977, where each agrees to a 'course of conduct' which would result in a crime. 'Course of conduct' takes in agreed results and circumstances. It is said that Alex does not go to the post office the next day, but the agreement is the *actus reus*. It is essential that Alex intended that the conspiracy be carried out (*Yip Chiu-Cheung v R* (1994)), but not necessarily to take part (*R v Siracusa*). On the other hand Alex must be proved to have had the intention to conspire, not simply the intention to steal (as indeed must all three) (*R v Siracusa* (1989)). Thus all three will be guilty of conspiracy to steal; this guilt is not dependent upon the theft actually occurring.

The third inchoate offence arises, not at the time of discussion, but later, and will be dealt with there.

The next possible offence is theft of the handbag under s 1 Theft Act 1968. Section 1 says 'A person who dishonestly appropriates property belonging to another with the intention of permanently depriving the other of it' commits theft. Sections 2-6 partly define each word or phrase in s 1.

The *actus reus* is satisfied with regard to 'property', which the handbag, as goods, is (and any money would have been); and with regard to 'belonging to another', which the bag does, as it is the woman's property. The main question in connection with *actus reus* is whether, in view of Bob's failure to carry it away, Bob does in fact appropriate it. Section 3 says that this means 'an assumption of any of the rights of an owner'. The House of Lords has clarified that appropriation can take place with the victim's consent (*R v Gomez* (1993), confirming *Lawrence v MPC* (1971), and disapproving on this point *R v Morris* (1983)), but clearly there is no issue of consent here; the woman clearly does not consent to the handbag being taken from her here. In *Corcoran v Anderton* (1980), on similar facts, the tug on the bag was held to be an appropriation, even though, as here, the thief ran off without it. In *R v Gomez* it was confirmed that the assumption can be of 'any' one of the rights of an owner, such as grabbing it. Thus *actus reus* of theft by Bob would be proved. (It is the lack of committing the *actus* while watching the old man which prevents theft existing at this time, despite the presence of *mens rea*. In *R v Deller* (1952), an unwitting statement of truth resulted in the lack of *mens rea* and accordingly a failure by the prosecution to prove the crime.)

With regard to *mens rea*, firstly as to Bob's 'dishonesty', and noting the sense of moral justification felt by all three, the case of *R v Ghosh* (1982) (actually on s 15, but on the same word) would be relevant. Lord Lane CJ for the whole Court of Appeal in this case said that in these cases of 'Robin Hood, or ardent anti-vivisectionists' who believe justified in their acts, the jury should be directed on two tests. Firstly, was it dishonest by the ordinary standards of the ordinary man? If so, was the defendant aware that by those standards it was dishonest? If the answer is yes, the defendant was dishonest. The decisions are for the jury.

Here, the question leans towards Bob's awareness of this; his furtiveness is indicative, and his co-actor is conscious that people may wish to call the police. The jury cannot convict on a reasonable test only, but they would almost certainly disbelieve Bob if he pleaded that he was not aware of others' ordinary standards.

The other part of the *mens rea* of theft is that Bob intended to 'permanently' deprive the other of it. This is possibly not satisfied as to the handbag, which he probably intended to throw away. On the other hand if he did so more than a hundred yards or so from the woman he might well be aware of the virtual certainty that she would be deprived of it (*R v Moloney* and *R v Nedrick*), thus proving this specific intent.

Thus there is, if the last mentioned *mens rea* can be proved, a theft of the bag. But if it cannot be proved, and there is no theft of any money (because there is none in the bag), then a prosecution under s 1 Criminal Attempts Act 1981 might be considered. Section 1 says that taking steps 'with intent to commit the crime ... which are more than merely preparatory' to committing the crime, commits an attempt to commit it, even if committing would have been impossible. Thus here, where the 'dishonesty' *mens rea* of s 1, above, applies equally (as set out in *R v Ghosh* (1982)), and there was an intention to permanently deprive the woman of any money, it could be said that the tug was an attempt at stealing the money Bob thought was in the bag.

A conviction here will not be defeated by the theft of money being impossible (by there being none). In *R v Shivpuri* (1986) a man was convicted of attempted smuggling when he thought the snuff he was 'smuggling' into the country was cannabis. Because it was not a drug, he was attempting the impossible, as is Bob, but Shivpuri was convicted of attempting the smuggling. Bob would therefore be convicted of attempted theft.

Two other crimes need consideration arising out of the grab and tug of the bag. Under s 8 Theft Act 1968 a theft by violence at or before the theft is robbery. As there may be no theft of the bag, so there may not be a robbery of the bag; but as there is an attempted theft of money, so there is an attempted robbery of the money. The facts of *Corcoran v Anderton*, above, similar to these, resulted in a robbery. Even a tug would constitute violence, even more so throwing the woman to the ground. Secondly, irrespective of there being a property crime, the violent tug and throwing to the ground of this woman would be both a battery, contrary to s 39 Criminal Justice Act 1988, and s 47 Offences Against the Person Act 1861 ('OAPA') ie 'an assault occasioning actual bodily harm'. 'Assault' here includes 'battery' (*DPP v*

Taylor & Little (1859)), and a broken finger would constitute actual bodily harm. The *mens rea* of both these crimes is intention to batter or *Cunningham* recklessness, the latter being actual foresight of some harm (*R v Savage; R v Parmenter*).

Having discussed Bob's liability, we now turn to Clare's liability as a secondary party to Bob's crimes, which he commits as principal. It will be recalled that Clare had gone to the telephone box and out of sight by the time Bob committed his crimes. Liability as a secondary party is dependent on a crime being committed (though as in *R v Bourne* (1952) and *R v Cogan & Leak* (1975), the dog buggery and sexual intercourse cases, no principal need be convicted, for a conviction of a person as secondary party). We have seen that attempted theft of money and possibly theft of a bag, and either battery or s 47 OAPA have been committed by Bob. The conduct which will secure liability is 'aiding, abetting, counselling and procuring' an offence (s 8 Accessories and Abettors Act 1861). The *mens rea* is the intention to aid etc, the knowledge that her conduct would aid etc, and the knowledge that the aiding etc would assist in either a specific crime (that is to say, a crime on a specific person, or a crime of a certain type: *Lynch v DPP* and *DPP v Maxwell* (1979)).

Clare's conduct would amounting to abetting the attempted theft of the money and the theft of the bag (if the specific intent is proved to exist). This is the type of crime she had agreed to and knew Bob would commit, as in *R v Bainbridge* (1960), where the secondary party knew that his torch would be required for a crime involving breaking into premises and disposing of stolen property. The particular bank in that case need not be known, and here the particular victim need not be known. Clare will be guilty as secondary party to the Theft Act offences. She would know that her presence would encourage Bob (as in *R v Coney* (1882), attending a boxing match). She is also aiding by taking steps to impede the calling of a policeman (which is a crime in itself under s 4 CJA 1967). Nor can she say that she had withdrawn from the venture by going round the corner. Withdrawal requires notice to the other parties and neutralising of the venture (not simply jumping through a window to escape: *R v Becerra* (1976)). This was part of the plan.

But the facts indicate that all discussion and understanding was to a property crime, and not to an offence against the person. Clare did not know that the battery or s 47 OAPA 1861 would be committed and will not be guilty of them. This principle of lack of awareness of the principal's intention or recklessness (which convicted the defendants in *R v Hyde* (1991) and *Hui Chi-ming v R* (1992)), will result in her acquittal as secondary party to the battery and s 47.

The final point is whether Alex can also be a secondary party to the Theft Act crimes. By intentionally counselling Bob as to a particular type of crime he would satisfy s 8 Accessories and Abettors Act 1861. In *DPP v Maxwell* (1979) it was said to be enough to convict, that the defendant had agreed to the commission of a particular type of crime, but had left the principal to decide when and where. On this basis, Alex would be convicted as secondary party to the Theft Act offence.

Question 37

The test for insanity in criminal law was set in 1843. Should it be up-dated?

General approach

This is a straight forward essay on the *McNaghten* rules (about 35 minutes would be allowed). You would need to first establish what the rules say, followed by your critique. Your exposition stating what the law is can simply follow your knowledge, and in the same order. But you have two options as to how to set out your commentary.

A discussion at the end of an essay, when time is short, will probably be almost an after-thought, and will not do well. Far better is a commentary as you move along through the test, taking the opportunity there and then to assess the point of law just described, and perhaps comparing this defence to diminished responsibility, under s 2 Homicide Act 1957 (though note that this is an essay of the defence of insanity; any reference to diminished responsibility should serve to emphasise the point you are then discussing in insanity).

Answer plan

- introduction; definition of rules; non-insane automatism compared
- defect of reason; *R v Clarke*
- disease of mind, not brain; memory; thought; understanding; *R v Kemp*
- external factors; *R v Quick, R Charlson, R v Kemp, R v Sullivan, R v Bingham*; stress?; confusion; *R v Clarke*; sleep-walking; *R v Burgess*
- definition in case-law; *R v Burgess*; cf s 2 Homicide Act 1957
- sentences; burden of proof; reversal
- conclusion

Answer

The present test for insanity in the criminal law are the rules prescribed by judges of the court of Queen's Bench after the defendant's acquittal in *R v McNaghten* (1843). He had been charged with murdering a civil servant (thinking his victim to be Prime Minister) but, being found to have no *mens rea* on account of his insanity, he was acquitted. The rules discuss the defendant's sanity or otherwise at the time of his crime. Statute covers his becoming insane by the time of trial (Criminal Procedure (Insanity) Act 1964, as amended by the Criminal Procedure (Insanity and Unfitness to Plead) Act 1991, which now allows the jury, after hearing both sides, to decide 'whether they are satisfied ... that he did the act or made the omission charged against him as the offence'. If they think he did, they must make a finding to that effect; if not, they must return a verdict of acquittal. Thus he is allowed now to clear his name, even though insane.)

The *McNaghten* rules, are, firstly, that every man is presumed to be sane; and to have a defence it must be proved that, at the time of committing of the act, the accused was labouring under such a defect of reason, from disease of the mind, as not to know the nature and quality of the act he was doing; or, if he did know it, he did not know that what he was doing was wrong.

These rules contain certain important points. Firstly, there must be a defect of reason, not just confusion, or temporary forgetfulness. In *R v Clarke* an old lady went shopping and put some goods into her own bag, forgetting to pay for them. Her husband was ill; she was pre-occupied. The trial judge jumped straight into insanity (as a judge is permitted in this defence to do), but on appeal her condition was said not to be insanity. After all she could still reason, and it should not be the aim of a criminal law to label as insane ordinary people who forget under stress.

The second important phrase is that the defect comes from a disease of the mind, not of the brain. In *R v Kemp* (1956) the mind was said to involve the faculties of memory, reasoned thought and understanding. It may well be that the defendant also suffers from a disease of the brain, but the test is concerned with the mind. A person whose brain is physically sound might easily have lost the normal powers of the mind, and should therefore be allowed to use this defence.

In *R v Quick* (1973) the Court of Appeal drew a distinction between internal factors, caused by the defendant's own body and counted as insanity, as opposed to external factors, caused by, say, a blow on the head from outside, and not being insanity, and allowing possibly the 'defence' of non-insane automatism (which strictly results in the prosecution failing to establish an *actus reus* that was voluntary).

These two types of factors have become an important test. In *R v Charlson* (1955) the defendant had a brain tumour, which was held to be an external factor. But cases since then have mainly been seen as internal factors. These include *R v Kemp* (1956), a case of hardening of the blood vessels in the head; *R v Sullivan* (1983), where the defendant was epileptic; and both *R v Quick* and *R v Bingham* (1991), cases of hypoglycaemia (too little blood sugar in a diabetic). This is where the credibility of this defence is called into question.

None of these victims of ill health would call himself 'insane', and yet that is how they are labelled. And even more surprising, sleep-walking was recently held to be insanity in *R v Burgess* (1991), even though merely caused by stress caused by a woman's rejection. The reasoning behind this decision was that such stress would be a result of the defendant's psychological make-up, thus being an internal mind. And the unfair label of 'insanity' put on these conditions was admitted by Lord Lane CJ in *R v Burgess* (1991) to be unfortunate and unfair, but that that was a result of the application of these rules, which only Parliament can now alter in view of their antiquity. It is satisfactory, however, to note that while sleep-walking and stress caused by a woman's rejection in *R v Burgess* was held to be insanity rather than non-insane automatism, the boundary is recognised, as evidenced by *R v Clarke*, where confusion and forgetfulness was not seen as a disease of the mind.

To summarise these cases, the Court of Appeal in *R v Burgess* defined insanity as arising from an internal factor (whether functional, eg brain tumour, or organic), which manifests itself in violence, and is prone to recur, and for which defendant ought to be detained in hospital (if only for curative treatment of some of these conditions), rather than be acquitted outright. It is surely generally agreed that a person who does not know what he is doing (for example a defendant cutting a throat under the idea that he was cutting a loaf of bread), or does not know that what he is doing is wrong in law, is a dangerous person to be left at large, not only for others' safety but also for his own.

Finally, it is interesting to compare the test of diminished responsibility under s 2 Homicide Act 1957, where the defendant need only plead an 'abnormality of mind' arising out of certain specified causes, and not a defect of reason or disease of the mind. The defence of s 2 has become the more popular defence in view of the fact that a verdict of manslaughter is brought in, for which the whole range of sentences is available, rather than a verdict of 'not guilty by reason of insanity', which would lead to detention at Her Majesty's pleasure. Section 2 is also a defence which can only be pleaded by the defendant, whereas the judge can argue that the defendant is insane if evidence of such arises in the trial. Indeed, it may sometimes happen that it is the prosecution who seek an acquittal by reason of insanity, and the defence seeking a conviction of manslaughter under s 2, for which a definite sentence would be imposed. Section 2 has recently become the refuge of battered wives suffering from a long history of violence and degradation, but who cannot plead the requirement of sudden loss of control of s 3, provocation, and do not want to have to declare themselves insane to avoid a conviction of murder. It is likely that s 2 will now lead the field in these mental stress defences, and fewer defendants will be happy to plead the defence of insanity. However, at present, s 2 only applies to charges of murder. Some of the cases mentioned above involve assaults (*R v Quick, R v Sullivan*), or property crimes (*R v Bingham* (1991): theft from shops). These defendants are barred from pleading s 2, which is restricted to murder, and have to plead insanity, or guilty to avoid the stigma and indefinite detention.

The penalty, call it what you will, of insanity is severe. While the defence may be useful in some cases, a more general defence, available to all defendants, along the lines of s 2's diminished responsibility is what is needed

Question 38

Historically the criminal sentencing system has focused on punishment of the offender. Is this still its main aim?

General approach

This is a straight forward essay on the aims of sentencing (about 35 minutes would be allowed). The sentencing system has now become a technical area, especially where minors are concerned, but the essay concerns the general aims, not the fine detail. Although the question only refers to punishment, you would widen your assessment by considering the extent that deterrence and protection, and rehabilitation were also central to sentencing.

Include your commentary on the relative importance of the various aims as you move along through your exposition of the theory, taking the opportunity there and then to deal thoroughly with each aim. Intentions to 'come back to this later, in my conclusion', are often left unfulfilled on account of lack of time.

Answer plan

- introduction; aims; *R v Sargeant*
- punishment; retribution/revenge; *R v Roberts*; victim's wishes?; CJA 1991; cf re-emergence from gaol
- deterrence; of defendant; of society; real deterrent; chance of being caught; proportion
- deterrence; theft and burglary and handling; CJA 1991
- discrimination; blacks and women
- reform/rehabilitation; especially victim support/reparation; CJA 1991; Rehabilitation of Offenders Act 1974
- conclusion; joy-riding; answer 'no'

Answer

There are many possible sentences ranging from absolute discharge at the lenient end and life imprisonment for murder at the other end. Most sentences are restricted in severity by the maximum sentence allowed by statute, but a conviction, say of manslaughter, would allow the judge or magistrates to impose any sentence he wished.

The choice of sentence will be influenced by the public perception of the crime and the criminal, and the needs of society and of the defendant. Despite the cries of indignation over differing sentences, no two sentences can ever be the same (unless by chance) as the court will have weighed these factors in all cases, but the balance in two cases will never be the same. In *R v Sargeant* (1974) the Court of Appeal said that there were four classic aims of sentencing: punishment or retribution; deterrence; protection; and rehabilitation or reform. In any particular case the balance of which aim is seen as prominent will always differ. In the Criminal Sentencing Act 1991, partly repealed in 1993, set proportion as an important factor in all these aims; but this has always been a test of a fair sentence, and is a necessary ingredient without which a criminal justice cannot be fair.

The first of the aims of sentencing mentioned by Lawton LJ in *R v Sargeant* (1974) is that of punishment, or retribution or revenge. This is a natural, though perhaps only human, response to a crime being committed against a victim. It is well known that the Old Testament recommends 'an eye for an eye' (even if the New Testament forbids it). This used to be one of the justifications for hanging ie he who has killed must in turn be killed.

One step further is to say that the 'punishment must fit the crime'. This would cause problems; the state cannot employ its own gang of perverted killers, solely to repeat the horrible crimes done by the defendant. The alternative, that people carried out their own revenge, would plunge society back to the blood feuds of Shakespeare's plays; Northern Ireland is a blunt reminder of the tit-for-tat killing motivated by revenge.

Clearly, to keep order, the aim of retribution or punishment must be institutionalised: instead of private punishment, there must, in fairness to society and to the victims, be state-applied punishment. If there is none, the unpunished defendant would appear to go 'scot-free'. Thus Lord Lane CJ in a rape case, *R v Roberts*, said that a rape conviction must attract an immediate custodial sentence to express society's condemnation of the defendant's act. Lord Taylor, succeeding Lord Lane as Lord Chief Justice, said that sentences should take account of public opinion, and that everyone felt that justice had been done.

This, however, raises a problem. Left to the public, all killers would probably be hanged. Who should decide, apart from the judge, what would leave society with a sense of justice? It raises the issue of whether the jury should express society's wish, or indeed whether the victim should be given a right of what he thinks would be a fair sentence sufficient to punish the defendant. In crimes concerning injury or damage, the victim is the most morally justified in deciding what is adequate punishment.

But a criminal system should be clear as to whether the punishment is for the moral blameworthiness or for the harm that is caused: the degree of fault, or the degree of harm. For example, a simple common assault might produce anything from a bruise to death. The moral blameworthiness is slight in common assault; but the harm could be severe. The law recognises the grading both of blameworthiness (murder is more seriously treated than manslaughter on account of its greater fault, even though both cause death), and of harm (grievous bodily harm is covered by more serious offences than is actual bodily harm); each of these systems of grading will qualify crimes for different grades of punishment.

But one problem will remain. Punishment by imprisonment will rarely last forever, and punishment by other means will not remove the defendant from the street at all. Punishment is a driving force, but should thought not be given to the fact that an undeterred and unreformed defendant will sooner or later be back on the streets? For this reason, if no other, it makes sense to consider the deterrence and the reform of the defendant.

Thus Lawton LJ's second principle is to protect the public, and to deter the offender and others. At its crudest, this can take place simply by the offender being put in prison, where he cannot be harmful, until, obviously, he comes out, and indeed the protection need is stressed by the Criminal Sentencing Act 1991. But a sensible system will seek to deter by discouragement, not only the particular offender who is sentenced, but also the rest of society, in particular those who might otherwise be tempted to commit that crime. However, it seems that sentences, both maximum and actual, are of little deterrent value. Defendants are unlikely to read the statutes and law reports, where maximum and actual sentences are reported; they need to be informed for 'deterrence by past sentences' to have any effect. Unless the local press, especially, informs criminals what the possible and likely sentence is, other criminals will stay ignorant and accordingly undeterred by criminal sentencing. In any case, there is some evidence that the defendant's perceived chance of being caught is the main deterrent, not the possible sentence.

Before considering the aim of reform, it is important to note that the fairness of both punishment and deterrence depend on the principle of proportion; that the sentence should fit the crime (in relative severity, not in method), if a sense of grievance is to be avoided. This is already built into the English system. Different sentences take account of whether the defendant is an organiser of the crime, and of the defendant's not using violence, or of using it. The Theft Act 1968 has several examples. For example, theft is often encouraged by the existence of a 'fence', a receiver or handler of the goods stolen. People who steal antiques know that there is a ready market for them; accordingly, the offence of handling stolen goods (s 22) carries a longer maximum sentence (14 years) than theft (s 1; seven years).

Offences accompanied by violence carry heavier maximum sentences too: robbery (s 8) more than ordinary theft; and aggravated burglary (s 10) more than burglary (s 9). The Criminal Sentencing Act 1991 requires that sentences be 'commensurate' with the severity of the crime. This is an important principle; if these crimes carry the same sentences, then the criminal may as well be hung 'for a sheep as a lamb'. He may as well use violence if it does not increase his sentence.

So far we have discussed maximum sentences, but proportion in actual sentences is also important. A man who receives a £200 fine in Manchester will feel aggrieved to hear that another man convicted of that offence in London had to pay only £100. This happens. All crimes committed are done under different circumstances. But too great variations are unfair, and in certain crimes unjustifiable. A violent rape should carry similar sentences in every part of the country. Linked to this are the perceived injustices of women and black people being more prone to receiving a gaol sentence on first conviction than male or white defendants. It is essential that fair play must be done, in order to create resentment, which could cause further criminal activity.

It has been seen above that deterrence, in addition to punishment, is now an important aim of sentencing. But whereas in former times it might have been said that gaol would both punish and deter, the latter aim is not borne out by the evidence. True, as Lawton LJ has said in the *Law Society Gazette* that of five defendants appearing before a criminal court for the first time, four will not appear there again. Thus it would appear that for many first offenders self-regulation thereafter seems adequate to keep them 'on the straight and narrow'. But criminals who serve a gaol sentence are likely to re-offend. Clearly spending time in gaol is not a deterrent to them. As some criminals have personal or psychological problems (for example the child-molesters), it seems that society, in its own interests if not those of the defendant, should look to a system of reforming the criminal to enable him to take his place in society again.

The final aim, to rehabilitate and reform the offender, is still controversial. It is close to, though distinct from, the 'nurture' argument, that environment is a powerful influence in making people commit crimes. Remove that influence and the problem is solved. This aim is sought to be met by the use of such sentences as probation or community service, by the parole system, discharge, suspended sentences, and the power of binding over to keep the peace. All these adopt a conciliatory approach, holding back the full force of the punishments also available, such as gaol and fines.

Linked to this approach are the Rehabilitation of Offenders Act 1974, whereby certain convictions become 'spent' after a while, the victim support system, and the reparation schemes whereby the defendant must physically help his victim, say by repairing the damage caused by his burgling and damaging the victim's house.

But attitudes differ widely. Some see these sentences as a 'soft option'; whereas others, taking into account the fact that even a term of imprisonment will, in most cases, end, with the result that the offender is again at large, seek to reform his character such that he leads a more useful, and reformed, life. Clearly, to make no attempt at reform is to simply allow back into society a person who is just as likely to commit the crime again, and, as figures show, does so. The Criminal Justice Act 1991 set out new sentencing principles to further this principle, for example that a sentence should only take into account one previous offence, and that a man should not be sentenced on account of his previous record. But pressure from magistrates, and adverse comment from the likes of Lord Taylor CJ, the Home Secretary changed some of the main provisions. Such a reversal is only evidence of the lack of coherent policy. The Aggravated Vehicle-Taking Act 1992, passed to cover the 'joy-riding' acts which caused death, imposed a maximum sentence of two years, and yet the Criminal Justice Act 1991 restricted the maximum possible sentence of an under-17 year old to one year, and yet many of the crimes committed under the 1992 Act are committed by under-17 year olds.

It is examples such as this which show that, while there is exploration into the areas of deterrence, protection and reform, there is no consistent system in existence. Criminal justice has always divided the punishment and reform adherents, and the nature or nurture adherents, but it now seems that, lacking the evidence of statistics, politicians certainly are not clear on the aims of sentencing, and have made this area a political football, as shown by the 'climb-down' on the Criminal Justice Act 1991.

Despite them, however, sensible sentences have been made available by Parliament to further the aim of reform and rehabilitation, and many judges are assisting that aim. It has to be said, however, that current sentencing policy among the judiciary is an attempt at implementing all the above-discussed aims.

Question 39

Discuss the importance of fault in criminal law.

General approach

You will here need to explain, firstly, the aim of the criminal law and the role of fault in that system, what fault is in its various forms (intention, recklessness and negligence), why there are these distinctions, and finally why there is strict liability in some crimes.

The argument along these lines should flow along quite nicely, but the better marks will be won by those who not only do this, but support their argument with case-law and statute-law as appropriate.

Answer plan

- the aim of the criminal law
- the role of fault in that system
- definition of fault: intention, recklessness, negligence, dishonesty
- why there is strict liability in some crimes
- conclusion

Answer

The aim of the criminal law is to mark out that conduct which is not generally acceptable in a particular society. But it is the fact that conduct can be committed innocently, or unknowingly, that will require further qualification in order that the boundary of what is acceptable and what is not, can be clearly seen.

The aim then, is not to make criminal all conduct, even that conduct which is prohibited, but to make illegal such conduct done with fault. It is only for special reasons that certain crimes are made possible irrespective of fault on a particular point. The latter crimes are those of strict liability, or liability without fault, and are exceptions to the general rule set by Coke, if not earlier, that conduct can only be criminal if accompanied by fault.

Every crime consists of an *actus reus* (consisting of a prohibited act, or a prohibited omission, or a prohibited state of affairs) and a *mens rea*. The *mens rea* is the fault and can consist of intention to commit the *actus reus*, or recklessness or negligence in bringing it about, and more special forms such as knowledge and dishonesty.

It should be understood that *mens rea* (for which some statutes use the word 'maliciously') does not mean evil or bad motive. In *Hills v Ellis* (1983), a man who had watched a football crowd incident and knew that the police were arresting the wrong man was convicted of 'wilfully obstructing' the police in the execution of duty after interfering in the arrest, though with good intention. His motive for interfering was irrelevant.

Before proceeding to look at the various forms of *mens rea*, on an evidence point, it used to be said that in establishing whether a man intended a result, or was reckless in that he should have foreseen it, it was said that a man intended or foresaw the natural and probable consequence of his act. This presumption was abolished by s 8 Criminal Justice Act 1967; the court must now decide whether he actually intended or foresaw a consequence on all the evidence, which includes any inferences it may make.

In many crimes the defendant will only be liable if he has committed the *actus reus* intentionally. Murder is an example, where the *mens rea*, called 'malice aforethought', is the intention to kill or cause grievous bodily harm, though the killing need be neither malicious nor pre-meditated.

There are two forms of intention: firstly, if it is the defendant's purpose to bring a result about (on purpose, or deliberately), he intends that result. Lord Bridge, in *R v Moloney* (1985), said: 'A man who, boards a plane which he knows to be bound for Manchester, clearly intends to travel to Manchester, even though Manchester is the last place he wants to be and his motive for boarding the plane is simply to escape pursuit.' (But purpose is distinct from 'desire'.)

The second form of intention arises where it is not the defendant's purpose to bring about that result (or so he says), but the result is something that could have been expected in the circumstances. In the 1980s this problem arose in connection with malice aforethought, described above. In *R v Moloney* a soldier at a family party shot his step-father's head off when the latter, in friendly rivalry, dared the soldier to fire a rifle which the soldier had just loaded. In *R v Hancock & Shankland* (1986), during the miners' strike, some striking miners dropped a concrete block from a bridge onto a taxi passing underneath, to frighten working miners who were travelling to work. The concrete block fell on, and killed, the taxi driver. The problem in both cases was that it was not the purpose to kill or cause grievous bodily harm either of the soldier or of the striking miners. Could the defendants in those cases be said to have nevertheless intended to kill or cause grievous bodily harm, on the basis that the results were foreseeable or likely?

Both cases used unclear language to express intention. So in *R v Nedrick* (1986), shortly after the other two cases, Lord Lane CJ refined the definition of 'intention' of causing an *actus reus* where there was no purpose in causing it. He explained it as the defendant's 'appreciation' that causing the *actus reus* was a 'virtual certainty' of his act or omission. The second type of intention clearly shows that if the defendant commits an act knowing that the commission of that act will cause a second act, he intends both acts. In *Arrowsmith v Jenkins* (1963), the defendant, making a speech in the street, did not have the purpose of obstructing the highway, but nevertheless was guilty of 'wilfully obstructing it', as she appreciated the virtual certainty of a crowd gathering to hear her, thereby blocking the highway.

A second form of *mens rea* is recklessness, found in manslaughter and the Criminal Damage Act 1971. A person who does not intend to cause a harmful result may nevertheless take an unjustifiable risk of causing it. If so, he will be held to be reckless. But as the social acceptability increases, so does the justification, of him taking that risk; for instance, evasive action in an emergency, in *R v Reid* (1992). If, on the other hand, the act is objectively unjustifiable, the defendant must have had one of three minds; the first two, below, will make him liable. (However, the test of liability will depend on whether the crime is statutory or common law, and whether, if the former, the statute which defines the crime requires that he acts 'maliciously' or 'recklessly'.)

The three states of mind are:

(a) that the defendant considered whether there was an unjustifiable risk, and decided that there was but carried on (thus, there was actual foresight of the risk);

(b) he did not consider whether there was an unjustifiable risk, but the risk was 'obvious' and he carried on (thus, there was reasonable foresight of the risk);

(c) he considered whether there was an unjustifiable risk, and decided that there was none, or that there was only a negligible risk, and carried on (thus, there was neither actual nor reasonable foresight): this is sometimes called the 'lacuna' or the 'loophole'.

The first state of mind will always amount to recklessness. In *R v Cunningham* (1957) it was held that where a statute requires a defendant to have acted 'maliciously', actual foresight of the risk is required for a conviction. 'Maliciously' is used in the offences of wounding or grievous bodily harm contrary to s 18 and s 20 Offences of the Person Act 1861, dealt with later, but actual foresight is required in any assault and in gross or criminal negligence manslaughter. In *DPP v K (a minor)* (1990) a school boy who took some acid from the laboratory and, in panic when he heard footsteps, put it in the hot-air dryer in the toilets, was convicted of assault occasioning actual bodily harm, contrary to s 47 Offences Against the Person Act 1861, after he had foreseen what in fact happened, namely that the acid flew into another boy's face who used the dryer.

Where the statute requires that the *actus reus* is committed 'recklessly', actual foresight of any risk will come within Lord Diplock's test of recklessness in *R v Caldwell* (1981). Thus in *Chief*

Constable of Avon & Somerset v Shimmen (1986), the defendant, a 'kung fu' expert, showed off by kicked at a window intending to miss it by two inches; in fact, he broke it. He was convicted of criminal damage; his argument that he thought he had eliminated the risk was irrelevant; it mattered only whether he had perceived that there was a risk.

Until *R v Caldwell* it was assumed that recklessness was based on actual foresight in all crimes. In that case the House of Lords held that where a statute requires the defendant to have acted 'recklessly', there is liability if, according to Lord Diplock, there is an obvious risk and the defendant has either not given thought to it or has recognised some risk and has nevertheless gone on to do it.

The defendant will be reckless if either (i) he has actually foreseen some risk of injury or substantial damage (though it need not be an obvious one), or (ii) the risk is in fact an obvious one, and he has not foreseen any (or some) risk of either of those things.

Initial doubt surrounded the question: obvious to whom? *R v Caldwell* leans towards the subjective ('he/she'), but *R v Lawrence* (1981) is objective: 'the ordinary prudent motorist'. In *Elliott v C* (1983), a mentally-subnormal 14 year old girl, who had stayed out all night, unintentionally committed arson (criminal damage by fire) to a shed. Was she reckless? She did not actually foresee the risk of arson and, while the risk might have been obvious to the reasonable man, this girl, young, mentally-subnormal and tired, could not have perceived the risk. The Divisional Court held that she was reckless.

This objective standard has caused criticism but Lord Goff in *R v Reid* (1992) said that reasonable foresight recklessness was justifiable, and included indifference to a risk and not caring whether one existed. Put in that light this form is perhaps more easily justified.

It follows from Lord Diplock's test that if the defendant has considered it properly, he cannot be reckless, though he may still be negligent. In *R v Reid* Lord Goff, with whom three Lords of Appeal agreed, confirmed *obiter* that the defendant might, through mistake, shock, illness or emergency, not recognise the risk of harm. Thus in *W (a minor) v Dolbey* (1983) a defendant who shot someone between the eyes with a slug-pellet gun, thinking that the gun was empty, was acquitted of s 20 of the Offences Against the Person Act 1861 as there was no actual foresight of personal injury. But the loophole only covers the defendant who has thought, but not recognised any risk (or has done, but assessed it as negligible). It does not cover the defendant such as that in the *Shimmen* case, above, who had recognised it, while also thinking that he had eliminated it. It is not clear, therefore, how a person who does think that he has removed a recognised risk can escape liability, if elimination is irrelevant.

Even in the cases where the defendant considers the risk and decides that there is no risk, ie the loophole, if the failure to recognise the risk was 'criminally negligent', then the defendant might be liable where the crime's *mens rea* requires it, but, as we have seen, this will not be where either 'maliciousness' or 'recklessness' must be proved. This form of negligence appears in manslaughter, where it is emphasised as requiring 'gross or criminal negligence'. In *R v Sulman, Prentice* (1994), *Adomako* (1994), *Holloway*, Lord Taylor CJ confirmed that this type of manslaughter still existed after *R v Caldwell*; it required proof of (a) a duty, (b) breach of that duty and causation of death, and (c) gross negligence which the jury considered justified a criminal conviction. Without purporting to give an exhaustive definition, he said that its *mens rea* might be any of: (a) indifference to an obvious risk of injury to health; (b) actual foresight of the risk coupled with the determination nevertheless to run it; (c) an appreciation of the risk coupled with an intention to avoid it but also coupled with such a high degree of negligence in the attempted avoidance as the jury considered justified the conviction; (d) inattention or failure to advert to a serious risk which went beyond mere inadvertence in respect of an obvious and important matter which the defendant's duty demanded he should address.

Another form of *mens rea*, found in the Theft Act 1968, and especially in s 1 of that Act, is 'dishonesty'. The offence of theft is 'dishonestly appropriating property belonging to another' (etc). In *R v Ghosh* (1982) the defendant maintained that he was morally justified in claiming for hospital work that he did not do. Lord Lane CJ likened this to the subjective test which would acquit 'Robin Hood' for thefts which he thought were justified. Lord

Lane said that the test should be a balance of subjective and objective tests: that if the jury regarded the defendant's conduct as dishonest by the standard of ordinary people, and the defendant was aware that it would be so regarded by those people, then he was dishonest. Thus 'Robin Hood' would be convicted, but a person who rides on a bus in London for free, having just come from a country where it is free, would be acquitted. Again the test would only convict those with a guilty mind.

We have seen that to assess the defendant's intention as to, and foresight of, a particular risk, s 8 CJA 1967 requires the court to assess what he actually intended or foresaw from all the evidence, and without assistance from any presumption. It may be then that the jury thinks that he did not intend or foresee a result. In the case of *DPP v Morgan* (1975) it was said that a defendant who honestly did not think that a circumstance part of the *mens rea* existed (such as that a person consented to an 'assault'), then he must be acquitted. The prosecution will not have proved the *mens rea* as to that part of the *actus reus* about which he is mistaken.

We have already said that some crimes are crimes of strict liability. Here, *mens rea* as to some, but not every, aspect of the *actus reus* is dispensed with. Very few common law crimes have strict liability. In *Sweet v Parsley* (1969), it was said that generally in important crimes there is a presumption that *mens rea* is required; thus it is only in the criminal forms of libel, eg criminal libel, blasphemous libel (*Whitehouse v Lemon*), public nuisance, and contempt of court, now statutory under the Contempt of Court Act 1981.

In contrast, many regulatory offences in areas of public safety, where the law is statutory, and especially if the criminal nature is relatively trivial, contain strict liability; examples include many offences in food safety (for example the Food Safety Act 1990) and consumer protection legislation, an example of the former being the sale of bad meat where the butcher has no reasonable means of checking for bacteria (*Hobbs v Winchester*). Many offences under the Licensing Act 1964, for example selling liquor to a drunken person (who did not appear to be so in *Cundy v Le Coq* (1884)), and many of the more trivial offences under the Road Traffic Act 1988 are strict.

Increasingly, there is also strict liability in the field of pollution. In *Alphacell Ltd v Woodward* (1972) the House of Lords held a river-side company guilty of pollution when an overflow channel became clogged up even though the company was not negligent in allowing it to happen or in failing to appreciate that it was happening because, otherwise, if fault were required, 'a great deal of pollution would go unpunished'. Clearly, the message for industry is: find out what you are using, or suffer for it. The courts presume a requirement of *mens rea* (*Sweet v Parsley* (1970)). But Wright J in *Sherras v De Rutzen* (1895) said that the presumption is liable to be displaced either by the words of the statute creating the offence or by the subject matter with which it deals.

Thus words such as 'knowingly', 'permitting' or 'possession' are usually taken to require *mens rea*, but those such as 'using' or 'causing', or phrases such as 'no person shall', are usually taken to denote strict liability. In *James & Son Ltd v Smee* the defendant, who was ignorant of a lorry's faulty brakes would have been convicted of 'using' it in its defective state (had he been so charged), but was not surprisingly acquitted of 'permitting' it to be driven.

The subject matter of the offence will also influence the court in whether to impose strict liability. In *Gammon (UK) Ltd v AG of Hong Kong* (1984) Lord Scarman, speaking for the Privy Council, said that the presumption of *mens rea* is particularly strong where the offence is 'truly criminal in character'. Thus, the courts will be more inclined towards strict liability where the purpose of the offence is merely to enforce a regulation, usually by imposition of a fine, and with little likelihood of causing disgrace.

However, the courts do maintain that social protection weighs more than injustice to the defendant. The Privy Council in *Gammon (UK) Ltd v AG of Hong Kong* (1984) stated that the court could rebut the presumption of *mens rea* in statutory offences of grave social concern, for example public safety, especially if it would encourage observance of the statute.

Strict liability is not without its problems. In practical terms, if the harshness of strict liability is to deter bad practice, might it not go further to deter a trader from trading at all? The case of *Hobbs v Winchester Corporation*, above, deters the selling of bad meat; but for the butcher unable to tell whether his meat is good or bad, might it not be easier for him to stop selling meat at all? The second problem is that, quite simply, strict liability is unfair. Under its principle, those who are blameworthy and blameless are convicted alike. Strict liability means ignoring the degree of blame when considering liability (as opposed to sentence). Thus all persons, whether intentionally harmful, recklessly or negligently so, or not at fault, are convicted alike.

Perhaps it is because of these elements of unfairness that statutory defences are becoming more common. They are usually of three types: that a third party caused the thing, and the defendant exercised all due diligence to avoid the *actus reus*; secondly, the unavoidable consequence of the process of collection or preparation, for example of food; and thirdly, that the defendant did not know, nor could reasonably have known, of the *actus reus*.

But these defences impose on the defendant a burden of proving both that he had no *mens rea* and that he took all reasonable precautions and exercised all due diligence to avoid the commission of an offence, and that while the provision of a defence is better than none at all, they are still a deviation from the fundamental principle that the prosecution must prove the whole of their case (either *actus reus* and *mens rea*, according to *Woolmington v DPP* (1935)).

We have seen that, though all crimes require *mens rea*, whether as to all parts of the *actus reus* or only some, the *mens* will show different mental attitudes to different degrees of harm.

Thus murder, committed with malice aforethought, an intention to kill or cause grievous bodily harm, carries a higher sentence, life imprisonment, than all forms of manslaughter, where any sentence is available. It is this degree of fault that the court's sentence in each case seeks to recognise in order to express the correct and proportionate amount of condemnation. It is only in the regulatory crimes that there is strict liability in general, but it is there that the main irrationality, and accordingly unfairness, exists in an otherwise sensible system.

Chapter 9

The Law of Civil Liberties

Introduction

This subject favours students. While it is a single subject, it can be treated as such or divided into sub-topics, each independent, eg freedom of expression. While problem questions generally hover around certain areas such as arrest and detention (which requires reasonable knowledge of the torts of assault, battery and false imprisonment, dealt with in Part Two of *Lecture Notes on 'A' Level Law Paper 2* (Cavendish Publishing Limited, 1995), and of criminal assaults), essays often leave it open so that you can select your best area or cases or statutes. These could be selected from across the whole subject, or from one area (subject to the question's requirement).

Favourite essays concern the balance between freedom and oppression, and the recent trend in civil liberties: does it show an improvement, a decline or a stable situation. The 1980s produced some, and so far the 1990s have produced many statutes for analysis of recent trends, but case-law is required too in most questions.

Topics which must be mastered are arrest and police detention; property (ie powers of entry, search and seizure); freedoms of assembly and expression; national security; and an essay should if possible contain a relevant reference to the European Convention on Human Rights.

Unfortunately this subject breeds unsubstantiated, and often political, generalisations (eg 'Europe is good', 'freedom to assemble is good' or 'bad', 'it is generally agreed'). Your essay should not read like a tabloid editorial; still less should it contain your prejudices and pre-judgments. Examiners look for: reasoned argument, and evidence, especially cases and statutes. Be impartial, and cite your legal evidence. This is a law exam, not a politics one.

You should also take note of the advice and comments contained in the introduction to Chapter 7 (p 197) about essay and problem answer styles.

Finally, it is 'nice' to start or end (or both) an essay with a quotation. But do not cram long-winded quotations into your head. Go for short but pithy ones, say half a dozen words at the most.

Question 40

How well does the law balance the competing interests of protection of the state and protection of the rights and interests of the individual, in areas such as public order and national security?

General approach

It is important to find the key words in an essay question. This is a fairly typical question in civil liberties, asking you to assess or evaluate the balance of competing interests in this subject between private rights and public or state regulation. Here the emphasis is on assessing whether the balance has been upset.

You should therefore choose areas which you can use to show either an upsetting of the balance or areas which show that the balance is being maintained. But it is your evidence, your analysis of the case-law and the statutes that will convince the examiner; avoid generalisations.

Answer plan

- introduction; balance is essential; Scarman; Art 10 European Convention on Human Rights
- obscene publications; balance upset by common law conspiracies, Customs Act, Post Office Act
- national security; expression and speech
- statutes; official secrets, data protection, interception of communications, security service, intelligence services
- theme:
  (a) ousting of jurisdiction of courts, separation of powers
  (b) court's attitude: *GCHQ, Cheblak, Liversedge, Spycatcher*
- conclusion; balance upset

Answer

In a civilised society neither absolute oppression nor absolute freedom is possible.

The former is a denial of civilisation itself and the latter leads only to oppression by the strong and powerful. Lord Scarman in the Red Lion Square Disorders Report said that 'a balance must be struck ... a compromise found'. He was discussing public order, but the principle applies throughout civil liberties.

This balance is now recognised at all levels of civil liberties. For example the European Convention on Human Rights recognises in Art 10 that there is a right of free expression, but that this can be justifiably restricted by the state on grounds of 'protection of health or morals' or 'national security'. We will examine evidence in two areas to assess whether this balance is still maintained or whether it is upset. These areas are obscene publications and national security.

The Obscene Publications Act 1959 creates an offence to publish obscene material, obscene being likely to 'deprave and corrupt' a person to whom published. Before the Act, literature such as *Boccaccio's Decameron* was ordered to be destroyed by magistrates. This was reversed on appeal, but the magistrates' decision shows the spirit of the old law. But the 1959 Act created three safeguards to provide a balance between pornography and artistic or medical material. These safeguards are: (a) how the material would appear to its likely audience; (b) that it must be taken as a whole; and (c) there was now a defence of public good to protect literature and medical material.

Soon after the Act, Penguin Books' acquittal of publishing *Lady Chatterley's Lover* showed that the new Act seemed to fulfil its promise.

But there also exist three other crimes in this area. Firstly, two common law conspiracies: to corrupt public morals and to outrage public decency. The former was established in *Shaw v DPP* (1962), where a 'ladies' directory', describing available prostitutes, was the subject of a conviction; and the latter was used in 1990 in *R v Gibson* (1990) to convict the defendant of publishing earrings made up of frozen human embryos. In *Shaw v DPP* (1962) Lord Simonds said there was residual power in the courts to protect the moral welfare of the state. Secondly, the Customs Consolidation Act 1876 allows Customs to seize obscene material, such as the medical books on AIDS and mediaeval poetry seized in a raid in the 1980s. And thirdly, the Post Office Act 1953 prohibits the sending of indecent, though not necessarily obscene, material through the post.

None of these crimes involve the three safeguards mentioned above, namely, the likely audience test, the requirement to take it as a whole, or the defence of public good. Consequently, prosecutors and customs are not restricted by the balanced planning of the 1959 Act.

Another area worth examining is that of National Security. Article 10 of the European Convention accepts that the right to freedom of expression can be restricted on grounds of protection of the state and national security.

Increasingly, this is a regulated field: the Official Secrets Act 1989 has recently replaced the notorious s 2 of the 1911 Act, and covers disclosure by civil servants of government information; the Data Protection Act 1984 regulates computerised information; the Interception of Communications Act 1985 prohibits 'phone-tapping' and letter-opening; the Security Service Act 1989 regulates the activities of the security service eg MI 5, and the Intelligence Services Act 1994 does the same regarding those services, ie MI6 and GCHQ.

The doctrine of separation of powers states that disputes are the province of the judiciary and the courts. In prosecutions under the Official Secrets Act it used to be arguable (according to *R v Ponting* (1985)) to claim that disclosure was not criminal if it was in the interest of the state. Whether this defence was properly available or not the right to argue it when prosecuted has now been abolished by the new Act, and a civil servant aware of ministerial chicanery must now report to a senior civil servant.

The Data Protection Act gives the citizen rights of access to material held about him and to correction of mistakes, but these are refused where a minister claims that the information is held for national security reasons. Further, the ministers claim of national security is final; there can be no judicial review.

The Interception of Communications Act prohibits interception except where the home secretary allows it. If there is a dispute, as indeed also if there is a dispute under the Security Service Act or the Intelligence Services Act, there is no right to take it to court; the right of access to court is abolished. Instead there is adjudication by a tribunal whose members have no security of tenure (and are therefore dismissible) who report to the Prime Minister (who has power to vet the report).

In case it is thought that the courts would take a more robust attitude to ministers' claims of national security where the courts do have jurisdiction, it can be seen from the case-law that this is not the case. The following two cases involve the right of natural justice to be able to put your case to an accusation; this presupposes a prior right to know the detail of the accusation, but this right was denied in two cases. In the *GCHQ Civil Service Unions* case (1984), where a minister claimed that trade unions should be banned at GCHQ in the interests of national security, the claim was not disputed by the House of Lords. In *R v Home Secretary ex parte Cheblak* (1991), where an Iraqi was deported during the Iraqi conflict on the same ground, but without further details, again the court did not dispute the minister's claim.

Only rarely do judges object, for example Lord Atkin in *Liversedge v Anderson* (1941) where he called the other Lords of Appeal 'more executive minded than the executive' and Lord Bridge in *AG v Guardian Newspapers* (1988), who claimed that the government, if it persisted in its claims, would be condemned at the bar of the free world. But these dissents are rare.

To conclude, and to assess the balance of freedom and restriction, we can note the by-pass offences around the carefully planned balance of the Obscene Publications Act 1959, thereby frustrating Parliament's careful considerations; and we can note the growing trend in statutes concerned with national security of ousting the jurisdiction of the courts. No longer in that area can the citizen take his complaint of wrongdoing by the executive to the courts of the land; he has to be satisfied with a tribunal which reports to the executive itself The checks and balances of the doctrine of separation of powers do not apply there. On this evidence, it is a fair assessment to say that the balance has indeed been upset against the citizen.

Question 41

(a) Lawyers and public alike talk about both civil liberties and civil (or human) rights. Explain the difference between civil liberties and civil rights. (10 marks)

(b) What evidence is there that civil liberties are less protected now than in 1980? (20 marks)

General approach

(a) The first part requires you not simply to define liberties and rights but also to compare them. But do not simply theorise; use examples from the law.

(b) This is a typical civil liberties essay, asking you to assess whether there has been a decline (another essay question might put 'improvement') in civil liberties. But it does not want generalisations; you are required to give evidence, ie cases and statutes, or instances from current affairs that do not reach the courts but which fit into some part of the law you have studied.

The 1980s were full of statutes in this subject, and case-law also has flourished, but assess them. You might agree, or not, but assess it for evidence of a decline. Do not simply explain or narrate it. And, again, in this subject, the choice of topic is yours; pick those you can remember, and can use best.

Finally, note the split of marks: apportion your time accordingly.

Answer plan

(a)
- liberty; residue of what is allowed; right; express capacity; irremovable; *Malone* and Art 11; guns in US constitution

(b)
- introduction; PCEA 1984; arrest; detention
- PCEA; arrest; ss 24, 25; *Rice, Ricketts*; detention; time; confession; *Gopee*

- PCEA; entry search and seizure; ss 15, 19, 8 and 9; *R v Leics CC ex parte DPP, Barclays v Taylor*
- conclusion; Blackstone; PCEA; sapping and undermining; Burke

Answer

(a) The popular understanding is that civil liberties (or freedoms), and civil rights (or human rights) are the same thing. They describe the same area of law, but there is indeed a difference between a liberty and a right, and now explained.

In *Malone v MPC (No 2)* (1985), the lawfulness of tapping telephones was questioned by the plaintiff. The Vice-Chancellor said that telephone-tapping was no crime as it had not been expressly forbidden, and that in England we can do anything unless it has been forbidden. His example was that we can smoke, not because we have the express right to, but because it has not been made unlawful. Thus we were at liberty to 'phone-tap (it has now been outlawed by the Interception of Communications Act 1985), and to smoke, these being examples of liberties. But, as has been said, the liberty to 'phone-tap has been abolished.

Similarly, the liberty to pass down the street has been eroded by statute, eg the Public Order Act 1986, and the Highways Ac 1980, which contain restrictions on assemblies, processions, ar obstructions. This, then, is the problem with liberties; they ⸺ what we are allowed to do, the residue of what is left to citizen by the state. And they can be restricted further by the ⸺ until the liberty is almost, or completely, extinct.

The European Convention on Human Rights, on th⸺ hand, contains rights. Article 8 gives the right of p assembly to everyone. Although Art 11(2) contains clause, this are expressly stated; the state cannot cre⸺ clauses at will.

In a country which has incorporated the Convention can only erode the right of assembly up to the l⸺er boundary, but no more. The citizen has his expre⸺ Art 11, and it cannot be taken from him.

Thus a liberty is what is left after the state has imposed its restrictions. A right is a definite, irremovable legal ability to insist on some advantage or capacity.

An example of a right which was justifiable when created (in 1791, in the Wild West), but which is outdated now is the American right to carry guns, enshrined in the Second Amendment to their constitution. As we have seen, English law is largely made up of liberties, which are continuously being squeezed, or eroded; the European Convention is made up of rights, admittedly with expressly stated but finite restrictions, but otherwise irremovable, even though social attitudes might change.

(b) Lord Scarman in the Red Lion Square Disorders Report said that 'a balance must be struck ... a compromise found'. He was discussing public order, but the principle of relative freedom or 'freedom under the law', applies throughout civil liberties. An assessment of whether a decline in civil liberties has taken place requires not merely an examination of the oppressive measures recently introduced, but also a weighing of those and the beneficial measures, in order to check the new balance and compromise, and to compare it with the old.

To make a complete assessment on whether civil liberties have declined since 1980 would entail a review of all aspects of civil liberties. However, governments and courts tend to be consistent in all areas, and a sample assessment could be made in a few areas.

The areas that will now be considered are the police powers of rrest and detention and entry, search and seizure, dealt with by e Police and Criminal Evidence Act 1984.

The Police and Criminal Evidence Act 1984 contains general ers of arrest without warrant. The power in s 24, exercisable oth police and citizen, for an arrestable offence is a repetition e previous law, with some alterations. Until the Act, the on on freedom of the person was clear: either you were rrest, or you were free to go on your way. Further, in *Rice lly* (1966), the court emphasised that where no arrest had le, although there was a social or moral duty to assist the en being questioned, there was no legal duty to do so.

(A refusal to give an address and the intended destination in that case was held to be justified.)

Such simple, clear rules have been blurred both by the Act and by the courts. The Criminal Justice and Public Order Act 1994 has also eroded *Rice v Connolly* in that the defendant's silence when questioned after caution can now be the subject of adverse inference at trial.

First, it is now possible for the police to stop and search a citizen even where there has been no arrest. Under s 1, the police can do this in public if he or she thinks weapons or stolen articles might be found. Further and secondly, it was held in *Ricketts v Cox* (1982) that, despite *Rice v Connolly* (1966), an abusive and aggressive refusal to give the name and an address was a wilful obstruction of the police in the execution of duty, an offence under s 51(3) Police Act 1964. Moreover, s 25 created a new national power of arrest without warrant for a suspected or alleged summary offence, where the police would not be able to serve the summons on you, among others, because he or she does not know your name or address, or disbelieves those you have given.

Thus, the simple distinction before 1984 between arrest and absolute freedom has gone. Powers to detain without arrest, or to require names etc from abusive persons, or to arrest for summary offences under certain conditions have whittled away the right to go free.

Let us now consider some rules of detention. Before the 1984 Act, the generally accepted maximum limit for detention was 48 hours. The Act, to its credit, shortened this to 24 hours for ordinary offences, but doubled it to 96 hours for 'serious arrestable offences'. No definition of 'serious' is given in the Act for the magistrates who might have to decide whether an offence was 'serious' at 36 hours, and 72 hours.

Granted that murder, rape, and others are serious and would cause no problem; but included, and likely to do so, are serious injury, serious harm to public order, serious financial gain or loss. The latter is decided on the loser's financial position, thus stealing a pensioner's total savings of £100 is 'serious financial loss', justifying 96 hours detention. Still in this area, the seven days maximum detention under the Protection of Terrorism (Temporary Measures) Act 1989, which raised eyebrows when first enacted in 1974, seems rather respectable now, when compared with the four days that a thief can lawfully be detained.

It is interesting to compare with these statutory provisions the hesitation with which the Scottish system of finite remand in custody (110 days maximum for indictable offences) was brought in certain areas for a trial period. It is noticeable therefore that a beneficial provision has to brought in, not by decisive statutory provision, but by a phased, cautious statutory instrument approach.

Finally, on the freedom of the person, it is worth noting the position since the Act on confession evidence. Before the 1984 Act, evidence of confession by the defendant which was challenged by him as obtained by oppression or induced by offer of reward, was dealt with by the 'judges' rules'. By these rules, the trial judge could decide on the evidence whether a confession should be admitted as evidence or not. Section 76 of the 1984 Act has taken a bold stance. Now, if a defendant claims that the confession was obtained by oppression, or by any means which might render it unreliable, such as by offer of reward (eg 'confess to this, and we'll drop those other charges'), the court 'shall not' admit it as evidence, unless the prosecution proves, beyond reasonable doubt, that it was not so obtained.

The second area of review is the part of the Act dealing with powers of entry, search and seizure.

Entry can, of course, be made under a warrant. But the courts have long seen the danger of general warrants, of the police walking around with a warrant for premises, without specifying any particular offence. In *Entick v Carrington* (1765), in the 18th Century, these were declared unlawful. Surprisingly, therefore, in *Rossminster Ltd v IRC*, where Inland Revenue officers had made dawn raids on private houses to obtain evidence of fraud, a warrant not specifying precise offences but only 'tax fraud' was held lawful. The reasoning was that until they got the evidence they did not know what the offence would be!

Parliament then had its chance to decide which case was preferable; s 15 has reinforced that warrants do not need to specify the offence.

The powers of search and seizure once entry had been effected had been confused under the common law; there was no authoritative statement as to whether the police could only seize goods specified in the warrant, or other goods as well. Section 19 has cut straight through these doubts, stating that the police 'lawfully on any premises' can take goods reasonably suspected to have been obtained as a result of 'an offence', whether or not that for which the warrant was obtained. Thus, police invited into a home can exercise this power.

As for the issue of warrants for entry and search, ss 8 and 9 provide a system for obtaining warrants in the case of suspected serious arrestable offences. The normal procedure is an *ex parte* application to a magistrate. But the statute wisely provides that in cases of 'excluded material' or 'special procedure material', that is personal records, human tissue or fluid, and journalistic material, the request justifies a hearing *inter partes* before a judge.

Unfortunately, what appeared to be a sensible provision has been undermined by the courts: *partes* means the police and the person holding the material not, if separate from the latter, the person under suspicion (*R v Leicester Crown Court ex parte DPP* (1987)); nor need a third person who is holding the material inform the person under suspicion that the police want to take his/her material (*Barclays Bank v Taylor* (1989)). It can be said that if either case had decided the other way, the suspect would immediately destroy his material (a fair point); but provision could have been made within this procedure for immediate immobilisation of the material pending argument before a judge on the legality of the seizure (perhaps on the lines of the *mareva* or *anton piller* injunctions procedures). Clearly, in a tricky area, the public interest has, perhaps inevitably, been seen as more important than the private interest.

To conclude on the Police and Criminal Evidence Act 1984, the Act was seen as a new balance, a compromise between the competing interests of private rights and the public interest of investigating crime. It has some beneficial points, such as s 76 on confessions, and the 110 day maximum for remand in custody outside the Act is of the same spirit. But it also contains widened powers of arrest, stop and search, relaxed requirements of warrants, wide police powers of seizure, and no provision of ensuring that applications over possession of a suspect's material are brought to his or her attention. Blackstone warned of the state 'sapping and undermining' the right to jury trial. Here, too, is a picture of gradual and hardly observable undermining of rights and liberties. Edmund Burke said, 'The price of freedom is eternal vigilance'. Tiresome as it may appear, we must still keep watch. The judicial right to make adverse comment on the defendant's silence after caution or arrest, allowed by Criminal Justice and Public Order Act 1994, shows that the erosion is still under way.

Another area worth examining is that of national security. Article 10 of the European Convention accepts that the right to freedom of expression can be restricted on grounds of protection of the state and national security. Increasingly, this is a regulated field; the Data Protection Act 1984 regulates computerised information; the Interception of Communications Act 1985 prohibits 'phone-tapping and letter-opening, the Security Service Act 1989 regulates the activities of the security service eg MI 5, and the Intelligence Services Act 1994 does the same with MI 6. The doctrine of separation of powers states that disputes are the province of the judiciary and the courts. But, in these statutes, there is a tendency to refuse access to the courts.

The Data Protection Act gives the citizen rights of access to material held about him and to correction of mistakes, but these are refused where a minister claims that the information is held for national security reasons. Further, the minister's claim of national security is final; there can be no judicial review.

The Interception of Communications Act prohibits interception except where the home secretary allows it. If there is a dispute, as indeed also if there is a dispute under the Security Service Act, there is no right to take it to court; the right of access to court is abolished. Instead there is adjudication by a tribunal whose members have no security of tenure (and are therefore dismissible) and who report to the Prime Minister (who has power to vet the report).

In case it is thought that the courts would take a more robust attitude to ministers' claims of national security where the courts do have jurisdiction, it can be seen from the case-law that this is not the case.

The following two cases involve the right of natural justice to be able to put your case to an accusation; this presupposes a prior right to know the detail of the accusation, but this right was denied in two cases. In the *GCHQ Civil Service Unions* case, where a minister claimed that trade unions should be banned at GCHQ in the interests of national security, the claim was not disputed by the House of Lords. In *R v Home Secretary ex parte Cheblak* (1991), where an Iraqi was deported during the Iraqi conflict on the same ground, but without further details, again, the court did not dispute the minister's claim. Only rarely do judges object, for example Lord Atkin in *Liversedge v Anderson* (1941) where he called the other Lords of Appeal 'more executive minded than the executive' and Lord Bridge in *AG v Guardian Newspapers* (1988), who claimed that the government, if it persisted in its *Spycatcher* claims would be condemned at the bar of the free world. But these dissents are rare.

To conclude, and to assess whether civil liberties in Great Britain have declined since 1980, we can note the growing trend in statutes concerned with national security of ousting the jurisdiction of the courts. No longer in that area can the citizen take his or her complaint of wrongdoing by the executive to the courts of the land; the citizen has to be satisfied with a tribunal which reports to the executive itself The checks and balances of the doctrine of separation of powers do not apply there. On this evidence, it is a fair assessment to say that the balance has indeed been upset against the citizen.

Question 42

Plod, a policeman in uniform, is walking his beat one night in an area where there has been a spate of burglaries when he sees Jones, who he knows is suspected of some of these crimes. Plod stops Jones and asks him his name. Jones says 'Smith'. Plod asks for some form of identity and asks him why he is out so late (at 2 am). Jones says he is on his way home from a late night film, and walks off. Plod catches up with him and, walking alongside of him, again asks him why he is out so late, whereupon Jones says, 'get lost, copper; okay?' Plod goes to restrain him when Jones pushes Plod and runs away. Plod radios for help, which arrives quickly. Jones is subdued, pushed into a 'black maria', and taken to the nearest police station. A police sergeant interviews him within 40 minutes of arrival, and decides to let Jones go without charge. Jones is leaving the station when Plod, seeing him, shouts, 'Stop that man!' Brown, a person on crutches and himself under arrest, trips up Jones with one of his crutches, causing Jones to fall, bruising his arm.

Advise Jones of his rights of redress against Plod and against Brown.

General approach

A problem question on powers of arrest is best tackled in chronological fashion. Simply work through the question event by event. It may well be the case that the lawfulness of some later event depends on an earlier finding. Do not worry that you may have been wrong in that earlier assessment; just carry on. The examiner is more concerned to see your account of relevant law, than that you decide correctly on points that, in court, could go either way.

For example, an early decision will be whether a lawful arrest without warrant has been made; this will depend on whether the policeman has 'reasonable suspicion', but the decision on reasonableness could go either way, affecting whether he is arrested or not, and affecting whether all the other powers dependent on a valid arrest, eg search, arise. So long as you tell the examiner the law, make a reasonable decision, and be consistent, that will usually satisfy an examiner.

Finally, remember that the rights of a person being wrongly treated lie in tort (eg trespass). A question on civil liberties does not require an elaborate discussion on torts, but you should identify the torts as and when committed.

Answer plan

- asking name; Jones walking off; no arrest (*Rice v Connolly*); abusive (*Ricketts v Cox*); s 51(3) Police Act 1964; power of arrest; ss 24, 25, 1 (all PCEA 1984); identity; walking off; silence; Criminal Justice and Public Order Act 1994

The Law of Civil Liberties

- Jones hitting T; if arrest by Plod, Jones obstructs; s 51(3) and assaults s 51(1); if no arrest, reasonable force to defend an assault?; arrest?; s 28 (*Christie v L*); no arrest (*Collins v Wilcocks, Donnelly v Jackman*)
- into van; battery; false imprisonment
- defamation; slander actionable *per se*; qualified privilege
- s 24; *Walters v WH Smith, R v Self*; citizen's arrest?; no arrestable offence committed; assault; battery and s 47 OAPA 1861

Answer

Jones has the burden of proving that any torts or crimes of assault, battery or false imprisonment, have been committed against him, but the police would have available any powers in the Police and Criminal Evidence Act 1984 under which they were lawfully acting.

It is within Plod's power to ask Jones his name, but the question arises as to his liability when Jones says he is Smith. In *Rice v Connolly*, it was held that though there is a social or moral duty to answer the police, there is no legal duty to do so if not under arrest.

However, under s 51(3) Police Act 1964 it is an offence to wilfully obstruct the police in the execution of duty, and in *Ricketts v Cox* it was held that an aggressive and abusive refusal to answer questions while not under arrest did constitute an offence under s 51(3). Thus, telling a lie (that Jones is Smith) would amount to s 51(3) (and the separate offence of wasting police time) but for the fact that Plod knows who Jones is. Though Jones may be wilful, he might not obstruct Plod in his investigation. Even if it is a s 51(3) offence, this section does not give a right of arrest. Plod could arrest Jones under s 24 Police and Criminal Evidence Act 1984 if Plod has reasonable grounds for suspicion that Jones has or is about to commit an arrestable offence, ie of at least five years imprisonment for a first offence, eg burglary (s 9 Theft Act 1968), but the facts are not clear as to whether Plod suspects this or simply wants to keep an eye on Jones to try to get evidence of burglary.

Plod could also arrest Jones under s 25 of the 1984 Act for the summary offence under s 51(3) if Plod fears that it would be impracticable to serve a summons because Plod does not know Jones' name or address or both. But Plod does know who Jones is, so the s 25 power is not available (nor does any other s 25 circumstance apply).

There is no power to stop and search Jones under s 1 of the 1984 Act unless the police have reasonable grounds to suspect that the person stopped has a weapon or stolen goods or tools used for burglary, which may be the case here although the facts do not indicate so, and say to the person what goods the police expects to find and on what grounds, which Plod does not do.

There is therefore no right to stop and search Jones. A request for proof of identity can be ignored under *Rice v Connolly*, provided it is done in a civil manner (as opposed to the abusive and aggressive manner in *Ricketts v Cox*, above). Probably it does not come within s 51(3) to say 'get lost, copper; okay?', as only aggressive or abusive behaviour is caught by *Ricketts v Cox* (1982). Further, as Jones has not been cautioned, no adverse comment can be made of his failure to answer under s 34 Criminal Justice and Public Order Act 1994.

The events of Plod putting out his arm, Jones hitting Plod and running off, create a complex and interwoven series of events, but two points should be noted: first Plod puts out his hand to take hold, he does not touch Jones; and second Jones hitting Plod is the first physical contact.

So far Jones has suffered no tort. With regard to these events, if there is an arrest, Jones must not resist it (he would commit s 51(3), above, even if he did this calmly, and if he did this violently he would commit various assaults, eg s 51(1) of the same Act, assaulting the police in the execution of duty). If there is no arrest, Plod is the tortfeasor and criminal and Jones is entitled to use reasonable force to resist Plod's wrongful act under s 3 Criminal Law Act 1967 and at common law. The first issue is: is there an arrest?

We said, above, that Plod had power of arrest if he suspected Jones of past or future burglary. To make an arrest, Plod must restrain Jones's person and, under s 28 of the 1984 Act, inform Jones that he is under arrest and the grounds for his arrest. (The grounds must be the true ones. If, as on similar facts in *Christie v Leachinsky*, Plod has power to arrest under s 24, but tells Jones that he is arresting him for a s 25 reason, the arrest is wrongful.)

Plod does neither of these but s 28 also states that the required information need not be communicated to Jones if it is not reasonably practicable to do so by reason of his having escaped 'from arrest' beforehand. It is probably the case here therefore that Plod had not arrested Jones, as Plod had not restrained Jones in any way, nor begun to communicate the s 28 information when he was perfectly capable of doing so.

Who, therefore, assaults whom? If there is no arrest, then does Plod assault Jones? In *Donnelly v Jackman* (1970) a policeman who tapped a person on the arm to attract his attention was held not to have committed a battery; but in *Collins v Wilcock* (1984) it was a battery to take someone's arm to restrain her. If Jones was aware of an impending restraint, ie a battery, then he was entitled to use reasonable force in his self-defence. Whether this is reasonable or not is a question of fact which it is not possible to make on the facts of the question; but, certainly, if Jones used unreasonable force, ie more than was needed, then he commits the torts and crimes of battery and, if Plod saw the hit coming, and the crimes of s 51(1) and (3) Police Act 1964 on Plod.

If, as we have said, Jones is not under arrest, then bundling him into a car is a battery and false imprisonment against him. Had he been arrested then a delay of half an hour would not have been unreasonable (a delay of one hour in *John Lewis v Tims* (1952) was held so). He is not under arrest and so is entitled to escape from his false imprisonment. To shout 'stop him' is not a re-arrest because, as stated above, there is no restraint on Jones, though, as he is escaping, it is not reasonably practicable to give him the s 28 information so as to complete the arrest. To shout this about a man not under arrest is also defamatory, as slander actionable *per se*; it is an imputation of an imprisonable arrest, although the police, who shouted honestly, would have an interest and duty in shouting, and would therefore have qualified privilege in doing so as Brown had an interest in hearing.

Finally, does Brown commit a tort or crime against Jones? Brown, as a private citizen, has power of arrest under s 24 if he reasonably suspects Jones to be committing an arrestable offence, which he cannot reasonably suspect here from a man simply walking, or if he reasonably suspects him to have committed one and one in fact has been committed. As in *Walters v WH Smith* (1914), where the defendant had not committed the theft of the books as the jury believed his intention to pay for them, or in *R v Self* (1992) where a shop detective wrongly thought the defendant's chocolate to be stolen, so here also, Jones has not committed an arrestable offence and Brown has no power of arrest. That being so, Brown commits the torts and crimes of battery against Jones, and possibly also of assault if Jones saw the trip coming. Brown has also committed the crime of s 47 Offences against the Person Act 1861, of assault (which includes battery) occasioning actual bodily harm, as bruising is a form of 'some physical harm', as held in *R v Savage, R v Parmenter* (1991).

Chapter 10

Family and Welfare Law

Introduction

What could you be asked? Ensure that you know your syllabus and have prepared sufficiently for the number of questions you are to answer. This gives you the most important and first information about what you could be asked.

Areas within the syllabus which tend to be popular areas for examination questions are cohabitation and the differences, legally speaking, between that and marriage, issues in divorce and property settlements and questions on children and parental responsibilities and the possibilities for the state's intervention in their welfare.

What are questions in family law actually like? Questions in family law at this level can appear quite daunting, but they are designed, like all questions at 'A' level, to see if you know the material and can actually apply it to the situation (in a 'problem' question) or in presenting a viewpoint (as in an essay question). You will find that problem questions are popular with examiners, because they allow them to present a reasonably 'lifelike' situation to you which you should regard as an opportunity to show what you know and what you can do.

You should also remember that questions could be subdivided with two, three or even four or more parts to them, although it is more common to have single questions or only two or three parts. If any of your questions are sub-divided, then you should check what marks are allocated to each part and answer the parts accordingly, bearing in mind the allocation as a 'weighting' of time and effort to be expended on each part of the question. If there is no separate indication of how many marks are allocated to each part, then you should assume that all parts have equal marks, and that all separate questions on the paper are worth the same number of marks as all the other questions.

What kinds of questions are there likely to be and how do you deal with them? There are likely to be both essay and problem questions on your examination paper.

The syllabus may have something to say about this matter, and you would find it helpful to obtain past papers from the examination board so that you are familiar with the kinds normally asked, and can practice on actual questions. There are sample questions in this chapter and they are like the types of questions commonly asked by examiners at 'A' level.

Remember that you may wish to tackle an essay question presented to you because it seems easier than a problem question at first glance; this might mean that you do not give yourself the opportunity to show your best approach; all that a problem question does is allow you to select your material as appropriate to that scenario rather than select your material in answering or presenting a viewpoint as you would do for an essay question.

The approach to adopt is to martial your material rather than attempt to put in as much material as possible - no question ever says 'write all you know about ... family law'!

Remember that you require legal authority for statements that you make about the law; it is no use simply writing what you know the correct answer is unless you are able to state the authority for what you have said - the authority will be, in most cases, the cases or the statutory references for 'A' level purposes. Try, as a general rule, to be in the habit of automatically giving the authority when you write what you consider is the applicable law.

What do you put into an answer? You must be accurate and relevant in what you write. This sounds simple, but it is all too easy to be tempted to write all you know about the topic area rather than be relevant. If you write all you know then the examiner will suspect that you are unable to select your material and cannot concentrate on the question; you will probably run out of time on that particular question and you may be rushed in getting through all that you must do in the time available.

In problem questions it will be easier to keep to the point because you will deal with the issues as they are in the problem, and usually in the order that they are presented in the 'story' so to speak. However, do remember that if asked to 'advise' one

Family and Welfare Law

person, then another person, you may deal with the issues for one, then the other. There will, then, usually be different issues to deal with as the legal viewpoint of your 'clients' has been highlighted by the examiners so that you are required to give the different positions in law. Keeping to the point in essay questions may be more difficult for you in family law for there may be temptations to wander away from the point and present your own view of what families are all about! Avoid this as it is likely that that was not what the examiner wanted you to do! You may be asked to present a view (of Divorce reform, for example) but your view should be informed by current opinion of lawyers, not what your bestfriend or your aunt said last weekend. Remember that the family law examination is not an opportunity to 'preach', even in an essay answer, but an opportunity to organise facts and present a legally supported view in a specific response to the question that the examiner has set.

Last advice: read the rubric (the instructions or advice to candidates) on the front of the paper (better still, get to know what to expect in advance) and answer the correct number of questions from the correct part if the paper is so divided.

Finally, you must remember to answer the question that the examiner set for the paper, not the one you wish you had read!

Question 43

Peter and Mary are engaged to be married but, in 1994, after being engaged for a year, they decide to postpone the marriage for a few years and to live together.

They buy a house and each put £200 towards the deposit and find that they are able to meet the mortgage repayments from their salaries. Peter earns £20,000 and Mary earns £18,000 per year. They take a share in the payments for expenses. They now want a child, but are unsure about whether they should marry or simply continue the relationship as it is.

They seek your help in deciding what they should do and the legal factors to be considered.

General approach

You could treat this almost as an essay question in the way the question is written.

You are being asked to deal with certain issues in the differences between married couples and those living together in terms of specific areas. Try to give advice to the couple, though, even though the question gives the appearance of an essay rather than a strict problem question.

Answer plan

- general introduction
- deal with the issue of married/unmarried in terms of legal requirements
- property rights and trusts needs to be discussed for the couple
- what happens with respect to the children?; if the couple are unmarried what difference will that make to the care of children?
- provision if the relationship breaks down;- division of property and maintenance
- advise on the making of a will and provisions after death if the couple are not married

Answer

There are different legal considerations where a couple decide to live together rather than marry. The term for living together is cohabiting. Advice has been sought because the law deals with married partners in a particular way. The Matrimonial Causes Act 1973 does not apply so that the couple need to look at joint property rights as they apply to family law.

There are legal requirements for those who wish to marry which are not required for those cohabiting. Those who are married may have stronger legal protection than those simply living together, although there are ways of providing for the legal establishment of the relationship.

Cohabitees will have to demonstrate to the court that they had a settled relationship intended to have a degree of permanence.

The engagement seems to indicate a degree of permanence about the relationship. Although not of itself a legally binding contractual arrangement, the engagement indicates an intention akin to marriage. The wish to establish a family together seems to support this. They have not, however, apparently been together for very long.

Peter and Mary 'buy a house' so the title deeds may indicate the ownership of the property (see *Goodman v Gallant* (1986)) but sometimes the beneficial interests are not clear. There is a rebuttable presumption that Peter and Mary are entitled to a half share each. We do not know whether this is what is meant by a 'share' or whether the share is in proportion to their incomes.

The deeds may indicate one owner only (possibly Peter?) so it may be necessary to see if there is a trust in favour of the other (Mary?). This may be an express trust created by a declaration of Peter or Mary (the person in whom the property is vested) or it may be a resulting, implied or constructive trust. The last three can be dealt with together since in family law there is not often a meaningful distinction made between them.

Both Peter and Mary have provided money towards the purchase price of the house so that even if it is in one name only there is a rebuttable presumption that it was intended that both should benefit from the ownership of the house; this is a resulting trust (*Sekhon v Alissa* (1989)). The principles of trusts are applied from *Gissing v Gissing* (1970) and *Pettitt v Pettitt* (1970) and the courts will look to see if there is a common intention that both parties should benefit from the house.

What did Peter and Mary intend when they purchased the house? Each has put down a deposit we are told, and each seems to share in the expenses of the house. What was intended can be indicated by direct contributions (preferably in terms of actual money) to the purchase price *Lloyds Bank v Rossett* (1990). The parties have acted to their detriment in making such contributions. There is even an indication of express agreement *Grant v Edwards* (1986) and *Eves v Eves* (1975).

Peter and Mary need to be advised about what should happen if the relationship breaks down and they wish to realise their 'share'. If married, this could be dealt with under the divorce legislation with the assumptions of equal shares and the requirements of the parties in divorce settlements. The Law of Property Act 1930 allows the court to order the sale of the property subject to a trust for sale, which applies to most jointly owned property. If, however, Peter and Mary bought the home for a purpose, which, here, might be the purpose of bringing up children, then the court will take the view that the trust is unfulfilled and will not order the sale, despite the breakdown in their relationship, if they have children as they plan. Occupation of the house (as a 'home' for the children, perhaps) would be 'protected' (*Tanner v Tanner* (1975)) in these circumstances, in the same way that the divorce settlement might permit one partner to occupy the home for a period in order to provide a home for the children of the erstwhile marriage.

In relation to any children of the relationship, if Peter and Mary remain unmarried, then s 2 of the Children Act 1989 assumes that Mary as the unmarried mother has parental responsibility for any children. As an unmarried father, Peter can 'acquire' parental responsibility through s 4 by a parental responsibility agreement with Mary which they should register with the court. This would give Peter 'standing' in matters relating to their children and he will be able to act alone in exercising that responsibility. *Re H (A minor) (Parental Responsibility)* (1993) supports the importance of this for Peter if he wants to play the fullest part in the upbringing of any children of the relationship, especially if he and Mary remain unmarried.

Both partners are liable to maintain any children they have. The absent parent, should Peter and Mary decide to break up their relationship after having children, is responsible under the Child Support Act 1991 for the payment of child maintenance to the parent with care. The payment of spousal maintenance will not apply if the couple are not married. In unmarried relationships the couple are not responsible financially for the other, so Peter and Mary may be advised to make another arrangement for such support, and to draft an agreement to cover those situations not already covered by existing legal provisions. They should remember that statutory provisions cannot be ousted by any agreement they make and it would have to be construed by the court in any dispute.

Finally, what about the untimely deaths of either of them? They must be advised to make wills for the law does not automatically provide for the cobabitee upon death of the partner. They ought to consider leaving their share of the house to each other and making provision for the remaining spouse, unless they want the existing law relating to intestacy to apply. The Inheritance (Provision for Family and Dependants) Act 1975 applies in the absence of a will, and would mean that the surviving spouse could claim a share, or, in this case, a surviving partner and children who could show dependency upon the dead partner while they were alive. It would be easier if Peter and Mary were to make wills providing for their deaths and what should happen to their property rather than depend upon the statutory provisions.

These are some of the major issues which Peter and Mary, in their cohabiting situation, ought to consider as they embark upon their long-term relationship.

Question 44

Bob and Alice have been married for 10 years and they have two children, Ted aged eight and Carol, aged six. Both have worked with the result that they own a large house, probably too big for their needs. Carol has reduced her hours of work as a secretary and has been able to take up tennis. Bob is an architect who has been very successful in the past but whose future work is not certain.

The relationship between Bob and Alice has deteriorated over the last five years with heavy drinking bouts on the part of Bob. Alice has begun looking for solace to the coach at the local tennis club, Fred, with whom she has a very friendly relationship.

The children dislike the air of tension that seems to be getting worse, and Carol has begun to wet the bed as a result of anxiety.

Alice comes to you for advice. She wants to know:

(a) whether she can divorce Bob, and on what ground, should she wish to develop her relationship with Fred;

(b) who would have the house; and

(c) what will happen to the children.

General approach

This is a typical question dealing with the issues surrounding divorce and the problems of care of the children and divorce settlements.

It may be convenient to deal with it in the three parts indicated in the question.

Answer plan

Parts (i) (ii) and (iii) in turn, dealing with the following matters in each:

- deal with the possible ground and facts of the divorce
- what are the 'best' options?; issues of these options with authority
- ownership and settlement of property with the likely orders; reasons for these orders and the possibility of a 'clean break'; spousal and child maintenance
- the care of the children and some of the principles of the Children Act 1989; any necessity to make orders at all?

Answer

(a) Can Alice divorce Bob and if so on what ground?

Their marriage must have irretrievably broken down (*Chilton v Chilton* (1990)) according to the Matrimonial Causes Act 1973 and this must be demonstrated along with one of the four facts which are adultery committed by Bob with Alice finding it intolerable to live with Bob, or that Bob has behaved in such a way that Alice could not reasonably be expected to put up with the behaviour, or that Bob has deserted Alice for two years without her consent, or that they have lived apart for two years and both want a divorce or they have lived apart for five years, which would not require the consent of them both.

The situation seems to suggest adultery and behaviour as being the most fruitful source, if Alice does not wish to wait a period before she can present a divorce petition. Alice and Bob have been married for longer than one year, so s 3 of the MCA 1973 is satisfied. There is some suggestion that Alice may have committed adultery with Fred, and the intolerability does not have to be caused by the adultery.

However, Alice cannot rely on her own adultery so will not be able to use this in demonstrating that the marriage has broken down. Section 1(2)(b) may be helpful to Alice if she can demonstrate that Bob's drinking problems are such that she cannot be expected to live with him any longer. The *Livingstone-Stallard* (1974) test applies in deciding whether a right thinking person could come to the conclusion that this person (Alice) could not reasonably be expected to live with this husband (Bob) taking into account the whole circumstances of the case. There is some doubt about Bob's conduct as such - is it 'sufficient' to justify s 1(2)(b)?

The alternative might be for the couple to live apart for a period before seeking a divorce under s 1(2)(d) if they agree and s 1(2)(e) if Bob does not agree.

According to *Mouncer v Mouncer* (1972) and *Fuller v Fuller* (1973) there would need to be an indication of living 'separate' lives, which might not be such a bad idea considering the effect on Carol of the increasing tension in the relationship of the parents. At least one of the parties must feel that the relationship is at an end; see *Santos v Santos* (1972).

(b) Who would have the house?

Clearly the children and the adults need somewhere to live. We are told that the house is 'probably' too big for them.

Property settlement may await the divorce, if there is to be one. Sections 23 and 24 of the Matrimonial Causes Act 1973 will be used for orders against either spouse for the benefit of the other, bearing in mind that both parents are responsible for the maintenance of the children under the Child Support Act 1991. Since Alice has specifically asked about the house, then a brief comment is all that is required for spousal maintenance. Section 23 provides for periodical payments either secured or unsecured and these can be made for a limited period of time. This may take into account which parent has the daily care of the children, how much and for how long they may require such care as might affect the possibilities of the parent caring for them not being able to secure employment so that they would not be able to, eventually, obtain a job in order not to need spousal maintenance. Orders for lump sums can also be made.

The same Act can be used in transferring property under s 24. This could be used to transfer the interest in the house, or in other property, such as shares, vehicles and jewellery. The various orders that could be used can be 'combined' to produce a 'package' appropriate for a particular situation. According to *Mesher v Mesher* (1980) a home in joint names could be settled so that it provided a home for the children until the youngest child reached 17 when it might then be sold to realise the assets; each party could then obtain their share of the capital in order to establish a new home for themselves. It may be that there is sufficient equity in the house (we are told it is large) for the house to be sold and the capital to be divided to realise the assets and for the former partners to buy new homes for themselves. In *Suter v Suter and Jones* (1986) first consideration will be given to the welfare of the children in trying to attain a result which is fair to both Bob and Alice.

In considering what settlement to make the court will consider such factors as the income, earning capacity, property and other financial resources of the parties. The court may wish to ask to what extent Bob's work will continue and whether Alice can be expected to return to full-time work eventually (perhaps giving her some time to retrain if she has been away from full-time work for a long period, so that her earning capacity can be improved) when the children no longer require so much of her presence at home; see *Leadbeater v Leadbeater* (1985) and *Delany v Delaney* (1990) where these factors were discussed. Financial needs and obligations of the parties will be accounted for so that if Alice starts to live with Fred then this might affect the maintenance she could expect, not necessarily because of any money which Fred has, but because Alice's living expenses might be reduced. This, in turn, may influence the court in deciding about the transfer of any property belonging to the couple. the standard of living of the parties and their respective ages and the duration of the marriage are all factors which may influence the orders that might be made. The conduct of the parties will only be relevant if serious and reprehensible (see *Kyte v Kyte* (1987)) and will not otherwise affect the settlement or maintenance payable to the spouse.

Finally, on this point, it must be remembered that although 'clean breaks' would seem to be 'encouraged' so that the parties can get on with the rest of their lives (see *Waterman v Waterman* (1989) and *Duxbury v Duxbury* (1990)), it is not usually going to be appropriate to make a clean break order if there are children. These orders were only meant to be clean breaks between partners and not parents and children. The provisions of the Child Support Act 1991 has dealt a blow to the use of these orders.

(c) What will happen to the children?

The Children Act 1989 assumes that parents are able to resolve difficulties without recourse to the courts to make orders.

Assuming that Bob and Alice were married when Ted and Carol were born then the Children Act s 2 says that both parents have parental responsibility for the children. This parental responsibility is retained after divorce on the assumption that this assists the parents in making appropriate arrangements for the children and allows the parents to continue their responsibilities as parents even though they may no longer wish to be married parents.

If necessary, where Bob and Alice are unable to agree on any matter relating to the upbringing of the children, they can use the s 8 orders in the Children Act 1989.

A residence order settles arrangements with respect to the living arrangements of the children and this order gives the person named in the order parental responsibility for the children. Time spent with that person could also be regulated if the order is made in favour of more than one person. Parental responsibility cannot be used to allow a person to act in a way that is incompatible with the residence order. A contact order could be used to regulate contact with any person named in the order, so that if Bob and Alice cannot agree 'visiting' or other contact this can be defined by the order. there is an assumption, however, that no orders are necessary unless making an order is better than not making any order at all. The court would expect

Bob and Alice to sort out their arrangements if possible (see s 1(5) of the Act).

The other two orders available are specific issues and prohibited steps which deal with individual issues in relation to the children where the parents are unable to agree. All orders can be made subject to conditions and directions (for example, living in a named town, if one party with daily care of the children wants to move and the other partner wants to ensure regular contact without travelling long distances).

In determining any question relating to a child's upbringing (and therefore, what will happen to Ted and Carol) the child's welfare is the paramount consideration and this is set out in s 1(1) of the Act. There are guidelines in s 1(3) called the 'checklist' which the court must use in deciding disputed areas of the law and among these factors the court would be interested in the ascertainable wishes and feelings of Ted and Carol, bearing in mind their age and understanding, their physical, emotional and educational needs (do they need to stay with their mother and attend a school where they have settled, for example?), the age, sex and background of the child including characteristics, harm suffered (has Carol 'suffered' as result of her father's drunken state such that she should live with her mother rather than her father?) and finally, how capable Bob and Alice are of meeting the needs of their children. The court will bear in mind all these factors, where appropriate, in deciding which of the range of powers it possesses it may use where the parties cannot agree.

Question 45

What alternatives are there if a person wants to become 'unmarried' and yet does not want to get a divorce?

General approach

What a strange question! This one must be about nullity and judicial separation since there are few alternatives other than death!

The general approach should be to spend the major part of your time looking at the issues of void and voidable marriages (since there is more to be gained from looking at the provisions of the Matrimonial Causes Act 1973) and then spend a short time looking at the provisions relating to judicial separation under s 17 MCA 1973.

Answer plan

- short introduction to establish what the parties may be attempting and what you will explore in your answer
- explain what nullity is; then look at the differences between void and voidable marriages
- the four grounds for nullity will be explored using s 11 MCA 1973 which deals with void marriages; this should be followed by the six grounds for declaring a marriage voidable under s 12 of the MCA 1973
- deal with the major issue of non-consummation
- finally, examine the bars to nullity
- judicial separation should be noted as a 'hybrid' in that it does not end the marriage but relieves the petitioner from cohabiting with the respondent and has 'similarities' with divorce

Answer

Very few marriages are now terminated by nullity petitions but the issues of nullity reveal the nature of marriage and so may reflect upon how the law approaches these important issues. A person may have a social or religious reason for not wishing to get divorced and these may be revealed by looking at the grounds for nullity in s 11 of the Matrimonial Causes Act 1973 or by turning to judicial separation which retains the actual marriage but which ends certain legal obligations under the marriage.

A decree of nullity declares the marriage null and void. The marriage is thus 'ended' in the same way as divorce ends the marriage. The parties are free to marry again after the pronouncement of the decree.

A void marriage is one that was never a marriage from the day of its celebration; it was void *ab initio*. However, people usually obtain a decree because it clarifies the issue of their marital state, even though in law they can be said to have been unmarried all along. Another good reason to obtain a decree is that financial relief under ss 23 and 24 is only available if a decree has been granted.

A voidable marriage is a valid marriage until it has been annulled by decree.

To obtain a decree of nullity (that the marriage is void) under s 11 MCA there are four grounds available. These are that the marriage is not valid under the provisions of the Marriage Acts, that at the time of the marriage either party was already married, (see the definition of marriage in *Hyde v Hyde* (1866)), that the parties are not male and female (see *Corbett v Corbett* (1970)) and, where the marriage is polygamous and entered into outside England and Wales, that either party regarded England or Wales as their place of abode (their 'domicile')(see *Alhaji Mohammed v Knott* (1968)).

If one of these grounds is successfully demonstrated, it means that the marriage is void. Children born to a void marriage can only be legitimate if, at the time of their conception (or celebration of the marriage if this comes later), at least one of the parties believed the marriage to be valid.

There are six grounds under s 12 MCA which are used for declaring a marriage voidable. These grounds are: that the marriage has not been consummated due to the incapacity of either party; that there has been non-consummation due to the wilful refusal of the respondent; that there was no valid consent to the marriage (this can include mistake a to identity and duress); if either party was suffering from mental disorder, that, too can be a reason; or that the respondent was suffering from VD in a communicable form at the time of the marriage, and the other party did not know about this at the time; finally, if the respondent was pregnant by someone other than the petitioner at the time of the marriage (and the petitioner was ignorant of this at the time), this can be used for a decree.

The most commonly used ground is that relating to non-consummation of the marriage. Incapacity and wilful refusal may be pleaded in the alternative. Consummation is one act of sexual intercourse after the celebration of the marriage and the law requires that the act be 'ordinary and complete, not partial and imperfect' (*W v W* (1967)). The use of condoms, the use of 'withdrawal' as a method of contraception, or the failure to ejaculate are not bars to a pleading.

Incapacity to consummate the marriage does not depend upon the reason; it may be physical or psychological but it must be 'incurable' in the sense that it may only be cured by a dangerous operation that is either refused by the party concerned or has a very limited chance of success. (See *Kaur v Singh* (1972) where the reason was the failure to complete the required religious ceremony knowing that the spouse would not allow consummation to take place without such requirements.)

A spouse may petition on the grounds of their own incapacity. Non-consummation due to wilful refusal must be 'settled and definite' and the decision must have been made without a good reason for the decision (see *Horton v Horton* (1947)) and the wilful refusal of the respondent must be proved for this ground.

There could not be a bar to a marriage that was never a marriage in the first place; so there is no bar to marriages that can be demonstrated to be 'void'. Section 13 MCA contains defences to petitions alleging that the marriage is voidable.

A decree will be refused if the respondent can persuade the court that the petitioner made the respondent think that he would not petition for nullity. How is this done? the respondent satisfies the court that the behaviour of the petitioner was such as made the respondent think that the marriage would continue and that it would therefore be unjust to end the marriage. This belief must be reasonably held and the petitioner must have known that he could have had the marriage annulled. In *D v D* (1979) the petitioner had agreed to the adoption of a child and this conduct was held to be sufficient to make the respondent think that there would be no petition for divorce. As the court heard, though, the respondent wanted the divorce, too, so there would be no hardship caused if the petition for nullity were granted.

Judicial separation may be used by those with a religious objection to being divorced who require a 'recognition' that their marriage is at an end and need to settle the arrangements with respect to maintenance and property as far as they are able to. A decree may be applied for at any time after the celebration of the marriage. Section 18 MCA states that the marriage is not at an end but the parties no longer have to live together. Financial orders are available in s 24 MCA. Section 17 MCA sets out the grounds and these are the same as for the decree of divorce but, obviously, there is no need to establish that the marriage has irretrievably broken down. There is a defence to the decree in that the respondent may claim that the ground does not exist.

Thus, there are ways of becoming 'unmarried' without seeking a divorce by using the provisions of the MCA to seek to establish that the marriage was never truly a marriage from the beginning, or that there was something fundamentally wrong with the marriage that it can be declared a nullity. Judicial separation does not legally end the marriage but gives the parties the formal recognition of the ending of the relationship and is as close to a divorce as those with fundamental objections to divorce may be prepared to proceed.

Question 46

To what extent does the state have a responsibility to ensure that children are properly looked after?

General approach

This is a very general essay question requiring a range of knowledge about the powers of the state in looking after children; the question especially seems to 'hint' to circumstances where the parents cannot or will not do so themselves. At a deeper level, the question is asking about whether there is some general standard in looking after children. References to the Children Act 1989 will be required.

The question refers to 'extent' so avoid simply reproducing notes on the powers possessed by the local authorities to ensure the welfare of children; to examine a 'balance' might be the better approach. The question uses the word 'responsibility' which is an echo of parental responsibility so a note on that may be helpful if this is linked with what powers the state exercises through local authorities.

Family and Welfare Law

Answer plan
- general introduction on the issue of children's rights establishes the importance of children in family law; are there any established 'standards'?
- section 17 assistance and s 20 accommodation in providing a 'partnership' with parents in the care of children
- types of orders under the Children Act 1989 available to local authorities and the circumstances under which they may be used
- the threshold criteria for care and supervision orders under s 31, and what happens in emergency situations under s 44
- how assessments may be made under s 43 and the use of this with other orders

Answer

Children are no longer regarded as the 'chattels' of their parents as they once were. A number of legal developments are responsible for ensuring that children's welfare is now regarded as important; the welfare of the child is specifically noted in the Children Act 1989 and there appears to have been a shift in emphasis from parental rights to the responsibilities. The age and maturity of the child is, however, important as the *Gillick* case (1985) suggests that the child's growing maturity means that the developing child may have a 'say' in how they are looked after in terms of the decisions that may be taken. This will affect the exercise of the responsibilities of both the parents of the child and what may occur when the state is required to step in.

Section 17 of the Children Act allows the local authority to offer assistance on a voluntary basis in the provision of services for children in need and for their families. Children in 'need' is defined by the Act as one whose health or development is likely to be significantly impaired unless such assistance is offered. This duty on local authorities is further supported by s 47 which requires the local authority to make appropriate investigations to provide such services. The Act encourages the offering of assistance voluntarily by stating that there should be a partnership between parents and the state with the best welfare of the child in mind.

Children can be accommodated by local authorities where this is done with their welfare in mind under s 20. Their general duties are underlined in s 22 which requires the authority to consult with relevant persons in the provision of services for such children.

It is only where the 'threshold criteria' in s 31(2) have been satisfied that a court can consider the local authority being given the power to act without the consent of the parents. The criteria requires the court to be satisfied that the child is suffering or is likely to suffer significant harm which is attributable to the care or lack of care received by the child (not being that which a reasonable parent would give) or that the child is beyond parental control. Only a care order (which commits the child to the care of the local authority and gives parental responsibility to the authority) or supervision order (which places the child under the supervision of the local authority) can be granted. The court can decide to grant another order altogether, considering all the circumstances of the case. Harm means ill-treatment or impairment of health or development (see *M v M* (1994)) so there are clear guidelines about what must be demonstrated before the local authority is allowed to exercise power which the parents may not want to be exercised over their child.

Clearly there is some indication of a 'standard' being applied with respect to the care of children.

A supervision order can also be used where it is apparent that the child concerned will not receive appropriate care unless help is given irrespective of the permission of those with parental responsibility for the child. Even when a care order is made out, the parents do not 'lose' parental responsibility for the child and must be consulted about the care plan for the child; they also have the expectation that contact with the child is maintained (see s 34).

Where authorities are unsure about the care of a child the Act provides s 43 which can be used where efforts to get the co-operation of the parents in having the child assessed have been unsuccessful. The kind of examination that is used with the child can be specified and the order is limited in time to seven days, as are the care orders which can last until the child is 18 unless they are discharged earlier, and supervision orders which usually last for one year. This is to be expected since the efforts are directed towards providing assistance where there has been a failure of co-operation in the 'partnership' between local authority and parents. The responsibility for the care of children rests with the parents first.

Where an immediate risk is perceived s 44 can be used, but this is strictly for emergencies as the name of the order suggests. They are limited to eight days with a possible extension for a further seven days, although a challenge can be made after only 72 hours. The local authority in these instances is only permitted to take such action as is necessary to safeguard and promote the child's welfare and such drastic measures are permitted only where there is a risk of the child suffering significant harm if he is not removed immediately from home, or if steps are not taken to prevent his removal.

After the Children Act 1989 it has not been possible to remove a child from its home unless it is by a court order, which, as we have seen, are set out in statutory form with particular requirements. A child is no longer the subject of a care order simply because the child is not attending school and the requirements in s 31(2) are 'threshold' which means that the court does not have to make the requested order; it need only 'consider' making the order for care or supervision once the criteria are demonstrated.

The orders have limited powers attached to them (even the exercise of the parental responsibility which the order may give cannot extend to the child's name or religion, for example) and they are further limited in time.

The continuance of the order requires further grounds to exist, and the local authority is required to produce a plan for the future care of the child which requires the involvement of the parents in that plan. The eventual aim is for the child to return home as soon as possible where that is in the interests of the child concerned.

Question 47

To what extent is there a 'right' to receive benefits under the present welfare benefit system and how does the system provide for those in severe need?

General approach

This is a general essay question which allows you to select relevant material in answer to it, but it would be very tempting to write all you know about benefits, produce a very long essay and still not achieve a high mark!

The question has two main parts to it, so remember to answer both parts in your response to the question, even if you combine your response rather than deal with the issues in separate parts.

Answer plan

- general introduction; what do we mean by 'right'?; entitlements through fulfilling the relevant criteria with examples
- where do those in 'severe need' fit in the criteria?; use the income support and allowances payments to illustrate this point
- perhaps try to come to some tentative conclusion

Answer

A person has a 'right' to benefits if they fulfil the relevant criteria for receipt of that benefit. Whether there is anything like a 'right' may be more of a political question rather than a legal one, but it can be said that the 'right' depends upon what has been set out in the statute as one of the criteria for the receipt of the benefit and if a person fulfils that criteria then they have a 'right' to that benefit under the law.

Rights to benefits are set out in two main Acts of Parliament: the Social Security Contributions and Benefits Act 1992 and the Social Security Administration Act 1992.

This means that although there are 'decisions' about whether a person satisfies the criteria or not (and these are set out in the decisions of hearings at the various tribunals that deal with benefit entitlements and payments and at the appeal stage with decisions from the Commissioners) the law is found in statutory provisions.

The regulations relating to benefits are very complicated and the statute itself may give only the 'outline' of the provisions with the detailed requirements (which can change from year to year). The right to a benefit is for that person only; it cannot be 'transferred' to another person. The right to receive a benefit may also be 'suspended' for a time if, for example, there is some doubt about whether the recipient continues to be entitled to receive that benefit according to the rules of entitlement. It can be reinstated and the payment backdated if the claim was correct in the first place.

There are different 'types' of benefits to which criteria for entitlement attach. Contributory benefits depend upon a sufficient number of the correct class of national insurance contributions having been paid over a period of time. Unemployment benefit is an example of this type of benefit so that a person who was unemployed could receive this benefit if they had previously worked for a period during which relevant contributions were made (just like an insurance system to entitle receipt of the benefit).

Contributions to the system are deducted from earnings as national insurance contributions and there are several kinds of contributions, not all of which allow the payer to receive benefits; basically, the most important types of contributions for the receipt of most benefits is the national insurance class 1 contribution which entitles a person to receive contributory benefits if they then satisfy the criteria for the individual benefit (like paying class 1 contributions and then registering as unemployed and actively looking for work before you can be entitled to receive unemployment benefit for a period).

Those who are out of work may make a claim for income support if they are in need. This is done if they are not entitled to unemployment benefit. Income support is a 'means-tested' benefit to which there is entitlement if a person has an income or has capital which falls below a level designated by the regulations made under the provisions under the Act. What actually 'counts' as 'means' and what can be taken into account is written into the regulations which are designed to 'target' benefits to those who need them most of all. There are also benefits to which a person may be entitled because they meet the 'circumstances' that have arisen and an example of this type of benefit is child benefit to which a person is entitled if they have the care of a child; this does not depend upon their income or whether they have paid sufficient national insurance contributions.

The 'right' to benefits is supported by an appeals system through the Social Security Appeals Tribunal and related tribunals that deal with appeals about entitlement under the system. This appeals system also uses a further appeal to the Commissioner which may result in changes to the law. Although legal aid is not available for an adviser to be paid to help a person to present their case at a tribunal (it is available for appeals higher up the system, though) legal aid can be sought for those entitled for the advice to help a person to prepare a case. Tribunals are designed for people to present their own case.

A person who is in 'need' will have to satisfy the criteria set out in the relevant legislation. In addition to the general requirements for benefits which define the extent to which there can be said to be a 'right' to the benefit, each benefit will have its own special requirements. For example, sickness benefit will be paid to those who have been sick for a period of time and can certificate themselves as such; it will not be paid to those who are well, for this would be a fraudulent claim.

There is no definition of 'severe need' as each benefit has requirements. The 'safety net' of benefit for those on low incomes which may be found within the provisions of the Social Fund payments. Those regarded as in severe need may not have paid sufficient national insurance contributions to receive a contributory benefit at all. They must therefore use the 'means-tested' benefits part of the welfare benefits system. Within this part of the system (sometimes referred to as the 'safety net') there are allowances for dependants and circumstances (like special clothing or bedding requirements) which may arise. These allowances are the amounts allowed for the state to pay out where a person is in need and they are generally regarded as the absolute minimum amounts required to deal with the situation.

The benefit system appears to be complicated and may, therefore, discourage claimants because of its complications. If that is so then it might mean that the benefits were not reaching those who had a right to receive them and needed to do so; benefits will only be paid where a correct claim is made. The more restrictive the criteria, the fewer will be the number who can make a correct claim. If the criteria are restricted then the 'right' to receive the benefit is also restricted and in that sense the absolute 'right' applies to a limited group in society.

Chapter 11

Labour Law and the Workplace

Introduction

What could you be asked? Ensure that you know your syllabus and have prepared sufficiently for the number of questions you are to answer. This gives you the most important and first information about what you could be asked.

Your syllabus coverage could suggest that there are quite limited opportunities for the questions that could be asked; there may be a stated limit per paper, so check.

Areas within the syllabus which tend to be popular areas for examination questions are the following: unfair dismissal, health and safety issues (which may require you to know about the welfare benefits relating to employment and unemployment) redundancy, discrimination and the contractual areas of employment which may suggest knowledge of the status of the worker as an employee.

Check your syllabus for the areas that the examiners could ask. Ask your tutor, if possible, to outline the areas for you, for it will depend upon what is written in your syllabus and what has been covered on previous written papers.

What are questions in labour law and the workplace actually like? Questions can appear quite daunting, but they are designed, like all questions at 'A' level, to see if you know the material and can actually apply it to the situation (in a 'problem' question) or in presenting a viewpoint (as in an essay question). You will find that problem questions are popular with examiners, because they allow them to present a reasonably 'lifelike' situation to you which you should regard as an opportunity to show what you know and can do.

You should also remember that questions could be subdivided with two, three or even four or more parts to them. If any of your questions are sub-divided, then you should check what marks are allocated to each part and answer the parts accordingly, bearing in mind the allocation as a 'weighting' of time and effort to be expended on each part of the question. If there is no separate indication of how many marks are allocated to each part, then you should assume that all parts have equal marks, and that all separate questions on the paper are worth the same number of marks as all the other questions. This is something you must check with the particular written paper that you are following.

What kinds of questions are there likely to be and how do I deal with them? There may be both essay and problem questions on your examination paper.

The syllabus may have something to say about this matter, and you would find it helpful to obtain past papers from the examination board so that you are familiar with the kinds normally asked, and can practice on actual questions.

Remember that you may wish to tackle an essay question presented to you because it seems easier than the problem at first glance; this might mean that you do not give yourself the opportunity to show your best approach; all that a problem question does is allow you to select your material as appropriate to that scenario rather than select your material in answering or presenting a viewpoint as you would do for an essay question.

The approach to adopt is to martial your material rather than attempt to put in as much material as possible; no question ever says 'write all you know about ... labour law'!

Remember that you require legal authority for statements you make about the law that applies, and it is no use simply writing what you know the correct answer is unless you are able to state the authority for what you have said. The authority will be, in most cases, the cases or the statutory references for 'A' level purposes. Try, as a general rule, to be in the habit of automatically giving the authority when you write what you consider is the applicable law.

What do you put into an answer? You must be accurate and relevant in what you write. This sounds simple, but it is all too easy to be tempted to write all you know about the topic area rather than be relevant. It is also tempting in employment areas to give comments about what you think the law ought to be, rather than what it actually is. This may be because it can be an area of law that most people have an opinion about! It is also an area that it often represented in the media, so there are many comments that can be made.

If you simply write all you know then the examiner will suspect that you are unable to select your material and cannot concentrate on the question; you will probably run out of time on that particular question and you may be rushed in getting through all that you must do in the time available.

In problem questions it will be easier to keep to the point and deal with the issues in the order they are given in the problem. However, do remember that if asked to 'advise' one person, then another person, you may deal with the issues for one, then the other. There will, then, usually be different issues to deal with as the legal viewpoint of your 'clients' has been highlighted by the examiners so that you are required to give the different positions in law.

Keeping to the point in essay questions may be more difficult since there are often temptations to wander away from the point and present your own view. Avoid this as it is likely that this was not what the examiner wanted you to do. You may be asked to present a view (of reform, for example) but your view should be informed by current opinion of lawyers, not what your bestfriend or a television news report said last weekend. Remember that the examination is not an opportunity to 'preach', but an opportunity to organise facts and present a legally supported view in a specific response to the question that the examiner has set.

Last advice: read the rubric (the instructions or advice to candidates) on the front of the paper (better still, get to know what to expect in advance) and answer the correct number of questions from the correct part, if the paper is so divided.

Finally, you must remember to answer the question that the examiner set for the paper, not the one you wish you had read!

Question 48

Mike, George and Julie were employed in a part-time capacity in a supermarket called 'Supashops'. They all began working at the shop when it opened about four years ago and each of them regularly worked at the shop performing the same hours each week.

Supashops has had a lot of general stock loss for the last year, despite efforts by management to identify the causes. Last autumn the manager of Supashops gave Mike, George and Julie a first warning under the disciplinary procedure in respect of these losses. The losses continued and a couple of months later a final warning was given.

Due to rescheduling of opening times and other staff matters, including the requirements over the Christmas period, all three staff were sent to other branches of Supashops for two months. During that time there were no substantial stock losses at any of the branches of Supashops.

After two months the three returned to the same branch and when the next stock check took place there appeared to have been substantial losses. On 31 January all three employees received notices of dismissal and the letter said that the dismissal was due to the failure to prevent stock losses.

Mike, George and Julie are considering what they should do. What advise are you able to give them about any claim they might have?

Assume that the date today is 1 April.

General approach

This question concerns the issue of unfair dismissal and the claim to an industrial tribunal.

Remember to show that you know about wrongful and unfair dismissal (and the difference between the two) and the lawful ways in which a contract of employment may be terminated.

You should not allow yourself to wander into commenting on the way that the three (ex-) employees have been treated other than to use the information to discuss the legal issues that have arisen.

Answer plan

Briefly deal with contracts of employment. Then examine the eligibility of the employees for a claim of unfair dismissal. The points you put forward must look at what would be relevant in determining a claim: has there been a 'dismissal'?; what was the reason?; does the employer have grounds for this?; has a reasonable procedure been used in the circumstances?; is it a reasonable response?

Answer

The contract of employment does not have to be in writing nor need it be found in one place, for the contract can refer to other documents which can determine the job and responsibilities of the employed person. Contracts can be terminated upon a number of grounds but here we should concentrate upon the possibility that Mike, George and Julie have been 'dismissed' for a reason which may fall within s 57(2) of the Employment Protection (Consolidation) Act 1978.

Are the employees eligible for a claim at an industrial tribunal? They appear to have had at least two years continuous service at Supashops. There is no indication given that their dismissal could be said to be on grounds of trade union activities, discrimination or pregnancy, so that it does not fall within that special group of reasons which are automatically 'unfair' reasons for dismissal. We assume that they are not over retirement age, otherwise it would mean that they were not eligible to make a claim that they have been unfairly dismissed.

We need to establish that they are making a claim within three months of being dismissed from their jobs. We are told that each has received a letter dated 31 January, so they must claim within three months; is it before the end of April? This requirement can be waived for a very good reason presented to the industrial tribunal.

We can establish that the three have received a letter that says they have been 'dismissed' (rather than made redundant) for the letter seems conclusively to refer to this, and furthermore it states the reason for the dismissal. We may note that otherwise we would have to consider whether a person had been told that they were dismissed during an argument which would need consideration of 'words said in the heat of the moment'. That does not appear to apply here because of the clear wording of the letters.

The reasons for the dismissal must fall within ss 57 and 58 of the Employment Protection (Consolidation) Act 1978 or must be 'some other substantial reason' for the dismissal. This would help the industrial tribunal to decide whether the reasons given were fair or not. Within this statutory provision are grounds of capability or conduct, that the job is no longer required to be done, that it is clear that there is a good reason for dismissing this employee. A single reason seems to have been given for the dismissals of Mike, George and Julie.

Were any other reasons given? Was it the responsibility of Mike, George and Julie to prevent the stock loss? On this last question, it may not have been the actual responsibility of Mike, George and Julie to prevent stock loss, but it could be implied within their contract of employment that this is what they were 'expected' to be doing.

The employer needs to show that he has grounds for the reason that he gives in the letter of dismissal, for he may simply be wanting to reduce his staff at a time when he wants to cut his costs.

Even if the reason appears to be a 'fair' reason for dismissal the actual procedure used prior to the dismissal must be considered. For example, were there any interviews to determine which employee was responsible, rather than dismissing all three who may have been involved in the affair?

Within the disciplinary code at Supashops there may be outlined the appropriate procedures to be used in such circumstances (see *Williams v Compair Maxim* (1982) and *Polkey v AE Dayton Services Ltd* (1987)). If the proper procedures were not used (warnings, letters of warning and appropriate checks may all be regarded as examples of proper procedures to be used) then the dismissal, despite there being a reason for it, might still be unfair.

Finally, it must be considered whether dismissal would be a reasonable reaction in all the circumstances of the case (see *Monie v Coral Racing Ltd* and *Saunders v Scottish National Camps* (1980)). If dismissal is reasonable then the dismissal cannot be said to be unfair.

If a claim went to the industrial tribunal they would need to be satisfied that a reasonable employer would have acted in the way that Supashops has done (see *Whitbread and Company v Thomas* (1988) a case from the Employment Appeal Tribunal).

From the facts it would seem that warning has been given and a procedure followed. The reaction does seem to be a reasonable reaction from the continuance of the stock losses.

Index

A
ABWOR scheme	45
ACAS alternative to litigation	4-10
ADR alternative to litigation	3-10
Actus rea	247-295
Administration of justice	
role of lay person in	20-26
Adult offenders	
sentencing	72-78
Animals Act 1971	221-227
Assault	248-256, 272-277
Assessors	20-26
Attempts	272-277

B
Barristers	
compared with solicitors	27-40
merging function with solicitors	27-40
Benefits	
right to receive welfare	334-337
Broadcasting Licensing Council	
challenging decision of	156-163
powers to grant licenses	156-163
Burden of proof	
distinguished from standard of proof	62-65

C
Children	
responsibilities of State	330-333
Civil liberties	297-314
contrasted with civil rights	302-309
introduction	297
powers of arrest	309-314
protection of	302-309
Civil rights	
contrasted with civil liberties	297-304
Common law	
adapting to needs of society	52-61
definition of	54
development of	52-61
Compensation	
personal injuries	235-245
Conspiracy	257-263, 272-277
Constitutional law	145-163
introduction	145
Consumer Protection Act 1987	214-220
Contract	
breach	166-171
employment termination	342-345
exclusion clauses	191-196
formation of agreement	171-176
limited liability clauses	191-196
misrepresentation	181-186
mistaken identity	186-190
offer and acceptance	171-176
poor quality goods distinguished from unsafe goods	176-181
Unfair Contract Terms Act 1977	191-196
void	186-190
Contract-based remedies	176-181
Contractual liability	
doctrine of frustration	166-171
Contract law	165-196
introduction	165
Coroners	20-26
Courts	
role in interpreting statutes	10-20
Criminal	
insanity in	277-281
Criminal and civil advice and assistance	40-52
ABWOR scheme	45
Legal Advice Service	50
Criminal Justice Act 1967	287-295
Criminal justice system	
defects	80-89
proposals for reform	80-89
Criminal law	247-295
importance of fault in	287-295
introduction	247
Criminal Law Act 1977	272-277

D
Defences	
intoxication	248-256
provocation	248-256
Dismissal	342-345
Divorce	321-326
Dworkin	
rules, principles and policies distinguished	100-112

E

EC Directive
  not implemented in UK   125-130
  reliance on directive
    not implemented in UK   123-130

EC law
  conflicts with UK law   119-125

EC Treaty
  relationship of European Court
    of Justice with national
      legal systems   114-119
  secondary rules   114-119

Employment
  termination of contract   342-345

English law
  general principles   79-112

English legal system
  introduction   1-65
  sentencing   78

European Court of Justice
  jurisdiction not updated because
    of Maastricht treaty   137-143
  relationship with national
    legal systems   114-119

European law   113-143
  introduction   113

European Parliament
  extent to which Maastricht Treaty
    extends role
      in legislation   130-136

Exclusion clauses   191-196

F

Family law   315-337
  introduction   315

Fault
  importance of in
    criminal law   287-295

I

Inchoate offences   257-263, 272-277
Incitement   257-263, 272-277
Individual
  rights of   298-301
Industrial Tribunal
  claim for unfair dismissal   343-345
Insanity   277-281

J

Judges
  selection, appointing and
    dismissal   146-156

Judicial separation   326-330

Judiciary
  constitutional position   146-156
  role in UK   146-156

Juries   20-26

Justice
  miscarriages of   80-89

Juvenile offenders
  sentencing   72-78

L

Labour law   339-345
  introduction   339

Law
  definition   91-100
  overlap with morality   89-100

Lay person
  role in administration
    of justice   20-26

Legal advice service   50

Legal aid   40-52

Legal system
  introduction   1-65
  relationship of national with
    European Court of
      Justice   114-119

Legislation
  ultra vires   12, 53
  void   12, 53

Limited liability clauses   191-196

Litigation
  effectiveness of alternatives to   2

M

Maastricht Treaty
  economic and
    monitory union   137-143
  extends European
    Parliament's role
      in legislation   130-136

Magistrates   20-26

Manslaughter   248-256, 264-271

Index

Marriage
  nullity 326-330
  judicial separation 326-330
Married couples 318-321
  children of 318-321, 321-326
  divorce 321-326
  property rights 318-321
  trusts 318-321
Mens rea 247-295
Miscarriages of justice 80-89
Misrepresentation 181-186
Mistaken identity 186-190
M'Naughton Rules 277-281
Morality
  definition 91-100
  overlap with law 89-100
Murder 248-256, 264-271

N
Nullity of marriage 326-330

O
Occupiers' Liability
  Act 1957 204-212, 213-220, 221-227
Offer and acceptance 171-176

P
Personal injuries I
  compensation for 235-245
Policies
  contribution to law 100-112
  distinguished from rules
    and principles 100-112
Poor quality goods
  distinction with
    unsafe goods 176-181
Powers of arrest 309-314
Principles
  contribution to law 100-112
  distinguished from rules
    and policies 100-112
Principles of English law 79-112
Punishment of offender
  aim of sentencing system 281-287

R
Reward
  offer and acceptance 171-176
Rights of individual
  versus rights of State 298-301
Rights of the State
  versus rights of individual 298-301
Robbery 272-277
Rules
  contribution to law 100-112
  distinguished from
    principles and policies 100-112
  ejusdem generis 10-20
  expressio unius est
    exclusio alterius 10-20
  golden 10-20
  literal 10-20
  noscitur a sociis rule 10-20
  secondary defined in
    EC Treaty 114-119

S
Secondary rules
  defined in EC Treaty 114-119
Sentencing 67-78
  aim of 74, 281-287
  principles of 73
  critically examined 72-78
  stealing from old lady 68-72
Society
  needs and the common law 52-61
Solicitors
  compared with barristers 27-40
  merging profession with
    barristers 27-40
Standard of proof
  distinguished form
    burden of proof 62-65
State
  responsibility for children 330-333
  rights of 298-301
Statutes
  role of courts in interpreting 10-20
Statutory interpretation
  main rules 14

T

Theft	272-277
Tort	197-245, 309-314
breach	199-203
common law negligence	199-203, 204-212
damage	199-203, 213-220
duty	199-203
introduction	197
Libel	228-234
negligence	213-220
private nuisance	204-212, 213-220, 220-227
public nuisance	204-212, 220-227
Tort-based remedies	176-181
Tribunals	20-26

U

UK law	
conflicts with EC law	119-125
Unfair Contract Terms Act 1977	191-196
Unfair dismissal	342-345
Unmarried couples	318-321
children of	318-321
property rights	318-321
trusts	318-321
wills	318-321
Unsafe goods	
distinction with poor quality goods	176-181

W

Welfare benefits	
right to receive	334-337
Welfare law	315-337
introduction	315
Working week directive	
reliance on when not implemented in UK law	125-130
Workplace law	339-345
introduction	339
Wrongful dismissal	342-345